Landmark Yiddish Plays

SUNY series in Modern Jewish Literature and Culture
Sarah Blacher Cohen, editor

Landmark Yiddish Plays

A Critical Anthology

Edited, Translated, and with an Introduction by
Joel Berkowitz and Jeremy Dauber

STATE UNIVERSITY OF NEW YORK PRESS

Published by
State University of New York Press, Albany

For information, contact State University of New York Press, Albany, NY
www.sunypress.edu

Production by Marilyn P. Semerad
Marketing by Fran Keneston

Library of Congress Cataloging-in-Publication Data

Landmark Yiddish plays : a critical anthology / edited, translated and with
an introduction by Joel Berkowitz and Jeremy Dauber.
    p. cm. — (SUNY series in modern Jewish literature and culture.)
    Includes bibliographical references.
    Contents: Silliness and sanctimony / Aaron Halle Wolfssohn — Serkele,
or, in mourning for a brother / Shloyme Ettinger — The two kuni-lemls /
Avrom Goldfaden — Miriam / Peretz Hirschbein — The duke / Alter Kacyzne.
    ISBN 0-7914-6779-1 (hardcover : alk. paper) — ISBN 0-7914-6780-5 (pbk. :
alk. paper) 1. Yiddish drama — Translations into English. I. Berkowitz, Joel,
1965– II. Dauber, Jeremy Asher. III. Series.

PJ5191.E5L34 2006
839'.12008—dc22   2005023939

ISBN-13: 978-0-7914-6779-4 (hardcover : alk. paper)
ISBN-13: 978-0-7914-6780-9 (pbk. : alk. paper)

10 9 8 7 6 5 4 3 2 1

Contents

Acknowledgments

We would like to express our gratitude to a number of people who have helped make the publication of this volume possible. Series editor Sarah Blacher Cohen expressed enthusiasm for this project from the start, and offered helpful suggestions that helped determine the contents of our anthology. James Peltz, interim director of State University of New York Press, was similarly encouraging, and we have enjoyed working with him and his fine staff.

Before the manuscript found its way to SUNY Press, several friends and colleagues asked questions and made suggestions that have helped determine the final composition of the book. Thanks to Esther Berkowitz, Charles Busch, Brad Sabin Hill, Dov-Ber Kerler, Judith Milhous, David Roskies, Joseph Sherman, Barry Trachtenberg, Jeffrey Veidlinger, Ruth Wisse, and Seth Wolitz for helpful feedback and assistance of various kinds.

We are grateful to the YIVO Institute for Jewish Research for providing us with both the cover image and the sheet music for this volume.

Those who participated in public readings of the plays helped us hear as well as see the dialogue in new ways, and asked many questions that led us to clarify the language of the plays. Bravo and thank you to our original cast of this translation of *Miriam*: Tiffany Anne Carrin, Stephanie Levine, Michael Rosenthal, Beth Saultz, Helene Scheck, Eileen Schuyler, Harry Staley, Karen Williams, and Peter Zalizniak. Special thanks to Ari Sholom Berkowitz and Noah Dauber, who took the time during several idyllic summer days to play multiple roles in a four-man reading of *The Two Kuni-Lemls*, and helped bring Goldfaden's comedy to life.

Our colleagues at Oxford University, Columbia University, and the University at Albany have provided great encouragement and helped create working environments conducive to moving this project forward. On the home front, our undying gratitude goes to both of our families for all their love and support.

Finally, having first come to the study of Yiddish as young adults, we are forever indebted to our Yiddish teachers, who inspired and enlightened us. It is to all of them that we dedicate this book.

Introduction

In the late nineteenth century, European Jewry began to experience a sea change. Beginning with the activities of a handful of German Jewish intellectuals, the Haskala, or Jewish Enlightenment, transformed the way that Central and Western European Jews identified as Jews, practiced their religion, and interacted with the wider society. Within a matter of decades, the Haskala made its way eastward into Poland and the Russian empire, bringing its secular ideals to a deeply traditional population. There was much resistance, to be sure, and a substantial part of the Eastern European Jewish population would carry on their traditional practices, or reinvent such practices in response to the Haskala and other new social and political movements. Yet the Haskala also effected profound changes in various facets of Jewish life, one of which in particular concerns us here. By successfully calling upon a portion of the Jewish population to embrace the intellectual and cultural achievements of the secular world, the Haskala opened up new areas of activity, including the writing and production of drama. A small number of *maskilim* (singular: *maskil*), or advocates of the Haskala, wrote plays that articulated their vision in dramatic form. After the middle of the nineteenth century, as the idea of Jews producing and consuming secular literature gained greater acceptance and an infrastructure of writers, journals, and publishers established itself, modern Yiddish literature began to flourish. It was in this atmosphere that the professional Yiddish theatre was born—a phenomenon that would quickly expand to become a lively medium for both entertainment and the exchange of ideas among Yiddish-speaking Jews everywhere, and one of the most dynamic and popular forms of Jewish expression in the modern world.

The five plays in this anthology represent highlights in the development of modern Yiddish drama, from its beginnings in late eighteenth-century Germany to the remarkable professional scene that thrived in interwar Poland. In between, we encounter satires written and performed in Poland and Russia. Some of the plays in this volume were little known

1

outside a circle of intellectuals, but exerted an enormous influence on later Yiddish drama. Others became part of an international repertoire that extended to Western Europe, the Americas, and Jewish communities in more distant locales, like South Africa and Australia. And still others, though performed infrequently, were given noteworthy productions at pivotal moments in the development of the Yiddish theatre.

All of these plays, in other words, are historically important. They will be of particular interest to anyone interested in Yiddish drama and theatre, but also to other readers and audiences, because of the remarkable degree of cross-fertilization that informed the creation of Yiddish drama, which transcended genre, language, and national borders. That is, Yiddish playwrights were rarely only playwrights, but also accomplished and popular writers of fiction, poetry, journalism, literary criticism, travelogues, and other forms of literature; they often wrote in other languages—particularly Hebrew—as well; they were influenced by, and exerted their own influence upon, theatre artists writing and performing in other languages; and their plays entered into the repertoires of troupes that traveled widely, creating an international exchange of performers, playwrights, and plays. The plays in this anthology, therefore, are the fruits of modern European Jewish writers, and can be placed simultaneously in a number of different artistic and historical categories.

While each of these works belongs to a specific time and place, we hope that readers, directors, performers, and audiences will come to share our belief that each also deserves to be revisited, to be read and performed from the perspective of a generation eager to learn more about the cultural legacy handed down to us by Yiddish playwrights from earlier times. There are many plays we could have chosen to reflect the development of modern Yiddish drama, and many considerations helped dictate the final selection of these five works. We wanted to include plays that would represent distinct moments in the history of Yiddish theatre and drama, and which reflect the changing nature of the modern Yiddish theatre from its earliest beginnings to the height of its popularity to its ultimate decline. We have chosen plays written in different genres, moods, and styles: satire, sentimental comedy, farce, naturalism, and grand historical drama. All of these works were written by writers who have been esteemed by literary and theatrical critics, and in some cases embraced by large and enthusiastic audiences. And just as important as any of the above considerations, we have included these plays because each is a masterpiece. They are by turns hilarious, thought provoking, startling, and moving. They spark lively discussion in the classroom. With effective productions, they can be just as stimulating in the theatre.

Despite their historical importance and artistic merits, none of the plays in this volume has ever been translated into English before;

indeed, most of their authors are completely unknown to English readers.[1] This sort of gap is familiar to teachers, students, and readers of Yiddish literature in any genre who are looking for worthwhile translations into English for themselves or their students, for only a handful of the many treasures of Yiddish literature are available in English. The dearth is even more pronounced for those interested specifically in drama. A number of major Yiddish playwrights have yet to have any of their work translated into English,[2] and only a handful of English translations of Yiddish drama have been translated in the past generation.[3] We hope that our anthology will

---

1. *The Two Kuni Lemls* has been freely adapted into English (*Kuni Leml*, Samuel French, 1985) by Nahma Sandrow, Richard Engquist, and Raphael Crystal, but ours is the first straight English translation of the play. The only other playwright from this collection whose work has been published in English before is Peretz Hirschbein, whose *Grine felder* (Green Fields) has been translated by both Joseph Landis and Nahma Sandrow, and several of whose other plays have appeared in English versions by Etta Block, Isaac Goldberg, and David Lifson. For further details, see note 3 below.

2. A few Yiddish plays are fairly familiar to English theatregoers, with two in particular receiving extensive attention in both published and staged versions. S. Ansky's *Der dibek* (The Dybbuk), arguably the most popular of all Yiddish plays and an absolute sensation when it debuted in 1920, has been translated, adapted, and performed in many languages, and English has produced its fair share of *Dybbuks*. For published versions, see S. Morris Engel (Los Angeles: Nash Publishing, 1974); Joachim Neugroschel, in *The Dybbuk and the Yiddish Imagination: A Haunted Reader,* ed. Neugroschel (Syracuse: Syracuse University Press, 2000); and Golda Werman, in *The Dybbuk and Other Writings,* by S. Ansley, ed. David G. Roskies (New York: Schocken, 1992). Neugroschel's translation was adapted by Tony Kushner as *A Dybbuk* (New York: Theatre Communications Group, 1998). *The Dybbuk* has also inspired music by Aaron Copland, a ballet by Leonard Bernstein, an opera by David and Alex Tamkin, and Paddy Chayefsky's popular play *The Tenth Man* (1959), which moves the story from Eastern Europe to a synagogue on Long Island in the 1950s. *The Dybbuk's* nearest rival for popularity in English is Sholem Asch's *Got fun nekome* (God of Vengeance). See translations by Isaac Goldberg (Boston: Stratford, 1918); Joseph Landis, in *The Dybbuk and Other Great Yiddish Plays,* ed. Landis (New York: Bantam, 1966; repr. 1972); and in *3 Great Yiddish Plays,* ed. Landis (New York: Applause, 1986); and Joachim Neugroschel, *Pakn-Treger* 23 (Winter 1996): 16–39. An adaptation by Donald Margulies (New York: Theatre Communications Group, 2004) premiered at the Williamstown Theatre Festival in 2002. Numerous other translations and adaptations of the play have been performed in both professional and university settings.

3. Translations and adaptations of other works by individual playwrights include Morris Freed, *The Survivors: Six One-act Dramas,* trans. A. D. Mankoff (Cambridge, MA: Sci-Art Publishers, 1956); Jacob Gordin, *The Kreutzer Sonata,* adapted by Langdon Mitchell (New York: H. Fiske, 1907); Sh. Harendorf, *Der kenig fun lampeduze / The King of Lampedusa* (bilingual edition), ed. and trans. Heather Valencia (London: Jewish Music Institute / International Forum for Yiddish Culture, 2003); Peretz Hirshbein, *The Haunted Inn,* trans. Isaac Goldberg (Boston: John W. Luce, 1921); Ari Ibn-Zahav, *Shylock and his Daughter,* adapted by Maurice Schwartz, trans. Abraham Regelson (New York: Yiddish Art Theatre, 1947); Kh. Y. Minikes, "Among the Indians or, The Country Peddler," trans. Mark Slobin, *Drama Review* 24 (September 1980): 17–26; I. L. Peretz, *The Golden Chain,* in Marvin Zuckerman and Marion Herbst, eds., *The Three Great Classic Writers of Modern*

help accomplish several overlapping goals: to introduce a new readership to some of the greatest achievements of Yiddish dramatists, in both comedy and tragedy; to help illustrate, through the combination of the plays and the historical introduction below, key trends in the development of modern Yiddish drama; and to offer new material to teachers, students, theatre directors, and audiences hungry to learn more about Yiddish theatre and drama. The rest of this introduction is designed primarily to provide background information on the five plays translated here: their authors, their textual history, and some analysis of the main themes. In that light, though this essay will not be able to serve as a full history of the Yiddish theatre, it will strive to treat many of the main issues surrounding not just these particular plays, but Yiddish drama more broadly.

Medieval Roots

Though theatrical performance was frowned upon by traditional Jewish authorities in late antiquity and the medieval period, in part due to its original connection with pagan religious festivals and a prohibition against male cross-dressing, this hardly meant that the concept of theatre was unknown to medieval and early modern Jewry.[4] On the holiday

3. (continued) *Yiddish Literature*, vol. 3: Peretz (Malibu, CA: Joseph Simon/Pangloss Press, 1996), 398–468; Peretz, *A Night in the Old Marketplace*, trans. Hillel Halkin, *Prooftexts* 12 (Jan. 1992): 1–71, and reprinted in *The I. L. Peretz Reader*, 2nd ed., ed. Ruth R. Wisse (New Haven, CT: Yale University Press, 2002), 361–432; David Pinski, *King David and His Wives*, trans. Isaac Goldberg (New York: B. W. Huebsch, 1923); Pinski, *Ten Plays*, trans. Isaac Goldberg (New York, 1920; repr. Great Neck, NY: Core Collection Books, 1977); Pinski, *Three Plays*, trans. Isaac Goldberg (New York, 1918; repr. Arno Press, 1975); Sholem Aleichem, *The Jackpot: A Folk-Play in Four Acts*, trans. Kobi Weitzner and Barnett Zumoff (New York: Workmen's Circle Education Department, 1989); and Sholem Aleichem, *Heaven, She Must Marry a Doctor*, and *It's Hard to be a Jew*, trans. Mark Schweid, in *Sholom Aleichem Panorama*, ed. Melech Grafstein (London, ON: Jewish Observer, 1948). For plays in anthologies, see Etta Block, ed., *One-Act Plays from the Yiddish*, 1st and 2nd series (Cincinnati: Stewart Kidd, 1923 and New York Bloch, 1929); Isaac Goldberg, ed., *Six Plays of the Yiddish Theatre*, 1st and 2nd series (Boston: J. W. Luce, 1916 and 1918); Joseph Leftwich, ed., *An Anthology of Modern Yiddish Literature* (The Hague: Mouton, 1974); David Lifson, ed., *Epic and Folk Plays of the Yiddish Theatre* (Rutherford, NJ: Fairleigh Dickinson University Press, 1975); Nahma Sandrow, ed., *God, Man, and Devil: Yiddish Plays in Translation* (Syracuse: Syracuse University Press, 1999); and Bessie White, ed., *Nine One-Act Plays from the Yiddish* (Boston: J. W. Luce, 1932). For Yiddish plays in general drama anthologies, see Sholem Asch, *Night*, trans. Jack Robbins, in Constance M. Martin, ed., *Fifty One-Act Plays* (London: V. Gollancz, 1934), 769–781; and David Pinski, *Laid Off*, trans. Anna K. Pinski, in *One-Act Plays for Stage and Study*, 7th series (New York: Samuel French, 1932).

4. On early Jewish and Yiddish theatre, see Shmuel Avisar, *Ha-makhaze ve-ha-te'atron ha-ivri ve-ha-yidi* (Jerusalem: Reuven Mass, 1996), 1–9; B. Gorin, *Di geshikhte fun idishn teater*, 2 vols. (New York: Literarisher Farlag, 1918), 1:7–63; Sh. Ernst, "Tekstn un kveln tsu der geshikhte fun teatr, farvaylungn, un maskeradn bay yidn," in *Akhiv far der geshikhte fun yidishn teatr un drame*, ed. Y. Shatzky (New York: YIVO, 1930); and Y. Shiper, *Geshikhte fun yidisher teater-kunst un drame fun di eltste tsaytn biz 1750*, 3 vols. (Warsaw, 1923–1928).

of Purim, the celebration of the salvation of Persian Jewry from the depredations of the evil vizier Haman through the heroic intercession of Mordechai and Esther, the public reading of the book of Esther and the commandment to celebrate joyously allowed Jews to take their first steps towards the incorporation of a theatrical tradition.

The dictum in Esther 9:1, "venahafoch hu" (lit. "and the matter was turned upside down"), allowed for the Judaization of the carnivalesque "king for a day" experience of medieval Christendom. Students of the rabbinical seminaries (yeshivas) performed parodic versions of Talmudic lectures, or *purim-toyre*, which showcased verbal dexterity. More important, however, was the development of the institution known as the *purimshpil* (plural: purimshpiln) or "Purim play."[5] This institution, certainly influenced both by the "high" Christian tradition of biblical miracle and mystery plays and the "low" tradition of the German *Fastnachtspiel* and the Italian commedia dell'arte, at first probably consisted of the performance of biblical stories both thematically related to the holiday (the story of the book of Esther) and unrelated (we know that the Joseph story was very popular, as was that of Jonah and the whale).[6] However, the performances were not limited to simple dramatization of religious fare. Aside from the improvisational nature of the performances, performers of the purimshpiln (believed, generally, to be yeshiva students boarding in the major Jewish cities of Western and Central Europe, notably what would become Germany and Italy) would also include anachronistic material, generally information related to local politics or personalities. Given the limitation of theatrical activity to the holiday of Purim (and, perhaps, the period immediately around it), it is unsurprising that the performances would generally occur after the holiday feast in the homes of wealthy Jews, who not only had the space in their houses to allow for a performance but also the means to provide a bit of charity to the impoverished student performers after the play was done. (One might add that there is a commandment on Purim to give gifts to the poor, a commandment that these players would certainly not have let their hosts forget.)

Though most of these plays were composed in Yiddish, the primary language of European Jewry in the premodern era, that was

---

5. For a recent in-depth study of the *purimshpil*, see Evi Bützer, *Die Anfänge der jiddischen purim shpiln in ihrem literarischen und kulturgeschichtlichen Kontext* (Hamburg: Helmut Buske Verlag, 2003), and the extensive bibliography there. See also Jean Baumgarten, *Introduction à la littérature yiddish ancienne* (Paris, 1993), 443–473; Ahuva Belkin, *Ha-purim-shpil: iyunim ba'teatron ha-yehudi ha-amami* (Jerusalem: Mosad Byalik, 2002); and Khone Shmeruk, introduction to *Makhazot mikraiim be-yidish, 1697–1750*, ed. Shmeruk (Jerusalem: Israel Academy of Sciences and Humanities, 1979).

6. Compare Bützer, esp. 23–30 and 153–201.

not universally the case. In fact, the first extant play to be performed on Purim, written by Judah b. Leone Somo (Leone de' Sommi) in 1515, is written in Hebrew.[7] Somo's play, *Tzakhut bedikhuta dekidushin* (An Eloquent Marriage Farce), is exceptional in many ways, not limited to its language of composition. The play is not based on a traditional Jewish story, and indeed superficially has little to do with Purim, though its plot, which turns on a series of complex and twisted interpretations of Jewish marriage law, may well have reminded the viewer of *purim-toyre* theatricalized, and upon closer examination of the play, the characters can be seen as representations of characters from the Esther story.

However, the main influences on the characters are clearly from commedia dell'arte, and many of the play's dramatic and theatrical motifs are borrowed directly from the theatre of the Renaissance. This is hardly surprising, given the author's prominent position as a theorist of theatre in Mantua: an intellectual who felt as much at home among the works of secular literature in European languages as in traditional Jewish texts. In this way, we see the first evidence of a theme which will become more and more apparent as the story of Yiddish theatre continues: the adaptation and Judaization of non-Jewish theatrical traditions, motifs, technologies, and even particular theatrical works. Somo, by dint of his own background and training, was an exceptional individual, but in fact much of the story of Jewish theatre—and, more specifically, Yiddish theatre—is the story of extraordinary individuals who attempt to transpose general theatre into a Jewish key for a Jewish audience, for both polemic and aesthetic purposes, as we will see.

Audience may well have been the reason for the failure of *An Eloquent Marriage Farce* to become a major influence on the lived history of Jewish theatre; the play's recondite Hebrew meant that few members of the general Mantuan population would have been able to understand it. In many ways, the fate of the play serves as an introduction to another of the major issues surrounding the development of Yiddish theatre: the linguistic knowledge of the playwrights' audiences. Though Jews in Eastern Europe were undoubtedly members of what scholars have referred to as a "linguistic polysystem"—a society in which many

---

7. See J. H. Schirmann, ed. *Tsakhut be-dikhuta de-kidushin: komediya be-khamesh ma'arakhot,* by Judah b. Leone Somo (Jerusalem: Dvir, 1965), and his introductory essay there. See also Alfred S. Golding's extensive introduction and notes to his English translation of the work, *A Comedy of Betrothal* (Ottawa: Dovehouse Editions Canada, 1988); Ahuva Belkin, ed., *Leone de' Sommi and the Performing Arts* (Tel Aviv: Tel Aviv University, 1997); and Avisar.

languages coexisted and were spoken and understood at various levels—a number of essential facts seem clear.[8]

First, in most of Europe, until the middle of the eighteenth century, the basic lingua franca of Jewry was Yiddish, though by this period significant divergences had developed between Jews living in Western Europe (the various German principalities, Italy, Amsterdam), and Eastern Europe (the Polish-Lithuanian Commonwealth). Second, Hebrew was the main liturgical language of all of Jewish society, as widely used for prayer as it was little understood by the general populace. Mostly used by educated elites, Hebrew also played a major role in the complicated mixture of rapprochement and alienation that marked the revival of Christian interest in Jewish texts and the Jewish religion that developed in the Renaissance and early-modern era (generally known as Christian Hebraism).[9] Third, Jewish knowledge of the coterritorial Western languages (German, Russian, Polish, and so on) varied widely, but roughly corresponded to the level of cosmopolitanism and urbanization of the Jewish community. With knowledge of Western languages came also knowledge of the culture and literature written in that language. Yiddish literature published in the sixteenth through eighteenth centuries, which includes a significant amount of material translated from other literatures (though often Judaized and censored to remove obscene or Christian elements), illustrates both the interest that readers of Yiddish literature had in these stories and, presumably, their inability or difficulty with reading them in the original.[10]

The complex linguistic situation would become particularly important to the history of the Yiddish theatre as the Jewish community of Europe began its uneasy encounter with modernity. Though many historians differ on the definition of "modernity" and its dating, it seems fair to date the changes in Western Europe to a period after the end of the Thirty Years' War (1618–1648), where an increasing philosophical interest in religious toleration combined with an improvement

---

8. There is a significant and fractious literature on the history of the Yiddish language. For two of the classic treatments, see Max Weinreich, *Geshikhte fun der yidisher shprakh: bagrifn, faktn, metodn* (New York: YIVO, 1973), trans. as *History of the Yiddish Language* (Chicago: University of Chicago Press, 1980), and Benjamin Harshav, *The Meaning of Yiddish* (Berkeley: University of California Press, 1990).

9. On Hebrew and Christian Hebraism, see Frank Manuel, *The Broken Staff* (Cambridge, MA: Harvard University Press, 1992).

10. This said, it is difficult to tell precisely where these books and pamphlets were intended to be sold and disseminated. For extensive discussion, see Sara Zfatman-Biller, "Ha-siporet be-yidish me-reshita ad 'shivkhei ha-besht,'" 2 vols. (Ph.D. dissertation, Hebrew University, 1983).

in the economic circumstances of a class of Western European Jewish bourgeoisie to provide new opportunities for Jewish acculturation. These opportunities were particularly visible in new "boom town" cities like Berlin, which saw an influx of Jewish settlement.[11]

During the next century, the trends towards acculturation continued and intensified. Jews became increasingly involved in and aware of Western culture, and began to develop the sense that real possibilities for social and political emancipation were available. The historical figure most symbolic of these possibilities was Moses Mendelssohn (1729–1786), the Prussian Jewish philosopher whose writings and personal experience suggested a new model of Jewish existence in the Diaspora: one based on a strong commitment to Jewish belief and action while simultaneously affirming the value of Western cultural values and ideals, particularly the rationalism highly prized by the proponents of the Enlightenment.[12] In his works, most notably *Jerusalem*, Mendelssohn attempted to illustrate not only how Judaism deserved toleration under the rules and values that enlightened Western society had set for itself, but also how Judaism was an excellent (perhaps the best) demonstration of those rules and values.[13]

In *Jerusalem*—written in German and addressed to a non-Jewish audience—Mendelssohn also demonstrates another idea: the way in which proof of Jewish suitability for being emancipated and given equal rights is contingent on the Jewish writer's mastery of contemporary Western cultural forms. Almost all of Mendelssohn's work, from his earliest *Kohelet Musar* to his *Philosophical Dialogues* to his *Jerusalem*, are modeled on contemporary Prussian genres: the "moral weekly," the

---

11. The historical literature on this subject is vast. Selected treatments of the subject include Azriel Shohat, *Im khilufei tekufot: reyshit ha-haskala be-yahadut germania* (Jerusalem: Mossad Bialik, 1960); Michael A. Meyer, ed., *German Jewish History in Modern Times, vol. 1* (New York: Columbia University Press, 1996); Michael A. Meyer, *The Origins of the Modern Jew: Jewish Identity and European Culture in Germany, 1749–1824* (Detroit, MI: Wayne State University Press, 1967); Jonathan I. Israel, *European Jewry in the Age of Mercantilism, 1550–1750* (Oxford: Clarendon Press, 1989); David Sorkin, *The Transformation of German Jewry, 1780–1840* (Oxford: Oxford University Press, 1987); and Steven Lowenstein, *The Berlin Jewish Community: Enlightenment, Family, and Crisis, 1770–1830* (Oxford: Oxford University Press, 1994).

12. See, for example, Michael L. Morgan, "Mendelssohn," in *History of Jewish Philosophy*, ed. Daniel H. Frank and Oliver Leaman, (London: Routledge Press, 1997), 660–681, and Moshe Pelli, "Moshe Mendelson kidmut ha-yehudi ha-khadash be-moral biografi shel yitzkhak aykhl," *Bitzaron* 45–48 (1990–1991), 118–127.

13. Moses Mendelssohn, *Jerusalem*, trans. and ed. Allan Arkush (Hanover, NH: University Press of New England, 1983), and Alexander Altmann's introduction there (3–29). See also Jeremy Dauber, *Antonio's Devils: Writers of the Jewish Enlightenment and the Birth of Modern Hebrew and Yiddish Literature* (Stanford: Stanford University Press, 2004), 138–163.

philosophical dialogue, the polemical pamphlet.[14] The German concept of Bildung, a word which in this context means something between "education" and "culture," was a vital one to Mendelssohn and his successors: Jewish acceptance by the non-Jewish minority, the maskilim felt, was contingent on the sufficient internalization of *Bildung*.[15] It is hardly surprising that the two main projects of what became known as the Berlin Haskala—the Hebrew language journal known as *Ha-me'asef* (the Gatherer), and the German translation and commentary to the Bible, generally known as the *Biur*—themselves participate in broader cultural traditions, even as they were addressed to primarily Jewish audiences.

The fact that these projects did not include Yiddish was hardly coincidental. The maskilim felt that there was a strong linguistic dimension to their project, not merely a literary and cultural one. It was not sufficient merely to demonstrate Jewish facility and excellence in the genres prized by the non-Jewish community; because of an eighteenth-century linguistic theory which divided languages into "pure" and "corrupt," one had to do so in a "pure" language as well. Hebrew, by dint of its classical status and its role as the language of a shared Jewish and Christian holy text, was not merely pure but also a potential vehicle for rapprochement between proponents of the two religions. Yiddish, on the other hand, was seen as a corrupt version of German, caught up in a larger controversy of the time about various dialects of German. Many of the maskilim felt that social and cultural emancipation among German Jewry also necessitated emancipation from Yiddish.[16] This strong stigma against Yiddish—a stigma also connected to the influx of Eastern European Jews into Prussia, which we will discuss later—would be maintained over the next century and would follow the spread of the Jewish Enlightenment into Eastern Europe, where it would have radically different consequences for the development of Yiddish literature and drama as a whole.[17]

---

14. See, for example, the discussion in Meir Gilon, *Kohelet musar le-Mendelson al reka tekufato* (Jerusalem: Israel Academy of the Sciences and the Humanities, 1979), 37–53, and Sorkin, 15–16.

15. See Steven E. Aschheim, *Brothers and Strangers: The East European Jew in German and German Jewish Consciousness, 1800–1923* (Madison: University of Wisconsin Press, 1982), 7–8.

16. For a full discussion, see Peter Freimark, "Language Behaviour and Assimilation: The Situation of the Jews in Modern Germany in the First Half of the Nineteenth Century," *Leo Baeck Institute Year Book* 24 (1979): 157–177; and Jeffrey A. Grossman, *The Discourse on Yiddish in Germany: From the Enlightenment to the Second Empire* (Rochester, NY: Camden House, 2000), esp. 75–90, 110–111.

17. On the development of this stigma, see Dan Miron, *A Traveler Disguised*, 2nd ed. (Syracuse, NY: Syracuse University Press, 1996), esp. 34–45; and Shmuel Werses, "Yad yamin dokhe yad smol mekarevet: al yakhasam shel sofrei ha-haskala le-lashon yidish," *Khulyot* 5 (1998), 9–49.

One difficulty with Hebrew and German, however, was that they were not by and large the languages of the Jewish populace. Research has indicated that contrary to the conventional wisdom, Mendelssohn's translation and commentary to the Bible was not intended to teach Prussian Jews German, but rather to familiarize them with the increasingly unknown Hebrew language.[18] German, fairly close linguistically to Western Yiddish, was certainly apprehensible to the Yiddish speaker, but the "narcissism of minor differences" meant that it was still perceived as a differentiated mode of speech. These differences would have major consequences for the representation of dialogue within the Yiddish theatre, as we shall see.

All of these factors combine to create the conditions that gave rise to the first Yiddish plays of the modern era. During the last decade of the eighteenth century, two members of the Berlin Haskala each composed a play focusing on contemporary Jewish life in northern Prussia, each of which featured a main character named Reb Henokh. (Some scholars have suggested that the similarity of the two plays resulted from friendly competition, or perhaps even a wager, between the two authors; history has yet to fully illuminate the issue.) Isaac Euchel's (1756–1804) *Reb Henokh oder vos tut men damit* (Reb Henokh, or What Is to Be Done About It, ca. 1792) and Aaron Halle-Wolfssohn's *Laykhtzin un fremelay* (Silliness and Sanctimony, ca. 1794) can be considered the first advances in the modern Yiddish theatre.[19] Compared to Euchel's *Reb Henokh*, which has a tendency to meander and squander its dramatic and satiric effect, Wolfssohn's play is dramatically taut and still eminently stageable, our reason for including it here rather than its contemporary.

Aaron Halle Wolfssohn's *Silliness and Sanctimony*

Aaron Halle-Wolfssohn's name already reveals some important historical information: born in the Prussian city of Halle in 1754, he took a name which was the German version of his patronymic.[20] His father,

---

18. Werner Weinberg, "Language Questions Relating to Moses Mendelssohn's Pentateuch Translation," *Hebrew Union College Annual* 55 (1984): 197–242.

19. On the two plays as a unit and their role as a reflection of the period, the classic (though tendentious) treatment remains Max Erik, *Di komedyes fun der berliner oyfklerung* (Kiev: Melukhe-Farlag, 1933), 5–67. On Euchel's play, see the discussions in Meyer, 118–119; Aviezer, 166–170; and Gilman, 110–114. On the meaning and the antecedents of the phrase *vos tut men damit*, see Dov Sadan, *A vort bashteyt* (Tel Aviv: Y. L. Peretz Farlag, 1975), 194–201.

20. For a fuller treatment of Wolfssohn's life and work, see Dauber, 164–206 and the sources cited there, especially Jutta Strauss, "Aaron Halle-Wolfssohn: A Trilingual Life" (D.Phil. dissertation, University of Oxford, 1994).

Wolf, the son of a merchant, had studied both Talmud and medicine, which illustrates the family's slow movement toward modernity. Wolfssohn himself grew up speaking German, not Yiddish, and may have already become familiar with secular works in his parents' home—affording him a kind of freedom from the necessity of a strong familial break which was to characterize so many of the later maskilim and have such powerful psychological consequences for their later work.[21]

Wolfssohn arrived in Berlin in 1785, joining the circle of Jewish intellectuals who were gathering around Moses Mendelssohn there. Like many of them, he participated in the main projects of the Berlin Haskala, including writing commentaries to the Song of Songs and translating the books of Lamentations, Ruth, Job, and Esther into German, as well as providing commentaries to them, and contributing numerous articles and notices to *Ha-me'asef*, most notably his dramatic dialogue from the mid-1790s, *Sikha be'eretz ha-khayim* (A Conversation in the Land of the Living). Wolfssohn became coeditor of the journal in the 1790s.

In keeping with the central position of *Bildung* in maskilic thought, Wolfssohn's interest in the dissemination of Enlightenment also expressed itself in pedagogical efforts; he wrote one of the first Jewish primers, *Avtalyon* (Berlin, 1790), which retold many of the biblical stories in simpler Hebrew and emphasized their universal moral lessons. Most important for our purposes, however, along with his fellow maskil, Joel Bril, he headed the Königliche Wilhelmsschule in Breslau, which taught Jewish and secular subjects according to new pedagogical principles and thus sparked controversy within the local Jewish community. As part of his work there, Wolfssohn composed plays for the students of the school to perform in the period around the holiday of Purim; whether *Silliness and Sanctimony* was one of those plays is a matter of speculation.[22] What is clear, though, is that both *Silliness and Sanctimony* and other plays by Wolfssohn exhibit polemic purposes beyond simple entertainment. In composing the play, Wolfssohn was attempting to create a replacement for traditional Purim plays which would accord with contemporary enlightened notions of appropriate Jewish dramatic creativity.

Though our previous discussion of the Purim plays ended in the early modern period, the plays themselves had continued—and had

---

21. See Alan Mintz, *"Banished from Their Father's Table": Loss of Faith and Hebrew Autobiography* (Bloomington: Indiana University Press, 1989).

22. A later play designed for this purpose, *Dovid der baziger fun Golies* ("David the Victor Over Goliath," 1802), seems to be a sign of the changing nature of Jewish linguistic patterns. Though the play is written in Hebrew script, it is composed entirely in German; see Strauss, 170–178. We also know that Wolfssohn composed a play, no longer extant, on the subject of early burial, a flashpoint for maskilic activity.

thrived—through the sixteenth and seventeenth centuries.[23] A few Purim plays, performed in the German cities and principalities and written in Yiddish, survive from the sixteenth and seventeenth centuries; looking at them, one can see why Wolfssohn would have thought the genre needed revising. The most striking characteristic, to modern eyes, is how the genre has not only continued its commedia dell'arte-inspired trends of improvisation and anachronism but has picked up on its ribaldry and obscenity as well. The 1720 *Akhashveyresh-shpil* is a case in point: its constant shift between high and low register, between the sacred biblical account and the profane interjections by the Mordechai character (who serves as a kind of outside commentator as well as a participant in the narrative action), provide exactly the kind of carnivalesque chaos anathema to the rationalist maskilim, hoping to show their refinement to their non-Jewish neighbors.[24]

Wolfssohn's own real affinities for traditional life (albeit a reformed and refined version of that tradition), as well as his canny sense of precisely how much transformation he could press on the Jewish community, certainly played a role in his maintaining the idea of the Purim story, not merely attempting to remove it entirely. Wolfssohn's own research and thinking on the book of Esther, done for his work on Mendelssohn's Bible translation project, must also have been extremely useful, for there are real continuities between the story of the book of Esther and *Silliness and Sanctimony*. Like the book of Esther, *Silliness and Sanctimony* features a hypocrite who has wormed his way into the good graces of the ruling authority and is finally unmasked due to the efforts of the main hero and heroine, in both cases at a place ostensibly designed for entertainment and pleasure (a feast or wine party in the Bible, and a bordello, where punch is regularly served, in *Silliness and Sanctimony*). Both works mix together comic and serious elements, and both attempt to depict Jewish existence in societies that seem to vacillate between tolerance and hostility. Wolfssohn's return to the biblical story as a template, rather than to its later expansion and transmuta-

---

23. Indeed, they remained popular well into the twentieth century, and can still be seen in many Hasidic communities today. For analyses of contemporary Hasidic *purimshpiln*, see Shifra Epstein, introduction to *"Daniel-shpil" ba-khasidut bobov: mi-makhazeh amami le-tekes purimi* (Jerusalem: Hebrew University, 1998), 7–73; Barbara Kirshenblatt-Gimblett, "Contraband: Performance, Text and Analysis of a *Purim-shpil*," *The Drama Review* 24 (September 1980): 5–16; and Shari Troy, "On the Play and the Playing: Theatricality as Leitmotif in the Purim Play of the Bobover Hasidim" (Ph.D. dissertation, City University of New York, 2001).

24. See Shmeruk, *Makhazot*, 20–44, and Shiper, 3:262–293.

tion, accords well with the maskilic love of classicism and bibliophilia, a sentiment which itself had ideological roots and effects.[25]

Reading Wolfssohn's play itself, however, those familiar with the theatrical tradition can easily find a much more straightforward analogue than the Bible story. As was first noted by an anonymous reviewer, the play is a Jewish adaptation of Molière's *Tartuffe* (1664).[26] In Wolfssohn's version, the wealthy German Jewish merchant Reb Henokh Yoysefkhe has hired a Polish rabbi, Reb Yoysefkhe, as live-in tutor for his young son—whom, intriguingly, we never meet. Reb Henokh, successful in business but with little Jewish knowledge, clearly enjoys studying with Reb Yoysefkhe far more than his son does, and as the play begins the father is very much in Reb Yoysefkhe's sway—so much so that the opening scene features an argument between husband and wife over the proper way to raise their children (an argument we will see echoed in Goldfaden's *The Two Kuni-Lemls*). Reb Henokh's wife Teltse and her enlightened brother Markus worry about the tutor's growing influence over his master. Their fears turn out to be well founded. Reb Yoysefkhe manages to plant the idea in his master's head that he should marry Reb Henokh's daughter, and then feigns surprise—but also genuine delight—at the idea. It is an odd couple if ever there was one, for Yetkhen, the daughter, is thoroughly assimilated. Where Reb Yoysefkhe laces his speech with references to traditional Jewish texts and ideas (albeit for purely self-serving purposes), Yetkhen speaks of nothing but rendezvous with her gentile suitors, the latest offering at the opera, and the pulp fiction that fills her shelves. When she learns—from none other than Reb Yoysefkhe himself!—of the planned marriage, she flees her father's house, invoking notions of rebellion against tyranny that would not sound out of place in the mouth of a Goethe or Schiller hero. She takes refuge with one of her suitors, who immediately shows his true mettle by handing her over to a brothel keeper, and is rescued from the brothel by her uncle, who before taking

---

25. See Dauber, 178–187.

26. Wolfssohn would have been familiar with *Tartuffe* from its German translation, which went through at least five printings between 1721 and 1784 and was performed at the court of Frederick the Great by a French troupe in the summer of 1776. See Bernard Weinryb, "Aaron Halle-Wolfssohn's Dramatic Writings in Their Historical Setting," *Jewish Quarterly Review* 48 (1957–1958): 35–50, esp. 47, and Y. Shatzky, "Vegn Arn-hale Volfsons pyesn (naye materyaln)," in Shatzky, ed., *Arkhiv*, 147–150, where the review, taken from the *Schlessiche Provinzialnblätter*, appears. On the performance of *Tartuffe* and other French comedies at Frederick's court, see Jean-Jacques Olivier, *Les comédiens français dans les cours d'allemagne au xviiiᵉ siècle* (Paris: Société Français D'Imprimerie et de Librairie, 1901–1905), 2:27–63, esp. 59–60.

her home fetches her father to show him the bitter fruits of excessive severity. Markus scores an added, unexpected victory when he and Reb Henokh find Reb Yoysefkhe in the brothel. The rabbi turns out to be a regular customer, who has been using the bordello's services on credit, based on his own vaunted prospects of marriage into a wealthy family. The end of the play finds him literally in the doghouse, while Yetkhen is reconciled with her father.

Aside from the inherent merits of Molière's satire as a model, Wolfssohn's attraction to *Tartuffe* was certainly based in part on his realization that its main plot device could be adapted to reflect a historical phenomenon then prevalent in certain German Jewish circles which neatly adumbrated his Enlightenment aims. At the time Wolfssohn wrote the play, a flood of Eastern European Jewish refugees was trying to make its way into German cities. Leaving the famine, instability, and poverty in their places of origin, many attempted to make a living by tutoring traditional Jewish subjects, particularly Talmud, in the houses of their wealthier but less traditionally educated counterparts.[27] In doing so, they hoped to win rare and valuable residence permits, optimally by marrying members of their host family. These Eastern European Jews became the flashpoint for a new shift in maskilic thinking at the end of the eighteenth century, which served as the root for attitudes between Western and Eastern European Jewry until the Holocaust. The maskilim, attempting to show to their non-Jewish neighbors their own fitness for adoption into general European culture and for political and social emancipation, hoped to demonstrate the difference between themselves and the Eastern European Jews, whose unfitness they attempted to portray in many ways: hygienic, cultural, moral, and linguistic. Currently, we may look at this approach and shudder, seeing in it the beginnings of a kind of Jewish self-hatred which has unfortunately flourished in the centuries since Wolfssohn wrote, but at the time the maskilim engaged in it with gusto, particularly after the death of the more restrained Moses Mendelssohn and in the political excitement of the time following the French Revolution.[28]

Wolfssohn, at the same time as he was composing *Silliness and Sanctimony*, was already thinking about the problem of the Eastern European Jew (or, as they were generally known at the time, the Polish Jew; Russia would gain a large Jewish community only with the various partitions of Poland in the last decades of the eighteenth century). His

---

27. See Meyer, *German-Jewish History*, 1:98.

28. See Aschheim, *Brothers and Strangers*, and Sander Gilman, *Jewish Self-Hatred* (Baltimore: Johns Hopkins University Press, 1986), esp. 124–132.

long work *Sikha be'eretz ha-khayim*, written in Hebrew and published in *Ha-me'asef* between 1794 and 1797, is an Enlightenment tract in the form of a philosophical dialogue between the spirits of Maimonides, Mendelssohn, and an unnamed Polish Jew. There Wolfssohn attacks the Eastern Jews' irrational and superstitious approach to Jewish tradition, as well as their unwillingness to delve deeply into the moral and philosophical principles which for Wolfssohn and other early maskilim were the most powerful proofs of Jewish fitness for emancipation. Though the genre of the philosophical dialogue is not designed for significant dramatic action, nor, for that matter, for characterization, Wolfssohn does a much better job than his mentor Moses Mendelssohn in crafting characters who both express opinions and personalities. As such, *Sikha be'eretz ha-khayim* becomes an important way station in the development of Wolfssohn's dramatic talents, as well as his articulation of the inferiority of the Eastern European Jew. [29]

Tartuffe, then, that pious hypocrite, becomes not only an Eastern European Jew but a Haman of an Eastern European Jew to boot: someone who, in maskilic eyes, is not only morally retrograde but, if he is able to continue and to flourish, responsible for the eventual destruction of the Jewish people. Reb Yoysefkhe, who on the one hand seduces the paterfamilias of the household with pieties while on the other sexually seducing the maid, is the strongest threat in the play, the restraining presence on the German Jewish march toward Enlightenment who must be revealed as the danger he is. Only when he is removed from the household can Jewish survival be ensured. As such, Wolfssohn's play can be seen not only as a recapitulation of the themes of the book of Esther, but a take on a literary classic and, in the style of the contemporary German *familien gemelde*, a picture of family life. [30]

One may additionally argue that Reb Yoysefkhe is not merely a Tartuffe and a Haman but also an actor, and that *Silliness and Sanctimony*, with its themes of masking and unmasking, is a play very much about the theatre itself; that, as in so many other works of theatre, it is the villain who gets the best lines and scenes, because he represents the anarchic spirit present in the play, or play itself. It may not be

---

29. *Sikha be'eretz ha-khayim* appeared in *Ha-me'asef* 7:54–67, 120–155, 203–228, 279–298. See Meyer, *German-Jewish History* 1:318–319; Aviezer 62, 80; Meir Gilon, "Ha-satira ha-ivrit bi-tkufat ha-haskala be-germania—anatomia shel mekhkar," *Zion* 52 (1987), 211–250, 246–250; and Yehudit Tsvik, "Reshit tsmikhato shel ha-sipur be-haskala ha-germanit: ha-takhbula ha-dialogit," *Kongres olami le-makhshevet yisrael* 11C3 (1994), 53–60.

30. On the "prose domestic drama" in contemporary German theatre of the period, see W. H. Bruford, *Theatre, Drama, and Audience in Goethe's Germany* (London: Routledge and Kegan Paul, 1950), 163–202.

insignificant to note that when Reb Yoysefkhe attempts to romance Yetkhen, he does so by complimenting her artistic endeavors, her playing; one performer recognizes the gifts of another. If the play operates on so many levels, then, it demands a closer look: how straightforward is the piece? Complicating the matter is that Wolfssohn wrote two versions of the play, an earlier version in Hebrew and a subsequent one in Yiddish; though there are many similarities between the two, there are significant differences as well, and these differences speak to the possibilities for both writing Jewish drama in these differing languages and developing a complex theory of the progress of German Jewry toward Enlightenment.[31]

Wolfssohn wrote his first, Hebrew version of the play in approximately 1794 under the title *Reb Henokh ve-Reb Yoysefkhe*, and wrote the Yiddish version at some point between his creation of the Hebrew version and 1796.[32] In the original version, the play is more schematic: on the one hand, we have the Hamanic Reb Yoysefkhe; on the other, we have Wolfssohn's attempt to rehabilitate the Mordechai figure, the maskilic Markus, who unmasks Reb Yoysefkhe for the hypocrite he is and wins the approval (and, one assumes, the ideological sympathies) of Reb Henokh, to say nothing of the hand of Henokh's daughter Yetkhen.[33] In his introduction to the Hebrew version, however, Wolfssohn writes of his attempt not only to replace the current Purim plays, but also to sketch the character types he sees in contemporary Prussian Jewish society. He mentions three types in particular: the well-meaning nonenlightened, the pious hypocrites, and the falsely enlightened. Though the first category is obvious and the second has been discussed, a bit more explanation is required for the third.

In the period of increasing liberalization following Mendelssohn's death and the French Revolution, some maskilim began to worry about the consequences of emancipation, not merely its prospects. These

---

31. For a fuller overview of this issue, see Jeremy Dauber, "The City, Sacred and Profane: Between Hebrew and Yiddish in the Fiction of the Early Jewish Enlightenment," *Jewish Studies Quarterly* 12 (March 2005), 1–18.

32. See Bernard Weinryb, "An Unknown Hebrew Play of the German Haskalah," *Proceedings of the American Academy of Jewish Research* 24 (1955), 165–170. The text of the play is included in the Hebrew section of the issue, 1–37.

33. For an excellent and extensive analysis of Wolfssohn's Hebrew play, see Dan Miron's introduction to the modern edition of the play, "Al Aharon Volfson ve-makhazehu 'kalut dat u'tseviut' (r' henokh ve-rav yosefkhe)," in Aaron Halle Wolfssohn, *Kalut Dat u'tseviut* (Israel: Seman Keriah, 1977), 5–55. On the figure of Markus as a rehabilitated Mordechai, see Khone Shmeruk, "Ha-shem ha-mashma'uti Mordekhai Markus—gilgulo ha-sifruti shel ideal khevrati," *Tarbiz* 29 (1959–1960), 76–98.

maskilim, who themselves were still committed to Jewish tradition and Jewish identity, began to see how some individuals were taking the freedoms that were given them in this new situation, and using it to abandon Jewish tradition—and, in some cases, the Jewish religion— entirely. This movement culminated in a series of baptisms known to contemporaries as the *Taufepidemie*. These baptisms were of men and women alike; much of the attention, however, both by contemporaries and later historians, focused on the acts of a few upper-class Jewish women who headed a series of salons which served as central social gathering points for Jews and non-Jews alike, some of whom would later convert to marry non-Jews.[34] Wolfssohn, well aware of the way social and sexual tension were combining in contemporary society, was able to create a story in which a female character's lack of true enlightenment was concretized in her near-disastrous decision to throw herself, literally and metaphorically, into the arms of non-Jews. This sexualization of religious issues was hardly innovative: since biblical times, Israel's turning astray to worship other gods had been rhetorically framed in terms of wantonness and prostitution,[35] and so using the contemporary landscape of bordellos (which indeed counted Jews among their patrons at the time)[36] to reflect Yetkhen's fate was unsurprising.

It is, however, possible to argue that Wolfssohn looked further. Certainly, Yetkhen is the clearest example of the "false Enlightenment." But there may be another as well. Wolfssohn may well have been concerned that false enlightenment was not merely the province of the uneducated and the foolish, but also of the overly educated and the wise. Could it also be that those who have internalized the moral tenets of the Enlightenment may themselves be at risk for leaving behind Jewish tradition? It seems significant that in the Yiddish version of the play, Markus is significantly less traditional than in the Hebrew version, and never uses a single Hebraism of any sort. Though the Hebrew Markus is clearly Wolfssohn's ideal maskil, the Yiddish Markus is an uneasier version of that paradigm. Overbearing, somewhat cruel, prone to long speeches and oh so certain of his rightness, Markus—as a foil to the play's undoubted villain—seems less heroic than we might feel comfortable with. If Wolfssohn did indeed wish to warn

---

34. On these historical events and their significance, see Lowenstein, 120–176; Deborah Hertz, *Jewish High Society in Old Regime Berlin* (New Haven, CT: Yale University Press, 1988), 119–203; and Reuven Michael, "Ha-haskala bi-tkufat ha-mahapekha ha-tsarfatit–ha-ketz le'haskalat berlin'?" *Zion* 56, no. 3 (1991): 275–298.

35. See, for example, Hosea 1:2.

36. See Shohat, 166, and Hertz, 76.

readers of the dangers of going too far in the opposite direction—leaving Reb Henokh as the play's true center, and, when he reforms at the end, the ideal model for the reading public—then perhaps it makes sense that he wished to include a more ambivalent Markus in addition to Yetkhen. It may also be that the difficulties of writing in the Hebrew language itself—a language which is constantly allusive, constantly reminiscent of classical Jewish texts—did not allow for the creation of a nuanced character halfway between the sacred and the profane. Perhaps this is one of the reasons that Wolfssohn turned from Hebrew to Yiddish: to more clearly express his ambivalence about the future of a wholesale adoption of the tenets of secularization.

One does not, however, need to go that far. Wolfssohn is clearly a dramatist, and is able to recognize how the Hebrew language, which affords far fewer possibilities for character differentiation, fails to provide the rich, multilingual environment he wishes to capture in his work. For *Silliness and Sanctimony*, in truth, is not a Yiddish play. It is a play which has Yiddish in it. Markus, the educated medical student, speaks a refined *Hochdeutsch*; Henokh and Teltse speak the Western Yiddish common among Prussian Jews of the period; and Reb Yoysefkhe, as befitting a hypocrite and an actor, is able to change his linguistic register depending on whom he is addressing, though his natural speech is an Eastern European Yiddish, studded with words from the Hebrew and Aramaic components of the language. In this rich mélange, which we have tried to preserve in our translation, the reader can begin to see Yiddish drama's realization that realism lies in differentiated language and its delight in the multiple possibilities of the Yiddish language to render that differentiation.

Wolfssohn's Successors

Though we have little detail about the performance history of *Silliness and Sanctimony*. Though it is reasonable to assume, given Wolfssohn's own biography, that there was some possibility for performance by members of the school he headed, the fact of the matter is that during Wolfssohn's lifetime—and indeed for the better part of the nineteenth century—theatrical pieces written in Yiddish had limited opportunities for performance. There were no professional actors to perform Wolfssohn's drama, nor were there professional spaces in which that drama would be performed. In fact, the chances are good that if there was any performance of the play at all, it would have consisted of a staged reading of what we might call a "salon drama," using the large rooms of bourgeois Jews as the performance space.

Even more likely, however, is the idea that Wolfssohn's play—as many other plays written by maskilim of the early nineteenth century, both extant and vanished—was rarely if ever performed even in this limited form, but merely circulated in manuscript and, at times, read aloud by both the authors and other like-minded individuals or groups.[37] There are a number of reasons for this lack of public performance and even more marked lack of theatrical publication, which, in turn, led to a lack of celebrity or notoriety among the writers of this period. In explicating them, we may begin to trace the development of Yiddish theatre as it moves eastward, from Prussia to Austria-Hungary and particularly the province of Galicia, and then from there to the massive Jewish population formerly of the Polish Lithuanian commonwealth.

Some of the reasons were economic: certainly the publication of theatrical material is often a financial risk, and this was more the case then than now, given the lack of theatrical venues for performance, as well as the lack of a traditional audience for printed theatrical material. Materials would have to be approved by censors. More important, though, were the limitations on maskilic printing in general: for most of the nineteenth century there were only two printing presses in Eastern Europe that would print Yiddish materials, both in the hands of Hasidim, who, naturally, were inimical to the maskilic project.[38]

The feeling was mutual: though Wolfssohn had had little good to say about the Hasidic Reb Yoysefkhe in *Silliness and Sanctimony*, the number of Eastern European Jews and Hasidim in Prussia was still comparatively small, enabling them to serve as much as symbol as actual phenomenon. Additionally, when Wolfssohn wrote in the 1790s, the Hasidic movement, while growing, had yet to reach the heights of population, influence, and power that it would in the nineteenth century. For all these reasons, it was unsurprising that among many of the nineteenth-century Eastern European maskilim, the war for enlightenment was often seen as a struggle against Hasidism.[39]

---

37. Two examples were the 1839 play *Teater fun khsidim* (Theatre of Hasidim) and the play *Gedules Reb Volf* (The Greatness of Rabbi Wolf), probably written in the first decades of the nineteenth century. Authorship of the former, whose name also indicates the similarities between theatricality and Hasidism discussed below, is ascribed by Erik to Ettinger's student Efrayim-Fishel Fishelson [Erik, "Shloyme Etinger, 1800 [01?]–1856," in *Sh. Etinger: geklibene verk*, ed. Erik (Kiev: Farlag fun der Ukrainisher Visnshaft-akademye, 1935), 7–33]. *Gedules Reb Volf* was erroneously ascribed to Joseph Perl but actually written by Khayim Malaga. See Shmuel Werses, "Tsvishn dray shprakhn: vegn Yoysef Perls yidishe ksovim in likht fun naye materyaln," *Goldene keyt* 89 (1976): 150–177, as well as Khone Shmeruk, *Prokim fun der yidisher literature-geshikhte* (Tel Aviv: Farlag Y. L. Peretz, 1988), 291.

38. The maskil Joseph Perl also controlled a Galician printing press, but very briefly. On Yiddish printing presses in Eastern Europe during the period, see Khayim Liberman, "Legende un emes vegn khsidishe drukerayen," in *Ohel Rokhl* (New York: Empire Press, 1980), ed. Liberman 2:17–160.

39. See Raphael Mahler, *Hasidism and the Jewish Enlightenment: Their Confrontation in Galicia and Poland in the First Half of the Nineteenth Century* (Philadelphia: Jewish Publication Society, 1985).

This was certainly the attitude of the author of the play *Di genarte velt* (The Deceived World), one of the most important transitional works between the plays of the Prussian Haskala and the rise of the Eastern European Yiddish theatre, and the first modern play written entirely in Yiddish.[40] In this play, probably written in the second decade of the nineteenth century in Galicia, Hasidic leaders are seen as actors par excellence: though they pretend to be pious, their religious activities are merely masks, put on to disguise their real agendas of cupidity and immorality. There are real continuities between this play and Wolfssohn's work: aside from the motif of the pious hypocrite, the play's setting—on Purim—reveals once more an attempt to fit a modern message within a traditional framework, and the play's odd reference to phylacteries as "the ten commandments," language used in Wolfssohn's play as well, may suggest some more direct lines of continuity.[41]

The full reasons that the author of *The Deceived World* remained anonymous may never be definitively known, but one possible factor may have been the inheritance of the embarrassment about Yiddish from the members of the Berlin Haskala and the resulting unwillingness to publicly present themselves as authors of texts in that language.[42] There were notable exceptions among maskilim (among them Shloyme Ettinger, the author of *Serkele*), but, at least rhetorically, such discomfort was the rule, only broken because of the necessities of speaking to the audience in a language they could understand. (Galicia and Poland were different from Prussia: there, the linguistic similarities to German meant that the writers could be emancipated from Yiddish; here, they were required to emancipate in Yiddish.) This may explain in part the fetish for anonymous production among the writers and dramatists of this early period. Also, many maskilim, who were generally poor educators reliant on communal positions, could not afford to risk public opposition by being revealed as antitraditionalists.[43]

This conventional narrative of the hidden nature of Yiddish literature (and Yiddish drama) in the early to mid-nineteenth century, cen-

---

40. See Meir Viner, *Tsu der geshikhte fun der yidisher literatur in 19tn yorhundert* (New York: YKUF Farlag, 1945), 1:50–63; and Khone Shmeruk, "Nusakh bilti yadua shel ha-komediya ha-anonimit 'Di genarte velt,'" *Kiryat Sefer* 54 (1979): 802–816.

41. It is possible, of course, that this was just a common phrase. Still, the figuring of phylacteries in both plays seems odd.

42. See Miron, *Traveler*.

43. For one account of the dangers of being discovered as a maskil in a small town (though significantly later in the nineteenth century), see S. Ansky's novella *Behind a Mask*, translated in S. Ansky, *The Dybbuk and Other Writings*, ed. David G. Roskies (New York: Schocken Books, 1992), 118–144. Ansky, one of Yiddish literature's major playwrights, was well aware of the theatrical and dramatic nature of the maskilic endeavor.

tering on a rhetoric of "Yiddish as Caliban," to use Miron's phrase, is, however, somewhat more complex when it comes to our admittedly limited theatrical material. If the rare plays that were written in the period were circulated among maskilic circles and read aloud, and not published, one must assume that there was both pleasure in the composition and the reading regardless of the language of composition (and, indeed, perhaps because of it), as well as a drastic limitation of the polemic effect of the material (given that it was, by definition, written neither for publication nor for performance, and that the reading circles we are discussing were essentially limited to the maskilim themselves—they were, in some sense, "preaching to the choir.") One might argue that the dramatic form was conceived of differently by the writers, given the mimetic necessities of dialogue, and it may indeed be that, despite this sense of limited circulation, some writers nonetheless had a sense that they were writing for larger audiences. Regardless of the answer, what literary historian Meir Viner writes in this regard about the plays of Israel Aksenfeld (1787–1866) applies to dramas by other maskilic playwrights as well:

> Aksenfeld knew full well that his plays would primarily be read; he thus included in them a great deal of description. We do not know to what extent Aksenfeld thought it possible that his plays would be performed (though the level of performance of *purimshpiln* was quite widespread and detailed!). It is possible that he had little hope for their production. But that is far from being evidence that they are parlor dramas. If we maintain that the plays are constructed with the full possibility of being performed on stage—that they can, or would then have been able to, have dramatic effect—we must consider them as "stage-dramas," though history may have dictated that they be mainly read. The genre of a work is not decided by its historical fate, but rather by its true essence.[44]

Thought of in Viner's terms, we suggest that the "true essence" of plays like *Silliness and Sanctimony* and *Serkele*—whatever their authors' original plans for them—is as performance texts.

All of this said, one should not be left with the impression that maskilic dramatists, influenced as they were by the material and the sensibility flowing eastward from Berlin, found nothing to influence

---

44. Meir Viner, *Yidishe literatur in 19tn yorhundert* (Moscow, 1939; repr. New York: YKUF, 1:118–119).

them in their native regions. The Hasidic movement itself, though not explicitly dramatic, was filled with rituals and customs which could be seen as highly theatrical moments, moments which themselves became the staples of fiction about them, both pro- and anti-Hasidic: the rabbi's delivery of his teachings, or *toyre*, the disciples' narrative rehearsal of their rabbis' miraculous deeds, the rabbis' encounters with their faithful when they accepted their requests and contributions in return for their heavenly intercession (*pidyonim*), and others.[45] Perhaps the most famous example of a type of Yiddish performance in the Hasidic milieu of that era was given by Rabbi Nachman of Bratslav, whose disciples, upon hearing the stories that he told between 1806 and 1810, did not merely write them down verbatim in order to preserve the hidden meanings within, but also attempted to find the meaning in Nachman's various gestures and facial expressions—both the script and its actor's interpretation, as it were.[46]

Other quasi-performative institutions that were developing in Eastern Europe as a part of Jewish traditional life would in later years become the roots of secular theatrical activity. Purimshpiln were performed annually in cities and towns, and there was a lively tradition of performance at weddings as well. The wedding jester (*badkhn*), for example, whose job was to entertain the married couple and their family, generally through the improvised composition of rhymed verses extolling the family's virtues, would provide a rich paradigm for later exploration by performers and writers alike.[47] Though the next major playwright in the history of the Yiddish theatre was neither a Hasid nor

---

45. On some of these rites, see Khaviva Fedye, "Le-hitpatkhuto shel ha-degem ha-khevrati-dati-kalkali ba-khasidut: ha-pidyon, ha-khavura, veha-aliya la-regel," in *Dat ve-kalkala*, ed. Menakhem Ben-Sasson (Jerusalem: Zalman Shazar, 1995), 311–374; and Barbara Kirshenblatt-Gimblett, "The Concept and Variety of Narrative Performance in East European Jewish Culture," in *Explorations in the Ethnography of Speaking*, ed. Richard Bauman and Joel Sherzer (Cambridge: Cambridge University Press, 1989), 283–308.

46. The standard biography on Nachman of Bratslav is Arthur Green, *Tormented Master: A Life of Rabbi Nachman of Bratslav* (Tuscaloosa, AL: University of Alabama Press, 1979). See also Arnold Band's introduction to Nachman of Bratslav, *The Tales*, ed. and trans. Band (New York: Paulist Press, 1978), 9–25; and Nathan of Nemirov's description of his master's storytelling, cited in David Roskies, *A Bridge of Longing: The Lost Art of Yiddish Storytelling* (Cambridge, MA: Harvard University Press, 1995), 29: "For by means of body movement—rocking his hands back and forth, winking his eyes and hands gesticulating—it was by these means in particular that the learned [listener] was enlightened to understand just a little."

47. For studies of the *badkhn*, see Ariela Krasney, *Ha-badkhan* (Ramat Gan, Israel: Bar-Ilan University Press, 1998); Y. Lifshits, "Badkhonim un leytsim bay yidn," in Shatzky, *Arkhiv*, 38–74; and an English version of the same article: E. Lifschutz, "Merrymakers and Jesters Among Jews," *YIVO Annual* 7 (1952); 43–83.

a badkhn, he would be able to draw these disparate strands together in his own work in order to create a play very much in the tradition of Wolfssohn's *Silliness and Sanctimony* and the German tradition from which it sprung, while providing a sensibility that was equally contemporary and local.

Shloyme Ettinger and *Serkele*

Shloyme Ettinger was born in Warsaw at the beginning of the nineteenth century,[48] at a time when the influence of the German Haskala was just beginning to make itself known in this largest of Polish cities.[49] The Ettinger family counted among its members fairly distinguished scholars and merchants: his grandfather, Itche Ettinger, was the rabbi of Chelm, and his father, Yoske Ettinger, had been asked to be the rabbi of Frankfurt am Main, but refused the commission because of his desire to remain in Poland. Yoske Ettinger died young, and Shloyme, an orphan like so many of the foundational figures of modern Yiddish literature,[50] was raised in the house of his father's younger brother, Mendel Ettinger. Mendel, the rabbi of Letshne, in Lublin province, had a reputation for his willingness to incorporate secular learning, particularly German, into his studies. Like Wolfssohn's childhood, then, Ettinger's upbringing involved traditional Jewish study and secular knowledge, thus sparing him from the perceived dichotomy between traditional Judaism and worldly education that was often the case with his maskilic contemporaries.[51]

---

48. Biographical information for Ettinger is taken from Max Erik, "Shloyme Etinger, 1800[01?]–1856," in *Sh. Etinger: geklibene verk*, ed. Erik (Kiev: Farlag fun der Ukrainisher Visnshaft-akademye, 1935), 7–33; Max Weinreich, "Shloyme Etinger, zayn lebn un zayn perzenlekhkayt," in *Ale ksovim [fun Shloyme Etinger]*, ed. Weinreich, 2 vols (Vilna: B. Kletskin, 1925), xiii–xlvii; and *Leksikon fun der nayer yidisher literatur* (New York, 1956–81), 6:574–583. A generally accepted date for Ettinger's birth is 1803 (see Weinreich, "Shloyme Etinger," xiii), though Erik dates differently; see Weinreich, "Vegn Etingers geboyrn-yor," in *Ale ksovim*, 585–588.

49. In 1802, a Jewish banker founded a separate synagogue for Warsaw's maskilic population, and within the decade Warsaw maskilim began petitioning governmental authorities for decrees supporting maskilic ideology. See Erik, "Etinger," 9–10.

50. In Eastern European Jewish society, one who had lost either or both parents was referred to as an orphan. Both S. Y. Abramovitch (Mendele Moykher Seforim) and Sholem Rabinovitch (Sholem Aleichem), two of the three classic Yiddish writers, were orphaned in childhood. See Ken Frieden, *Classic Yiddish Fiction: Abramovitsh, Sholem Aleichem, and Peretz* (Albany: State University of New York Press, 1995).

51. *Leksikon*, 6:574. Ettinger would, as an adult, employ German for personal correspondence; see Miron, *Traveler*, 7.

It also began to give him the familiarity with German culture which would influence his later work so greatly.

Ettinger married at fifteen, a marriage his uncle had arranged for him with the daughter of a Zamosc magnate, Yude-Leyb Volf. As was customary at the time for traditional educated males throughout Eastern Europe, Ettinger went to live with his in-laws, and spent his days in the study house. What was, perhaps, less usual was Ettinger's involvement in the gradually increasing enlightenment movement in Zamosc;[52] Ettinger regularly visited the house of Reb Yosef Tsederboym, a meeting point for local maskilim, where he read secular literature and developed his understanding of German and Polish.[53] Apparently, it was here that Ettinger first received the reputation for good humor and merriment, as well as for rhymed poems and songs, which would last him (rightly or wrongly) for the rest of his life and into literary history. When Ettinger's father-in-law died, cutting off his support, his wife opened a store specializing in glass work and windowpanes, but Ettinger still needed to find a means of making a living. After a brief and abortive stint in Odessa, his brother-in-law's home, attempting to take advantage of the city's rising role as a trade center to succeed in business, Ettinger and his family decided that he would go to Lemberg to attend medical school.[54]

Ettinger arrived at the Medicinisch-Chyrurgische Lehranstalt zu Lemberg in 1825, having divested himself of his traditional Jewish clothes.[55] He seems to have been a *succès d'estime* at the university, known both among colleagues and the Lemberg maskilim as the "merry Solomon." Ettinger completed his studies in the beginning of 1830[56] and returned to Zamosc, where, though he was granted the title of *mediker*, was unable to practice before passing the official government examination at Warsaw University. Soon, however, the November Upris-

---

52. On Zamosc as a center of maskilic activity, see Erik, "Etinger," 11, and Weinreich, "Shloyme Etinger," xv. Compare I. L. Peretz's comments on Zamosc and its Enlightenment presence in "My Memoirs," in *The I. L. Peretz Reader*, ed. Ruth Wisse (New York: Schocken Books, 1990), 267–359, esp. 305–330.

53. Yosef Tsederboym's son, Alexander, would become the publisher of the famed Yiddish supplement *Kol mevaser*, where some of Ettinger's work would be posthumously published.

54. Part of this decision seems to have been catalyzed by the economic crisis in Odessa around the time of Ettinger's arrival there in 1825. See Weinreich, xvii, who suggests that Ettinger's stay there lasted about four months.

55. Weinreich ("Shloyme Etinger," xix–xx) seems to present this change of dress, and indeed the study of medicine more generally, as an unwilling concession to necessities rather than modernizing desire. If this is true, then one must once more be reminded of how complex the negotiation between traditional desires and reformist impulses are in the history of the Haskala.

56. Weinreich, however, could find no records at the university indicating Ettinger studied there, though he doesn't doubt that he did so; see "Shloyme Etinger," xxii, n. 9.

ing of 1831, which led to the belief that the walled city of Zamosc would be besieged, led Ettinger to settle with his family in the glass-works of his brother in-law, Yaakov Gold, near Yanov.

The Russians who came into Poland to suppress the rebellion brought cholera with them, which developed into a full-fledged epidemic in the summer of 1831. The Polish government, desperate for aid, called on Ettinger to do medical support work; he rose to the task with such dedication that when the revolt ended, the government presented no impediments to his practicing medicine, directed local pharmacists to fill his prescriptions, and even supported his candidacy for the position of *ordinator* of the Zamosc Municipal Hospital (in the division of venereal diseases).[57] Ettinger also worked in the Jewish poorhouses and at the same time prepared for the governmental exams, which he had yet to pass. When Ettinger did go to Warsaw to take the exams, however, he became dangerously ill and took them insufficiently prepared, with the result that he received only the title "Doctor of the Second Degree"—without the right to heal internal diseases.[58] Despite these obstacles, he managed to maintain a thriving medical practice, though not a highly profitable one.

Over a decade later, the "half-legal" doctor, now a family man with seven children, would attempt to take the exams once more, after a change in local government meant that local pharmacists refused to fill his prescriptions. Around 1847, Ettinger attempted the exams in Kharkov University, but was forced to return home empty-handed because his official papers were not in order.[59] After another brief attempt at practice, Ettinger bought a piece of property in Zhdanov, about four kilometers from Zamosc,[60] and settled there with his family in 1848, working the land and living there for the rest of his life.[61] Though his material circumstances improved significantly and he entertained often, he seems to have been unhappy: in a letter from that period, he complains, "I don't

---

57. Perhaps alone among most of the townspeople and later Yiddish literary critics, however, Ettinger apparently never referred to himself as "doctor," since he had not passed the required examinations. See Weinreich, "Shloyme Etinger," xxv–xxvi.

58. Weinreich ("Shloyme Etinger," xxvi) dates this to around 1833–1834.

59. On the details of this trip, which took almost a year in total, see Weinreich, "Shloyme Etinger," xxxvii–xxxviii.

60. Peretz describes the small village: "Zhdanov, three miles past the Lemberg gate, had been founded some years back as a Jewish farm colony. To attract Jews to agriculture, the Polish government offered certain inducements: long-term credit, and, more important, exemption from the draft. The colony's founder, Dr. Shloyme Ettinger, had worked the land himself, along wth his children, but that was before my time." Peretz, "My Memoirs," 279.

61. A brief exception was in July 1855, when Ettinger once more assisted Polish authorities during another cholera epidemic.

pose any great demands from life, I want only a bit of familial happiness
and that simple thing has not been given me by fortune. I am a husband,
a father, a landowner, a farmer, but to me is destined only the sorrow of
all of these."[62] One might suggest that, like many known for their cheerful
temperament and comic sensibility, there is a significant difference between outside and inside. His family life was also apparently unhappy,
though it seems reasonable also to suggest that at least some of his unhappiness had come from his perceived failure at his other love: writing.

Ettinger had begun to write while still a medical student in
Lemberg.[63] While there, he became acquainted with the Yiddish Bible
translations of Mendl Lefin, as well as *The Deceived World* and a Yiddish
adaptation of Robinson Crusoe called *Alter Leb*.[64] From these two works,
Ettinger presumably learned the ideological importance of writing in
easily understandable Yiddish, as opposed to the dialectally different
Yiddish of the translations Lefin's work came to replace, and became
aware of the ideological and dramatic possibilities of writing in Yiddish.
Ettinger later wrote, "I saw that the books found favor with a great
number of people; that is, they pleased both the connoisseurs and the
uneducated. . . . For a number of reasons I would rather not say whether
they were well-written or not. In any case, the idea to write in plain
Yiddish appealed to me; that everybody can see, for I immediately
decided to find out whether I possessed the talent to write in that
language and in that literature."[65] Though Lefin's first writings seem to
have been parables and epigrams along the lines of eighteenth-century
German writings, *Serkele* was almost certainly written at this early stage
in Ettinger's life.[66] We know from a letter Ettinger wrote that by 1836
or 1837 he was already considering publishing his Yiddish work,[67] and
was planning several other literary works in Yiddish, including a my-
thology and a world and natural history.[68]

---

62. Cited in Weinreich, "Shloyme Etinger," xlii.

63. Apparently Ettinger also had artistic ambitions; a painting he did from memory of his
friend Jacob Aykehnboym is still extant and is reprinted in Erik, "Etinger," 13. See Weinreich,
"Shloyme Etinger," xxi, for a discussion of the circumstances.

64. This information appears in a prospectus for potential subscribers to Ettinger's works,
presumably written in the 1840s. Ettinger—interestingly, in light of our discussion of *Silliness and Sanctimony* and its relationship to later maskilic drama—refers to *Di genarte velt* as
"Tartuffe in German." Ettinger's prospectus appears in *Geklibene verk*, 368–369; translated
excerpts appear in Miron, *Traveler*, 12.

65. Translation taken from Miron, *Traveler*, 12.

66. See Erik, "Etinger," 15.

67. Excerpts from the letter appear in Weinreich, "Shloyme Etinger," xxx.

68. See Weinreich, "Shloyme Etinger," xxxi.

We also know that on May 24, 1843, his good friend Anthony Eisenbaum, previously the founder and editor of the Warsaw Polish-Yiddish newspaper *Der beobachter an der vaysl*,[69] submitted a request to the curator of the Warsaw Scholars' Circle for permission to publish Ettinger's *Serkele* and *Fables*. Eisenbaum's arguments for publication—that "these works are accessible to all classes of Jews, they present in living colors their failings and their lacunae, they picture pointedly and comically the entire Jewish way of life and therefore they can have a redeeming effect on the brain"[70]—suggest the role that Ettinger and his circle felt literary materials could play in the role of enlightenment; perhaps even more important, though, they implicitly acknowledge Ettinger's Yiddish as a useful medium for achieving that task, given both the audience's ability to read the language and, most powerfully of all, the possibilities for realistic depiction that Yiddish affords.

In submitting his works to the authorities for publication, Ettinger relied on the support of the then Jewish censor of Warsaw, his friend Yankev Tugendhold (1794–1871).[71] Ettinger's faith was misplaced, however: Tugendhold so bowdlerized his writings that Ettinger refused to allow their publication in that form.[72] Since publication was impossible without the censor's approval, Ettinger engaged in a campaign of self-promotion: he read his works aloud whenever possible and made dozens of manuscript copies of his work, with the result that during his lifetime he became well known (at least in maskilic circles) not only in Zamosc, but throughout Poland. Still, the author never saw a single published line of his own Yiddish work in his lifetime, and though he would certainly have been gratified to see how much of the city of Zhdanov accompanied him to his resting place after his sudden death at home on the last day of 1856, he might well have thought that his only posterity would have been the self-composed Hebrew epigraph on his gravestone.[73]

As it was, however, Ettinger's work would begin to appear in book form less than a decade after his death. The first of his works to appear

69. On Eisenbaum and his multiple roles in the Warsaw community—editor, rabbinical school director, informant—see Erik, "Etinger," 10–11.

70. Cited in Weinreich, "Shloyme Etinger," xxxii. See also 588–590 for the original document.

71. Tugendhold was the head of three modern Jewish elementary schools in the Warsaw area. See Erik, "Etinger," 10.

72. For example, the censor refused to allow "king" as an epithet for a lion in one of Ettinger's fables, because it might affect the honor of the czar and bring about republican ideals: he demanded almost 100 changes to *Serkele*. See Erik, "Etinger," 17–18 and Weinreich, "Shloyme Etinger," xxxii–xxxv.

73. The escorts included the traditional *bet din*, or Jewish court, once more illustrating a closer relationship between enlightenment and tradition than might be thought. For details, as well as the reprinted epigraph, see Weinreich, "Shloyme Etinger," xliii.

in print, fittingly enough, was his masterpiece *Serkele*, published in an
error-filled edition in 1861 in the Prussian city of Johannesburg.[74]
Ettinger's work in rhyme was better served: beginning in the early 1860s,
many of his fables, poems, and epigrams had been published in the
new explosion of Yiddish newspapers and newspaper supplements, such
as Tsederboym's *Kol Mevaser*, the *Varshever yudishe tsaytung*, and the
Yudisher folksblat; a collection in book form was published by his son
Wilhelm in Petersburg in 1889.[75] Ettinger's literary and historical
importance remained undoubted ever since, attracting some of the
most noted scholars in the field: in 1925, Max Weinreich, the dean of
twentieth-century Yiddish studies in Europe and America, published a
critical edition of the material with a biographical and bibliographic
introduction and with notes;[76] and when the indefatigable critic and
editor Shmuel Rozhansky began his one-hundred-volume edition of the
masterworks of Yiddish literature, he placed an anthology of Ettinger's
work as the first volume, before Sholem Aleichem or Peretz.[77] Yet Ettinger
never achieved the height of popularity that these two authors did. While
one might suggest that some aspect of this has to do with the dynamics
of celebrity during one's lifetime as opposed to posthumously, and the
significantly greater opportunities that means of production afforded to
later authors and dramatists—of which Ettinger had no means of taking
advantage—one must agree with Max Weinreich's conclusion that Ettinger
"remained the *great-grandfather* of Yiddish literature, the less well known,
half-forgotten great-grandfather."[78] This being said, historians and critics

---

74. Published by A. Goncharovski under the title *Komedye in 5 aktn fun Serkele oder di falshe
yortsayt geshen in lemberg shnas tkts"h*. The work was reprinted in Warsaw in 1875. For more
information on the editions of Ettinger's work, see M. Dubilet, "Etinger-oysgabes," in *Sh.
Etinger: geklibene verk*, 349–367, and Weinreich, "Shloyme Etinger," xlv–xlvi, xlix–lix.

75. *Mesholim, lidlekh, kleyne mayselekh un kesuveslekh eygene un nokhgemakhte* (Petersburg,
1889; 2nd ed. 1890). A new edition only of the *mesholim* was published in Warsaw (Nayer
Farlag, 1920).

76. See Weinreich, ed., *Ale ksovim*. The edition contains previously unpublished material of
Ettinger's, including two unfinished plays, *Der feter fun amerike* (The Uncle from America)
and *Di freylekhe yungelayt* (The Merry Youngsters), some of Ettinger's letters, and a useful
bibliography of early sources on Ettinger.

77. Sh. Rozhansky, ed., *Oysgeklibene shriftn fun Shloyme Etinger* (Buenos Aires: Alveltlekhen
Yidishn Kultur-kongres, 1957). Other editions of Ettinger's work are listed in *Leksikon*, 6:578:
Serkele oder di yortsayt nokh a bruder, "an entirely new theatre piece in five acts" (Vilna: Naye
Yidishe Folkshul Farlag, 1929); *Geklibene verk* (Kiev: Farlag fun di Ukrainisher Visnshaft-
akademye, 1935); and *Mesholim* (Kiev: Ukrainisher Melukhe-farlag, 1938).

78. Though one might not agree with Weinreich's reasons. He suggests that had Ettinger "possessed the temperament of a revolutionary, he might have become the grandfather of our literature. If he stands behind Mendele in terms of talent, he certainly stands higher than him in the
details of formalistic excellence, though he wrote thirty years earlier. But as it turned out, he was
not able to transcend his character." Weinreich, "Shloyme Etinger," xlvii–xlviii.

of Yiddish literature and drama have pointed out many admirable aspects of Ettinger's work. Most interesting to us, though, is Ettinger's attitude toward Yiddish. As the eminent critic Shmuel Niger memorably put it, "He did not find it necessary to justify his writing in plain Yiddish and not Hebrew or German. He did not need any excuses. He did not feel guilty, just as the bird who sings or the tree that blooms does not feel guilty. And [this was] truly astonishing . . . right in the middle of the flourishing of the Haskala, when Yiddish, or, as it was called, 'jargon,' was, in the best case, a means to civilize the Jewish masses or, as I. M. Dik put it, a *lom*, a battering ram, to break down the walls of the ghetto."[79]

This comfort with Yiddish, this lack of self-defensiveness, may help to explain the unbridled freedom and linguistic virtuosity that character- ize Ettinger's Yiddish poetry. Niger himself considers Ettinger's true con- tribution to be in the poetic sphere, writing that "no one had yet written poems, parables, and epigrams like his in Yiddish. . . . Ettinger had a cultivated sense of sound, of rhythm, of form. . . . If in the longer parables, which are more narrative, we see Ettinger's cleverness, his life-wisdom and life-knowledge, what is revealed to us in the shorter parables and in the even shorter epigrams is his craftsmanship, his mastery of the word."[80]

Ettinger's few dozen parables, though written in "beautiful, naïve, melodic, picturesque, well-rhymed" Yiddish, owed significant debts to the Aesopian fabulist tradition, with themes taken from classical fables and complete with a moral ending;[81] parables were also, however, a favored genre of the Berlin Haskala, authored by Mendelssohn and Wolfssohn, among others.[82] Ettinger had also written longer poems and ballads, which revealed the influence of various German writers and balladeers, most notably Schiller; his famous thirty-three-page poem *Dos likht* (The Light) follows Schiller's "Die Glocke" (The Bell) in using the object in question to serve as the leading metaphor in chronicling the events that demarcate the ebbs and flows of a human life.[83] "Just as there the poem

---

79. Niger, quoted in *Leksikon*, 6:578–579. Miron (*Traveler*, 13) writes that "Etinger's very 'normality' made him exceptional."

80. Niger, quoted in *Leksikon*, 6:578–579. Ettinger, following in Lefin's footsteps, also trans- lated certain psalms and selections from the liturgy, which also serve as testament to his literary virtuosity. See the translations of Psalm 67 and of the prayers *Yigdal* and *Ma Tovu* in Weinreich, 550–551.

81. Other European writers whose fables may have influenced Ettinger included La Fontaine, Schiller, Gellert, Hagedorn, Florian, and others. See Erik, "Etinger," 21–26, for a full discussion of the fables.

82. See Erik, "Etinger," 19.

83. Ettinger considered this poem, written in 1846, to be his best work. See Erik, "Etinger," 26, and Erik, "Parafrases fun shilers 'lid funem glok' in der yidisher haskole-literatur," in *Sh. Etinger: Geklibene verk*, 370–383, which includes selections from similar works by A. B. Gottlober and Hirsh Reitman.

is of a human life, whose refrain is the bell, that rings always—birth, holi-day, wedding, celebration, tragedy, funeral . . . so too in the Yiddishized version of Shloyme Ettinger's *Dos likht* the eternal accompaniment of a Jewish life. . . . At birth a light, at the circumcision a light, holidays—a light, the Sabbath—a light, Sabbath's end—a light, wedding candles and after death a memorial candle."[84] One might also add that, in transforming the metaphor, not only is Ettinger engaging in a centuries-old process of Judaization of secular (and in Schiller's case, somewhat Christian) mate-rial, but is also engaging in the maskilic trope of privileging an image of light as the most important key to understanding Judaism.

Ettinger uses his poetry not only to get to moral truths, particu-larly in the epigrams, but also, as in these ballads, to reveal or to char-acterize certain ethnographic truths as well. It is not surprising that Ettinger is prized by certain critics not only for his Yiddish style, but his ability to render the language and life of the people, of the folk. It is here, then, that we may observe the shifting balance between the Yid-dish theatrical work as polemic and as mirror (or site of nostalgia), and the importance that critics (and, perhaps, audience) place on Yiddish theatre not so much as a medium of change for the future but as a reflection of life present or past. Ettinger's comfort with Yiddish may help explain his willingness to and ease in creating neologisms through-out the play, particularly in terms of theatrical vocabulary, which would be used by generations of Yiddish playwrights and actors after him.[85]

Ettinger's contributions to the field of Yiddish theatre, however, are hardly limited to the technical sphere, for *Serkele* is populated with a vivid array of comic characters, situations, and language. The play opens in the home of Reb Moyshe Dansker, the *nouveau riche* husband of the title character. It takes only a moment for us to realize that it is Serkele who runs the household, with a combination of physical and verbal intimida-tion and emotional manipulation, particularly in the form of her hilari-ously over-the-top hypochondria. Serkele has darker deeds to answer for, however. The play's Yiddish subtitle is "a yortsayt nokh a bruder"—literally, the anniversary of a brother's death. The entire action takes place on the anniversary of the day Serkele's brother Dovid reputedly died at sea. After his ship disappeared when he was on a business trip, Serkele had a fake will drawn up. She and Moyshe were in fact named as guardians for Dovid's

84. Melekh Ravitch, quoted in *Leksikon,* 6:579–580.

85. Zalmen Reyzen writes, "The consciousness in Ettinger's attitude to the Yiddish language is truly remarkable. Knowing German himself, he would nonetheless eliminate every trace of Germanisms in his Yiddish work. If he lacked words for a certain concept in Yiddish, he tried to create them in the spirit of the language, and his neologisms were very often successful." Quoted in *Leksikon,* 6:580–581; see also Weinreich, "Shloyme Etinger," xxxi.

daughter Hinde, and he provided a substantial fortune to see that she would be raised as befit a girl of her station. The fake will, however, redirected those funds into the guardians' own pockets, while Hinde lives a Cinderella-like existence, more overworked servant than adored niece. Hinde even has an unattractive foil in the person of Friederika, Serkele's own daughter, a foolish creature on whom her mother dotes elaborately. Friederika is being courted by a sly young fortune hunter named Gavriel Hendler, who also steals a box of Serkele's jewels and then helps throw the blame on Hinde and her beloved, the enlightened Markus Redlekh. Things look grim for our heroes until a Stranger comes to town, who of course turns out to be none other than the long-lost brother. By the end of the play, the falsely accused have been cleared of wrongdoing and given Dovid's blessing, the true villains have been punished, and Dovid magnanimously forgives the sister who had gone to such great lengths to steal his fortune at his daughter's expense.

Serkele itself illustrates the flexible and virtuosic nature of Ettinger's Yiddish: as in Wolfssohn's *Silliness and Sanctimony*, characters use various versions of Yiddish both as a means of character differentiation and—in a manner profoundly different from that of the earlier play—as a source of humor. The innkeeper Shmelke Troynik's peculiar dialect[86] not only marks him as a Litvak, but also allows Ettinger and his characters to engage in fun at the expense of one or another of the subgroups of Jewish Eastern Europe—mockery based on a trait other than the group's tendency to accept or reject the tenets of enlightenment.

Ettinger's dwelling on dialect humor also shows, incidentally, how certain types of humor have not worn particularly well; though presumably Ettinger and nineteenth-century Yiddish audiences found humor based on dialect, stuttering, and mental retardation funny, it seems fair to say that most contemporary audiences would be greatly offended if this were placed in the middle of a play by, say, Neil Simon, or even Neil LaBute. Ettinger, of course, was hardly the first to draw on these sources for humor, and his doing so illustrates once more how *Serkele* draws directly on both the Western European dramatic tradition and its mediation through the (limited) earlier maskilic drama. As Dan Miron points out, *Serkele,* as well as Ettinger's dramatic fragment *Der feter fun amerike,* uses "the conventional comic sequence of errors and misunderstandings following the appearance of an unknown traveler (who is no less than the missing son, relative, lover, husband) and which leads to

---

86. As a *litvak,* Troynik speaks a dialect that lacks the *sh* sound. The litvak dialect acquired the nickname *sabesdike losn*—literally, "Sabbath language," but used to illustrate its peculiar sound, for the same phrase would be rendered *shabesdike loshn* in other dialects. See our discussion of this issue in the Note on Translation.

a comic 'recognition': a procedure begun by the Middle and New comedy writers of Greece and Rome and revived during the Renaissance in numerous 'comedies of errors.' "[87] Aside from these characteristics taken from Plautus, Terence, and others, one might also add the archetypes of the clever servant, dialect humor, and verbal tics. The title character's "Oy, mayne koykhes!" (translated by us as "Oy, I feel faint!" but literally meaning "Oh, my powers!") is a constant refrain by a character who perpetually complains of her ill-health and her misfortune.[88]

But Serkele herself is, as we see, quite physically powerful, as is clear from her ability to knock around the servants (itself a staple of the Old and New Comedy, as well as a precursor of the physical comedy which would become prevalent in Yiddish theatre more generally). In this falsehood, which serves as the mere background for the moral falsehood and hypocrisy that emerges as one of the play's major themes, we can see another pious hypocrite. Serkele's real secret, though, is not that she is healthy, but that she has manufactured a fake will disinheriting her niece.[89] As such, Ettinger is drawing on the somewhat limited history of Yiddish drama so far, as well as what Miron refers to as "the characteristic middle-class comédie larmoyante."[90] Ettinger himself referred to it as a *familien gemelde*, the same genre as Wolfssohn's *Silliness and Sanctimony*.[91]

Enlightenment themes are plentiful here, some previously in evidence and some new ones coming to the fore. Certainly much of the play, as in *Silliness and Sanctimony*, revolves around questions of marriage and the fitness or appropriateness of a particular groom for the innocent bride (who can be seen as metonymic for the Jewish populace)—though in *Serkele*, at least, there is no question that the appropriate groom is the enlightened figure, who once more is called Markus. And Markus, who aspires to adoption of Gentile culture as well as language, points the way away from current society, as symbolized by the arranged marriage system and the reliance on both *yikhes*—a word roughly akin to "lineage"—and money. One may, incidentally, suggest that given the vicissitudes of Eastern European Jewish society—a far

---

87. Miron, *Traveler*, 101.

88. In his memoirs, Peretz claimed, "I had a nasty aunt. . . . [T]he Yiddish writer Dr. Shloyme Ettinger based his portrait of 'Serkele' on her. She was a tall, thin woman, pale and sickly, forever yelling: 'Give me strength!' " (Oy, mayne koykhes!) Peretz, 276.

89. See Erik, "Etinger," 16, and Dubilet, 39.

90. Miron, *Traveler*, 249. For an extensive comparison of *Di genarte velt* and *Serkele*, see Erik, "Etinger," 16 and 28; for further discussion about the play, see Erik, "Etinger," 28–33.

91. See M. Dubilet, "Vegn etingers dramatishe verk," in *Sh. Etinger: geklibene verk*, 34–40, esp. 35, where the play's melodramatic elements are also addressed.

less cosmopolitan and integrated society than Prussia's—the kind of ambivalence about the total transformation of Jewish society and the integration of Western culture is less prevalent than in Wolfssohn's work, though we still do have evidence of some ambivalence about foolish and false enlightenment. Given the unhappiness of Ettinger's own arranged marriage, there may have been other reasons for him to foreground such an issue. One might also suggest that Ettinger's own orphanhood finds some reflection in the trope of abandonment that extends throughout the play. Not only is it a narrative device, but the evocations of longing and solitude strike a theme which will be a commonplace of much of Yiddish melodrama in the future. Some of these emotions are also expressed in song, a medium not seen in *Silliness and Sanctimony*, but an increasingly prevalent part of the Yiddish theatrical scene in Eastern Europe, as local and contemporary modes of dramatic presentation become incorporated into the Yiddish dramatist's repertoire.[92]

There are some other surprises and new elements to be found in *Serkele* as well. Serkele's own power, symbolic as it is of her hypocrisy, also illustrates an early treatment of a theme to be found over and over again in Yiddish literature: the powerful woman and the passive man. Serkele's husband is tormented by guilt and moral ambivalence over what they have done; the goal-oriented and financially rapacious Serkele, only wishing for improved status, a good marriage for her daughter, and never to return to her life as a mill woman, lacks any such scruples. Additionally, in a movement continuous with the archetype of hypocrites like Tartuffe and Reb Yoysefkhe, Serkele is revealed to be sexually rapacious as well, lusting after the young doctor Markus—such a character trait, though, may be seen as significantly more shocking when the gender of the hypocrite in question is switched. One hesitates to ground this simply in a recognition of the conventional Eastern European Jewish social structure involving women as the breadwinners and men as the effete, impotent intellectuals, but certainly this line of criticism was carried forward by S. Y. Abramovitsh and many other writers, sometimes for comic purposes and sometimes to illustrate the pressing unfairness of the treatment of women given their obvious capabilities for social equality.

This allows us to return to a final question: how realistic, indeed, is *Serkele?* Recall that Eisenbaum's claim to the censors was that Ettinger's works "picture pointedly and comically the entire Jewish way of life;" recall, also, that the censor rejected the works as they stood. The linguistic differentiation of the characters can be seen not simply as a

---

92. Additionally, Ettinger's own talents as a poet and balladeer make the addition of rhymed work to his plays unsurprising.

realistic device reflecting sociological reality, which includes linguistic code switching and sociologically rooted responses to that actual phenomenon within a lived society,[93] but a kind of archetypal a priori division, suggesting to us attitudes we as protoenlightened readers should take toward the particular characters. Miron points out that the characters in *Serkele* can be divided into three groups: those who "stubbornly stick to the traditional way of life and speak fluent, idiomatic Yiddish"; the "mouthpieces for their creators" who speak " 'educated,' bookish, anemic German;"[94] and a "smaller, third group who seem to adhere to the ideas of the Haskala but who are mere fellow travelers . . . frivolous, superficial characters."[95] This tripartite division, so similar to the one in Wolfssohn's *Silliness and Sanctimony,* can be seen as evidence of an antimimetic structure imposed from without. Even Zalmen Reyzen, who argues that "Ettinger also remains an objective depicter of Jewish life, artist, not a publicist of Haskala ideals, in his drama *Serkele*" notes the "maskilic tendencies here in the exaggerated idealization of the representatives of the new generation in the character of the 'enlightened,' the student Redlekh."[96]

Similarly, though critics have often praised Ettinger's dialogue for its realistic nature, it is possible to suggest that with the frequent verbal

---

93. For example, when the stranger returns to town, while he speaks German the innkeeper flatters him in the most elevated Germanic language he can muster; when it is revealed that the stranger is a Jew, the innkeeper "immediately relaxes his strained rhetoric and switches to the most unceremonial familiarity." Miron, *Traveler,* 102. This peculiarly Jewish version of familiarity breeding contempt was sufficiently noteworthy for Freud to tell his readers the following joke: "A Galician Jew was travelling in a train. He had made himself really comfortable, had unbuttoned his coat and put his feet up on the seat. Just then a gentleman in modern dress entered the compartment. The Jew promptly pulled himself together and took up a proper pose. The stranger fingered through the pages of a notebook, made some calculations, reflected for a moment and then suddenly asked the Jew: 'Excuse me, when is Yom Kippur (the Day of Atonement)?' 'Oho!' said the Jew, and put his feet up on the seat again before answering." Sigmund Freud, *Der Witz und seine Beziehung zum Unbewussten* (1905), as *Jokes and Their Relation to the Unconscious,* trans. and ed. James Strachey, Pelican Freud Library, vol. 6 (London: Routledge & Kegan Paul, 1960; repr. Penguin Books, 1983), 121.

94. Even here, though, as Weinreich points out, Ettinger inserts some ambivalence as to this group's linguistic choices: Hinde says of Markus that "he speaks just like a book," which may be taken as less than flattering, and when Freyde–Altele speaks her (admittedly mangled) German, one of the positive characters, David Gutherz, asks her why she doesn't speak Yiddish.

95. See Miron, *Traveler,* 257–258. Certain of these characters, like Freyde-Altele, try to speak German but make numerous mistakes.

96. Z. Reyzen, quoted in *Leksikon,* 6:580–581. This said, Reyzen's general assessment is that "*Serkele* is a lively realistic comedy, written in a fluid, for that time truly extraordinary folklike language, and in terms of its construction it stands at the height of the dramatic art of the early nineteenth century."

tics, the stutters, the set speeches and frequent monologues, the elevated Germanicisms, and the highly symbolic names,[97] what we see in *Serkele* is less a realistic middle-class comedy than a work perched uneasily between a snapshot of the bourgeoisie and a move into stylization. After all, Serkele herself is a wild, horrifying caricature, a woman who consumes scenery as easily as she does the innocents around her: it stands to reason that from a dramatic perspective this unbalances the play—not only in performance, but on the page as well.

Serkele was performed for the first time in 1863 by the students of the Zhitomir Rabbinical Seminary at a Purim celebration (among the students, twenty-two-year-old Avrom Goldfaden, who played the lead role). The first performance of *Serkele* in a theatre was produced by Y. Y. Lerner in Odessa on August 11, 1888. In 1923, *Serkele* was performed at the Central Theatre in Warsaw under the direction of Zygmund Turkow. That performance was turned into a celebration of Yiddish theatre and elicited enthusiastic reviews in all the Yiddish press. It was also performed in the Yiddish theatre of Communist Poland.[98] The play's enduring freshness—the best argument of all for bringing it to the attention of new audiences—has been described as follows by one of the leading critics of the Yiddish theatre: "*Serkele* shows almost no sign of the fact that it was written almost two generations before Goldfaden laid the cornerstone of Yiddish theatre. Hundreds of such plays are performed on the Yiddish stage even to this day. They are cast in the form of *Serkele*, no more—in *Serkele* the language is fresher, more lively, more Yiddish. Serkele is written in a pure, modern Yiddish. *Serkele* was the example for the later Yiddish playwrights, and, to tell the truth, they imitated it poorly."[99]

Avrom Goldfaden and *The Two Kuni-Lemls*

Much of the "imitation" of *Serkele* that critic B. Gorin had in mind was undoubtedly unintentional, a rehashing of comic tropes that had hardened into nearly inescapable tradition by the time the professional Yiddish stage came to life in the last quarter of the nineteenth century. The person who initiated all that activity, however, modeled his first full-length comedy directly on *Serkele*—and in his case, the imitation was quite a skilled one. Avrom Goldfaden (1840–1908) then went on to lay the foundations of the professional repertoire, and in the process brought countless innovations to Yiddish drama, theatre, music, and performance.

---

97. Such as David Gutherz (or Goodheart), and Markus Redlekh, whose surname means "honest" in German.

98. *Leksikon*, 6:578.

99. Gorin, 1:95.

At the start of his literary career in the 1860s, however, Goldfaden seemed headed down a path fairly typical of maskilic writers. Like many of them, as well as contemporaries like the so-called "classic" Yiddish writers, S. Y. Abramovitsh (1836–1917), Sholem Aleichem (1859–1916), and I. L. Peretz (1851–1915), Goldfaden was equally at home in both Yiddish and Hebrew and published works in both languages. In the tradition of Wolfssohn and Ettinger, as well as other early nineteenth-century maskilim like Israel Aksenfeld and Avrom Ber Gottlober, young Goldfaden turned to drama among other genres. Had all gone according to plan, Goldfaden might have led a life much like Wolfssohn's and written dramas much like Ettinger's. That is, he might have secured a job as headmaster of a Jewish school, or some other respectable service career, giving him the financial stability to pursue his writing on the side— writing that, like, Ettinger's, started out being less strident than was the case with many other maskilic playwrights.

Goldfaden's life took surprising turns, however, in ways that would forever change Yiddish culture. Goldfaden's father was a watchmaker, a respected artisan who was receptive to the winds of the Haskala that had by then blown eastward from Germany. In his memoirs, Goldfaden described his father as "the only craftsman in the shtetl who enjoyed opening up a Jewish book, and did not spare his last hard-earned penny to teach [me] Hebrew."[100] His father's involvement in Jewish letters went further, in fact: he and one of Goldfaden's brothers both published letters in the Hebrew and Yiddish press when Avrom was a young man. Unlike some of his forebears in Yiddish culture—and unlike not a few of his contemporaries and successors—Goldfaden's subsequent choice of career, however impractical, would not have been regarded by his family as an act of heresy, or even of rebellion.[101]

---

100. Avrom Goldfaden, "Goldfadens kurtse oytobiografye." *Goldfaden-bukh*, ed. Jacob Shatzky (New York: Idish Teater-muzey, 1926), 43.

101. Goldfaden's life and work have, understandably, attracted a great deal of attention— though his full biography has yet to be written. For biographical studies, see, inter alia, *Leksikon fun der nayer yidisher literatur*, 2:77-87; Nachman Mayzel, *Avrom Goldfaden: der foter fun yidishn teater* (Warsaw: Farlag Groshn-bibliotek, 1935); Nokhem Oyslender and Uri Finkel, *A. Goldfadn: materyaln far a biografye* (Minsk: Institut far Vaysruslendisher Kultur, 1926); Yitskhok Perkof, *Avrom Goldfadn: mayne memuarn un zayne brif* (London: Jouques Print Works, 1908); Nahma Sandrow, *Vagabond Stars: A World History of Yiddish Theater* (New York, 1977; repr. 1986 and 1999), 40–69; Yitskhok Turkov-Grudberg, *Goldfaden un Gordin* (Tel Aviv: S. Grinhoyz, 1969); Zalmen Zylbercweig, *Leksikon fun yidishn teater* (New York: Farlag Elisheva, 1931), 1:275–367; Zylbercweig, *Avrom Goldfaden un Zigmunt Mogulesco* (Buenos Aires: Farlag Elisheva, 1936); as well as both biographical and critical materials in two volumes of essays edited by Jacob Shatzky: *Goldfaden-bukh* (New York: Idisher Teater-Muzey, 1926), and *Hundert yor Goldfadn* (New York: YIVO, 1940).

In the meantime, however, Goldfaden received a fairly conventional Jewish education, except that at the advanced level he was trained in a new sort of institution: a government-run rabbinical seminary in Zhitomir, Ukraine. As mentioned above, Goldfaden would enjoy fleeting notoriety as a performer in a student production in 1863 of none other than *Serkele*, with Goldfaden himself playing the title role. The production was the brainchild of the sophisticated wife of the school's headmaster; according to a friend and classmate of Goldfaden's, "The plan to stage a Yiddish drama seemed crazy to the Zhitomir intelligentsia, but Madame Slonimskaya stuck fast to her plan. . . . She assigned the roles, organized, rehearsed, worried about suitable decorations. . . . The production caused an uproar. The students performed their roles well, but most outstanding of all was Goldfaden, who played the hardest role, Serkele."[102] Goldfaden's biographers conclude that his schooltime performance experience taught him "how to adapt to the minimal scenic possibilities of an improvised theatre, as would later be the case in his own theatre."[103]

Goldfaden had no reason at the time to take such lessons to heart. There was no professional Yiddish stage for which to write as of the early 1860s, but the rabbinical student was already beginning to make a name for himself as a poet and literary dramatist. After publishing Yiddish poems in the new Yiddish literary journal *Kol mevaser*, he produced a volume of Hebrew poems, *Tsitsim u'frakhim* (Blossoms and Flowers, 1865), followed in short order by two volumes of Yiddish verse, *Dos yidele* (The Little Jew, 1866) and *Di yidene* (The Jewish Woman, 1869). The latter included his first efforts at writing drama, in the form of a dialogue called "Tsvey shkheynes" (Two Neighbors) and a full-length comedy, *Di mume Sosye* (Aunt Sosya, 1869). Critic Isaac Goldberg deemed the former "thoroughly enjoyable satiric farce, with a genuine insight into human nature," while saying that *Aunt Sosya*, "despite its evident indebtedness to Ettinger's *Serkele*, contains some of Goldfaden's best work."[104]

We can draw another, more biographical connection between Ettinger and Goldfaden. Among Dr. Ettinger's patients was the noted maskilic writer Avrom Ber Gottlober. A well-known story has Ettinger reading aloud his manuscript of *Serkele* to Gottlober, who visited Zamosc in 1837 and became ill with cholera, saying, "What's all this cholera business? Better I read you my Serkele," and, Gottlober said, "He read

---

102. A. Y. Paperno, "Di ershte yudishe drame un der ershter yudisher spektakl (mayne erinerungen vegn A. Goldfaden)." *Der pinkes*, 1913.

103. Oyslender and Finkel, *A. Goldfaden*, 18.

104. Isaac Goldberg, *The Drama of Transition: Native and Exotic Playcraft* (Cincinnati: Stewart Kidd, 1922), 345.

it to me and I got better."[105] Gottlober would become one of Goldfaden's teachers, and in his memoirs, he remembered his student as "a very young boy . . . who studied privately with me at home in addition to the school. He would pay special attention when I wrote Yiddish: it was his great passion."[106]

Though Gottlober does not specify which Yiddish writings Goldfaden saw him working on, his student clearly became familiar at some point with Gottlober's scathing anti-Hasidic farce, *Der dektukh, oder tsvey khupes in eyn nakht* (The Bridal Veil, or Two Weddings in One Night, 1838), which would serve as a direct influence for Goldfaden's own satires. *The Bridal Veil* features two impending mismatches. Yosele and Freydele, two intelligent and attractive teenagers, seem to have been made for each other, but their parents are planning strategic rather than romantic attachments for the young lovers. This has led to Yosele's involuntary engagement to a blind girl, while Freydele has been forcibly betrothed to Leml, a young man without a nose. While Freydele agonizes over the situation, Yosele manages to joke about it, since he is confident of his plan to thwart the parents' intentions. Most of the rest of the play involves Yosele's clever use of the traditionalists' superstitions to his own ends. Ambushing the groom's party in the woods, he convinces them that he is a spirit and dons the groom's clothes after everyone else runs away. The final curtain leaves us in no doubt that Yosele and Freydele are about to marry.

Goldfaden obviously knew Gottlober's play, and made little effort to disguise his debt to it—particularly in *The Two Kuni-Lemls*, though there are elements of *The Bridal Veil* in an earlier Goldfaden farce, *Shmendrik* (1877), an important step in Goldfaden's development as a farceur. *Shmendrik* was adapted from a popular Romanian comedy of the time, *Vladutsu Mamu*, and also bears the influence of early Russian satires, particularly Denis Fonvizin's *Nedorosl* (The Minor, 1782). Fonvizin's influential comedy revolves around the efforts of an ambitious mother to marry her foolish son to her ward, who has just inherited a fortune. *Shmendrik* revolves around the efforts of an ambitious mother to marry her foolish son to a beautiful, intelligent young woman, though not for her money, as we shall see. Shmendrik, like Gottlober's Leml and Fonvizin's Mitrofan, is not only unworthy of his intended bride, but preposterously so. Goldfaden describes his titular antihero as "15 years old, not tall, a *yarmulke* on his head and two long, straight earlocks, in red underwear that buttons in back. Over the

105. See Weinreich, "Shloyme Etinger," xxvii.

106. Avrom Ber Gottlober, "Zikhroynes vegn yidishe shrayber." *Di yidishe folks-bibliotek* (1888), 1: 255.

underwear a *talis-kotn*, and a long string of lead amulets, parchments, and wolf's teeth hangs around his neck, and a silver hoop in one ear. His foolish face is framed by large black eyebrows, with redness around his nose and various scratches scattered about his face and neck. He says "s" instead of "sh" and "t" instead of "k.'"[107]

Offsetting these unattractive characteristics, in the eyes of the traditional community, is Shmendrik's family's money, which can essentially buy him a bride from a family with *yikhes* (lineage). The familiar plot that grows out of this—a beautiful, intelligent young woman who is forced to accept a match well beneath her because her family has fallen on hard times, but is then rescued by her beloved, who hatches a scheme to marry her himself—diverts us while sending a clear message. Shmendrik embodies all that is wrong with the old way of doing things; the old ways are every bit as spiritually stunted and aesthetically ugly as he. Now, young people must be given the freedom to choose for themselves, or mismatches like the one narrowly averted here might continue to occur.

The message of *The Two Kuni-Lemls* is essentially the same. The two comedies have so much in common that they have been called "to a degree variations on one work"[108]—this despite the fact that *Shmendrik* was based on a Romanian comedy, while the plot of *Kuni-Lemls* was taken from a German comedy, *Nathan Schlemiel*.[109] Certainly many of the core ingredients of the two Goldfaden farces are similar: the efforts of parents to choose mates for their children based on the potential partner's social standing rather than on love; the stark contrast between the attractiveness and eligibility of one party to the match—in both cases a young lady—and the pronounced physical and mental shortcomings of the other; the plays' assortment of broad comedy and musical numbers; and the mixture of comic types taken from everyday Eastern European Jewish life. Yet the most important insight we gain from comparing the two plays is how far Goldfaden advanced in the writing of comedy in just a couple of years.

Shmendrik, to be sure, is itself a comic masterpiece, notwithstanding its creator's later attempts to all but disown it: "*Shmendrik!* . . . What sort of diseased notion got into my head? I frightened myself, was ashamed of myself, like a young, healthy woman who had suddenly

---

107. Avrom Goldfaden, *Shmendrik* (Odessa: Ulrikha, 1879), 3.

108. Bilov and Velednitski, 52.

109. J. Rosenzweig, *Nathan Schlemiel, oder Orthodoxe und reformirte Juden.* Ein Tendenz-Lustspiel in 3 Acten (Pressburg: C. Angermayer, 1873). Goldfaden's rival playwright, Joseph Lateiner, is said to have first borrowed Rosenzweig's play as the basis for a comedy of his own, *The Two Shmuel Shmelkes*, which is unfortunately no longer extant.

given birth to a mooncalf—some sort of monster."[110] Yet we should feel free to take Goldfaden's assessment, written near the end of his life, with a pillar of salt, for here he was trying to convince his readers that he was capable, when his career as a professional playwright began, of writing much more sophisticated stuff, if only his audience had been polished enough to sit still for it. Upon reading or seeing *Shmendrik*, one might thank Goldfaden's muse for not offering up a more high-brow audience. The play is a fast-paced farce with lunatic energy, radiating outward from its foundling of a protagonist.

As Fonvizin had done in *The Minor*, Goldfaden has great fun showing off his protagonist's idiocy—most strikingly by having him butcher a lesson in Torah while his proud mother beams over what she takes to be great cleverness. Shmendrik is too absorbed in childish games to think about what marriage really means—a fact that becomes glaringly obvious when he is interviewed by his prospective bride:

> RIVKE: What good would a bride do you? What do you need a bride for?
>
> SHMENDRIK: What do you mean, what good would a bride do me? Get a load of her, the trazy girl! My rebbe bought me a dreydl, so I'll play dreydl with her! Heh heh heh— . . .
>
> RIVKE (*Cries*): Oh, all is lost!
>
> SHMENDRIK (*Also cries*): Mommy, where is my Mommy?![111]

Fortunately for Rivke—and undoubtedly for Shmendrik too—she is rescued from this dire situation by her lover and co-conspirators, who substitute a different bride for Rivke at the last minute, so that Shmendrik's marriage is a *fait accompli* before anyone can complain.

All these influences—the plays of Gottlober and other Haskala playwrights, farces and operettas written in other European languages, and Goldfaden's own experience of writing for the theatre, which amounted to some thirty plays by 1880—would serve Goldfaden in direct and indirect ways in the writing of *The Two Kuni-Lemls*. The very name Kuni-Leml pays undisguised tribute to Gottlober's antihero. To Leml (Yiddish for "lamb") of *The Bridal Veil*, Goldfaden adds the seemingly meaningless prefix "Kuni," which heightens the impact of Kuni-Leml's severe stutter by having him spray a volley of *k-k-k*'s every time he said his own name. Goldfaden also borrowed the device—not original with Gottlober, of course—of a physical disability as manifestation of spiritual shortcomings. Gottlober had deformed his Leml not only grotesquely, but also, perhaps, syphilitically. Goldfaden

---

110. Avrom Goldfaden, "Fun 'Shmendrik' biz 'Ben Ami,'" *Amerikaner*, March 29, 1907. Reprinted in Jacob Shatzky, ed., *Arkhiv*, 266.
111. Goldfaden, *Shmendrik*, 24.

restored the nose to his protagonist's face, but then gave him physical characteristics found elsewhere in *The Bridal Veil*'s cast of characters, which includes a stuttering rabbi with a blind daughter. The result of all this reshuffling of names and physical characteristics is Kuni-Leml, "blind in one eye, lame in one foot, and with a stutter."

However indebted Goldfaden was to the Haskala dramatists who preceded him,[112] however, he parted company with them in one important respect—in fact, on a matter that Goldfaden himself brought about. By establishing the first professional Yiddish theatre troupe, he created the need for a different kind of play than had been written in Yiddish before—a play that could satisfy a live, paying audience.[113] Practical considerations would need to be kept in mind, and some of the excesses of writing works for the salon—like three-page speeches summing up the previous ten years of a character's life—would have to be avoided. The didacticism of most Haskala plays would also have to be toned down if such works were to enjoy any success on stage. The cardinal rule for didactic literature, dating back to the first-century Roman writer Horace, is that it should be *dulce et utile*—sweet and useful. Though Goldfaden was deeply engaged with social and political issues, when writing for a live audience he would need to go heavy on the *dulce*, light on the *utile*. It is an approach that he clearly takes in *Kuni-Lemls*.[114]

---

112. While less obvious in terms of content, Israel Aksenfeld's *Di genarte velt*—not to be confused with the anonymous play by the same name discussed above—bears many similarities to both *Shmendrik* and *The Two Kuni-Lemls*. For more on this connection, see the introduction to Sh. Bilov and A. Velednitski's *Goldfadn: geklibene dramatishe verk* (Kiev: Melukhe-farlag far di Natsyonale Minderhaytn in USSR, 1940), 3–64.

113. At the same time, it is important to keep in mind the extensive publication history of Goldfaden's plays. Like many of his most popular dramas, *The Two Kuni-Lemls* was published in numerous editions, and under alternate titles (note that it was often billed as *The Fanatic, or, The Two Kuni-Lemls*). In roughly chronological order (for the publication dates are not always clear), they are: *Der fanatik, oder, di beyde Kuni Lemil* (Warsaw: n.p., 1887); *Der fanatik, oder di beyde Kuni-Lemil: opereta* (Warsaw: Boymritter va-khatano Gonshar, 1887; repr. 1902); *Der fanatik, oder di beyde Kuni-Lemil* (New York: J. Saphirstein, 1893); *Fanatik di beyde Kuni-Lemels* (Warsaw: Y. Lidski, 1905); *Fanatik, oder di beyde Kuni-Lemil: opereta* (Warsaw: F. Kantorovitsh, 1922; repr. 1927); *Di beyde Kuni Lemels: Opereta in 4 akten un 8 bilder* (New York: Hebrew Publishing Company, n.d.); and in Bilov and Velednitski, 199–261. Alyssa Quint emphasizes Goldfaden's interest in the publication side of his dramatic work as central to our understanding of his place in Yiddish cultural history; see "The Botched Kiss: Abraham Goldfaden and the Literary Origins of the Yiddish Theatre" (Ph.D. dissertation, Harvard University, 2003).

114. The fact that the practice of arranged marriage was less widely accepted, and the critique thereof somewhat less controversial as a result, helped foster a different role for this issue in the professional theatre than it had been among earlier maskilim. As Uri Finkel has observed, "For other maskilic writers, the topic of arranged marriages was filled with contentious themes. For Goldfaden it was no more than entertainment." See "Sotsyale figurn in A. Goldfadns ershte verk," *Tsaytshrift* 1 (Minsk, 1926), 87–103.

Not all of Goldfaden's early works—his first compositions for live performance, written in the mid- to late 1870s—had a social agenda at all. As often as not, they were burlesques, vaudevilles, and other types of light comedies, but the best of his early works show not only growing self-assurance as a playwright, but a talent for conveying a clear message in an entertaining manner. By the time he wrote *Kuni-Lemls*, Goldfaden had completed an initiation period of several years writing for a theatre troupe built on the foundation of two cabaret-type performers known as Broder Singers, and growing into a stock company typical in the nineteenth-century European and American theatre. Goldfaden and his troupe toured Romania and Russia throughout the second half of the 1870s with a repertoire of light comedies of varying length and quality, as well as operettas like *Di kishefmakherin* (The Sorceress, 1878), a musical masterpiece that would, like *Kuni-Lemls*, become a fixture in the Yiddish dramatic repertoire for decades to come, inspiring imitation, adaptation, and reinvention by some of the leading Yiddish playwrights and theatre companies.

As in *Silliness and Sanctimony*, the conflict in *Kuni-Lemls* is first aired in an argument between husband and wife. Reb Pinkhesl, a wealthy Hasidic merchant, looks forward to marrying his daughter to a suitably religious young man, while Rivke, his traditional but "more worldly" wife, is more concerned about their daughter's feelings than about some abstract notion of *yikhes*. Unlike the raisonneurs in Wolfssohn's play, though, Rivke is scathingly funny, tearing into the excesses of the Hasidic world and labeling her husband and his fellow Hasidim as so many horses and oxen. Into this rift enters the *shadkhn*, the matchmaker, straight out of Jewish folklore, which immortalized this archetypal figure in countless jokes about his ability to heap effusive praise, without exactly lying, on even the saddest matrimonial prospect. Goldfaden's Kalmen clearly can hold his own, as he scoffs at the notion that anyone could find fault with a catch like Kuni-Leml: "[A]re you going to make a big fuss of such nonsense? So what, one of his eyes doesn't see, and he limps on one leg. Show me, Reb Pinkhesl, where it's written in the *shulkhen orekh* that a Jew has to see with both eyes, or walk equally well on both legs. He speaks with a bit of a lisp. Well, do our holy books say that a Jew has to speak perfectly? A Jew must know that he is a Jew; beyond that, nothing matters."

It takes nothing away from Goldfaden to point out that he borrowed this joke, again from *The Bridal Veil*. Here is Gottlober's hero, Yosele, teasing his Freydele about the arranged marriage her parents are attempting to foist on her: "Would your father embarrass that holy man, the Kanaver Rabbi [Leml's father], over such a trivial matter, a bit of nose, and turn him away with his precious only son? 'Disgraceful!' he would say. 'Where is it written that every Jew must have a nose? What, can't one be a Jew without a nose?' "[115]

Even when Goldfaden is obviously recycling material—perhaps especially at such moments—we can appreciate his comic artistry. He realizes that the joke will be funnier if played straight, rather than spoken by a character who implicitly calls attention to the absurdity of the situation. And Kalmen's punch line sums up much of what the maskilim found wrong with the traditional world: the privileging of Jewish tradition at the expense of all earthly happiness.

Goldfaden also does more in *Kuni-Lemls* than any previous Yiddish play had done to illustrate not only the backwardness of traditional Eastern European Jewish life, but also the vitality of the enlightened world. Rather than simply tell us that enlightenment bears much-wanted fruit by introducing a maskilic *raisonneur* to critique religious fanaticism, Goldfaden takes us out to the maskilim. We first meet Max in a garden, where he and his classmates from the university are celebrating the end of exams with singing every bit as spirited as in the Hasidic gathering that opened the play. Just as he is complaining to his friends that he has been barred from seeing Carolina, she enters, and they sing a duet that shows them to be a more whimsical couple than their predecessors tend to be, for the song revolves around the singing of the word "Cuckoo!," their signal for calling each other. When Carolina tells Max about her father's intentions to marry her off, Max realizes that he knows Kuni-Leml, and like Yosele in *The Bridal Veil*, plans to sabotage the father's wishes by disguising himself as the intended groom. Gottlober, though, had made his antihero so grotesque that he could not really have the character interact with everyone else; in fact, Leml never says a word, so he feels more like a prop than a person. The "real" Kuni-Leml, on the other hand (as opposed to his fraudulent double in the form of Max), is brimming with personality, and we may even find him lovable for all his backwardness.

Goldfaden introduces Max's disguise early enough in the action to have both Kuni-Lemls running around—or limping, as the case may be—for much of the play, causing no end of confusion not only for the traditionalists, but for the young lovers themselves. Max courts the matchmaker's homely daughter in the guise of Kuni-Leml, while the real Kuni-Leml is first meeting Carolina, whose mistaken belief that he is the fraudulent version makes her treat him with a familiarity that confirms his worst fears about what a "heretic" she is. Goldfaden's master stroke is to bring the true and the ersatz versions face to face in Act 3,

---

115. Avrom Ber Gottlober, *Der dektukh, oder, tsvey khupes in eyn nakht* (Warsaw: Yozef Verbleynski, 1876), 20.

scene 6, a scene that is the apotheosis of a nearly century-long tradition of satirizing religious fanaticism in Yiddish drama. Goldfaden put
the Haskala in Hasidic clothing and made the old world of the shtetl
confront itself. As a result, Kuni-Leml concludes pathetically (and,
depending on one's point of view, poignantly), "So he r-really is Kuni-
Leml, and I am . . . me." One can argue that Goldfaden had brought
the satirization of Hasidism to its logical conclusion; in his hands,
Hasidism had seen itself in the mirror, and was left with no identity
of its own.

That there can be any poignancy in such a moment, as opposed to merely making a mockery of an outmoded belief system as
embodied in the central character, further confirms Goldfaden's
maturation as a playwright. The character Shmendrik is a marvel-
ously effective comic target, but he is little more than that, for he is
too detached, too caught up in his own childish games, for us to
empathize with him. Kuni-Leml, however, for all that he similarly
represents the "crippled" world of loveless, arranged marriages, has
been endowed with a humanity that allows him to transcend the
mere functionality of his symbolism. One line that may illustrate
Kuni-Leml's humanity better than anything else is almost buried in
the climactic encounter between the "real" Kuni-Leml and his im-
postor. Having earlier courted the matchmaker's daughter while in
disguise, Max now tries to convince Kuni-Leml that the latter actually did the wooing:

> MAX: Y-you yourself s-swore to her that you love her.
>
> KUNI-LEML: Who? I s-swore? In my whole l-life, I've n-never
> sworn more than once. J-just once, I swore that I would
> never eat p-prune jam with bread. That was because my dog
> snatched it away from me once, and t-took a bite out of me
> at the same time. But b-besides that, I've n-never sworn.

Kuni-Leml recalls this incident in passing, out of sheer befuddlement.
His articulation of this memory helps add a dimension to him that has
nothing to do with the play's politics, and everything to do with giving
the actor playing this character an emotional life beyond the play. Not
incidentally, in our experience in staged readings and in the classroom,
this line always gets a laugh. It is such moments that allowed as great
an interpreter as Maurice Schwartz, who in 1924 directed his own adaptation of the play at the Yiddish Art Theatre in New York and played
the real Kuni-Leml, to emphasize levels of the character often over-
looked by other actors. "Just as Hamlet asks the eternal question, 'To

be or not to be?',", Schwartz recalled in his memoirs, "I tragicomically asked myself, 'Am I Kkkuni-Llllemel or am I not Kkkuni-Llllemel?'"[116]

By the time of Schwartz's production, *The Two Kuni-Lemls* had been a fixture on Yiddish stages for nearly half a century. The very name "Kuni-Leml" was by then "a byword for an awkward, inconsequential simpleton [. . .] just as well known to Jews as is, for instance, among the English, Pooh-Bah as a type of grasping politician,"[117] and the play enjoyed an enduring place in the repertoire of Yiddish theatre companies all over the world.

By modernizing the play in certain respects, Schwartz risked offending critics and spectators who had come to see Goldfaden's works almost as the property of the Jewish people rather than as works for the theatre subject to different interpretations over time. Works like *Kuni-Lemls* had become so familiar to actors and audiences alike that at least in some circles, it was not even deemed possible—or at least desirable—to depart one iota from how the master used to stage the play, as actor and theatre historian Jacob Mestel illustrates in the following scenario:

> We are at a rehearsal of *The Two Kuni-Lemls*—the scene in Pinkhesl's house. The "young" director places the table "left of the actor." An actress insists that the table should be on the right.
>
> DIRECTOR: This time we'll play the scene with the table on the left.
>
> ACTRESS: That feels awkward to me; I've always played it with the table on the right.
>
> "*Where does the table go in Reb Pinkhesl's?*" This question is soon posed to an older actor who still remembers how Goldfaden directed. And wherever Goldfaden put the table is where it will stand now as well.[118]

Such rigidity not only put a damper on artistic creativity; it obscured the new insights one could have into Goldfaden's work if old traditions should be followed too rigidly. By breathing new life into *Kuni-Lemls*, Schwartz brought out dimensions of the play that had not been appreciated before.

116. Maurice Schwartz, "Moris Shvarts dertseylt," February 14, 1942. For a detailed discussion of the production and reception of Schwartz's Goldfaden revivals, see Joel Berkowitz, "The Tallis or the Cross?: Reviving Goldfaden at the Yiddish Art Theatre, 1924–26," *Journal of Jewish Studies* 50 (Spring 1999): 120–38.

117. Goldberg, 353–354.

118. Jacob Mestel, "Goldfaden als traditsye af der bine," *Goldfaden-bukh* (New York, 1926), 12.

Among these was a statement from critic Nokhem Buchwald that might then have seemed almost heretical, for he compared it to arguably the most popular Yiddish play of all time, S. Ansky's *The Dybbuk*, which had premiered to rapturous reception in 1920, and had since then become widely known and loved in both Yiddish and Hebrew versions:

> *The Two Kuni-Lemls* is in fact nothing less than *The Dybbuk* in a funhouse mirror. Ansky and Goldfaden both draw upon the same material, taken from the same environment. *The Dybbuk* deals with *lamed-vovniks* and so does *The Two Kuni Lemls.* In *The Dybbuk*, Hasidim walk around in fur hats, black overcoats, and white socks, and in *The Two Kuni-Lemls* too. The supernatural plays a role in *The Dybbuk* and in *The Two Kuni-Lemls.* Ansky brings the dead out onto the stage and so does Goldfaden. In *The Two Kuni-Lemls* we see a Hasidic engagement party and in *The Dybbuk* a Hasidic wedding. . . . Ansky took all these Hasidic materials and made a symbolist, mystical, legendary, sanctified, frightening stew, and Goldfaden stuck out his tongue and broke out into impertinent laughter at all the fur-hatted sanctimony. The same environment, the same Hasidic culture, so to speak, appears in *The Dybbuk* as something right, deep, and beautiful, and in *The Two Kuni-Lemls* as foolishness and humbug.
>
> Say what you want—for me, Goldfaden's caricature and cheerful nonsense is not a drop less valuable than Ansky's idealization and deeply spiritualized nonsense.[119]

The Two Kuni-Lemls, then, is even more than one of the great Jewish comic plays of all time. It deserves an honored place among the literary works depicting the world of Eastern European Jewry entering the modern era.[120]

---

119. Nokhem Buchwald, "Goldfadens a shpil modernizirt," *Frayhayt*, February 1, 1924.

120. Besides its ubiquitous place in the repertoire of Yiddish troupes throughout the world, *The Two Kuni-Lemls* has inspired a number of adaptations. In 1933, the Warsaw-based avant-garde company Yung Teater staged *Trupe Tanentsap: a Goldfaden-shpil in a galitsish shtetl* (The Tanentsap Troupe: A Goldfaden Play in a Galician Shtetl), written by Yung Teater's founding director, Mikhl Weichert (the play was later published in Tel Aviv by Hamenorah in 1966). Weichert's play sets out to recreate the performance conditions of the early days of the wandering troupes in Eastern Europe while subtly criticizing authorities like the ones that censored Yung Teater's previous offering, *Boston,* about the trial of Sacco and Vanzetti. The most detailed study of Yung Teater is Elinor Rubel's "Lahakat ha-'Yung Teater'" (M.A. thesis, Hebrew University, 1990). In the 1960s, *Kuni-Leml* was adapted for the screen in one of the most commercially successful Israeli films up to that time. *Shnei Kuni Leml* (1966) spawned two sequels as well: *Kuni Leml b'tel aviv* (Kuni-Leml in Tel Aviv, 1976) and *Kuni-Leml b'kahir* (Kuni-Leml in Cairo, 1983). In English, the play was adapted into a new musical, *Kuni Leml,* by Richard Engquist, Raphael Crystal, and Nahma Sandrow. The play won three Outer Critics Circle Awards in 1984–1985, including Best Off-Broadway Musical.

Goldfaden's Successors

It would not be entirely accurate to call *The Two Kuni-Lemls* the last Haskala satire, but in some respects the play marks the end of an era. Shortly after its premiere, Tsar Alexander II of Russia was assassinated, triggering the outbreak of pogroms in Russia that would spark large-scale westward emigration of Russian Jewry—and of the Yiddish theatre itself. Goldfaden would not leave Russia immediately, but he moved away from writing satires in favor of grand, nationalistic spectacles of Jewish heroism, such as *Shulamis* (1881) and *Bar Kokhba* (1883), both of which would become as ubiquitous as *Kuni-Lemls* in the Yiddish repertoire. In the last two decades of his life, Goldfaden would become increasingly drawn to Zionism as a cure for Jewish ills. While later plays like *The Messianic Era?!* (1891) and his last work, *Ben Ami* (1907), are not his strongest efforts as a dramatist, they show him continuing to grapple with Jewish issues, in this case trying to illustrate the merits of Zionism in dramatic form.

While Goldfaden's plays would continue to be popular on Yiddish stages around the world, their author's own prominence in the theatre world would slip several notches when the center of gravity shifted from Russia to New York. Goldfaden's chief competitors, Moyshe Hurwitz (1844–1910) and Joseph Lateiner (1853–1935), sailed for New York City years before he did, and established themselves as house dramatists for rival troupes performing in theatres across the street from each other on the Bowery in lower Manhattan. Hurwitz and Lateiner were skilled not only at meeting the demands of their new environment for new plays—at least providing a high quantity of plays, if not usually plays of high quality—but also at winning the loyalty of their actors and thereby making it difficult for any competitors to get their work staged. Even the man who would come to be known as the "Father of the Yiddish theatre" failed to gain a foothold in New York. After meeting with a cool reception upon his arrival in 1887, Goldfaden toured other American cities, wrote a couple of important new plays,[121] published a short-lived Yiddish newspaper in New York, and returned to Europe. Plagued by illness and poverty in his later years, and undoubtedly demoralized by professional disappointments, Goldfaden would never again be as productive as he had been in his first half-dozen years as a playwright. He died in New York in 1908.

Much of the Yiddish repertoire, throughout the heyday of the Yiddish theatre that would last until the Holocaust, would continue in the

---

121. These were *Kenig Akhashveyresh* (King Ahasuerus) and *Akeydes Yitskhok* (The Binding of Isaac), musical comedies based on biblical themes—and among his half dozen or so best works for the stage.

direction that Goldfaden first mapped out, though unfortunately not always with nearly the same degree of inventiveness as he had shown in his best works. That is, Yiddish audiences overwhelmingly sought out broad comedies, musicals, and sentimental melodramas. They also craved novelty, creating a never-ending demand for new offerings that tended to leave playwrights little time to craft their plays. And at least in the first couple of decades of professional theatrical activity, the performances were extremely uneven. The first generation of actors included a number of remarkably talented performers, including Jacob Adler and Sarah Adler, Sigmund and Dina Feinman, David Kessler, Keni Liptzin, Sigmund Mogulesco, and Boris and Bessie Thomashefsky. But for every world-class star, there were dozens of lesser actors, not always possessing any great claim to talent.

European theatre and drama in other languages, meanwhile, was enjoying something of a renaissance. A new wave of realist and naturalist playwrights and directors striving for greater consistency and professionalism was beginning to eclipse the lighter fare that had dominated for decades—fashionable drama that George Bernard Shaw scathingly characterized as nothing but "a tailor's advertisement making sentimental remarks to a milliner's advertisement in the middle of an upholsterer's and decorator's advertisement."[122] Shaw lauded the efforts of a new generation of English dramatists, as well as Scandinavians like Henrik Ibsen, to bring social issues, natural dialogue, and well-constructed plots back to prominence. Shaw and Ibsen were at the vanguard of a remarkable flowering of dramatic writing that included Scandinavians August Strindberg and Bjornstjerne Bjornson; Émile Zola and Henri Becque in France; Gerhart Hauptmann in Germany; and Anton Chekhov, Ivan Turgenev, and Maxim Gorky in Russia.[123]

The new writing was accompanied by new stagecraft, and just as important, by new venues for producing plays that could never have gotten

122. Quoted in Martin Meisel, *Shaw and the Nineteenth Century Theater* (Princeton, NJ: Princeton University Press, 1963; repr. New York: Limelight Editions, 1984), 71.

123. Among the many works surveying the dramatists of this period, see Eric Bentley, *The Playwright as Thinker: A Study of Drama in Modern Times* (San Diego: Harcourt Brace Jovanovich, 1946); Oscar R. Brockett and Robert R. Findlay, *Century of Innovation: A History of European and American Theatre and Drama Since 1870* (Englewood, NJ: Prentice-Hall, 1973), esp. chapters 2–9; Robert Brustein, *The Theatre of Revolt* (New York: Little, Brown, 1964); Barrett H. Clark, *Contemporary French Dramatists* (Cincinnati: Stewart and Kidd, 1916) and *The Continental Drama of To-Day* (New York: Holt, 1914); Toby Cole, ed., *Playwrights on Playwriting: The Meaning and Making of Modern Drama from Ibsen to Ionesco* (New York: Hill and Wang, 1960); Ludwig Lewisohn, *The Modern Drama* (New York: Viking, 1915); Maurice Valency, *The Flower and the Castle: An Introduction to Modern Drama* (New York: Macmillan, 1963); and Raymond Williams, *Drama from Ibsen to Brecht* (London: Chatto & Windus, 1968).

an airing in mainstream theatres. The independent theatre movement was spawned in 1887 by André Antoine, a clerk at the Paris Gas Company who took part in amateur theatrical activity as a hobby. That year, he persuaded his theatre group, the Cercle Gaulois, to sponsor an evening of new plays, but the conservative organization became less and less enthusiastic when it sensed that at least some of the material on the four-play bill—particularly Zola's *Jacques Damour*—threatened to be controversial. Antoine persisted, creating a new entity he called the Théâtre-Libre. Favorable notice in the press prompted him to continue, and for the next seven years, Antoine presided over his productions with an exacting professionalism that dramatically raised the level of production standards. After leaving the struggling theatre he created, Antoine would run the Théâtre Antoine from 1897 to 1906. By this time, Antoine's efforts had inspired important imitators elsewhere in Western Europe, most notably the Freie Bühne, Freie Volksbühne, and Neue Freie Volksbühne in Germany, and J. T. Grein's Independent Theatre in London. Such theatres, and others like them, championed new drama that at its best broke new artistic ground, provided socially conscious alternatives to the superficiality common on nineteenth-century stages, and strove for ensemble acting rather than productions designed to serve largely as vehicles for star performers.[124]

The professional Yiddish theatre, then, was born under one dominant mode of theatre just as the modern European and American theatre performed in other languages was beginning to shift to another. And while Yiddish audiences came largely from the working class, Yiddish playwrights were more likely to be aware of the intellectual and artistic trends of the day. One pivotal figure who was keenly aware of new developments in society and in the theatre was Jacob Gordin (1853–1909), a Russian Jewish intellectual who had been involved in radical politics before emigrating to the United States in 1891 to escape the Tsarist police.[125] Gordin sought to further his agrarian utopian efforts in America, but failed to secure funding. He thus turned to journalism. Before settling in New York, Gordin had written some theatre criticism in Russian; he had never written in Yiddish,

124. For an introduction to key figures and developments in the Independent Theatre movement, see, in addition to Brockett and Findlay's *Century of Innovation*, André Antoine, *Memories of the Théâtre-libre*, trans. Marvin Carlson (Coral Gables, FL: University of Miami Press, 1964); Toby Cole and Helen Krich Chinoy, eds., *Directors on Directing: A Source Book of the Modern Theater* (1953; repr. New York: Macmillan, 1985); Anna Irene Miller, *The Independent Theatre in Europe, 1887 to the Present* (New York: Benjamin Blom, 1931); Maxim Newmark, *Otto Brahm: The Man and the Critic* (New York: G. E. Stechert, 1938); and Oliver M. Sayler, *Inside the Moscow Art Theatre* (New York: Brentano, 1925).

125. Steven Cassedy discusses this facet of Gordin in *To the Other Shore: The Russian Jewish Intellectuals Who Came to America* (Princeton, NJ: Princeton University Press, 1997).

and never written a play before his first drama, *Siberia*, in 1891. With a large and growing family, however—he and his wife ultimately had fourteen children—he needed ways to supplement his income, and took up a colleague's suggestion that he write for the Yiddish theatre.[126]

There was just one problem—not so much Gordin's complete lack of playwriting experience, which does not seem to have fazed him. What did bother him was the Yiddish theatre itself, which he described as being "far from Jewish life . . . coarse, unaesthetic, false, mean, and vulgar."[127] Gordin had in mind the popular dramas in the Hurwitz / Lateiner vein that had come to dominate the Yiddish stage—a kind of drama loosely labeled by critics as *shund*—literally, "trash." It was a kind of theatre that made the Yiddish critics perpetually wring their hands and worry aloud about how to bring "better drama" onto Yiddish stages. Of course, other theatrical cultures had their own versions of *shund*, and Gordin's artistic heroes—figures like Hauptmann, Ibsen, and Gorky—also had to overcome audiences with low artistic expectations and poorly staged productions. Gordin set out to write in the same spirit of reform that was sweeping Europe. Histories and memoirs of the Yiddish theatre in New York in Gordin's day are filled with stories of his clashes with actors, of bewildered audiences, and of a handful of actors and critics who understood what Gordin was trying to do, and tried to convince performers and theatregoers of the merits of his project. While many of these stories became the stuff of theatre legend, there is no question that Gordin became second only to Goldfaden in terms of his impact on the Yiddish theatre. His contributions were many: adapting works by prominent European playwrights, including Shakespeare, Goethe, Schiller, and Ibsen;[128] championing socially engaged dramas with coherent story lines and three-dimensional characters; writing lively dramatic dialogue largely free of the *daytshmerish*, or bastardized German, that plagued many of the plays of his predecessors and contemporaries; creating powerful roles for the best Yiddish actors, most notably Jacob Adler, Keni Liptzin, David Kessler, and Bertha Kalish; inspiring a new generation of playwrights who emulated his methods, led by writers like Leon Kobrin (1872–1946) and Zalmen Libin (Israel Zalmen Hurwitz, 1872–1955); and writing some

---

126. For biographical and critical studies of Gordin, see in particular *Leksikon fun der nayer yidisher literatur*, 2:142–53; Kalmen Marmor, *Yankev Gordin* (New York: YKUF, 1953); S. Niger, *Dertseylers un romanistn* (New York: CYCO, 1946), 193–203; Zalmen Reyzen, *Leksikon fun der yidisher literatur, prese un filologye* (Vilna: B. Kletskin, 1928), 1:519–30; Nahma Sandrow, *Vagabond Stars*, 132–63; Zylbercweig, *Leksikon*, 1:392–461; and Zylbercweig, *Di velt fun Yankev Gordin* (Tel Aviv: Farlag Elisheva, 1964).

127. Jacob Gordin, "Erinerungen fun Yankev Gordin: vi azoy bin ikh gevorn a dramaturg?", in *Di idishe bine*, ed. Chanon Minikes (New York, 1897), n.p.

128. On Gordin's reform efforts and his adaptations of *King Lear*, see Joel Berkowitz, *Shakespeare on the American Yiddish Stage* (Iowa City: University of Iowa Press, 2001), 31–72.

hundred plays, including several that would become staples of serious Yiddish drama, including *Der yidisher kenig Lir* (The Jewish King Lear, 1892), *Mirele Efros* (1898), *Sappho* (1899), *Got, mentsh un tayvl* (God, Man, and Devil, 1900), *Kreutzer Sonata* (1902), and *Khasye di yesoyme* (Khasye the Orphan, 1903).

For all his considerable achievements, Gordin did not manage to drive *shund* from the Yiddish stage altogether. Besides the fact that popular theatre always carries on alongside new artistic movements—however much history focuses on the latter at the expense of the former—Gordin's reforms had their limits. He did not jettison "lines of business" for particular actors, who sometimes rebelled against dramaturgical changes that they felt might cost them their livelihood. He carried on the "Oy, I feel faint" tradition established by Ettinger—that is, giving various characters verbal tics repeated ad nauseam throughout the play, like the fishmonger who speaks fishmongerese in *Sappho,* or the elderly jesters addicted to speaking in rhymed couplets in *The Jewish King Lear* and *God, Man, and Devil.* The speeches delivered by his characters can be powerful, but can just as easily descend into tendentiousness or bathos, and the dénouements to all but a few of his plays feel contrived. The most discerning of Gordin's contemporaries noted that the line between his dramas and *shund* was not always clear-cut (and that is even when he was not writing popular entertainment himself, which he often did under pseudonyms like "Dr. Jacobi from London"). Had Gordin never written his reformist agenda down in black and white, he might have been spared some of this grief; it is the perennial plight of playwrights to be chastised for failing to live up to rules of dramaturgy that they may or may not have ever subscribed to. Rules are for critics, after all; working playwrights have to put food on the table, and overattentiveness to aesthetic principles is often inversely proportional to the amount of food a writer brings home.

Peretz Hirschbein and *Miriam*

It is no accident, then, that a more radical break from Yiddish theatrical tradition would have to await the arrival of a playwright who cared less about pleasing audiences than about satisfying his own artistic ideals. Peretz Hirschbein's plays would mark another turning point in the development of Yiddish drama. As Jacob Mestel has observed, "What Avrom Goldfaden was for Yiddish theatre as a whole, and Jacob Gordin was for Yiddish folk drama, Hirschbein was for *modern* Yiddish theatre and for Yiddish folk comedy."[129]

---

129. Jacob Mestel, *Literatur un teater* (New York: YKUF, 1962), 87.

Unlike the three playwrights whose work precedes his in this collection—indeed, unlike perhaps any significant Yiddish writer before him[130]—Hirschbein came from a poor, rural background. He grew up in a water mill in a small village in Grodno province, was given what rudimentary Jewish education his surroundings would allow, and then made his way to the city of Grodno, and shortly thereafter to Vilna, as a young man. In Vilna—known as *Yerushalayim d'lite*, or the Jerusalem of Lithuania, because of its rich network of yeshivas, Jewish printing presses, libraries, and other manifestations of a prominent religious infrastructure—Hirschbein joined a circle of yeshiva students who studied the Bible, Hebrew grammar, and Jewish history together. While living in poverty, eking out a meager living as a Hebrew teacher, he followed the blossoming literary scene, learned Russian, and in 1901 published his first Hebrew poem in David Frishman's (1859–1922) literary journal *Ha-dor*.[131] Our anthology contains Hirschbein's first major work, the naturalist drama *Miriam* (Hebrew 1905; Yiddish 1906); we will explore the circumstances under which that play was written in a moment. At about the same time he wrote *Miriam*, he wrote another Hebrew play, but shortly thereafter, feeling that Vilna had limited opportunities for an aspiring writer, he made his way to Warsaw, then a mecca for Yiddish writers.

During early 1900s, Hirschbein would continue writing naturalist dramas in Hebrew, including *Nevelah* (Carcass), which in Yiddish (*Di neveyle*) would become one of Hirschbein's most successful works. *Olamot bodedim* (Lonely Worlds, 1906) marked a new symbolist phase in his career, as well as the end of his practice of writing originally in Hebrew. Like many other Yiddish playwrights working at the time, Hirschbein was then deeply influenced by the symbolist movement, and wrote a number of plays in that vein, including the one-act *Kvorim-blumen* (Graveyard Flowers), *Di erd* (The Earth), *In der finster* (In the Dark), and *Der tekies-kaf* (The Handshake).[132]

---

130. Yisroel Osman suggests that Hirschbein "was perhaps the first of our writers to come from simple people, from the mill and the village." See "Perets Hirshbayn (biografye)" in *Perets Hirshbayn (tsu zayn zekhtsikstn geboyrntog)*, ed. Shmuel Niger (New York: CYCO, 1948), 5.

131. Concise discussions of Hirschbein's life and work can be found in the *Leksikon fun der nayer yidisher literatur*, 2:147–58; Zalmen Reyzen, *Leksikon*, 839–47; and Zylbercweig, *Leksikon*, 1:613–28. The fullest sources for Hirschbein's biography are his own memoirs, *Mayne kinderyorn* (New York: Perets Hirshbayn Bukh-komitet, 1951), and *In gang fun lebn: zikhroynes* (New York: CYCO, 1948). A variety of essays on the many facets of Hirschbein's career—as playwright, director, novelist, poet, and so on—can be found in Niger, *Perets Hirshbayn*. Biographical and critical essays accompany a selection of Hirschbein's writings in *Perets Hirshbayn: teater, velt-rayzes, zikhroynes* ed. Shmuel Rozhansky (Buenos Aires, 1967).

132. For selected assessments of Hirschbein's dramaturgy, see Jacob Glatshteyn, *In tokh genumen: eseyen, 1948–1956* (New York: Farlag fun Idish Natsyonaln Arbeter Farband, 1956), 70–82; Isaac Goldberg, "The Yiddish Drama," in *The Drama of Transition* (Cincinnati: Stewart Kidd, 1922); Jacob Mestel, "Perets Hirshbayn, a pioner in yidishn teater," in *Literatur un teater* (New York, 1962); Dovid Pinski, "Perets Hirshbayn der dramatiker," and Maurice Schwartz, "Dikhter-dramaturg," in Niger, *Perets Hirshbayn*, 118–23, 260–67.

Many of these plays were published, but in 1908, when Hirschbein moved to Odessa, he began taking a more active role in staging them. That year he wrote the drama *Yoel* (Joel), and the respected director David Herman staged *Der tekies-kaf* in Lodz. Soon afterward, *Af yener zayt taykh* (On the Other Side of the River) was produced in Russian in Odessa. In the autumn of the same year, Hirschbein—with the encouragement of Hebrew poet Hayyim Nahman Bialik and students from an acting conservatory in Odessa—founded the theatre company that would become known as the Hirschbein Troupe. The ensemble stayed together for only two years, during which it staged a number of important dramas, including works by Hirschbein, Sholem Asch, David Pinski, Sholem Aleichem, and Jacob Gordin, as well as translations of plays by Semyon Yushkevitsh and Herman Heijermans.[133]

It was only after the troupe disbanded in 1910, however, that Hirschbein reached his zenith as a dramatist, with works that Jacob Glatshteyn has called "the four greatest plays in the Yiddish repertoire:"[134] *Di puste kretshme* (The Idle Inn, 1911), *A farvorfn vinkl* (A Distant Corner, 1912), *Dem shmids tekhter* (The Blacksmith's Daughters, 1918) and *Grine felder* (Green Fields, 1918). In these and other dramas, Hirschbein left symbolism behind and returned to his rural roots, dramatizing the lives and loves of simple Jewish peasants. Critics have tended to agree that the shift was for the better; as one put it, "The best of Hirschbein's longer plays are those in which he himself establishes a restorative contact with the earth that his early years have known, with the simple folk among whom he was reared, with the bumpkins and hoydens of peasant life as he saw it and felt it."[135]

Although Hirschbein might have seemed to have found a successful formula by this point, he would never sit still, either professionally or geographically. In 1914 he helped found the New York Yiddish daily newspaper *Der tog*, to which he would contribute extensively for the rest of his life, starting with dispatches from Latin America.[136] After marrying a poet named Esther Shumiatsher in 1918, Hirschbein traveled with her for two years in Australia, South Africa, Tahiti, and New Zealand,[137]

---

133. On the Hirschbein Troupe, see Hirschbein, *In gang fun lebn*, 279–418; A. Mukdoyni, "Zikhroynes fun a yidishn teater-kritiker," in Jacob Shatsky, *Arkhiv*, 341–421; Nokhem Oyslender, "Der veg fun dem odeser yidishn 'kunst-teater,'" in *Yidisher teater: 1887–1917* (Moscow: Emes, 1940), 237–58; Avrom Reyzen, "Di vanderndike yidishe trupe" and Mendl Elkin, "A bintl zikhroynes," in Niger, ed., *Perets Hirshbayn*, 204–31; and Zalmen Zylbercweig, *Leksikon*, 1:612–13.

134. *In tokh genumen*, 76.

135. Goldberg, 407.

136. *Fun vayte lender* (New York: Tog, 1916).

137. Chronicled in *Felker un lender: rayze-ayndrukn fun nay-zeland, oystralye, dorem-afrike, 1920–1922* (Vilna: B. Kletskin, 1929).

and later in the 1920s, they spent five years traveling through Asia,
Europe, and the Near East.[138] He also wrote two novels[139] and two highly
regarded books of memoirs, the first (*My Childhood Years*) dealing with
his rural youth, the second (*As Life Goes On*) chronicling his first years
as a writer and man of the theatre. After a long and debilitating illness
that nearly paralyzed Hirschbein, whose physical strength had always
been a topic of wonder to his friends, he died in 1948.

The work that helped launch Hirschbein's reputation was *Miriam*,
and students of modern Jewish literature may find the drama behind
the making of this drama as compelling as anything the action that
unfolds in the play. The process by which *Miriam* came to be published
is a tale of two literatures, and of yet another striking new direction in
Yiddish drama. Two of the leading Jewish writers of the early 1900s
were the play's midwives, and other important artists helped determine
its circuitous route to publication and production. According to
Hirschbein, a chance encounter with a prostitute as he was returning
from a Hebrew lesson one evening changed the course of his literary
efforts from lyric poetry to naturalism. In his account, Hirschbein comes
across like one of the endearing rural naïfs who would come to popu-
late so many of his plays. Not fathoming the girl's intentions, he even
asks, "Why do you need me to come home with you?"[140] A moment
later, apparently overcome with shame, she bursts into tears. Hirschbein,
haunted by the encounter and unable to sleep, was immediately inspired to write a Hebrew drama exploring the path that leads an innocent young girl to a life of prostitution.

The strangest part of this account—as Hirschbein was well aware—
was the language in which the play was written. As we know by now,
Wolfssohn's quasi-Yiddish satire and Ettinger's deliciously Yiddish comedy were written and published during a period before professional
Yiddish troupes existed. Such troupes were established by Goldfaden
and his contemporaries, providing a living theatre for works like *The
Two Kuni-Lemls*. Hirschbein, therefore, could have found Yiddish companies to stage *Miriam* had he written it in the language of the Jewish
street—the language, as he points out, that these characters would have
spoken—but he could not bring himself to do so. This was not because
he regarded Yiddish as a linguistic Caliban—or not exactly:

> [W]henever I had enough money for a ticket, I loved to go
> to the Russian theatre. Visiting companies, guest performers

---

138. See *Arum der velt* (New York, 1927) and *Indye* (Vilna: B. Kletskin, 1929).

139. *Bovl* (New York, 1942) and *Royte felder* (New York, 1935).

140. Hirschbein, *In gang fun lebn*, 11.

from the world theatre, used to come through Vilna, performing plays by Chekhov, Hauptmann, Ibsen, Shakespeare,
and Maeterlinck. The language onstage sounded clear and
musical. Sitting in the theatre, I learned from the actors how
to speak Russian beautifully.

Yiddish troupes often traveled to Vilna, and when I went to
see what they performed, going with the same eagerness
with which I went to the Russian theatre, I emerged ashamed,
spiritually bereft. Even *Shulamis*, which I saw then for the
first time, drained my spirit as I sat in the theatre. I could
not for the life of me understand how, writing for the stage,
one could move so far from artistic and living truth. I therefore wrote my ultra-realistic drama *Miriam* not in Yiddish, as
such subject matter demanded, but in Hebrew.[141]

Hirschbein's initial encounter with Yiddish theatre echoes Jacob Gordin's
experiences of just over twenty years earlier. Yet rather than being driven
to reform the Yiddish stage, Hirschbein initially took a different high
road—so high, in fact, that had he continued to take it, his theatrical feet
would never have touched the ground.

He soon wrote a second Hebrew drama, *Shovevim* (Shards; later translated into Yiddish as *Der inteligent*), "the inner tragedy of an intellectual
who did not win the trust of the masses, and for whom the psychology of
the simple worker was truly foreign."[142] But what to do with his two most
recent literary products? He wrote, "In Vilna there were no connoisseurs.
When I read them to my friends, Hebrew teachers, they shrugged their
shoulders, blinked their eyes, and did not know what to say. At the time,
drama was a virtually unknown entity in our literature."[143]

Feeling that his work would find a warmer reception in Warsaw,
Hirschbein saved up the four rubles for a train ticket, and headed for
the Polish capital. It was also once a Jewish literary capital, boasting a
circle of talented writers and a bustling literary scene with important
printing presses and journals. An almost obligatory destination for any
Eastern European Jewish writer at the time was the home of Isaac Leib
Peretz, nearly as famous for nurturing young talent as for his own
stories and other writings. Hirschbein planned to visit Peretz as well as
Peretz's friend Hayyim Nahman Bialik (1873–1934), the Hebrew poet
already world famous for beautiful lyric poems like "El ha-tsipor," and

141. Peretz Hirschbein, "Vegn a gruntshteyn oyf dem idishn teater-bodn (zikhroynes un
batrakhtungen)," Peretz Hirschbein Papers, YIVO Institute for Jewish Research Archives, RG
833, folder 116.
142. Hirschbein, *In gang fun lebn*, 13.
143. Ibid.

for "Ba'ir ha-haregah" (In the City of Slaughter), his incendiary response in verse to the Kishinev pogrom of 1903.

Upon arriving in Warsaw, Hirschbein quickly befriended another famous Hebrew writer, the realist novelist Isaiah Bershadsky (1871–1908). Learning that his new companion had written a play, Bershadsky invited Hirschbein to his apartment and sat down to read *Miriam*. Hirschbein, with some time on his hands, looked around Bershadsky's lodgings and picked up a new Yiddish play by Sholem Asch, a young sensation in the world of Jewish letters, with several Yiddish and Hebrew stories whose publication had drawn warm reviews from important critics. Hirschbein was impressed by the Asch piece at hand, partly because it was a serious drama written in Yiddish.[144] Bershadsky, meanwhile, had spotted a new literary talent, and complimented Hirschbein on his achievement. As for Asch, Bershadsky remarked that he had "great talent; though I myself am drawn to simple realism, without any ornamentation."[145] He did not have to spell out that he preferred the work of the as yet unknown Peretz Hirschbein to the rising star Sholem Asch.

There were still others to convince, of course. Perhaps the most important of them was I. L. Peretz, a literary angel to Asch as he was to so many other writers of Asch's and Hirschbein's generation. Peretz's door was open to visiting writers for an hour every afternoon, and one day Hirschbein took up the general invitation. Warmly welcoming him, Peretz asked to see Hirschbein's plays—which the young man had not brought with him. Peretz paid for the coach to take Hirschbein to his lodgings and back again, so he could start reading the young man's work right away. Impressed with *Shards*, Peretz asked Hirschbein to leave *Miriam* with him overnight, and took the young man out to a café for the evening.

The next stop for Hirschbein was the home of Hayyim Nahman Bialik who, in addition to his accomplishments as a Hebrew writer, was an important literary editor as well. Arriving at Bialik's apartment, Hirschbein was astonished to find the poet greeting him by name; Peretz had already spoken to Bialik in glowing terms about Hirschbein, and the two older writers had read *Miriam* together the night before. Bialik declared, "I've decided to publish your *Miriam* in *Ha-shiloakh*," Bialik's literary journal. This should have been cause for celebration, but the reasons Bialik went on to give for his decision gave Hirschbein pause: "He emphasized the places that contained a bit of humor, or something like a joke. I was not

---

144. Hirschbein says that the play was *Der zindiker* (The Sinner), but this one-act play was not published until several years later. He may have confused this with an earlier play, such as *Tsurikgekumen* (Returned), first published in 1904 and later staged by the Hirschbein Troupe under the title *Mitn shtrom* (With the Current).

145. Ibid., 25.

pleased with this. I expected that he would emphasize moments of tragic experiences, which that drama had in sufficient measure, but he did not do so. It seemed to me at the time that he focused on superficial details. It was my opinion then that the virtues he mentioned were no basis to give a novice the privilege of being published in the famous *Ha-shiloakh.*"[146]

Hirschbein's doubts about Bialik as a critic—despite his great admiration for Bialik the poet—were reinforced a moment later when he noticed a manuscript sitting on Bialik's desk, covered with editorial comments and deleted passages in red ink. The work was a novel, *Mi-saviv le'nekudah* (Around the Point), by no less a writer than the pioneering novelist Yosef Hayyim Brenner (1881–1921), then being published in installments in *Ha-shiloakh*. Seeing Brenner's words changed so radically, and in ways that Hirschbein felt were not always improvements, made him feel as if Bialik "had hit me over the head with a hammer."[147] Making an excuse about wanting to polish his manuscript, he took *Miriam* home with him rather than leave it with Bialik for publication.

Hirschbein and Bialik would later become close friends, but Bialik would not have the chance to publish *Miriam*. Hirschbein soon returned to Vilna, and in 1905—four years after the publication of his first poems—he published *Miriam* in installments in a new monthly literary journal, *Ha-zman*. At first it seemed that the fourth and last act would not make it into print, for Joshua Steinberg, the stern Hebrew censor in Vilna, considered it immoral. Hirschbein tried in vain to convince Steinberg that *Miriam* fit within a respected literary tradition. Citing Russian writers like Gorky, Andreyev, and Tolstoy, Hirschbein argued the merits of exposing social injustice by depicting the seamier side of society. Steinberg was unimpressed, declaring that if he were the Russian censor, "I would tear their scribblings to pieces. It's their luck that I have no jurisdiction over them."[148] Nevertheless, a supporter of Hirschbein's ultimately convinced Steinberg that *Miriam* criticized rather than excused prostitution, and the fourth act was allowed to appear in *Ha-zman*. Hirschbein was soon persuaded by a number of friends in artistic circles to translate his Hebrew dramas into Yiddish, and before long, he began writing his plays only in Yiddish, with a few exceptions. *Miriam* was published in an American Yiddish journal in 1906, and in several later editions, at times under the title *Barg arop* (Downfall).[149]

---

146. Ibid., 37–38.

147. Ibid., 39.

148. Ibid., 67.

149. *Miriam, Der idisher kemfer* (1907), 22–29; *Barg arop*, in *Gezamelte shriftn*, vol. 5 (New York: Literarish-dramatishe faraynen in amerike, 1916), 5–88; and *Miriam*, in *Ale verk*, vol. 1, *Elnt un noyt: dramen* (Vilna: B. Kletskin, 1923), 1–85. We have based our translation on the latter text.

Steinberg was being prudish about the prostitution theme in *Miriam*, but Hirschbein's treatment of such subject matter is noteworthy for other reasons, and closer examination of it helps shed light on what he accomplished in this play. The brothel in which *Miriam* finds herself at the end of the play is not the first one we visit in this collection, and the issue of licentiousness will surface again, with very different overtones, in Alter Kaczyne's *The Duke*. In *Silliness and Sanctimony*, written over a century before *Miriam*, Wolfssohn had used the brothel as a clear moral contrast to the world of Jewish ideals—particularly the intellectual and moral education, derived from both Jewish tradition and secular learning, that promises to save modern Jewry from either the blindness of religious fanaticism or the dissolution of a completely assimilated life.[150]

The naturalist writers whom Hirschbein admired, however, took a very different view. Émile Zola, the movement's most influential theorist, articulated a view of the writer as a kind of scientist, who "collects observed facts, chooses a point of departure, and establishes a solid ground upon which characters can walk and phenomena develop."[151] Elsewhere, Zola insisted that naturalist writers "tell everything, we do not make a choice, neither do we idealize; and this is why [our critics] accuse us of taking pleasure in obscenity. . . . [T]here is no morality outside of the truth."[152] This outlook, shared by many of the leading novelists and playwrights of Zola's generation, was behind some of the most controversial and influential plays of the late 1800s, including several that assessed prostitution and sexual disease with the kind of scientific detachment that Zola advocated. Foremost among these were Ibsen's *Ghosts* (1881), Arthur Wing Pinero's *The Second Mrs. Tanqueray* (1893), Shaw's *Mrs. Warren's Profession* (1894; first performed 1902), and Eugène Brieux's *Damaged Goods* (1902). And as Hirschbein tried to explain to Vilna censor Joshua Steinberg, Russian writers had made their own contributions to the naturalist literary canon. Most germane in terms of drama was Maxim Gorky's *The Lower Depths* (1902), set in a flophouse and peopled with an array of social outcasts. The Moscow Art Theatre, under Konstantin Stanislavsky's direction, staged the play with such exacting attention to detail "that spectators in the first few rows were said to fear being infected with vermin."[153]

---

150. For a discussion of the role of brothels in these and other Yiddish dramas, see Joel Berkowitz, "The Brothel as Symbolic Space in Yiddish Drama," in *Sholem Asch Reconsidered*, ed. Nanette Stahl (New Haven: Beinecke Rare Book and Manuscript Library, 2004), 35–50.

151. From *Le roman expérimentale* (1880), quoted in Marvin Carlson, *Theories of the Theatre* (Ithaca, NY: Cornell University Press, 1984), 274.

152. "Naturalism on the Stage," trans. Belle M. Sherman, in *Dramatic Theory and Criticism: Greeks to Grotowski*, ed. Bernard F. Dukore (New York: Holt, Rinehart and Winston, 1974), 703.

153. Brockett and Findlay, *Century of Innovation*, 246.

Like Gorky, Hirschbein takes us down into the cellar, but the people we find there could hardly be more unlike Gorky's thieves, prostitutes, and drunks. Quite the contrary: as Hirschbein's contemporary, playwright and critic David Pinski (1872–1959), observed, Miriam and the other inhabitants of the basement dwelling where she lives and works "are characters from the Jewish masses, whose profound goodness and compassion Peretz Hirschbein set out to illustrate."[154] Hirschbein lets the action unfold slowly; indeed, there is very little of what most theatregoers would call "action" for much of the first half of the play. For most of act 1, we simply become acquainted with Hirschbein's vividly drawn characters: Shimen the shoemaker and his wife Dvoyre; their small children as well as an older daughter, Leah; her fiancé, Jonah; and two lodgers: Moyshe, an elderly porter, and Miriam, a sweet, vibrant young orphan, who recently moved to the big city from her small home town. The first words we hear are the folksong she sings; we cannot know it yet, but we will later discover that the song, and the brief discussion it sparks, help establish the play's central themes:

> I am lonely as a stone;
> I've been abandoned, all alone—
> Please take pity, gentle friends,
> Don't let me meet an early end.
>
> (*To Dvoyre.*) Once I start singing that song, I forget all about the machine; then the thread goes and breaks on me.
>
> DVOYRE: What sort of fool dreamed up that song? Even if I knew I was going to kick the bucket, I wouldn't go complaining about it in public. Do you really think there are good people like that in the world?
>
> MIRIAM: Here it's a blind orphan girl complaining. Probably came up with the song herself. (*Long pause.*) There are still plenty of good people.

The play's events, like a Zolaesque experiment, will ultimately test Miriam's thesis.

To the extent that act 1 contains any dramatic tension, it is contained in the relationship between Miriam and Jonah, who bicker with an intensity that can only come from two people who care about each other—and though nothing untoward ever occurs between them, perhaps there is an element of sexual attraction there too? In any case,

---

154. Dovid Pinski, "Perets Hirshbayn der dramatiker," in Niger, *Perets Hirshbayn*, 119.

Jonah fancies himself a man of the world, and immediately stakes out a contrarian position: "Ech, what a little goat! In your *shtetl* you had plenty of beans and noodles. Here you won't eat so well; the red in your cheeks will disappear, and your lips—fyu-fyu! Then, *ketsele*, you'll find out if there are any good people." It is hard to take much of what Jonah says as anything more than boyish swagger, but the characters in Shimen's basement will soon find this debate more real than they might ever have expected.

Yiddish has a lovely expression for high society—a part of the world so alien to most Jews of Eastern Europe: *di hoykhe fenster*: literally, the "high windows."[155] Hirschbein literalizes this figure of speech in *Miriam*, when into Shimen's shop saunters Zilberman, the spoiled rich kid from upstairs whose family owns the premises. He has come on the pretext of fixing an ice skate, but everyone but Miriam can see that he is just using this as an excuse to see her. For the rest of act 1 and much of act 2, we watch the attraction between Miriam and Zilberman blossom into a romance, while Miriam's friends in the basement look on apprehensively, at times teasing her, at times warning her seriously about the potential consequences. Sure enough, when Miriam becomes pregnant with Zilberman's child, his family keeps her from seeing him, and literally throws her down the stairs that lead to their fancy dwellings (an event we hear rather than see). After having left the basement and staying away for some months, Miriam returns just in time to go into labor; act 3 ends with her howling in pain while a religious neighbor brought in to help with the delivery clucks incessantly at the immorality of it all.

Act 4 takes us out of the basement for the first time, except in the dreams and longings of the people who live there. The play's final act follows Miriam to the brothel where she now works. There Hirschbein manages a remarkable dramaturgical balancing act, neither soft-pedaling the place's function nor dwelling on it pruriently. The only characters we see in act 4 are Miriam and two fellow prostitutes, one of them intelligent, the other a simpleton who speaks in bursts of isolated words and half-sentences. Throughout the act we hear would-be customers knocking at the door, but the women have decided to take the afternoon off and spend most of the rest of the play sharing their stories, tales of how they landed where they are. Hirschbein neither romanticizes nor judges the prostitutes here, but tries to understand them—the abuse they have suffered at the hands of parents and others, the seemingly small but fateful choices that have decided their path in life, their loneliness, longing, and desperation. Neither do the characters wallow in their own suffering; they cling to each

---

155. In act 4, the prostitute Grunye uses this term, which we translate as "high society."

other—quite literally—but Miriam, even after all she has been through, believes, "There are still good people in this world, Grunye." The drama's quietly powerful finale contains no grandstanding, no plot contrivances, no chewing of scenery. In *Miriam*, Hirschbein achieves what many naturalist writers formulated in critical essays and a number managed to achieve in fiction, but few accomplished so gracefully in drama.

Alter Kacyzne and *The Duke*

The final play in this collection has flashes of humor and naturalistic touches, but speaks in a completely different register than we have witnessed so far: the grand manner of a historical drama, buzzing with action yet filled with philosophical and theological ideas. Alongside the Yiddish theatre's extensive repertoire of comedies, musicals, and melodramas, historical drama was every bit as important—and indeed, intersects with every possible dramatic genre of Yiddish play.

Alter Sholem Kacyzne was born on May 31, 1885, in Vilna, the only child of a working-class family; his grandfather was a blacksmith, his father a bricklayer.[156] Though Kacyzne would go to traditional *kheyder* and a Russian Jewish elementary school for several years, he was primarily an autodidact; he knew Yiddish, Russian, Polish, German, French, and Hebrew. At fourteen, with the death of his father, Kacyzne was sent to Yekaterinoslav (Dnepopetrovsk) in the south of the Ukraine, where he spent the next eleven years as a photographer's apprentice. During this period, he also engaged in intensive self-study and began to write; however, his first literary works were composed in Russian. It was, perhaps, unsurprising that he would send his first works to another noted Jewish writer who, though raised in Yiddish, had begun his distinguished literary career in Russian: it was S. Ansky who first published two short stories by Kacyzne in the Russian journal *Yevreyskii mir* (The Jewish World) in 1909, around the time of his marriage to Khana Khachanov, who would later assist him in fulfilling his many responsibilities.[157]

---

156. Biographical information, unless otherwise noted, is taken from Melech Ravitch, "A bagleyt-vort fun a khaver," in *Alter Kacyzne: gezamlte shriftn*, 4 vols. (Tel Aviv: Y. L. Peretz Farlag, 1967), 1:7–13; Nachman Mayzel, "Alter Kacyzne," in idem, 1:313–318; Dov Sadan, "Tsvishn revolt un kidesh-hashem," in idem., 2:7–20; *Leksikon fun der nayer yidisher literatur* (New York: Congress for Jewish Culture, 1981), 8:117–119; and Marek Web, introduction to *Poyln: Jewish Life in the Old Country*, by Alter Kacyzne (New York: Metropolitan Books, 1999), xi–xxiii. The various accounts differ on minor details; we have chosen in such instances to rely on Web's account, the most recent. A bibliographic list of works about Kacyzne by Yefim Yeshurin and with additions by Dov Sadan can be found in *Gezamlte shriftn*, 2:329–344.

157. See Ravitch's warm words in "A bagleyt-vort," 8.

Like Ansky and so many other Yiddish writers, Kacyzne's literary life changed dramatically when he discovered the writings of I. L. Peretz. A short time later, in 1910, Kacyzne moved to Warsaw, where he became part of the circle that surrounded Peretz.[158] Kacyzne "became Peretz's most devoted disciple; his adulation was legendary"; perhaps it was because he was so impressed by Peretz that he published nothing from his move to Warsaw until Peretz's death in 1915.[159] Kacyzne would later describe this period as one in which "I was learning how to write from Peretz, working on it very methodically. What was the method? I kept writing, and he kept erasing. This went on for more than two years, week after week."[160]

His first literary activity to speak of was, appropriately enough, memories of Peretz published after his death; his first belletristic work in Yiddish appeared in 1918, a fragment of his "dramatic poem" *Der gayst der meylekh* (*The Spirit-King*), published in book-length form a year later.[161] In the next few years, he published another dramatic poem, *Prometeus* (Prometheus, 1920), as well as a book of stylized novellas and short stories, *Arabeskn* (Arabesques, 1922), which were heavily influenced by both the *Song of Songs* and the *Arabian Nights*.[162] In 1926, Kacyzne published *The Duke* with the prestigious publisher B. Kletskin in Vilna, and published *Hordos* (Herod), a tragedy, that same year. His most notable prose work is his two-volume novel *Shtarke un shvakhe* (The Strong and the Weak, 1929-1930), set in Jewish Warsaw during and after the First World War,[163] and his last work

---

158. The Kacyznes first lived on Świętojerska Street, in the center of Jewish Warsaw; after the birth of their daughter, in 1925, the family moved to a larger apartment in Nowolipie, across the street from the offices of the Yiddish newspaper *Folkstsaytung*. They also had a summer house in Świder, which became, after 1920, a summer retreat for Yiddish writers, who would rent the house from Kacyzne for rates they constantly complained about. One of the guests was Isaac Bashevis Singer, who stayed with his older brother, a member of the Khalyastre, and then wrote, "Here I'm surrounded by literature, by knowledge, by poetry." (Web, xv).

159. Web, xii; Mayzel ("Alter Kacyzne," 314) compares Kacyzne to an ardent Hasid at the home of his rebbe.

160. In *Di yudishe velt*, April–May 1915; translation here from Web, xii.

161. The excerpts appeared in the anthology *Eygns* (Kiev, 1918); the full 312-page work was published in Warsaw in 1919. The work itself, according to Ravitch, is highly influenced by the classic Polish writer Juliusz Słowacki (sharing a title with one of his works, *Król Duch*), and it was notably unsuccessful, perhaps because of its style of "enigmatic symbolism" (Web, xiii); see also Ravitch, 10.

162. See Ravitch, 10.

163. See Sadan's generally positive comments about the novel on pages 11–12.

to be published during his lifetime was *Baladn un groteskn* (Ballads and Grotesques, 1936).[164]

Kacyzne also wrote numerous poems and folk ballads as well as articles about literature, art, and theatre and social issues in *Literarishe bleter*, the seminal literary journal he cofounded with I. J. Singer, Peretz Markish, Melech Ravitch, and Nachman Mayzel. He also published in numerous other representatives of the flourishing press of the interwar period, including *Bikhervelt*, M. Shalit's *Lebn*, *Ilustrirte velt*, *Folkstsaytung*, *Vilner tog*, *Varshever shriftn*, *Undzer expres*, *Lebns-fragn*, and *Naye tsayt*. He also edited or coedited *Di teyve*, *Di glokn*, *Ringen*, *Literatur*, and the Communist *Der fraynd*.[165] Between 1937 and 1939, he published the biweekly *Mayn redendiker film*, containing articles, feuilletons, translations, and photographs; it was, apparently, regularly confiscated by the Polish censors.[166] He was also a board member of the Yiddish Writers and Journalists' association, chairman of the Yiddish PEN Club, and executor and editor of both Peretz's and Ansky's literary estates. Kacyzne scored a great success with S. Ansky's *Tog un nakht* (Day and Night), which he completed from the author's discarded notes from the first two acts, adding entire scenes and composing a new third act. Despite a harsh critical reception from the Vilna Yiddish press and later from the noted critics Alexander Mukdoyni and Shmuel Niger, among others, the play quickly became a staple of the Yiddish theatre's classic repertory.

Kacyzne wrote many songs for Yiddish *kleynkunst* (cabaret) theatres, the music for the film version of Jacob Gordin's drama *On a heym* (Homeless, 1939) and, most famously, the screenplay for the film of Ansky's play *The Dybbuk* (1937). He also worked on a film version of Abramovitsh's *Travels of Benjamin III*, which was never made. Kacyzne also constantly

---

164. A volume of his selected works was published in Warsaw in 1951 [A. Kacyzne, *Geklibene shriftn*, ed. D. Sfard (Warsaw: Yiddish Bukh-Farlag, 1951], and his complete works in four volumes, published by his daughter Sulamita Kacyzne-Reale, were published in Tel Aviv between 1967 and 1972. It is this version of *The Duke* which serves as the basis for our translation. Some of his other plays remained unpublished during his lifetime, including *In krizis* (In Crisis, 1933), *Dem yidns opera* (The Jew's Opera, 1937), set in Portugal among the forced Jewish converts there, and *Shvartsbard* (Schwarzbard, 1937), about the historical figure who assassinated Ukrainian nationalist leader Symon Petliura, all of "which were dominated by themes of Jewish destiny and anti-Jewish persecution" (Web, xiii). See also Sadan, 15–16.

165. Though some of these journals only appeared for a single issue, the record is still remarkably impressive. See Sadan, 17–18.

166. Among Kacyzne's translations were Aleksandr Blok's *Twelve* (Warsaw, 1920) and, in *Glokn* in 1921, selections of Anatoly Lunacharsky's *The King's Barber*; Sadan (16) also refers to him as one of the best Yiddish translators of Pushkin. On Blok's influence on Kacyzne, see Mayzel, "Alter Kacyzne," 315.

worked on his photography, operating a studio on Długa Street, which moved several times until the Kacyznes fled Warsaw in 1939; he specialized in individual portraits, weddings, bar mitzvahs, and confirmations, and became the photographer of choice for Warsaw Jewish society.[167]

Though Kacyzne's archives were destroyed during the Holocaust, some photographs, the majority of which were sent by Kacyzne to America during the 1920s, survived. After taking his first photographs for American audiences as a result of a commission by the Hebrew Immigrant Aid Society (HIAS) to document Jews' difficulties leaving Poland, he was hired by Abraham Cahan, the editor-in-chief of the New York Yiddish daily *Forverts* (Forward), to take pictures of life in "the old country" for American Jewish immigrant readers. Hired for the then substantial sum of 150 dollars a month, he traveled throughout the length and breadth of Poland looking for suitable photographic subjects; the pictures of Poland in the *Forverts* come from over 120 different places. Cahan was so impressed that when he made his trip to Palestine in 1925, he asked Kacyzne to come along as the official *Forverts* photographer. Kacyzne would also visit Romania, Italy, Spain, and Morocco.[168] When Kacyzne was asked how he had the time to do everything he did, he joked that he kept two pocket watches, and so his time was doubled; to drive the joke home, he would actually produce the two pocket watches in question.[169]

As the Second World War was about to begin, though Kacyzne had received a U.S. visa, in the end he decided not to use it. When the Germans invaded Poland, Kacyzne and his wife and daughter left for Lemberg, which was then under Soviet occupation. There he became involved in Soviet-run Yiddish theatre and radio, working as an editor of Yiddish-language broadcasts and artistic director of the local Yiddish theatre. After the Nazi advance toward Lemberg following the German violation of the Nazi-Soviet Pact in June 1941, the Kacyznes tried to head further east. Unable to get a place on the Soviet train heading east, the family split up, Kacyzne believing that the Germans were seeking him out because of his work for the Soviets and so heading toward Tarnopol on foot, while his wife and daughter remained behind. Five days later, he reached Tarnopol, only to find the Nazis and their Ukrainian collaborators carrying out a five-

---

167. One of his assistants was Israel Joshua Singer, who described Kacyzne's studio in his first short story; see Web, xv.

168. A selection of Kacyzne's Polish photographs have been published in *Poyln: Jewish Life in the Old Country*; the photographs in the book were taken between 1924 and 1929—the same period of the publication of *The Duke*. On the methods of Kacyzne's travel, from his own letters to Cahan, as well as his arguments with Cahan over money, using him as a writer, and his desire to send him to the Soviet Union, see Web, xvii–xix. Cahan refused to publish any of Kacyzne's writing, which naturally upset him greatly.

169. Ravitch, 8.

day pogrom that would kill five thousand Jews. On July 7, Kacyzne was marched to the Jewish cemetery, forced to dig his own grave, and tortured and beaten to death there by Ukrainian collaborators with the Nazis.[170]

While some early critics have implicitly drawn comparisons between the martyrdom at the culmination of *The Duke* and Kacyzne's own death because of his own Judaism, such a connection is at best rhetorical; this said, it is unquestionable that Kacyzne's constant reflection on the nature of Jewishness and of anti-Semitism is a major preoccupation in this dramatic work. *The Duke* is based on the legend of Count Valentine Potocki (d. 1749), the righteous convert (*Ger Tsedek*) of Vilna, who was martyred for his love of Jewishness and the Jewish people.[171] The theme had received previous treatments in Jewish literature, both as storybooks written by Isaac Mayer Dik and Y. Y. Krashevski, and as a ballad written by S. L. Gordon, but had never received as full a treatment as Kacyzne gave it. Dov Sadan suggests that Kacyzne, as a native of Vilna, may have had a particular interest in the subject.[172] However, as Sadan also suggests, it seems just as likely that Kacyzne's treatment of the subject speaks volumes about his method of incorporating—and making his own—the lessons about folklore, history, and Jewish literature he learned from his two major Yiddish literary influences, Peretz and Ansky. As mentioned earlier, Kacyzne was first published by Ansky and was one of Peretz's most ardent admirers, the literary executor of both writers' estates and responsible for transforming some of Ansky's work into better-known literary forms (by completing *Tog un nakht* and writing the screenplay for the film version of *The Dybbuk*). Dov Sadan writes that people jokingly referred to him as "Peretz's widow" and "Ansky's widow,"[173] and the critic Nachman Mayzel suggests that Kacyzne turned to Peretz and later Ansky so intensely because of his own lifelong need for affection after having received none from his parents.[174]

---

170. Knowledge of Kacyzne's death comes from the eyewitness account of the Yiddish poet Nakhman Blitz, who published it—one of the first Holocaust testimonies—in *Dos naye lebn*. Khane Kacyzne died in Belzec in August of 1942; and his daughter survived the war disguised as a Gentile and later married Poland's Italian ambassador. See Ravitch, 9, and Sadan, 18–20.

171. According to legend, Potocki and another Polish aristocrat asked to be taught about Judaism when they met a Jewish innkeeper studying Talmud in Paris. The two promised to convert to Judaism if convinced of the error of Christianity. Both later converted, separately, in Amsterdam. Potocki once scolded a boy for disturbing the prayers in synagogue, prompting the boy's father, a tailor, to turn Potocki in to the authorities. Potocki was tried for heresy and refused to recant despite the pleas of fellow aristocrats. On the second day of the holiday of Shavuot in 1749, he was burned at the stake. See *Encyclopedia Judaica* (Jerusalem: Encyclopedia Judaica, 1972), 13: 934–935.

172. Sadan, 13.

173. Ibid., 10.

174. Mayzel, "Alter Kacyzne," 313. See, however, Sadan's caution about accepting this psychological hypothesis on pages 7–8.

Whatever the reason for Kacyzne's attachment to the two writers, the fact remains that the attachment was there, and Kacyzne was intensively exposed to the two writers' intense interest in the revitalization of Jewish literature through a return to Jewish folk materials, albeit reframed in a modern fashion. One can see this most powerfully in Kacyzne's use of the most modern technology in a quasi-nostalgic manner: his photography. Moshe Dluznowsky, speaking about his photography, wrote, "He plucked his subjects from the exotic reaches of folklore, cloaked them in the ordinary and the festive, and let them stand with their dreams and their reality, their prayers and their woes, their great burdens and their painterly beauty."[175]

This outlook emerges in Kacyzne's writings as well. Kacyzne was greatly inspired by Peretz's 1911 essay "What Our Literature Needs,"[176] which demands that the Yiddish writer "leave the ghetto, see the world—yes, but with Jewish eyes . . . consider his problem from a point of view that's Jewish" and "to come back to the Bible" and Jewish history. Melech Ravitch wrote that Kacyzne had, like Peretz, "searched for the integral line between the secular and religious path of Yiddish literature. . . . [H]e was always occupied with something, not simply doing something, but creating, experimenting. . . . Kacyzne is one of the first writers to see that all of Jewish history—all four thousand years of it, beginning from Abraham—is a kind of pearl necklace around the throat of Jewish reality. The task of the Yiddish writer is [according to Kacyzne] to seek whatever he finds most appealing [in all of Jewish history] and integrate it into our literature."[177]

It seems eminently understandable, then, that Kacyzne would search through Jewish history for his theme, and find a story which stems not only from eighteenth-century Poland, but, as in a set of nested boxes, draws on Jewish literary material before that as well. The action begins on the eve of the Sabbath. We learn of rumors that the Young Duke, recently returned from an extended period of study and travel abroad, has learned Hebrew, and possibly even converted to Judaism. Nekhamele, the innkeeper's daughter, tells a friend of a startling recent encounter with the Young Duke, who showed up at her family's tavern recently and, finding Nekhamele alone, kissed her numerous times on her face and lips. When the Young Duke returns to

---

175. Quote from Web, xx, n.7. Web notes that even in the cities, Kacyzne focuses on the more traditional figures.

176. First appearing in the anthology *Yiddish* in 1911; a translation by Nathan Halper can be found in *Voices from the Yiddish: Essays, Memoirs, Diaries,* ed. Irving Howe and Eliezer Greenberg (Ann Arbor: University of Michigan Press, 1972), 25–31.

177. Ravitch, 7–8, 10–11.

the tavern, he is greeted by Nekhamele's parents, who fawn upon him in the most subservient manner. They try in vain to convince him that their daughter is plain, and not worth seeing. When Nekhamele arrives a moment later, the Young Duke makes her parents dance for him while her grandfather, a fiddler, accompanies them with a Jewish song. Nekhamele, defying her parents, sits on the Young Duke's lap. A moment later, though, after nearly shooting someone with his rifle, the Young Duke tires of his own antics and rides off, leaving Nekhamele yearning for him.

The action soon shifts to the castle, where the Clown, dusting ancestral pictures, vows to get revenge on the noble family for all they did to harm and humiliate his family. He tells the Bishop of the dukes' latest antics: the rumors of the Young Duke's attraction to Judaism while abroad, and the Old Duke's latest coup from a hunting expedition. He captured an enormous bear and is forcing the town's tailor, Yoshke, to make the bear a pair of trousers. A moment later, Yoshke comes to the Bishop, begging him to appeal to the Duke to release him from this dangerous and difficult assignment. It soon becomes a moot issue. The bear escapes, and the Young Duke, intervening to stop the creature from harming a Jew nearby, kills it with his own knife. The Old Duke is impressed with his son's exploit, but the Bishop warns the old man that the Young Duke is playing with fire; the Bishop has seen him with Jewish books that could bring charges of heresy, and hopes the Old Duke will steer his son back to a safer path. The merry Old Duke, though, essentially shrugs off his son's interests as youthful antics, particularly when he hears that a girl is involved—though we soon see Nekhamele in the arms not of the Young Duke, but of his father. The Young Duke, meanwhile, continues on a now inexorable path away from his origins, and circumcises himself.

The fortunes of both the Jews and the noble family begin to unravel after that point. The Old Duke shows up at the home of Yoshke the tailor, offering him a substantial reward to return his son to him. The religious authorities soon lay siege to Yoshke's place, tying him and Nekhamele to posts, and accusing both of them of immoral behavior. Nekhamele remains contemptuous throughout the proceedings, threatening to seduce all the young men in the yeshiva—particularly a talented student named Avremele, who soon arrives himself. Nekhamele realizes that this scholar is in fact the Young Duke, who in his earlier incarnation had made advances to her that unhinged her moral compass and set her on a course toward complete wantonness. Yet the town still needs her, for they conclude that she is the only one who can persuade the Old Duke to reinstate the fair that is the bread and butter of the community. She and Yoshke are untied, but before she can go, Avremele is arrested, since Yoshke had reported Avremele to the authorities. The rest of the action revolves around the efforts of noblemen to get the Young Duke to recant, but he refuses. The Old Duke returns from Rome, having secured a written reprieve from the pope. When he learns that his son has chosen martyrdom willingly, though, he refuses to do anything more to intervene, for "his honor is preferable to me than his life."

In the willingness of the old Duke to sacrifice his son for his principles, one sees the transmuted echoes of the sacrifice of Isaac, a subject on which Kacyzne had hoped to write a play;[178] in the move of a Jewish girl from her own home to the world of a foreign noble, then pressed by her townspeople to intercede with that noble, we see how this play, like and unlike so many before it, also borrows tropes from the book of Esther. In doing so, though, Kacyzne is not only (and not primarily) participating in the Purim-based theatrical tradition, but rather drawing on Esther as a biblical source in a Peretz-approved fashion and citing it as a seminal text in the history of Jewish/non-Jewish relations.

Despite his fidelity to Peretz and to certain aspects of his theoretical system, Kacyzne, a relentlessly searching, constantly restless individualist,[179] also needed to make these ideas his own. As late as 1936, Kacyzne would dedicate most of the introduction to his last book published during his lifetime, *Ballads and Grotesques*, to a discussion of the influence that Peretz has had on him and on many others: "Peretz understood best of all that beneath the language of our literature lies another vein, a true vein of gold: the language of deep expressiveness and great zest: the folk tale, the folk dream, the half product of artistic creation of great unknowns, which must serve as the cornerstone of the young literature, so it can gain its authenticity and uniqueness."[180] However, Kacyzne, in a classic case of the anxiety of influence, charges most of the writers with reaching into the Jewish past not through a method inspired by Peretz's folkloristic work, but through those particular works themselves, and presents his own turn toward the grotesque as the natural evolution of the Peretzian model and himself as Peretz's honest literary heir.[181]

---

178. This according to Yitskhok Turkov-Grudberg; see Sadan, 16.

179. See D. Sfard, "Kurtse kharakteristik," in *A. Kacyzne: geklibene verk*, ed. D. Sfard (Warsaw: Farlag "Yidish-bukh," 1951), 3–12, 3–4.

180. Reprinted in *Gezamelte shriftn*, 1:221.

181. Sadan considers this effort to find one's own essence the hallmark of Peretz's style of mentorship; see Sadan, 10.

The Duke, written a decade earlier, has not quite reached the level of the grotesque. And yet elements of it are unquestionably there, and employ techniques of historicization—an ideal not particularly prized by Peretz or Ansky, who tend to set their works in a kind of folkloristic never-when—to provide an added emotional heft. Aside from the historical basis of the story, whose broad outline, as Kacyzne suggests in his introduction, remains largely factual, the Young Duke refers to an earlier historical figure, Shlomo Molcho (ca. 1500–1532), another convert, as a paradigm for his own experiences. And certain aspects of the play, particularly the complicated mixture of subservience and resentment that constitutes the Jews' behavior toward the non-Jews, and the delicate combination of blackmail, violence, and contempt that composes the reverse of the relationship, seem to be grounded in a realistic recovery of the historical record.

This said, the sensibility of the play can hardly be described as an entirely straightforward work of historicized folk literature. Ravitch describes Kacyzne's early failure of *The Spirit-King* as impressing on him the importance of remaining grounded (and comprehensible) even while engaging in poetic and rapturous endeavor,[182] and one can see these efforts in *The Duke*. Kacyzne never really managed to leave behind the symbolism of his youth. Symbolic elements loom large in the work—the constant reference to brilliance and light, the bear and the attempt to make trousers for it, the dancing in circles, indeed the characters themselves—all of which leads to the constant sense that the play is about archetypes and larger issues, not about a group of actual people.[183] It may be for this reason that certain critics, such as Zalmen Reyzen and Shmuel Niger, were less than flattering about the play. Reyzen wrote that "though psychologically the drama suffers from serious flaws . . . [Kacyzne] has certainly enriched the modern Yiddish repertoire with a strong, colorful, theatrical work."[184] Others, however, such as Sadan and Mayzel, were more forgiving, and audiences apparently agreed with them: *The Duke* was a success theatrically, playing in Warsaw, Vilna, Lodz, Riga, Buenos Aires, and also in America, and was taken on by actors and directors like Avrom Morevski, Maurice Schwartz, Joseph Buloff, and Clara Segalovitch.[185]

---

182. Ravitch, 10.

183. Compare Sfard, 9.

184. *Leksikon* 8:119. Bal-Makshoves (Isidor Eliashev) wrote after Kacyzne's debut, "The motifs aren't particularly original, but they are carried out masterfully. . . . [H]e has achieved such beauties, which establish him as a poet."

185. On this split, see Sadan 14, who also talks about critical efforts to compare it to Asch's short story "Kidesh hashem" and Lion Feuchtwanger's novel *Jud Süss*. See also Mayzel, "Alter Kacyzne," 315.

Perhaps audiences and actors were particularly drawn to the archetypal nature of the work. Certainly the author is unapologetic about this characteristic; the characters are well aware that they stand for much more than their own personalities, and say so frequently throughout the play. Not only do their actions somehow resonate allegorically—that is to say, that in a historical period of fragile democracy and possibility in interwar Poland increasingly threatened by rising anti-Semitic activity, investigation into the roots of anti-Semitism and its inherency somehow seems entirely of the moment—but their speeches also suggest traces of the Ibsenesque "problem play." In this sense, the Young Duke, the Old Duke, and other characters are aware that they are faced with general philosophical problems, such as "Is there anyone by virtue of birth or character who is allowed to overstep the bonds of conventional morality?" (the Old Duke); "Can one change one's essential nature, and, indeed, is there such a thing?" (the Young Duke); and "How can pleasure and sensuality exist without transforming into sin?" (Nekhamele). This awareness (and the way they talk about it) does not necessarily transform them into fully realized psychological characters; it does, however, make them relevant not in their humanity, but in their roles as philosophical provocateurs. But if this reflects a touch of Ibsen, it also, in its own way, channels *King Lear*, with its clown, old father, and rebellious child. And, from the pen of a writer who had dramatized the Prometheus myth, it also resonates with the aura of classical tragedy, for one feels from the start that destiny has set these characters on a path where there is no turning away from the ultimate end.

Such a philosophy of historical determinism is essentially congruent with Communism, and it may also be that Kacyzne's own attraction to Communism may be related to his interest in characters as archetypes.[186] Though this seems to conflict with his sense of individualism, one must remember that Kacyzne's work is all about contradictions and paradoxes. Those paradoxes are not only general and philosophical, but personal and biological as well: critics have made much of the point that Kacyzne, who moved from Vilna to Warsaw, seemed in his personal nature to combine the stereotypical aspects of both a Lithuanian Jew and a Polish Jew.[187] The Ansky play he completed, *Day and Night*, features a rabbi whose parents were a Jewish woman and a Cossack who had raped her, and the center of the drama revolves around his struggle between his desires to be a Jew and his non-Jewish impulses which serve as the center of the drama. This can be compared to *The Duke*, where

---

186. Compare Sadan, 17.

187. Ravitch, 7.

we have the figure of a non-Jew who has converted to a Jew and struggles to determine what this means.

Conversion, the central theme of *The Duke*, is not merely theological, but also somehow existential: the question is whether or not one can unmake oneself and remake oneself again, to utterly break down the essential characteristics of that former self and replace them. In this case, the ultimate characteristics of non-Jewish life are violence and immorality (at least as defined as transcending the bonds of conventional morality, and mistreatment of Jews, particularly sexually), and the ultimate characteristics of Jewish life are scholarship, sublimation, and powerlessness. The Duke's martyrdom, then, can be seen not merely as a Pyrrhic victory, but also as an ultimate evocation of Jewish powerlessness.

One may well wonder which side Kacyzne ultimately takes on these questions. On the one hand, the young Duke is portrayed as the hero of the piece; on the other hand, it is the convert who becomes the best Jew. Most of the Jews in the play are hardly positive figures; while one might argue that it is their precarious position in Eastern European life and their maltreatment at the hands of non-Jews that is responsible for their hypocritical, cringing, stunted state, one also may simply shudder at the zealotry, the wildness, the folly, that Kacyzne elicits from his Jewish characters. This is deeply reminiscent of the dynamics that suffuse Wolfssohn's world and Wolfssohn's play. And let us not forget that prostitution once more plays a major factor in both works, along with what we may suggest to be a certain type of Jewish self-hatred.[188]

So we have come full circle, from Warsaw in the 1930s back to Berlin in the 1790s, and we see that these landmark Yiddish plays are significant in the way that they speak to Jewish history and Jewish reality, and how the development of Yiddish literature is not a story of increasing sophistication and complexity, but rather a constant flow of talented creators focusing on recurring ideas and conditions to achieve remarkable results.

---

188. See Sadan, 13–14.

Translators' Note

Every translation is a balancing act, and in that sense, our task is like that of any other translator of drama: the quest for that narrow patch of ground where fidelity to the source overlaps with a readable or stageworthy work in the target language. As scholars of Yiddish literature and drama, we feel a responsibility to offer accurate English counterparts to the Yiddish originals, but not at the expense of texts that can stand on their own for readers, performers, and audiences.

Translating from Yiddish poses special challenges. As the noted scholar and translator Benjamin Harshav has remarked, Yiddish is in some respects "a Slavic culture with a German-based language living in a Hebrew library."[1] Although the authors of these plays, as we have discussed in our introduction, were active over the span of 150 years, worked under very different conditions from one another, and expressed diverse sensibilities, they would have shared certain broad assumptions about their audiences that would have informed—both consciously and unconsciously—the content of their dramas. All five wrote for audiences and readers that were at least bilingual, if not multilingual. Wolfssohn is a special case, writing a play only partially in Yiddish for readers familiar with the German spoken by their neighbors, and who would have had a grounding in Hebrew as well. The other four playwrights wrote for native Yiddish speakers who would have had at least some basic Hebrew literacy; most of the original audiences for these four works would have spoken at least one Slavic language as well. It was natural, then, for Yiddish writers seeking to capture their language's rhythms to have their characters speak in the many different registers that language was spoken. A character learned in traditional texts, for example, could be expected to lace his Yiddish with words from Hebrew and Aramaic. A young woman who cannot get enough of German

---

1. Benjamin Harshav, *The Meaning of Yiddish* (1990; repr. Stanford University Press, 1999), 29.

romance novels might speak very much like the heroes and heroines whose fortunes she reads about. And the speech of a young man who has been serving in the Tsar's army for the past few years might be closer to Russian than to Yiddish.

The linguistic mixture is particularly diverse in Wolfssohn's *Silliness and Sanctimony*, which illustrates as well as any of these plays the potential pitfalls of turning what is really a multilingual, multilayered German/Yiddish play into a viable English version. In the dialogue of Wolfssohn's eight characters—as well as a short but telling note one of them reads aloud from a character we never see—we can map a sociolinguistic spectrum from the Germanic to the Hebraic components of Yiddish, with assimilated characters speaking *Hochdeutsch*; servants speaking a simple, everyday Western Yiddish; and a Polish-born rabbi dropping numerous references and allusions to the canonical Jewish texts in Hebrew and Aramaic.

Certainly Wolfssohn's students, or fellow maskilim invited to a reading of his drama at a literary salon, would have had no difficulty recognizing and understanding the many textual references made by the tutor, Reb Yoysefkhe. We, on the other hand, would like to imagine audiences and readers not confined to the rosters of yeshivas and rabbinical schools. Indeed, while all five plays in this collection vividly reflect the world out of which they arose, we hope our texts will be sufficiently clear, in translation and annotation, to stand on their own for audiences who are not necessarily knowledgeable in Jewish religion, history, or languages—and for that matter, are not necessarily Jewish either. This desire to reach as broad an audience as possible would be impeded if we clung too closely to passages like the following, uttered by Reb Yoysefkhe early in *Silliness and Sanctimony* (with Hebrew/Aramaic words transcribed in italics, reflecting the Ashkenazi[2] pronunciation of Hebrew):

> *Yitsri takfa alay*!: "My evil impulse triumphed over me!" But it's as our sages say: *aveyre goreres aveyre*. I come in, I think you're home—for all of my sins, I'm going to have to isolate myself, oy, vey, oy vey! May God in his oneness preserve us and save us! Nu, I was going to take my medicine *before* I got sick—I took a *Gemorrah* down and I learned: *im paga b'kha menuvl ze mashkhehu l'besmedresh*. That's what I learned, but

---

2. Ashkenazi Jews trace their ancestry to Central and Eastern Europe, as opposed to Sephardi Jews, whose lineage descends from the Jews of the Iberian Peninsula. Modern Hebrew uses the Sephardi pronunciation.

what can I tell you? It was an evil hour! Oh, woe, my sins!
(*He begins to beat his breast.*) Oh, woe, my transgressions!

While we do not think it is fatal to the enjoyment of a performance not
to catch every single reference, hearing a string of quotations in the
original language would be a bewildering and frustrating experience
for all but a tiny handful of spectators. In such instances, we have
followed the lead of translators like Hillel Halkin, who, in his translation of Sholem Aleichem's *Tevye the Dairyman*, interpolates a number of
translations of textual quotations that did not appear in the original.[3]
It is a liberty with the text that strikes us as warranted, if not dictated,
by the realities of the very different linguistic environment for which we
are providing these translations.

The actual languages these characters draw upon are only one of
the ingredients of the flavor of their individual speech, and it is here
that an English translation, without the kind of polyglot readership
Wolfssohn would have taken for granted, can find other ways to suggest
the rich texture of the original dialogue. For German-speaking characters like Yetkhen and Markus (whose counterparts we meet in Ettinger,
in characters like Redlekh, Hinde, and Gutherz), who tend to speak in
either a flowery or a stilted manner, we have tended not to use mono-
syllabic words where multisyllabic words will do just as well, and we have
taken few if any steps to curb their verbosity. Take, for example, this
pronouncement by Markus from near the end of *Silliness and Sanctimony* (act 3, scene 4):

> In this awful house, this residence which is all lasciviousness
> and indulgence, the daughter of my sister! In this grave of
> innocence, perhaps hers has already been murdered? Ah,
> these are the fruits of blind religious zealotry! Unchange-
> able as death, timeless as the tomb, you pile sacrifice upon
> sacrifice, trampling over them in order to honor your mas-
> ter, to fit in with his master plan. But is she then entirely
> guiltless? Must she, in order to escape her own insult, turn
> directly to the worst possible insult? Isn't it simply the silli-
> ness, impetuousness, and other modish pleasures of our
> contemporary youth, that have paved the way to this trag-
> edy? And nevertheless, I still feel, when I consider it more
> deeply, that the blame should return to the parents! Do not

---

3. Sholem Aleichem, *Tevye the Dairyman and the Railroad Stories*, trans. and ed. Hillel Halkin
(New York: Schocken, 1987).

neglect the education of your children, be more watchful of their moral education than their physical education, and teach them early to have an affinity for what is noble and good, then you will never have to worry about your children's foolishness.

The result is stiff, removed from everyday speech. If this stiffness were not part of the fabric of the play—indeed, part of the very meaning of the play—we might have tried to make Markus's speech more colloquial. Instead, we have tried to keep it every bit as removed from ordinary speech as it feels in the original. This will undoubtedly pose a challenge to performers trying to find an emotional life for characters like Markus, who in rehearsal may find themselves envying those playing the servants, whose English will feel more natural (not to mention, in the tradition of comic servants from Plautus to Stoppard, sassier).

While *Serkele* contains a substantial Germanic element as well, this side of the linguistic spectrum occupies proportionately less of a play that is well over twice the length of Wolfssohn's. Ettinger also makes the Hebrew-Aramaic component less of an issue, but adds layers of his own: the overblown pseudo-German of Friederika, another character in furious, desperate flight from all things Jewish—and Yiddish; the dialect humor found in Yerakhmiel's severe stutter and the innkeeper Reb Shmelke Troyniks's regional elision of the *"sh"* sound so common in Yiddish; and the endlessly repeated verbal tics exhibited by certain characters. Characters who stutter pose far less of a challenge in terms of translation than they do to our notions of what is funny, but someone like Shmelke Troyniks is a different story altogether. As a speaker of the Lithuanian Yiddish dialect, Shmelke substitutes "s" for "sh" in the many Yiddish words that contain the latter consonant (given its own letter, *shin*, in the Hebrew and Yiddish alphabet). To the ears of a Polish Jew like Ettinger and his local readership, the foreign quality of Reb Shmelke's speech comes across in countless ordinary words that he pronounces differently from the rest of the characters: *dayts* rather than *daytsh* (German), *seyn* rather than *sheyn* (pretty, nice), *safn* rather than *shafn* (make, create), and on and on. Oddly, Shmelke's pronunciation is complicated by the fact that he occasionally—but not consistently— makes the reverse substitution: that is, saying "sh" where a Yiddish word contains an *s* sound. Ettinger is clearly having fun with the otherness of Shmelke's regional dialect, and compounding this with the character's own speech idiosyncracy.

If "sh" were as common in English as in Yiddish, we might have conveyed this characteristic simply by transferring it into English. Not only did there turn out to be few "sh"-words in Reb Shmelke's English, but even had there been more, the pronunciation shift would have been confusing rather than funny to English readers. Another possibility we tried as a provisional solution was, rather than just dropping the "sh," turning "sh" into "s" and vice versa. The result, in an early draft, yielded moments like this:

> Yesh indeed, my good shir! Please accshept my very warmesht welcomesh, your grache! What can we do, what doesh your grache command! A beautiful, gorgeoush, painted, light-filled room, a magnifishent shtable, fress hay, a good sock of oatsh, a hearty meal and lotsh to drink, whatever your grache could posshibly wiss, shome good old-fassioned mead, a glassh of wine, from the very besht short of grapesh. Just shnap your fingersh, your grache! I am your grache's to command!

When it proved impossible to deliver such passages without adopting our best W. C. Fields impressions, it became clear that this route was more a distraction than a solution. Another option was to emphasize a dialectal rather than an aural difference, but this meant finding the English equivalent to a Lithuanian voice in Lembergian ears: what should be the English regional norm from which Shmelke departs, and how should he depart from it? Should he be a Chicagoan among New Yorkers? A Yorkshireman among Londoners? Once more, this seemed to introduce issues that would impose something foreign on the play, and we finally reluctantly concluded that in this case to omit something Ettinger included was better than to insert something he never intended. Since Ettinger also makes an issue of Reb Shmelke's social class and his homespun simplicity, we opted instead for a folksy quality to his language that contrasts just as strongly with the speech of the other characters as his *litvak* dialect did in the original.

The most obvious new challenge Goldfaden's *Two Kuni-Lemls* poses is its music, so that a substantial part of the text involves not only finding English equivalents, but marrying them to the rhythms and rhymes for which the words were originally written. This additional demand undoubtedly helps account for the fact that so few Yiddish musicals have been translated into other languages, despite the prominence of musical plays in the Yiddish repertoire. Goldfaden's characters also speak a language deliciously rich in idiom. It is another device that Goldfaden may have learned from Ettinger; where the former has Serkele constantly moaning, "Oy, I feel faint" and the matchmaker Reb Yoykhenen exclaiming, "Let me tell you something," Goldfaden has his Kalmen the Matchmaker continually interrupting others with "Hold your horses!" The Yiddish phrase he uses, "Khapt nit!," means "Don't interrupt" in this context, but Goldfaden cleverly gave him a stock phrase that allows for endless punning, for the verb *khapn* also means, among other senses, catch, grab, and snatch. As a result, we wanted something more figurative than simply "Don't interrupt," something that would afford us a similar flexibility for wordplay to Goldfaden's. Take, for example, when Kalmen urges Reb Pinkhesl, "Don't dilly-dally and hold onto this gem so you don't find someone else holding him first, hold your horses!"[4]

The Kuni-Leml trait most troubling to the translator is his foolishness, or more precisely, his ignorance. To be fair, he is at a disadvantage. He has no more reason to understand why Carolina should be calling him Max than she should understand why Kuni-Leml (who she thinks is Max at that moment) is so unresponsive when she treats him with her usual affection. Goldfaden creates more than just comic confusion in the Yiddish, which has Kuni-Leml mishearing the name Max to be *makes* (pronounced MAH-kess), or plagues, scourges (the same word used for the ten plagues in Exodus, for example, but also used in homespun curses like "a make af dayn kop," literally "a plague on your head"). Kuni-Leml is confused partly because he has become a pawn in an elaborate ruse, but he is easily duped because he is so unaware of the secular world, and therefore has probably never even heard the name Max before. This cannot be fully conveyed by changing the pairing from *Max/makes* (Yiddish) to *Max/mocks* (English), but at such moments, the translator is constrained by the serendipity of the available sounds. Carolina's exchange with Kuni-Leml (act 3, scene 3) is full of such misunderstandings, with which we took numerous liberties to try to preserve the combination of the misunderstanding itself and the overall arc of the exchange.

Hirschbein's *Miriam*, a naturalistic drama devoid of puns, dialect humor, and other gags, was in many ways the easiest work in this collection to translate. The only character whose speech sounds entirely unlike any other's is the prostitute Natalka, but it is not difficult to find an English counterpart to her stunted Yiddish (and the sprinkle of Russian in the prostitutes' dialogue can be preserved with the occasional footnote). The double-edged sword of naturalistic language, however, is that it must sound natural if nothing else. The best thing the translator can do at such moments is to get out of the way of the language, to be as invisible as possible.

Though we hope not to be intrusive at any time, invisibility is less of a concern in translating Alter Kacyzne's *The Duke*, whose lofty, philo-

---

4. "Makht nit keyn shies un *khapt* oys dem even tov, kedey me zol im bay aykh nit oys*khapn*, *khapt* nit!

sophical language (albeit interlaced with the occasional more naturalistic scene) sounds no more like what our next-door neighbor would
say than does Wolfssohn's Markus, Ettinger's Reb Shmelke, or
Goldfaden's Kuni-Leml. This type of writing, too, has a central place in
the repertoire, alongside the broad comedy, weepy melodramas, and
escapist spectacles. By Kacyzne's time, Yiddish audiences had seen
numerous plays exploring questions of faith, heresy, redemption, Israel's
covenantal relationship with God, the idea of the messiah, and other
philosophical and theological subjects. The grandeur of Kacyzne's language is likely to feel far more alien to us, after decades of realism and
naturalism as the dominant modes in our serious drama, and in much
of our television and film as well. *The Duke*, mind you, is a great work
of theatre, not a philosophical treatise, and it has its share of ordinary
language, and of earthy dialogue. It might not seem surprising for an
aristocrat who has just come back from studying abroad to speak in
elevated language, but Kacyzne's more ordinary (at least socioeconomi-
cally) characters also have a habit of doing so. Though Kacyzne's grand
drama could hardly be a more different creature than Wolfssohn's
compact satire, the range of registers brings us back to the question of
maintaining the texture of the original. With Kacyzne, it is important
to let changes of language carry drastic changes of mood: from the
brooding scholasticism of the Young Duke communing with a spiritual
brother "across the generations" to the self-assured hedonism of his
father, whom we first meet just after he has trapped a huge bear; from
the cringing obsequiousness of Jewish tavernkeepers and tailors to the
authority of aristocrats and clergy; from the pious indignation of Jewish
authorities to the sexual abandon of Nekhamele.

We hope that we have been able to express those changes in the
differing registers in a way that does justice to Kacyzne's vision. Ultimately, that was our goal for all these plays: to provide, as best as
possible, access to these universally great plays while still providing their
local and particular flavor.

Silliness and Sanctimony

A Family Portrait in Three Acts

by Aaron Halle Wolfssohn

Cast of Characters

REB HENOKH, *a rich householder*

TELTSE, *his wife*

YETKHEN, *his daughter*

MARKUS, *his brother in-law and Teltse's brother*

REB YOYSEFKHE, *the rabbi hired as domestic tutor*

SHEYNDL, *Reb Henokh's cook*

A HAIRDRESSER

LEMGIN, *a madam*

The action takes place in a large city in the northern part of Germany, during the last decade of the eighteenth century.

Act 1

Scene 1

(*Reb Henokh's living room. Reb Henokh sits at a table, upon which there are several open religious books. Teltse is standing in front of a mirror, arranging her cap and scarf.*)

REB HENOKH. *Nu,* onward—so then he asks '*b'may ka mafligi,*' what are they arguing about? So Rebbe Eliezer says . . . (*Thinks.*) I don't understand this at all; there must be some sort of misprint here—maybe the Maharsha[1] makes something out of it. (*After looking at the Maharsha's commentary.*) Nu, simple, what's so new about that? Didn't I just say that? Amazing! Sha! Sha! I've thought of something else, which I swear, is *mosek midvash*—sweeter than honey![2] (*Exults.*) This is something for my Shmuel to see. He'll love it for sure. (*Calls.*) Shmuelke, Shmuelke!

TELTSE. Nu, why are you shouting like that?

REB HENOKH. Why am I shouting? I want Shmuel to come here. I have something to show him. (*Calls.*) Shmuelke! Shmuelke!

TELTSE. It must be something remarkable for you to shout like that. The child's not at home.

REB HENOKH. What does that mean, he's not at home? News to me—is it Shabbes or the New Moon today or something, he has to disappear?[3]

TELTSE. What's the matter? I let him go myself. He begged me to let him see our Pinkhes; it's his birthday, and he's throwing a party. The poor child hasn't gone out of doors for a week.

REB HENOKH. Again with your leniency! What good are all my speeches, all my rebukes? With your mercy, you're ruining everything; such a jewel of a child, he could be a great prodigy, but (*Indignantly.*) here is the very devil of it: you're not allowing the child to learn. But I swear to you by the Holy Letters[4]: it's going to be very different around here, or my name isn't Reb Henokh!

TELTSE. Just tell me, what sort of a man are you? How can you get so angry over this? Must the poor child spend the entire day toiling

---

1. Polish Talmudist Shmuel Eliezer Edels (1555–1631), whose commentary *Khidushey halakhot* is included in most editions of the Talmud.

2. See Judges 14:18 and Psalms 19:11, but a common saying among Jews of the period.

3. Reb Henokh may be referring (jokingly) to the practice of going to visit religious leaders on holidays. See 2 Kings 4:23 for the biblical source of this custom.

4. The phrase appears in early Hasidic teachings and resonates with the kabbalistic idea of the sanctity of the Hebrew alphabet.

away? He looks so thin and so pale that my heart aches every time I see him. Why shouldn't the child have a little fun every once in a while? Markus himself interceded with me on his behalf.

REB HENOKH. (*Heatedly.*) Do I care about Markus? What do I care if he intercedes? Thank God, I know what it is I have to do. Obviously, Markus doesn't like it; if the boy took after him, he would also turn into an anti-Semite. He'd go around in a short coat and in a round hat[5] just like his uncle does. Oy, oy, I wouldn't wish that on my worst enemy! Hasn't he already ruined the girl?

TELTSE. What do you want from her? What has she done to you? Everyone else—Gentiles and, *lehavdil*,[6] Jews—are perfectly happy with her, but you always have something to grumble about.

REB HENOKH. (*Mocking her.*) Gentiles and, *lehavdil*, Jews . . . "What's good for the goyim is better for the Jews . . ." I'd be willing to bet you that the Rebbe isn't so happy with her! What does she do all day long? Does she say blessings? Does she pray? Does she open a Yiddish Bible or a prayer book? All you hear around here, all day long, is singing and music, music and singing, enough to drive a person crazy. And when the beloved Sabbath finally comes around, you wouldn't remember it's holy, God forbid! This is a sin that I'm getting more and more concerned about. (*Sighs.*)

TELTSE. A fine thing! What's the matter? I'm leaving too . . .

REB HENOKH. Listen to what the Hasid[7] said as well; he complained to me, poor fellow, that he can't learn the whole day long with all her singing and playing.

TELTSE. A new decree! What business of his is her singing?

REB HENOKH. What business of his? Because, you ignoramus, our Sages tell us: *kol b'isha erva*—the voice of a woman is her nakedness.[8] And even when she's not singing, there is always such hustle and bustle around her that it's a shame and a disgrace in front of the neighbors. But what am I supposed to do? Whenever I have anything to say, Markus, our esteemed teacher, comes along and knows better.

---

5. Contemporary fashion trends, marked by traditionalist Jews as signs of sinful modernity.

6. Literally, "to make a distinction"; generally used to excuse any unintended blasphemy when comparing a sacred object to a secular or profane one, e.g., "The Second Temple was as beautiful as, lehavdil, the Parthenon."

7. One of the members of the pietistic movement begun in Eastern Europe in the mid-eighteenth century; the word can also mean "a pious individual," and the two meanings are often ironically juxtaposed in the play.

8. A Talmudic dictum, often used by traditionalists to prevent female singing in public (and, not incidentally, as part of the reason for prohibiting general female participation in theater). See BT Kidushin 70a.

But (*Heatedly.*) God will be my support! It has to change! And after
today, it will! I know what I have to do. *Leoylem yisoy odem es bisoy
l'talmid khokhem*—a man should always marry his daughter to a
scholar;[9] we couldn't make a better match. The only question is
whether he will be satisfied; he'll be able to turn her to the good,
such a Hasid he is . . .

TELTSE. You're not so crazy as to give her to Reb Yoysefkhe—that would
be a fine way to treat her . . .

REB HENOKH. What is that supposed to mean? What—you think I should
ask for her advice?

Scene 2

MARKUS. Good God, why are you making such a racket? I could hear
your bickering from the stairway.

TELTSE. And what do you think he's so angry about? He's upset because
Shmuelke is at our Pinkhesl's now—is that such a big deal? That's
what he's been going on about this whole time. And to calm himself
down—get this—he wants to marry off our Yetkhen to Reb Yoysefkhe
today.

MARKUS. An eminently sensible idea! (*To Reb Henokh.*) Did you come up
with it all by yourself?

REB HENOKH. (*Hurt.*) How am I supposed to answer that? Believe me—
I may not wear my hair long, but I'm just as clever as you. Say what
you like; Reb Yoysefkhe must have my daughter, and today at that.

MARKUS. But for heaven's sake, where did you get such an idea? How
can you give your daughter to a man you hardly know, who has been
in your house just a couple of weeks, and who probably is forbidden
to go near a woman anyway? You're going to marry off your own
child just like that?

REB HENOKH. That's none of your business—it's for me to worry about.
Reb Yoysefkhe is a scholar, and where there's Torah, there's wisdom.
I'm rich enough, thank God, that I can support a son-in-law very
comfortably. But so what? (*Scornfully.*) I suppose you'd have me follow the latest fashions, wear a powdered wig, go to the theatre, and
all that other nonsense. Well, that will never happen as long as I'm
around, God forbid!

TELTSE. But consider . . .

REB HENOKH. Consider this, consider that—never mind that; I know
what I want. I've already wasted enough time on this business. And
don't forget to tell Shmuelke that he has to come home. Reb

---

9. A Talmudic dictum, taken as a norm rather than a law. See BT Pesakhim 49a–49b.

Yoysefkhe is coming to give his lesson, and Shmuel has to come hear it. (*Calls.*) Sheyndl! Sheyndl!

TELTSE. I sent Sheyndl out for coffee.

REB HENOKH. Well, I'll go myself, right away. (*Runs out quickly.*)

Scene 3

TELTSE. Good God! You're right! What I have to go through with that lunatic! He never used to be like this, but ever since that Hasid came to stay with us, we argue about everything.

MARKUS. As the saying goes, "From one fool come many fools," and if you want my opinion, that Reb Yoysefkhe is a one-man fool factory.

TELTSE. Certainly not. Reb Yoysefkhe is an honest, upright, respectable man. It's not his fault that Henokh has gone soft in the head and wants to make him our son in-law. God in heaven! When Yetkhen hears about this, I'm afraid the poor girl will worry herself to death! The poor child! (*Cries.*)

MARKUS. Calm yourself, dear sister. This is just a passing fancy of your husband's. He's not himself—it's his enthusiasm talking, I assure you. When he cools down, he'll sing a different tune—he'll see how wrong he's been.

TELTSE. Oh, sure, he'll see. You don't know him as well as I do, my dear Markus! When an idea gets stuck in his head, the Messiah himself wouldn't be able to shake it loose. You should have heard how he insulted the girl, as if she were the worst sort of creature imaginable.

MARKUS. As far as your daughter is concerned, we would be better off not talking about it. I have given you my opinions on her education many times. You know that I wanted to teach her myself at first, but instead of letting me do that, you are always so eager to train her, and she has become extremely impertinent.

TELTSE. Listen to how you talk! Of course men will swarm around her, but why are you making these demands except out of jealousy? She is lovely beyond description, quite charming, and is always surrounded by lords and princes, each one trying to outdo the others. You should have heard what Baron Von Ox and Count Mount said to me, and the tall officer—you know him—his name has just flown out of my head for the moment. That one's really crazy about her. He's asked me a thousand times to send her to pay his wife a visit, but I mustn't; that nasty woman wouldn't give a Jew the time of day.

MARKUS. Oh, quiet, my dear sister! You really don't see the danger your daughter is in. Believe me, my heart just aches for her when I see her on the promenade and have to behold the swarm of barons, counts, and officers buzzing around her, each one with his own foolishness, burying her with smiles—and she accepts it all as the height of sincerity. And what is the result? She comes back home, every inch the grande dame, fritters away her time on trivial things, neglects what really matters, does not deign to lift a finger around the house—in short, is turning into the most useless creature on God's good earth.

TELTSE. Go on, go on! You always see the worst in everyone. You just want to . . .

Scene 4

SHEYNDL. I need one more kreuzer—it came to fourteen paym and two kreuzers.[10]

TELTSE. Thank God you're back! What took you so long? I wanted to go out with Markus, but had to wait for you. Here's the key to the cupboard. There's coffee in there; when my husband comes, make some for him and the Hasid.

MARKUS. If only we could get rid of the Hasid . . .

SHEYNDL. Some Hasid he is!

TELTSE. What do you know, you simpleton? You always have to put your two cents in. (*To Markus.*) Let's go, it's late. She'll be waiting for us. (*She and Markus exit.*)

Scene 5

SHEYNDL. What do I know? (*Smiling.*) While I was upstairs making the beds, he chased me all over the place, like cat and mouse! (*Moves the chair aside.*) What am I supposed to think? Why does he need the house key from me every night at eleven o'clock? Can't he control himself? I've told him a thousand times already, but he always finds some excuse to come into the kitchen. Oh, yes, you're a good boy! (*Starts to go.*)

Scene 6

REB YOYSEFKHE. (*He creeps and crawls, his head deeply bowed, his eyes fixed on the ground and his hands folded. As he enters the room, Sheyndkl comes up to him, and he pushes her away.*)

---

10. The kreuzer was a small coin in use in various eighteenth-century German principalities.

SHEYNDL. Hey, hey! The Rebbe almost knocked me down! (*Without answering or looking at her, Reb Yoysefkhe sits on a stool near the table and begins to look at a volume of Talmud.*) The master isn't home. He went out. Would the Rebbe like to have his coffee now, or should I wait until the master comes back?

REB YOYSEFKHE. (*Stands up quickly and approaches her.*) Reb Henokh isn't at home? That was why I pushed you away. (*Pause.*) I haven't, God forbid, hurt you?

SHEYNDL. Nah, nah, you scratched me a little here under my arm—the Rebbe must have needles for nails.

REB YOYSEFKHE. I swear on my life, I am so sorry! Let me see it for a minute. Oy, oy—nu, it'll get better soon. All right? You're not angry?

SHEYNDL. Why should I be angry? The Rebbe hasn't drawn blood!

REB YOYSEFKHE. By my life—hasn't drawn blood! I pushed you! God forbid that you should be angry with me. Nu, nu, give me your hand as a sign that everything is good between us again. (*He strokes her cheeks.*)

SHEYNDL. I'm not angry at all. (*She gives him her hand, which he clasps in his own, and as they stand next to each other this way, Reb Henokh enters the room.*)

Scene 7

(*Sheyndl quickly runs out of the room; Reb Yoysefkhe assumes his pious manner once more, and embraces Reb Henokh.*)

REB YOYSEFKHE. *Borekh hamokem, borekh hu*—Blessed is the Omnipresent, blessed is He![11] That you've come, that is! You are my savior. *Ki hitsalta nafshi mimaves es ragli midekhi*: "For you have saved my soul from death, and my steps from downfall!"[12]

REB HENOKH. (*Stands paralyzed.*) What does all this mean?

REB YOYSEFKHE. What? My dear Reb Henokh! *Ma enosh ki tizkerenu*: "What is man, that Thou art mindful of him?"[13] What is man? A stinking drop,[14] a nothing, a less-than-nothing! If you hadn't come in when you did, God only knows what might have happened!

---

11. Taken from the Passover Haggadah. Also appears in Tana Debe Eliyahu, chapter 1.

12. Psalms 116:8 (omitting the middle clause); familiar to traditional Jews from the Hallel, the extra prayer of praise recited on holidays.

13. Psalms 8:5. This passage also appears in the High Holiday service.

14. Of semen.

REB HENOKH. Just tell me what did happen.

REB YOYSEFKHE. What happened? (*Sighs.*) "For our manifold sins!" *Yitsri takfa alay!*[15]: "My evil impulse triumphed over me!" But it's as our sages say: *aveyre goreres aveyre*—if you do one sin, you're going to do another.[16] I come in, I think you're home—for all of my sins, I'm going to have to isolate myself, oy, vey, oy vey! May God in his oneness preserve us and save us! Nu, I was going to take my medicine *before* I got sick—I took a *Gemorrah*[17] down and I learned: *im paga b'kha menuvl ze mashkhehu l'besmedresh*—if this evil impulse hits you, then drag it to the house of study.[18] That's what I learned, but what can I tell you? It was an evil hour! Oh, woe, my sins! (*He begins to beat his breast.*) Oh, woe, my transgressions! The Evil One with all of his tricks must have possessed me! Nu, when I was standing there, my intent was good, I was going to spit right in the Devil's eye; I grabbed her hand, but in my heart I was praying to the Holy One, Blessed be He: Master of the Universe, take all of these evil thoughts away from me, and let me commit no sins, and, God forbid, do not let me become defiled—and what can I tell you, the Holy One, blessed be He, had mercy on me and sent you in just like an angel. Thank God, it is all over, but what do you think—I need to make sure that I repent. I'll eat nothing all night and I will perform the 310 ritual immersions.[19] *Hirhurey d'aveyre kashin me'aveyre*—the warnings of sin are harder than sin, that's what our holy sages say.[20]

REB HENOKH. I see more and more every day that what our sages said was the true Torah of Moses! I've seen this happen to you a number of times; why is it I've never been possessed by the Evil Impulse this way? But never mind, *kol hagodl mikhaveyro yitsro godl*—the greater of two friends has the greater desire as well.[21]

REB YOYSEFKHE. No, my dear Reb Henokh, a thousand times no; if you'll pardon me for saying so, you are mistaken; believe me, you are certainly my superior, since *eyno doyme mi sheyesh loy*—you can't

---

15. Calqued on BT Nazir 4b.

16. Ethics of the Fathers 4:2.

17. In this context, a volume of the Talmud.

18. BT Suka 52b.

19. Jewish mystical thought and practice often suggested immersion in a ritual bath to cleanse oneself of sin; the number of immersions, whose value could numerologically translate into particular letters and words in the Hebrew alphabet, was believed to have particular mystical significance.

20. BT Yoma 29a.

21. BT Suka 52a.

compare someone who's got it to someone who hasn't . . .[22] You have a wife, may she live to be a hundred, and I am a bachelor.

REB HENOKH. (*To himself.*) Even though that was a coincidence, it's a sign that this might be a good time to talk to him about my daughter. (*To Reb Yoysefkhe.*) I have to tell you the truth, it's always surprised me: why have you never gotten married? You're certainly over eighteen.[23]

REB YOYSEFKHE. Pardon me for speaking this way, but what should I do? Maybe if I were some sort of rich man, then I could learn and still support my wife, but how can one put his nose to the grindstone and study at the same time? And if—God forbid—I was going to have to give up the study of Torah, it would be better for me to have no wife at all. Am I right? Tell me.

REB HENOKH. What would you say, though, if I told you about a really perfect match? Where there's money, *yikhes*,[24] family—everything.

REB YOYSEFKHE. What should I say? I'm sure that if you're involved, it's undoubtedly good. After all, one should always impute goodness to the good—*megalglin zkhus al yedey zakay*.[25] Let me hear what it is.

REB HENOKH. It's my daughter, in fact.

REB YOYSEFKHE. (*Joyfully.*) What did you say—your daughter?

REB HENOKH. Yes, yes, my daughter, praise God, is ready to be a bride now. She still has a little foolishness in her—that is, she sings and dances. But she'll give all of that up, especially once she's in your hands. She's still a child—how old do you think she is? She'll only be about nineteen years old; you'll see, she'll go along with you in everything. So, are you satisfied?

REB YOYSEFKHE. What sort of a question is that? What do you think? *Mi anokhi*—who am I?[26] Certainly this has come from God—*mehashem yatsa hadavar*,[27] I see that clearly. What should I tell you? There may be a tiny bit of flattery here, but believe me, my heart has told me: I will always remain here. I always knew that, from the very first hour that I had the honor to meet you and teach you.

---

22. See BT Yevamot 37b and BT Ketubot 63a; the original phrase, "You can't compare one who has a loaf of bread in his basket to one who lacks it," is by then extended from its original nutritive sense to apply to the comforts of marriage and family.

23. A reference to the traditional belief (as seen in Ethics of the Fathers 5:24) that "eighteen years old is time for marriage."

24. Good (or distinguished) family lineage.

25. BT Bava Batra 119b.

26. Exodus 3:11. Moses's real humility has been replaced by Reb Yoysefkhe's mock deference.

27. Genesis 24:50. The phrase is spoken by Laban, generally considered by traditional Jews to be one of the Bible's arch-hypocrites.

REB HENOKH. (*Comforted.*) Well, so let it be blessed with good luck—and if it's not too much trouble to you, we'll announce the betrothal soon, because, I have to tell you, I have this brother in-law, he would like to have her for himself, but—why should I slander him?—it's enough to say that he is one of those newfangled people, he goes around in a rounded hat and long hair—

REB YOYSEFKHE. What? With long hair? Feh! God forbid, the daughter of a *talmid khokhem*[28] like you should take a longhair in marriage? Heaven forbid! Better you should drown her in the sea! What is a longhair? Do you know, my dear Reb Henokh, do you know what a longhair is to me? What can I tell you? A longhair is—God protect us—an act of Satan! Certainly That One has long hair himself. What is a longhair? I'll show you what a longhair is: if you've got long hair, you go around waxing it, and powdering it, and once you go around powdering it, you're walking around full of frivolity, and once you start walking around frivolously, then you start acting like the goyim, and once you start acting like the goyim, then you actually start going among them, and once you're actually among them, then there's no sin in the world you won't do, since everything has been made permissible. Am I right?

REB HENOKH. You're right, don't you think I know that already? I'm also not going to give her over to him. I simply have one favor to ask you: if you are going to marry my daughter—may it bring good luck and blessings—that you do something about my beloved Shmuelke. This is going to do me in, I don't even know what I should begin to do about it. I've already had a broken heart about it today; my wife sends the child out to a party, just lets him run off, and what am I supposed to do? I've shouted enough, I have even run over there myself, but when I got there and made my announcement, then . . .

REB YOYSEFKHE. With God's help, you don't need to have a worry in the world. I'll take care of him and, with God's help, make something out of him. But there's still one thing that bothers me.

REB HENOKH. What? Tell me, tell me!

REB YOYSEFKHE. You are, thank God, a learned man; you know very well that *oser leodem lekadesh ishe ad sheyirena*—it is forbidden for a man to marry a woman until he has seen her.[29]

REB HENOKH. What do you mean; you still haven't seen my daughter? And you two eat at the same table?

REB YOYSEFKHE. No, my dear Reb Henokh. *Ma esbonen es bsule?*[30] Why should I look upon a maiden? I have never laid eyes upon her—one

---

28. A religious scholar.

29. BT Kidushin 41a.

30. Job 31:1.

never knows, the temptations of sin, the *hirhurey aveyre*, what they can do . . .

REB HENOKH. Well, never mind, that can be arranged; tomorrow, God willing, you can go, so to speak, to her. It's actually much better that way, that when the women see you, they will, so to speak, have respect, and especially my women, who don't have any respect . . .

REB YOYSEFKHE. (*Comforted.*) Whatever you think best. Tomorrow I'll—so to speak—go to her.

REB HENOKH. But wait one minute, we completely forgot one thing; we forgot that this can't be done, because you're not allowed to be alone together. That's *yikhud* . . .[31]

REB YOYSEFKHE. (*Slightly taken aback, but quickly recovers himself.*) I'll tell you something: this can in no way be called *yikhud*. Why? Because this is for the sake of a commandment, and *shlukhey mitsve eynam nizokin*—no harm can come to someone fulfilling a commandment.[32]

REB HENOKH. You're right. (*Looks at the time.*) We have completely forgotten our lesson in the course of this discussion. But what can you do? This was also about a commandment. It's already time for afternoon prayers; we have to go to shul. (*They leave.*)

Act 2

Scene 1

(*In another room. Yetkhen wearing a smock; the Hairdresser behind her, preparing her curls.*)

HAIRDRESSER. Well, Mademoiselle Yetkhen, what should I tell him your answer is?

YETKHEN. You already heard: it's no.

HAIRDRESSER. Well, it's always better to see for oneself. You know that better than me—you're so cultivated. (*Cuts off a curl from the back of her head.*)

YETKHEN. Oh, go on, go on!

HAIRDRESSER. But do tell me, how can you be so cruel as to torture the count?

YETKHEN. Doesn't he deserve it? Such naughty behavior! Went strolling by me five times yesterday, and didn't tip his hat once—as if he didn't know me.

---

31. A traditional prohibition against men and women being alone in the same room together, for fear that sexual impropriety will result.

32. See BT Pesakhim 8a–b, Kidushin 39b, Hulin 142b.

HAIRDRESSER. I'm telling you, that only happened because of his old lady. He has to go with her, poor guy. And the Baroness absolutely hates you people. Believe me, he was plenty sick about it, and he assures me that he couldn't sleep a wink because of it that whole night, the poor count!

YETKHEN. But how did he find out I was angry with him?

HAIRDRESSER. My God! I already said: Herr Von Schnapps[33] told him.

YETKHEN. I assure you, Herr Von Schnapps wouldn't dare do that.

HAIRDRESSER. Well, I assure you that the count will never do it again. Forgive him just this once. Please! Please!

YETKHEN. Oh, alright. I'll let it go this time, but tell him not to come to me again, or else . . . (*The Hairdresser starts to go, but she calls after him.*) One more thing! If the count asks where I'll be this evening, just tell him this: you heard me say something about going to the theatre, and about sitting in loge number twenty. But don't let on that these instructions came from me.

HAIRDRESSER. Very well, Mademoiselle Yetkhen. Don't you worry about a thing. I understand exactly what to do. Trust me.

Scene 2

YETKHEN. (*Alone, sits at the piano.*) That was a mistake, taking him back so quickly. He should have to beg more. He was so rude! Didn't greet me once—and when he comes to see me, he fawns and smiles incessantly. (*Gets up and goes to the mirror.*) That goddamned hairdresser! While he was babbling away, he gave me a horrible haircut! What kind of a 'do is this? (*Runs to the window.*) Isn't that Herr von Schnapps riding by? (*Looks out.*) How genuine he is!—He's making some gesture to me, but I don't know what he's trying to say. (*Comes away from the window.*) Oh, I don't much feel like playing today. (*Throws herself onto the sofa, opens a book, and reads aloud.*) "Amelia, or, the Good Housewife; a book for women."[34] You call this a book? They're always sending me nonsense like this! I need a whole new library.

Scene 3

SHEYNDL. (*Enters, carrying a note and a package.*) Herr von Schnapps has sent these with his compliments.

---

33. The German *schnappen* can mean "to kidnap."

34. Though there seems to be no direct novel of the period with this title and subtitle, it is very possible that the work referred to is one of the numerous German translations of Henry Fielding's last novel, *Amelia* (1751), which revolves around a faithful wife and her improvident husband.

YETKHEN. (*Opens the note and reads.*) "Charming girl! I have taken the liberty to enclose herein some music I admire: several arias from the opera *Oberon* that I just got from the music shop.[35] As thanks, all I ask of you—my dear!—is the permission to hear you sing and play them. In any case, take this little token as a sign of my undying esteem and affection, and with that I remain with admiration, Yours sincerely, Von Schnapps." Who brought this note?

SHEYNDL. The servant. He had to go, but he'll be back soon for your answer.

YETKHEN. Good. When he comes, send him straight to me. Go to Mama and ask her whether she wants to go to the theatre today; they're putting on a new show.

SHEYNDL. Your mother and Markus are talking about something secret; I mustn't interrupt her.

YETKHEN. Ask her later, then, when my uncle leaves. (*Sits at the piano. Sheyndl starts to leave, but comes back.*)

SHEYNDL. I almost forgot to tell you something—you'll be quite surprised. You're getting an important visitor today—someone you can be proud of.

YETKHEN. Well? Who is it?

SHEYNDL. Who? None other than our very own Rebbe; he already asked if you're alone. I think he'll be coming this morning.

YETKHEN. You're out of your mind. What would that swine want with me? Go play your pranks on someone from your own class, you hear me?

SHEYNDL. May I drop dead if I'm lying—he's coming to see you. Why are you so surprised? Our Rebbe is quite the ladies' man.

YETKHEN. You are the very height of humor! Very well, let him come— I have some time to kill.

SHEYNDL. He's coming already. He's coming, I hear him. (*Exits.*)

Scene 4

YETKHEN. Do come in!

REB YOYSEFKHE. (*Friendly, but somewhat embarrassed.*) Good morning, good morning. So diligent!

YETKHEN. (*Curtseying.*) Welcome. (*Takes a chair for him.*) Please, have a seat.

---

35. Perhaps referring to *Oberon, König der Elfen*, a *romantisches Singspiel* in three acts by Paul Wranitzky to a libretto by Karl Ludwig Gieseke after Sophie Seyler's libretto *Hüon und Amande* (1788), which was itself based on Christoph Martin Wieland's epic poem *Oberon* (1780). The opera premiered in Vienna at the Theater auf der Weiden on November 7, 1789. The more famous opera of the same title by Webern did not premiere until 1826, decades after the composition of this play.

REB YOYSEFKHE. (*Grabs the chair out of her hand.*) While I don't want to do anything forbidden, I don't want to be a boor either; what I mean by that is, that I can take my own chair. There's no need for you to trouble yourself. (*Sits down.*) Am I disturbing you, perhaps?

YETKHEN. Absolutely not; I was just playing some little trifles.

REB YOYSEFKHE. So, you were playing? That's wonderful, I swear, absolutely wonderful.

YETKHEN. Are you also a music lover, then?

REB YOYSEFKHE. What do you mean? Music is my life! I let food and drink go untouched while I hear singing and dancing, and especially when someone plays the piano. Believe me, I have spent many an hour standing outside your door listening to you sing.

YETKHEN. Really? If I had known that, I would have practiced more diligently.

REB YOYSEFKHE. (*To himself.*) That's quite a good sign. (*Aloud.*) May I possibly be permitted to trouble you to ask you to sing something? You have such an incredibly beautiful voice.

YETKHEN. I'm not in the mood to sing today, but I will play something for you. (*She plays; Reb Yoysefkhe draws himself very close to her.*) You must not sit so near to me . . . you'll get powder on your clothes, you see?

REB YOYSEFKHE. Don't worry, you can get me all powdery if you like.

YETKHEN. How do you like the piece? Isn't it something?

REB YOYSEFKHE. What do you mean—beautiful? May God make my days and years as long as that piece is beautiful! And what is most amazing to me is that all of this can be made by those tiny and slender fingers of yours!

YETKHEN. (*Laughing.*) You are truly very gallant. But do tell me something, to what do I owe the honor of your presence today?

REB YOYSEFKHE. The honor is all mine; as your neighbor, I hope to have the honor in the future as well.

YETKHEN. I thought that you couldn't look into a lady's chamber. . .

REB YOYSEFKHE. I most certainly *can*; I'm just not allowed to.

YETKHEN. Well, it certainly pleases me that you have made an exception in my case; but you must have some particular reason for visiting me today of all days.

REB YOYSEFKHE. There is a reason, of course.

YETKHEN. Am I not permitted to know? I'm so curious . . .

REB YOYSEFKHE. Why not? You're going to hear it anyway. Yesterday, I (*Stuttering.*), I—I —hasn't your father mentioned anything to you? He hasn't said anything at all?

YETKHEN. My father? Not a word—what should he have mentioned to me?

REB YOYSEFKHE. (*To himself.*) *Kol haskholes kashes*—all beginnings are difficult.[36] I must act as her advisor. (*To her.*) Tell me, truthfully, from the very depths of your heart—would you like to be married?

YETKHEN. (*Laughingly.*) That's a matter of conscience—do you have a match for me, then?

REB YOYSEFKHE. Your father and I know a very good match for you, and things have progressed so far, that the betrothal can be announced soon—maybe even today, God willing.

YETKHEN. I find that impossible to believe; my father would certainly not betroth me without my opinion and willingness to participate in the match. Who is this person, anyway?

REB YOYSEFKHE. You're an extremely clever person—take a guess.

YETKHEN. How am I supposed to guess? There are so many men in the world—just give me the name of one!

REB YOYSEFKHE. (*To himself.*) She's as big a heretic as she seems to be. (*Aloud.*) Why shouldn't you know it? You might as well hear it from me. Nu, I'll tell you: I am your bridegroom.

YETKHEN. (*Jokingly.*) Well, if it were you, then I'd be ecstatic.

REB YOYSEFKHE. (*Joyful.*) Truly? I swear, your father told me what a wonderful child you were! May the Holy One, blessed be He, grant us only good luck and blessings and may we only live to see happy occasions. Believe you me, I don't want to brag, but I know what to do with a woman. Your father is going to be overjoyed. I'm going to go down there right now and tell him what sort of wondrous creature he has for a child. (*Tries to clasp her hand.*) Nu, nu, mazl tov! Mazl tov!

YETKHEN. (*Breaking away.*) You have become very bold. Either you refrain from such jokes, or I will show you the door. (*She moves away from him.*)

REB YOYSEFKHE. What is this? Do you think I'm simply fooling around? (*He approaches her.*) On my life and soul, there's no fooling around here! What do you think—do you think I would kid you about this? Do you think this is foolishness? Your father has agreed to it; what do you think? (*Grabs her hand again.*)

YETKHEN. I'm telling you now for the last time, remove yourself, or I will throw you out of my chamber. What sort of audacity is this from a drunken Polish swine?!

REB YOYSEFKHE. (*Sorrowful.*) What? I'm a drunk? I will not make your father's honor into a sham; I will show you whether I'm a drunk. But it is already taken care of, all taken care of. I'm going to go to your

---

36. The phrase is originally from *Mekhilte derabi Yishmael*, Masekhte Debakhodesh 2, but had entered the standard Yiddish lexicon.

father this very minute and you will see that you will have to accept me against your will. Against your will, I tell you, against your will!

YETKHEN. You can go straight to the devil; neither you nor my father will be able to force me to marry anyone. (*Sits down at the piano and tries to play.*)

REB YOYSEFKHE. (*As before.*) What an impudent woman she is! Her father can't force her—is that the way for a child to talk about her father? Shame on you! You're impudent! If I were your father, I would make you take me, even if you said no a thousand times. (*Strikes the piano with his fist so that the sides shake.*)

YETKHEN. (*Claps her hands together and cries.*) God have mercy: *mein schönes Klavier is ganz kaput!*[37] (*Sinks powerlessly.*)

Scene 5

(*Teltse, Markus, and Sheyndl burst into the room together while Reb Yoysefkhe tries to get out. Markus grabs him and shakes him vigorously, while Teltse and Sheyndl tend to Yetkhen.*)

MARKUS. What did you want with the mademoiselle?

REB YOYSEFKHE. (*Anxiously.*) I beg your pardon, but please let me go. I haven't done anything.

MARKUS. You'd better tell me what's going on here right now, or...

TELTSE. Do me a favor and let him go—you already know the whole story. (*To Yoysefkhe.*) Go, just go! (*Markus lets go of Yoysefkhe, who exits.*) Sheyndl, go downstairs and make sure no one robs the house; the doors are wide open. (*Exit Sheyndl.*) This is what comes of his stubbornness! He thinks he can just do whatever he wants. (*To Yetkhen.*) Well, how are you, Yita? Feeling a little better?

YETKHEN. A little. But for God's sake, get that despicable person out of my room.

TELTSE. He's already gone, my dear child, he's already gone. Calm yourself. Do you want anything? Tell me, does anything hurt?

YETKHEN. No, I'm feeling much better, I was just very upset. Did you see that, Uncle dear? How that scoundrel smashed my piano?!

MARKUS. It's always painful when such expensive things are smashed to smithereens, but to sink into despair like this, I believe, is being overly sensitive.

YETKHEN. Always the moralist!

TELTSE. Don't you worry, my dear child! Where does that get you? It will be alright, you'll get another piano—there are more where that one came from.

---

37. "My beautiful piano is completely destroyed!"

YETKHEN. And how crude he was with me! He wants to arrange with Papa to marry me! How do you like that? I'd like to meet the man who'll force me to marry someone! No! No father can do that— I have a will of my own. Papa may do whatever he likes, but there's no way I'm going to marry that man.

Scene 6

(*Reb Henokh furiously barges into the room as Yetkhen is finishing the previous line.*)

REB HENOKH. What? There's no way you'll have him? What do you think you're doing? Where do you get the nerve? You have the chutzpah to say that you won't have him? It's taking everything I've got to keep from tearing you to pieces! You spoiled brat! I'll teach you manners. You think I'm afraid to? I'll break every bone in your body. (*Runs around the room, grabs the music and books, tears them up, and flings the pieces at Yetkhen.*) I'm fed up with your nonsense!

MARKUS. Get a hold of yourself, for heaven's sake! You're acting like a raving lunatic!

REB HENOKH. Leave me alone, leave me alone. I'll tear her to pieces! (*Goes after Yetkhen, but Markus holds him back.*)

TELTSE. Get him out of here, my dear Markus! Get him out, he doesn't know what he's doing—he'll make things even worse! (*Markus drags him out.*)

Scene 7

(*Teltse and Yetkhen are both crying. Pause.*)

YETKHEN. (*To herself.*) I'm in an extraordinary situation; I need to find an extraordinary solution. I'll use all my wits, risk everything—I've got nothing to lose. (*Aloud.*) Mama dear, crying will get us nowhere. We'll have to do something if we want to get out of this danger. I've read many stories, and Uncle has told me many others, about cruelty to children. But a father like this is unheard of! To persist so stubbornly—such a tyrant!

TELTSE. (*Absentmindedly, having only heard the last few words.*) What do you know about his stubbornness? I can tell you stories! When an idea gets stuck in his head, God himself couldn't come knock it out of him. Get this: just yesterday afternoon . . .

YETKHEN. What if he comes back? I shudder at the very thought! Dear Mama!—go downstairs and make sure he doesn't come back up.

TELTSE. How come? Markus is down there with him.

YETKHEN. He acts differently with you—you'll have more chance of detaining him than Uncle will, so please go, Mama dear! Talk to him, at least get him to calm down for a couple of days. In time, cooler heads will prevail. (*Pleading.*) Go to him!

TELTSE. I'll do it if it makes you happy (*Going.*), even though I know that talking to him won't do any good. (*Exits.*)

Scene 8

YETKHEN. I am finally alone again, thank God! (*Locks the door.*) At least he will not take me by surprise, and I can think calmly about what to do. (*Thinks as she walks back and forth, stopping to contemplate the torn books and music.*) Look at all of this! He ruined everything! Is this any way for a father to behave? May a father do whatever he likes? Doesn't he have certain duties to his children? But if he does not feel obligated to anyone, I do not want to know about duties any more either! I will not even have a father any more! (*Pause.*) Yes, that's fine, but my mother? Oh well, that will probably be better for her than it is now—she is also suffering so much! (*In the process of picking them up, she finds a piece of the ripped up arias from Herr Von Schnapps. She picks it up, contemplating it sadly.*) You cannot escape his tyranny either! What behavior: forcing someone on me whom no maid would have, just because *he* is in love with him! (*Laughs wildly.*) Ha, ha! Imagine people's reactions on the promenade if I were to appear there with a man like that at my side! And Herr von Schnapps! He's asked for my hand countless times, and I would go to the ends of the earth for him. (*Pause.*) But what am I waiting for? I'm not accountable to my father any more—he is a tyrant! Yes, that's it, I have made my decision, and mustn't waver any more. I will leave this house today, I will throw myself into his arms today—today! I'll get everything together right away. (*Unlocks the door and exits.*)

Act 3

Scene 1

(*10 o'clock in the evening in Reb Henokh's living room. Reb Henokh sits at a table, his head resting in his hands. A volume of Talmud lies open in front of him. He frequently interrupts his studies with deep sighs. Teltse sits in a corner, sobbing. Pause.*)

REB HENOKH. I can't hear myself think; what good does all of this crying do? It's true, it is—because of our manifold sins—a great misfortune, but since we're Jews, we have to consider: *kol ma d'oved rakhmone l'tav oved*: everything that the Merciful One does, he does for good![38] It could have been even worse.

TELTSE. What are you talking about? What do you mean, even worse? What could possibly be worse?

REB HENOKH. How should I know what could be worse? It could be worse—that's enough. And a Jew always has to find the silver lining in every cloud—a *gam zu letoyve*.[39]

TELTSE. May God in his seventh heaven have mercy! A fine *gamzel letoyve* this is! The poor, poor child! Wherever she might be all of this time, she might even cause herself harm! The poor child! (*Cries.*) And such a husband! It's all because of you! All your insanity, you're driving me right into the grave, and yourself too, because of this craziness. May God have mercy! (*Cries.*)

REB HENOKH. I'm begging you to give it a rest—don't drive me completely out of my mind. (*Sighs.*) What should I do? God has clearly willed it to be so! Presumably, He knows what needs to be done! And what does that mean? I have to stay here silent while I'm terrified for my child? This is insane! Why would I think that she would run away? Who would think she would run away? Maybe if I was going to give her to some buffoon, some stripling, it would make sense, but as it is, what more could she possibly ask for? I know where all of this is coming from, though—I know it's for the sins, with which you and your brother ruined her!

TELTSE. (*Jumps up from her chair.*) Don't be so high and mighty; she also ran away from you. Divine decrees aren't solely to blame . . .

Scene 2

(*Sheyndl enters with a bowl of soup.*)

SHEYNDL. Won't you have a bit of soup? It's already so late, and you haven't eaten a thing today.

---

38. BT Berakhot 60a.

39. Literally "this too is for the best." The Talmudic source (BT Taanit 21a) discusses the figure Nachum Ish Gamzu, so called because of his propensity, when misfortune occurred, to utter the eponymous phrase. Though he is taken advantage of by a crooked innkeeper, God intervenes miraculously and all works out for the best. Teltse seems to mangle the phrase in the next line.

TELTSE. No, I can't. Just put it away. I don't want to eat; I've lost my appetite. (*Cries.*)

SHEYNDL. But what does all of this crying help? You're simply going to make yourself sick. You'll see, everything is going to work out; Herr Markus has sworn that he's going to do everything he can to bring her back.

TELTSE. Yes, yes . . . who knows where she is? She could really do something to herself, God protect us . . .

SHEYNDL. There's no need for you to get yourself in such a state; she is not going to hurt herself. Mam'selle Yetkhen is too much in love with herself for that.

REB HENOKH. And did you completely fail to notice the fact that she was leaving? How is it that you did not see who was going in and out to her?

SHEYNDL. I should know? How is that? Do you think that there's just the one visitor a day? It was a madhouse all day long. As soon as one *sheygets* arrived, there's another *sheygets*[40] at the door. I didn't have a single minute to stay in the kitchen—it's a miracle that the food wasn't burned to a crisp! And had I said something, there would have been big trouble. (*Knocking is heard.*) I think someone's at the door; I'll go down and get it. (*Leaves.*)

Scene 3

REB HENOKH. Did you hear that? Did you see what the girl said? The whole day, she was surrounded by goyim, and all of this was hidden from me—oy, the shame! How can I stand it all? What does this mean? My daughter's spending her time with goyim! Oy vey, oy vey! (*Markus enters.*)

TELTSE. (*Running over to him.*) Markus, dear Markus! What's happening? Still no news of her?

MARKUS. As of now I still haven't heard anything; I hope to receive some information soon, though.

TELTSE. So did you go to see Herr von Schnapps, did you ask the good-for-nothing if he knew anything?

MARKUS. Certainly I went there; I even did a little asking around among the servants, and I found out from them that last evening, he went riding around with some woman in a closed coach. Where exactly they were going, they didn't know.

TELTSE. That's a good sign already.

---

40. Yiddish, non-Jewish male, generally meant pejoratively.

MARKUS. With this information, I went straightaway to one of my friends, revealed my suspicions to him, and asked him for his support in this risky affair. He's one of those friends who is an old enemy of Von Schnapps, and so I was fairly sure that he would make every effort, do everything possible in order to obtain detailed information and to bring the matter to light and make sure that the scoundrel gets his just desserts.

TELTSE. May God reward you, my dear Markus! I can't thank you enough—my gratitude is too meager. (*Cries.*)

MARKUS. What is all this for? Can an action which was merely my duty deserve such effusive thanks? Whatever I did, I was required to do as a brother, as a man.

REB HENOKH. But what does it help? Woe—for our manifold sins!—she has gone off with a goy, the dirty trollop! And she'll defile my whole house as well.

MARKUS. Now is not the time for speeches. What we need to do now is determine how we can free her from the clutches of these seducers. There's no way to change what happened in the past, and what happens in the future is up to each of us.

REB HENOKH. Why, do you think that maybe she'll come back? I would forgive her everything right away! I'll beg for atonement like a dog, God should forgive me all of my sins, I almost cursed her myself! But she's still mistaken. She'll have to marry Reb Yoysefkhe, if only for spite, and I don't care if she stands on her head.

MARKUS. You have to learn to speak more gently! All of your threats and curses are forgiven, but she is still not here. When we have her back home, God willing, I advise you as a friend to speak to her sternly but sensibly. If you ever try to keep her here by force, you shall regret it. You have seen how well strictness works; maybe you shall learn to bend a little now. To be perfectly open and frank with you, if I were your daughter, I would not marry this Reb Yoysef, and so she resists the idea of this marriage as well!

REB HENOKH. This doesn't come as any news to me; you're the only one she ever listens to! *Aval ko yihyeh*—But thus shall it ever be . . . [41] (*Sheyndl enters with a message, which she hands to Markus, and quickly exits again.*)

MARKUS. Everyone be quiet for a moment; this message may tell us something new! (*Reads.*) "With the greatest of friendship I hurry to write you that I am finally on the trail. The wolf has finally arrived, but the sheep is as of yet completely unharmed. Come to me as soon

---

41. Possibly calqued on Genesis 15:5 (where the context is about Abraham's children).

as possible; I wait for you at my house. Come whenever you wish; if you want, you can speak to your niece. More to follow." I have no time to lose; I will hurry there and soon I will have spoken with Yetkhen, and then I will return to you. (*Leaves.*)

TELTSE. God be praised and thanked! That that's all! A huge stone has been lifted from my heart, and I'll have a little soup now. Do you want some too?

REB HENOKH. If you like, but you know what, we'll set the table just like usual; I didn't have a proper lunch today. Come, Sheyndl will prepare something for us.

Scene 4

(*In Lemgin's lodgings. Yetkhen, her clothes disheveled, sits at the table crying, her head in her hands.*)

LEMGIN. When will you stop your crying? Silly thing! Laying it on a little thick, aren't you? After all, it's not as if you've been captured by a band of robbers. You're with decent people—no harm will come to you as long as you're good and play along! Come here, little fool— always be merry and cheerful. When you make faces like that, you'll scare people off. You'll never move a Christian soul that way. Here! Here's my glass of wine—drink, it gives you courage, and then we'll dance a little waltz! (*Goes to take her by the hand.*)

YETKHEN. Oh, let me go. I'm not in the mood for waltzing or drinking.

LEMGIN. Look here, you silly thing. How will you ever attract a lover that way? Let yourself be happy—you'll find more than enough lovers here. Only the finest clients come here; you can have your pick. But as I said, you have to behave differently, be very friendly, to entertain the young gentlemen so they'll fork over plenty. Play your cards right, and nothing will happen to you.

YETKHEN. (*Resisting.*) Then why are you keeping me here? I think you want to make a strumpet out of me. No, I haven't fallen so far, thank God—I still have parents, thank God, who will take me back.

LEMGIN. Yeah, yeah, I've heard that one before! I'm sure you're parents are just great. Why did you run away from them, then? And why did the Mademoiselle spend time with that cream puff Von Schnapps? Heh! She's silent! (*Knocking is heard.*) Take my advice, really cheerful and happy! (*The knocking gets louder.*) Okay, okay— this one can't wait. (*Going.*) Put on something nice—take my advice, you hear? (*Exits.*)

Scene 5

YETKHEN. (*Alone.*) Oh God! The punishment is too hard! Is my crime so terrible that I should have to suffer so? Me, in a brothel! A trophy for every hedonist! Ach!—she's coming. Oh God, stand by me and save my honor. (*Goes into an adjoining room.*)

Scene 6

LEMGIN. (*Entering.*) Yes, yes, mein Herr! That's my name. I've been living here over five years now, and have always been visited by honest folk. Believe me, I know what gentlemen want.

MARKUS. Do you have any girls in the house?

LEMGIN. Yeah, yeah, a freshly baked one—just came to me this evening! In truth, she's still a little aloof, but that will pass. She'll attend on the Herr shortly, she just went in to get herself together. Would the gentleman like something to drink? Punch, hot chocolate, wine? You may have whatever you like.

MARKUS. Punch.

LEMGIN. Good, it will be ready soon. One ladle or two?

MARKUS. Whatever you like. (*To himself.*) If I can just speak to her soon.

LEMGIN. I'll bring it in a moment. The Herr won't have to wait long. As I said, the Mademoiselle will be here soon. (*Exits.*)

Scene 7

MARKUS. (*As she exits.*) In this awful house, this residence which is all lasciviousness and indulgence, the daughter of my sister! In this grave of innocence, perhaps hers has already been murdered? Ah, these are the fruits of blind religious zealotry! Unchangeable as death, timeless as the tomb, you pile sacrifice upon sacrifice, trampling over them in order to honor your master, to fit in with his master plan. But is she then entirely guiltless? Must she, in order to escape her own insult, turn directly to the worst possible insult? Isn't it simply the silliness, impetuousness, and other modish pleasures of our contemporary youth that have paved the way to this tragedy? And nevertheless, I still feel, when I consider it more deeply, that the blame should return to the parents! Do not neglect the education of your children, be more watchful of their moral education than their physical education, and teach them early to have an affinity for what is noble and good, then you will never have to worry about your children's foolishness. Well, I'm forgetting the purpose of my being here; the woman told me that she is in the chamber; why should I tarry? (*He approaches the chamber and calls out.*) Yetkhen! Yetkhen!

YETKHEN. (*Comes out of the chamber and embraces Markus.*) Ach, my uncle! My savior!

LEMGIN. (*Comes in with punch and a ladle.*) Well, you silly thing, didn't I tell you it would be okay? And if it starts off well, it will end even better. (*To Markus.*) Shall I pour you some?

MARKUS. Allow us to be alone right now; we will be able to serve ourselves perfectly well.

LEMGIN. As you wish; there's no need for me to stay around here. For these sorts of things, three's a crowd, hm? (*Laughing, exits.*)

MARKUS. Ah, my dear niece! Answer for all of us the most important question: how did you come to be in such an awful house? Did this happen of your own free will, or against your will? Answer me perfectly honestly; you know me, and you know that I know all about human frailties and failings.

YETKHEN. (*Miserably.*) Of my own free will? God, how low I must have sunk in your eyes, that you can even ask me this question! (*Cries.*)

MARKUS. I apologize if I have insulted you by asking that; that was certainly not my intention. I am only asking in your own best interest, and depending on what the answer is, that will determine how I shall be able to help you. So tell me, then, how did you come to be here?

YETKHEN. I am truly too weak to tell you the whole long story.

MARKUS. Then make it as brief as possible, and just tell me who has brought you here.

YETKHEN. That despicable Schnapps! Right after I had made the unfortunate decision to abandon my father's house, I hurried to this place and flew in, in my temptation to be protected. I believed myself justified in this and in even further steps, since he had so often assured me of his everlasting friendship. He received me in an extremely friendly fashion as well, offered me his assistance in the kindliest manner, and constantly behaved toward me in a way most eager to please. "In the meantime," he said in the most honest tone, "I will bring you to a safe place, to one of my relatives, where you can lead a quiet, comfortable, and secure life, out of any sort of danger, out from under your father's power. He will take care of your clothing; I'd better keep hold of your money or whatever else you were able to take in your flight, because it will be safer with me than anywhere else." My heart was too full, and my head too empty, for me to have found something suspicious in this proposal; I gave him everything, and was taken out in the evening twilight. I was placed in this house after he had taken great precautions with the lady of the house.

Markus. And he—where did he go?

Yetkhen. Only God knows that! He only stayed with me for a brief moment; then he excused himself with some necessary visit that he had to pay in the city, and he promised me that he would return soon, but . . . (*Cries.*)

Markus. May this whole affair serve as a cautionary example for the rest of your life! May you learn a lesson from all of this, that the punishment always follows in the end! However, I am not going to chide you any more about this matter right now; your misfortunes are returning to me once more, and your better accomplishments in the future can and will completely wipe away this small blot of shame. Now I must hurry and bring your parents news of you.

Yetkhen. And will you simply leave me here by myself? Impossible, dear uncle! I beg you, in heaven's name, take me with you!

Markus. This is impossible for me right now; it is necessary for you to stay here for the time being. I give you my word, however, that within half an hour I will return to you; in the meantime, do not worry.

Yetkhen. But why can't you take me with you?

Markus. Because I think that it is beneficial to you; because I may have the opportunity as a result to get your father to change his mind about marrying you to the Pole. (*He goes out of the door and calls Lemgin.*)

Scene 8

Lemgin. What's the matter, mein Herr?

Markus. Listen, little mother, a fatal blow has befallen me. In my hurry I forgot my purse, and with respectable people like you one must pay for everything up front. I would like to run home and fetch my purse. (*Lemgin makes a long face.*) Since you do not know me, though, I want to leave my gold watch with you as security in the meantime. I will be back in just half an hour.

Lemgin. (*Taking the watch.*) As the gentleman wishes.

Markus. I will probably bring a good friend with me, and then we shall have a grand time. Today I want to spend a few Fredericks.[42]

Lemgin. That would suit me just fine. The gentleman may do whatever . . .

Markus. Listen, though: do not let anyone—I care not who he is—come to the mademoiselle in the meantime. For tonight, the mademoiselle belongs to me alone. You hear? I will pay you for that as well.

---

42. An apparent reference to the Frederick d'or, an eighteenth-century Prussian gold coin.

LEMGIN. The gentleman needn't worry about a thing. I understand my work and know how to please. But would the gentleman like a glass of punch first? (*Offers it to him.*) It won't cost you anything—it's on the house!

MARKUS. When I return. (*He hurries out.*)

Scene 9

LEMGIN. That's an enchanting man, *nicht wahr?*[43] You can still get something out of that sort of man, but whenever these Jewfolk come, it's like letting the devil in here; that sort of vermin can go begging for bread.

YETKHEN. Do Jews come here as well?

LEMGIN. And why shouldn't they? Foolish thing! Are they different creatures than we are? Yes, yes, the Moyshe-goat is twenty times wilder for the ladies, but what difference does it make? The goat still doesn't pay his bills. In fact, there's one Polish Jew who comes here practically every night, and stays here 'til one or two in the morning, and he already owes me twenty-four thalers!

YETKHEN. But why do you let him have so much credit?

LEMGIN. What, should I start something with the Moyshl?[44] I know that he lives with one of the richest Jews in town, and I've found out enough to know that he's very well liked there, and so I think he's still going to pay up in time. But the rascal is draining me dry from one day to the next. If he comes here this evening and doesn't bring me any money, then I'm going to give him such a beating that he'll think he's been in a duel. (*Knocking is heard.*)

YETKHEN. Someone's knocking—it must be the young man.

LEMGIN. Ah, no, it's much too soon, he won't be back for another half hour at the very least; it must be the Polish Jew, he always comes at about this time. He can wait outside for a little while, cool his heels for a bit, he's hot enough . . .

YETKHEN. If it is him, then I shouldn't stay here; I'm going to my room.

LEMGIN. You can do that. You know what? The Jew can stay here in the salon, and when the young man returns, I'll lead him straight down the corridor and through the other door into your room. (*Knocking is heard again.*) Devil take it! I'm coming! (*She leaves. Yetkhen goes into her room.*)

---

43. German, "Isn't that so?"
44. Probably not only a generic reference to a Jew ("a little Moses"), but also to the *Mauschel*, a stock Jewish character common on stages of the period.

Scene 10

REB YOYSEFKHE. (*Entering.*) You should be very sorry, making me wait so long; I was so cold that my teeth were chattering. (*Crosses to the table.*) What's that there? Punch? Have you had company? (*Drinks.*)

LEMGIN. Other company just like you; you see that the punch is made, and we celebrated. It was very nice, but when you come, the free-loading begins.

REB YOYSEFKHE. I beg your pardon, but don't I spend something every night at your place? You know, you've already cost me forty thalers in four weeks—what am I saying, forty?—over fifty you've cost me; this should be poison that I'm drinking right now if what I'm saying isn't true! (*Drinks.*)

LEMGIN. You and your fifty thalers can go straight to the devil! That's a laugh—in four weeks, I figured once that every week has eight nights, and each night you're here for at least three hours. With what one hour here costs, you've hardly paid for your candles!

REB YOYSEFKHE. Don't drive me crazy with your figures, just make me something.

LEMGIN. I'll fix you something good, but first I want my money. You owe me more than twenty-four thalers.

REB YOYSEFKHE. I'm not going to run away from you; you know quite well that I'm living with a rich man. And if you have any doubts, then I will give you a pledge (*Takes out his tefillin.*)[45] Here, take my Ten Commandments.

LEMGIN. What should I do with your Ten Commandments? Money's what I want. You promised me that you were going to bring money today; don't try any nonsense!

REB YOYSEFKHE. Don't get upset! Here, in the meantime, is six thalers, and tomorrow I will bring you more. Just hurry, I don't have much time; I'm not going to stay very long—I must get back home tonight. Hurry!

LEMGIN. Well, well, just have a little bit of patience, until I've finished my glass of punch. (*Someone knocks.*) Yes, yes, right away!

REB YOYSEFKHE. Let me do it for free, I'm asking you; otherwise I will never set foot over your threshold again. (*Lemgin leaves. From offstage, we hear Reb Henokh saying, "Why shouldn't I go inside? I'm going right in. Well, that's news to me." and demanding to be served refreshments.*) God have mercy!

---

45. "Phylacteries" in English; ritual objects traditionally worn by male Jews on the arm and head during morning prayers. They are small black boxes with selections from the Bible inside them. In antiquity, though not since then, those passages were the Ten Commandments (see BT Berakhot 12a), which may be why Reb Yoysefkhe refers to them in this fashion.

(*Claps his hands together.*) I hear Reb Henokh's voice! What should I do? What can I do? (*Runs around the room like a madman, and then gets the idea to hide himself under the bed as Reb Henokh, Markus, and Lemgin step inside, the latter two supporting the former as he enters.*)

Scene 11

REB HENOKH. (*Entering.*) Nu, where is she? (*Notices Reb Yoysefkhe, then turns back to Markus, astonished.*) What, then? Reb Yoysefkhe is already here with her? This is a bad sign.

MARKUS. What makes you say that? (*Also notices Reb Yoysefkhe.*) What's this I see? A Hasid in a whorehouse? (*Approaches him.*) Scoundrel! What are you doing here? (*Reb Yoysefkhe retreats anxiously; his profound embarrassment robs him of speech, and this embarrassment and anxiety last throughout the scene.*)

LEMGIN. (*Gets between Markus and Reb Yoysefkhe.*) Mein Herr! Let the man go, I don't allow any scenes in my house. He spends his money here like anyone else, he's a good customer: comes here every evening and . . .

MARKUS. What do you say to that, brother in-law! Do you know the man you promised your daughter to? (*To Lemgin.*) Don't worry, little mother, there won't be any scenes, I won't do this man any harm. Just go and bring the mademoiselle here; she knows already. (*Exit Lemgin.*)

REB HENOKH. What can I say? What can I say? I am *nivhal u'meshtumem*— too shocked for words![46] How could this be? I believed in him to the ends of the earth! In all my days, such a hypocrite . . . (*Lemgin enters with Yetkhen.*) Nu, she's here? Come, see, if I didn't . . .

MARKUS. (*Aside to Reb Henokh.*) Remember what you solemnly promised me: be gentle, and do not give her more reasons to rebel.

REB HENOKH. Come here, Yita. Come! (*She approaches timidly and fearfully.*) Come, I want to show you something that will amaze you. (*Takes her by the hand and points to Reb Yoysefkhe.*) Do you know this man? Tell me, do you know him?

YETKHEN. (*Afraid.*) Papa, dear Papa, for God's sake! Everything is just . . .

MARKUS. Don't worry, dear niece! You have nothing to fear from this man, he has been exposed, the hypocrite!

REB HENOKH. Listen, brother in-law, tell the lady here not to let the hypocrite go tonight. I'll pay her for her trouble, and tomorrow, God willing, I'll show him what I'm capable of.

---

46. This phrase appears in the responsa of Joseph Karo, the author of the Shulkhan Arukh (*Bet Yosef Dinei Ketuvot* 50); however, it seems to be a general colloquial phrase rather than a citation.

MARKUS. Listen, little mother. This is what I owe you. (*Gives her money.*) But don't let this scoundrel leave your house tonight, for he has treated my brother in-law shamefully. I will pick him up tomorrow, and will pay you for your effort.

LEMGIN. That's just fine. He won't get away from me—he already owes me a lot of money, and where else am I going to get it? He always tells me how he's staying at a rich man's house, and that he'll get as much money from him as he wants. But from what I've just heard here, it sounds like he's quits with the rich man too! *Nicht wahr?*

MARKUS. Absolutely. This is the man in whose house he has been staying.

LEMGIN. (*To Reb Yoysefkhe.*) I hope you burn in Hell, you rascal! How will I get my money from you? But just you wait: you won't get this (*Points to the tefillin.*) back until you pay up.

REB HENOKH. What do you have there? Tefillin? How did you get that?

LEMGIN. The rascal gave it to me as security. He says they're his Ten Commandments, but who knows whether that's true now? He'd probably lie about that too.

REB HENOKH. You hear, brother in-law? He pawned his tefillin! That enemy of Israel! I must say, I never would have dreamed such a thing in all my days. Such a heretic and an apostate! And now what he was doing with the maid comes back to me! Well from now on, I'll never believe people like him again—they're clearly impostors! I prefer these modern types a thousand times better; at least they act openly, while people like him do everything in secret, and are *goynev das hamokem vedas habriyes*—deceitful before God and man.[47]

MARKUS. We're chatting away here, while my sister is waiting anxiously for us.

REB HENOKH. You're right, we'll go. (*To Yetkhen.*) If you behave yourself from now on, I promise to forgive you, and I'll never bring it up again. (*To Markus.*) And you haven't gone to all that trouble for nothing—you've taught me a lesson. *Rov bonim holkhin akher akhey ha'em*—most children follow their mothers' brothers, say our Sages.[48] I hope my child follows her mother's brother as well. (*Exits with Yetkhen.*)

---

47. Literally "steals the mind of God and of man," the phrase generally refers to a kind of financial fraud through misrepresentation. See BT Shavuot 39a and Tosefta Sota 7:2. The form of the clause is probably modeled on *Mekhilte derabi Yishmael Mishpatim* 13, which speaks of "stealing the mind of people and of the Most High" or *Masekhet Kala Rabati* 9:9.

48. Calqued on BT Bava Batra 110a.

MARKUS. Don't worry, little mother, I'm a man of my word. You won't be disappointed. Just don't let him get away. (*Exits.*)

LEMGIN. Look how the rascal stands there, rooted to the spot! Ha ha ha! You see, Jew—that's what happens to all rogues! But if you think I'm keeping you in my house overnight, you've got another thing coming. You'll have to sleep in the woodshed tonight. It's plenty cold there, but you're full of hot air. March, march, get a move on. (*She drags him out the door.*)

Curtain.

Serkele, or, In Mourning for a Brother

An Entirely New Theatrical Piece in Five Acts

by Shloyme Ettinger

Cast of Characters

REB MOYSHE DANSKER, *a nouveau riche*

SERKELE, *his wife*

FREYDE-ALTELE, *their daughter, who calls herself Friederika in German*

HINDE, *an orphan, Serkele's niece through her brother*

REB GAVRIEL HENDLER,[1] *a speculator*

MARKUS REDLEKH,[2] *a medical student*

REB YOYKHENEN, *a matchmaker*

A STRANGER

A DOCTOR

REB SHMELKE TROYNIKS, *a Lithuanian, the owner of "The Spies" guesthouse.*

BERL, *his servant*

CHAVA, *a maid*

CHAIM, *a servant at Reb Moyshe Dansker's*

YERAKHMIEL, *Reb Gavriel Hendler's servant, a stutterer*

BEADLES *and* POLICEMEN

---

1. Yiddish for "businessman, speculator."

2. German for "honest."

Prologue

What is itself completely pure
And good, the world cannot endure;
It surely will not be too long,
'Til it hears evil's siren song.
Wise enough to know my place,
'Twill be enough to save my face,
If you will, of tonight's affair,
Find but a bit of goodness there.
Serkele! Come! Reveal yourself!
And grace us with your charms a while.
One viewer will toast your good health,
Another, spew out bile.
I beg you, gentles, one thing more,
A trifle, that's all, I assure.
Say of Serkele what you will
Concerning me, though, please keep still.

—The Author

Act 1

A room in Reb Moyshe Dansker's house. Three doors: one stage right, exiting to the rest of the house; one stage left, leading to Serkele's bedroom, and one stage center leading to the street. The room has a few pieces of furniture: a sofa with several small chairs surrounding it, a bookcase, a chest of drawers; a mirror hangs on the wall, and another, larger one stands against the door stage right; a round table is in the middle of the room.

Scene 1

(*Chaim stands by the door to the street and closes it. Afterward, he counts some coins, transferring them from one hand to the other.*)

CHAIM. One, two, three twenty-groschen pieces! Oh-ho, I swear, pure coins every one of them! He's a good man! It's an absolute pleasure to be of service to a householder like Reb Gavriel—completely different from my boss, you hardly have to lift a finger and you've earned yourself some money. Heh? He was here today and Monday—two days, two coins. Ay, Altele is no fool, that's for sure; if I were a woman, I'd fall in love with him too. And why not? He's a

good man, after all, a smart man, a fine man . . . If only someone
said half as many nice things about me, Chava would be singing
quite a different tune . . . What's in that head of hers, there's no
figuring out, that's for sure . . . (*Stands in front of the large mirror.*)
After all, I'm no little boy—there's already some gray in my beard.
Well, and if I'm a little bit pockmarked, what of it? Hm? At night all
cats are black . . . (*Takes another look in the mirror.*) I just wish I knew
what sort of expression I could use that she'd really go for! Like this?
Nah. Maybe this? Ah, feh! It makes me look all bitter and nasty. Oh
ho! This? Doesn't do a thing for me. (*Chava enters through the stage-
right door very quietly, watching Chaim make faces in the mirror. He does not
turn around, but continues speaking to her image in the mirror.*) Chava my
dear! I'm burning up with love for you—why don't you love me
back? Just take a look at me, I'm not hideous, that's for sure. You're
just being stubborn. And look! (*Jingles the coins in his hand.*) I've got
money, too! (*Chava laughs loudly and runs off. Chaim runs after her
reflection in the mirror, running into it and knocking himself backward onto
the ground, breaking the mirror and scattering his coins.*)

Scene 2

SERKELE. *Oy vey iz mir*! What happened? What happened? Leave for one
minute . . . (*She clutches herself.*) Oy! I don't even have the strength to
scream this way. Have you gone mad? What have you done? My good
mirror! May my very worst nightmares come true and happen to
you, you thief! You fiend! A plague on you—oh, oh, I feel faint! The
boy is going to be the death of me! The little brat spends all day and
all night ogling himself. At least if he were good looking it wouldn't
bother me so much, but such an eyesore? . . . Oh, wait, you just wait
'til my husband comes home, my Moyshe's going to give you what's
coming to you! God knows that I don't have the strength, now that
people like you have taken my health away. Oh, oh, I feel faint!
CHAIM. (*Slowly begins to gather the coins and the shards of the mirror together
and quietly says to himself*): Just my luck that Mrs. High-and-Mighty
here should come in right after this disaster. (*More loudly, he whines.*)
Oh, my head! My aching head! I've practically killed myself!
SERKELE. If only you had finished the job! What business did you have
with the mirror anyway?
CHAIM. Oh! The mirror? That mirror? I just wanted to give it a little bit
of the old spit and polish, that was all! And in my great hurry, I
fell. . . . I almost killed myself!
SERKELE. Were you too sick to call Chava for help? What else does she
have to do with her time, that impertinent bitch? It's ridiculous! One

more incompetent than the next! Oh, oh, I feel faint! If I weren't so old and broken down. The whole damn day, the maid sits with that troublemaker, that disaster, her darling little Hinde, and helps her carry out her nasty little tricks! Oh, wait, you just wait until my Moyshe gets home, oh, oh, I feel faint!

CHAIM. Most gracious madam, please! Don't get angry. Chava's done nothing, I assure you . . .

SERKELE. (*Interrupting, slyly.*) Maybe the two of you are in cahoots! Who's the guilty one here, me? Oy, if I could live long enough to get rid of all of you, then maybe I wouldn't feel so faint.

CHAIM. Just don't be angry with me, that's all, my gracious madam! From now on, I'm going to follow you in everything, even through fire, just don't get mad at me!

SERKELE. Oh, you've become so sly! You think I'm not going to be angry? How could someone not be angry? What sort of excuse do you think I'm going to give to my Moyshe, ha?

CHAIM. Ah, the master won't notice a thing. He comes in and out of here day in and day out with his head in the clouds, lost in thought.

SERKELE. (*Grilling him.*) What are you saying? He's going around thinking? What does he have to think about? What? What's he thinking, huh?

CHAIM. Do I know what he thinks? What could it possibly have to do with me? I'm merely a humble servant. What do I care what the master thinks?

SERKELE. Well, if you had dared to investigate what the master is thinking of, I would have sent you packing. And the way I found Chava behind the door a while ago—I wouldn't want to be in your place, that's for sure.

CHAIM. Ah, my dear madam! I'm telling you, Chava being behind the door—she must have been looking for me.

SERKELE. And an idiot like you, you're such a find? Just pay attention—what was I going to tell you? Oy, oy, I feel faint—yes, look—I mentioned it myself—pop over to Redlekh's and tell him I would be ever so grateful if he were to call on me this evening in my bedchamber, because I am simply falling to pieces. I used to send for a different doctor, but he simply didn't understand my nature . . . oy, oy, I feel faint! But listen up, pay attention, make sure you don't let the walking disaster know—you know who I'm talking about, right?

CHAIM. Oy, oy, oy! If I could only guess! You must mean the master, certainly?

SERKELE. Go on! You should be ashamed of yourself! (*She says to herself quietly.*) The fool has a bit of sense in him—that was pretty sly . . . (*Louder, to Chaim.*) Don't you know I mean Hinde? Always have to correct him, the idiot. Well, go on already, go—someone's coming!

Scene 3

REB GAVRIEL. Good morning, my dear Serke! How are things going with you? My word, you do look wonderful today, knock on wood. But what is this? Why aren't you wearing your kerchief today?

SERKELE. (*Gracefully*.) Oh, I look so wonderful—go on, just go on! It's true, if I could just return to my old self, that would be something very different, but now—alas—where is the old Serkele I used to know? Ha, ha! The radiant Serkele that every man used to die for— no more. Oy, I feel faint! Ha, ha, ha, I remember how I put on my very first veil as if it were yesterday, and when I was led into the shul—what a tumult there was then! Young and old alike followed me with wide eyes—you should have heard, the richest men in town were saying to each other, "There goes that beautiful Serke, that beautiful Serke"—but how do I look now? The day grows cold, and I grow old . . .

REB GAVRIEL. Eh . . . what's the matter today, then? You should only be healthy! (*To himself.*) When is it ever anything else with her? (*Aloud, to Serkele.*) So why aren't you wearing your kerchief today?

SERKELE. What, don't you know? Today marks four years, to the very day, that my golden, beautiful, one and only brother died abroad. To- day—alas—is my dear Dovid's *yortsayt*[3] . . .

REB GAVRIEL. Well, does a weak and feeble person like yourself really need all this crying? You've shed enough tears over this news. What more do you want?

SERKELE. Believe me, my dear Reb Gavriel, I have cried, wept, wailed; I thought that I would never be able to survive since this black, bitter, evil news had sapped the last bit of strength from these old bones— oy, I feel faint! It's no small thing ever to lose a brother, but what a brother! Such a pure soul! Such an educated man! Such a saint! (*She wipes her eyes and cries some more.*)

REB GAVRIEL. Ah, Serkele! Feh, you should be ashamed of yourself. You're crying? What did you just say to me? A wise woman like you should cry? You should be ashamed of yourself . . . Nu, enough . . . stop it, I can't bear to see you crying.

---

3. Traditional Jews commemorate the anniversary of the death of a parent, child, or sibling. The day is referred to as a "yortsayt" (literally, "year time"), and is generally marked by certain symbols of mourning, such as the lighting of memorial candles and the saying of kaddish (though in traditional Eastern European society, as Serkele sug- gests, only men said kaddish; if the deceased only had surviving female relatives, then a husband or male relative would say kaddish for them).

SERKELE. (*Cries.*) Oy, oy, I feel faint! If only he had left a son to say kaddish for him—at least that would have comforted me. My Moyshe, God protect him, says kaddish for him every year.

REB GAVRIEL. And won't Hinde turn out to be a decent person?

SERKELE. Not even close. She's trouble, a disaster, and who knows what else—it's just a shame, a scandal. All she knows how to do is talk, talk, talk . . . Believe me, if he—may he intercede for us, God rest his soul—were to stand before us right this minute and look at the jewel of a daughter he left behind, he would, I swear, drop dead a second time from sorrow.

REB GAVRIEL. Well, that's news! She sounds truly awful. Together with Freyde-Alte, this must be too much trouble for you to handle . . .

SERKELE. Excuse me one minute, what are you doing comparing that troublemaker, that nuisance, to my dear Alte? My goodness gracious! What a difference! On the other hand, do you think she hasn't cost me my health? Oy! What do you think saps my strength so? Take those new clothes of hers—she sewed a pair of pockets on them completely by herself! And her shirts, and her piece work? Did you see the Polish alphabet she needlepointed? And the way she talks? And her handwriting? And the way she reads—isn't she a treasure? French and German, smooth as silk!

REB GAVRIEL. How old is she? I mean, isn't it time to start looking for husbands?

SERKELE. What, do you mean because she looks so grown up—there should be no evil eye? She isn't more than—than thirteen.

REB GAVRIEL. True. (*Aside.*) Not counting Sabbaths and holidays.

SERKELE. How old do you think I am, after all? People can say whatever they want, but I'm really no older than—than twenty-seven . . .

REB GAVRIEL. Also true. (*Aside.*) Give or take ten years.

SERKELE. It's only my brother that has aged me. And that parasite, that Hinde, takes away my last bit of health, oh, oh, I feel faint! At my wedding, I was a beautiful maiden, a gorgeous sapling, I shined like the sun in July; no one would have believed that I was only thirteen years old.

REB GAVRIEL. (*Aside.*) I don't believe it myself. (*Aloud, to Serkele.*) And you were married so young? I swear! Well, the daughter's reached the age when her mother got married . . .

SERKELE. Yes, no question, as long as we find the right person.

REB GAVRIEL. What? Just make sure that you give her to a good merchant, someone who'll be able to support her. These days, no one's looking at family any more—when you're dealing with a father-in-law, you're stepping right into the lion's mouth.

SERKELE. What? Family? What does she need to worry about family for? Isn't my side of the family distinguished enough, after all? After all, the Rovshitzer Rabbi—heh? how about that?—a close relative, and the Preacher of Suaranyer, may he rest in peace, was related—a blood relation—to my uncle's mother-in-law, and the Chacham Zvi's mother-in-law's grandmother and her great-grandfather were on my mother's side . . . they were close relatives.

REB GAVRIEL. (*Aside.*) She's told me this a thousand times already. (*Aloud, to Serkele.*) All that aside, all I'm saying is that you should find someone who looks good. A good merchant.

CHAVA. (*Enters stage right.*) Madame! Come inside, the master has arrived.

SERKELE. Go, give him his sinful bit of coffee. He's just come from prayers, poor thing. Don't take this personally, Reb Gavriel, but I have to go in to my husband.

REB GAVRIEL. Not at all, go, go.

SERKELE. Oy, oy, I feel faint! (*Exits with Chava.*)

Scene 4

REB GAVRIEL. (*To himself.*) Thank God I'm finally rid of her—she's already given me the whole family tree ten times, how the Preacher of Posner was related to her sister's kid, some Berdichev cantor. But that's how it goes: as long as you've got money, you're beautiful, smart, a saint, and take a few years off your age while you're at it. After all, what was Serke a few years ago, when she was still sitting in the middle of all that corn and meal? Who would have even given a moment's notice to Serke the meal dealer? Who would have thought? But now—she has money and who's her equal? That daughter of hers, the green-faced nuisance, from out of the blue has become the sum of all virtues. But what do I care? All that matters to me is that she's got money. I'm planning to get married myself, so I might as well bag her. Let her be green—all the easier to get money out of her. Sha! That's her now. (*Adjusts his sidecurls and his collar in the mirror and takes off his fur hat.*) Ah, the best of mornings, my dear Fräulein! How goes it with you?

FREYDE-ALTELE. (*Speaks with a certain charm.*) And a very good morning to you, Mr. Hendler, thank you kindly. *Wie haben sie geshlafen diese nacht?*[4]

---

4. Freyde-Altele is asking "How did you sleep last night?"; Reb Gavriel misunderstands *Wie* ("how") for *Wo* ("where").

REB GAVRIEL. What? Where else would I have slept? I slept at home last night, the way I always do.

FREYDE-ALTELE. (*Laughs.*) Ha ha ha, you see, my teacher told me that if someone asks, "*Wie haben sie geshlafen?*" you answer, "Well," and if someone asks, "*Wo haben sie geshlafen?*" you must answer, "At home."

REB GAVRIEL. Well, my dear young woman, what difference does it make whether you say "Vi" or "Vo"? I'm telling you that the teacher is a fool, an idiot, it's all the same thing whether you say "Vi" or "Vo" or "Vey"—as long as you sleep.

FREYDE-ALTELE. (*Puts two chairs together and sits on one of them.*) Please, take a seat. What did you dream about last night?

REB GAVRIEL. (*Sits near her.*) Look here, my dear young woman! The whole night long I dreamed only of you; it seemed to me that my wagons of merchandise had already arrived from Lipsk and I had received some beautiful material for a new dress for you.

FREYDE-ALTELE. Material for just one dress? I ask you, why just one? Is it possibly à la Valter Shcott?

REB GAVRIEL. Yes, precisely: à la altered stock.[5] Besides that, though, I've brought you a pair of bracelets, beautiful ones. But you've never accepted what I've brought you, what I've begged and pleaded you to. And I still don't know why.

FREYDE-ALTELE. I haven't accepted anything? From you? No, that can't be. You see, my dear Mr. Hendler, my teacher always says that I may accept anything from you in a dream—and he is absolutely right.

REB GAVRIEL. Is that so? (*He takes the material and a pair of bracelets out of his pockets and gives them to Freyde-Altele.*) Now we'll see if you're telling the truth!

FREYDE-ALTELE. (*Quickly grabbing for the things.*) Oh, they're beautiful! Thank you!

REB GAVRIEL. No, my dear young lady! There is no need to thank me for such poor trifles; I would give away to you every one of my possessions—and do you know why? Because I truly, deeply love you.

FREYDE-ALTELE. (*Looks him right in the eye and smiles gracefully.*) And does this truly come from the heart? You see, then, I can no longer disappoint you—(*Gives her hand for him to kiss.*)

REB GAVRIEL. (*Grabs her by the hand and kisses her on the cheek.*) My golden Altenyu! I do love you so.

---

5. Literally "*à la alter shtok*" ("like an old piece of material").

Scene 5

CHAVA. (*Sees them kiss, then runs around. She says to herself.*) I swear, that's a fine pair! (*Aloud, to Freyde-Altele.*) Freyde-Alt . . . (*She stops herself and begins again.*) Fräulein! Come inside, the teacher has arrived and is calling for you.

FREYDE-ALTELE. Who, Redlekh? That fool! Tell him to come tomorrow. I've waited a long time for him, now he can wait. (*Chava begins to clean the room.*) Well? Why aren't you going? You cow! I've never seen a bigger fool in all my life! You should be ashamed of yourself.

CHAVA. What have I done that the mistress should curse me this way? Why shouldn't I clean here?

FREYDE-ALTELE. (*Angrily.*) What a dumb animal! You see that I have a guest here, and yet you're standing around and cleaning! Whenever Hinde tells you to do something, you hop to it, but as for me, even if I tell her a thousand times what she should do, she doesn't follow me. (*Takes Chava by the hand and throws her out.*) Go, you ox!

REB GAVRIEL. Enough already, stop being so cross, my dear young lady! It can only embarrass you! Are you still angry?

FREYDE-ALTELE. Ah, no, no. Once she goes away, I calm down. One must always make sure that the servants treat one with the greatest respect.

REB GAVRIEL. Oy, my servant, my Yerakhmiel—he's such a silent young man, it's as if he doesn't even know how to talk—but he has such respect for me that it gives him fits.

FREYDE-ALTELE. If it were up to me, I'd only employ Christian servants—they know how to behave themselves, *nicht wahr?*[6]

REB GAVRIEL. When will that ever come to pass, though? As a matter of fact, I spoke yesterday with Reb Yoykhenen the matchmaker. And he told me that he's going to speak with your father and mother today. Believe you me, my dear young lady, that as far as money is concerned, there's nothing to worry about! I just received a payment from the Suchard brothers in Trieste that I'm already getting a hundredweight of coffee and a hundredweight of sugar, besides what's coming back to me from the Vienna groceries and other products.

Scene 6

YERAKHMIEL. (*Takes off his fur hat.*) M-m-m-m-master! Go h-h-home already! (*Freyde-Altele laughs heartily.*)

---

6. German "isn't that so?"

REB GAVRIEL. See, as a result of his great respect for me he can hardly get the words out! (*To Yerakhmiel.*) What do you want?

YERAKHMIEL. C-c-c-come home already. Whenever you're w-w-w-wanted, someone always has to go looking for you. The m-m-m-mailman has arrived with a letter.

REB GAVRIEL. Well, go tell him to wait a minute—I'm just about to leave. Or—tell him to leave the letter with you.

YERAKHMIEL. I h-h-h-had the same idea, but he got furious at me a-a-a-and cursed you w-w-w-with the filthiest curses, because y-y-y-you o-o-o-owe him for several letters, and haven't paid him for a long time.

REB GAVRIEL. (*Grabs him and tries to throw him out.*) Nu, go to hell already.

YERAKHMIEL. Nu, I-I-I-I'm going—will y-y-you come with m-m-m-me, though?

FREYDE-ALTELE. (*Laughs heartily.*) That's what I call respect, all right!

REB GAVRIEL. (*Throws Yerakhmiel out.*) Get going already, you deaf dog. (*Yerakhmiel leaves.*) The reason he's so stubborn is because he earns so much money out of me from tips; do you think it's a small amount that the rat takes from all of the business that I do each week? You wouldn't believe it.

FREYDE-ALTELE. Ah! I believe you. I know that you are quite well-to-do. You see, they have approached me concerning a—concerning a— (*Tries to remember the word.*) concerning a—ah! I have forgotten how one refers to a—what is it called in Yiddish? A—a . . .

REB GAVRIEL. Might you mean, God forbid, a *shidekh*?[7]

FREYDE-ALTELE. Yes, that's what the Jews call it! You see, the bridegroom is also quite extraordinarily wealthy. He has his own money, quite a lot of it, silver and jewelry and one of the largest inns here in Lemberg.

REB GAVRIEL. Ah! Don't you believe it. It's all a big lie. That's just what that swindler the matchmaker is telling you so that he can get his commission. I bet he's got no money, no house, no jewelry—I know these swindling matchmakers pretty well!

FREYDE-ALTELE. But I happen to know for myself that he has an extremely large house, and Mother tells me that he is very, very rich.

REB GAVRIEL. And I swear to you that he's a beggar, a scoundrel, a swindler, and the matchmaker is a liar and a villain!

FREYDE-ALTELE. Do you know the groom, then?

REB GAVRIEL. What do I need to know about him? What I do know is that he's a pauper, he's broke—and that's enough for me. Just so I can be sure, what's his name, hm?

FREYDE-ALTELE. His name is Reb Shmelke Troyniks.

---

7. Yiddish "an arranged match."

REB GAVRIEL. (*To himself.*) Uh oh! I'm in it deep this time: he really is loaded! Only a brilliant young man could get out of this one. (*Laughs aloud.*) Ha ha ha! Well, what did I tell you? That Litvak![8] That swindler! That pauper! I should have as much property as the difference between what he earns and what he owes. (*To himself, quietly.*) I'm being a fool, but what can I do? (*Aloud.*) And that rascal, that old dog, that's who you want to take for a bridegroom? (*Laughs heartily.*) That scoundrel of a Litvak? That villain who drove his first wife, poor woman, into the grave?

FREYDE-ALTELE. Did he truly cause her to pass away? She was always perfectly healthy; she accidentally fell down a flight of stairs and passed away. How is he to blame for that?

REB GAVRIEL. How is he to blame? Who knows? When a Litvak hates his wife—it's possible, believe me, that the murderer threw her down the steps himself, just so that he could be rid of her!

FREYDE-ALTELE. But he was not even here in Lemberg—

REB GAVRIEL. (*Interrupting her and speaking very quickly.*) But his servants were here, hm? But he sent her letters, the old thief, ha? Nu, nu, nu, he already knew what sort of advice he needed to give, that killer! (*Pretends to get angry.*) Nu, so leave me already and take the Lithuanian as your groom, believe you me, I'll also get a fine bride—I won't be a bachelor for long, that's for sure. It's nice to have met people like you. Now that I've seen you, may I please leave now? (*Pretends to get ready to go.*)

FREYDE-ALTELE. (*Grabs him by the hand and prevents him from going.*) But, my dear Herr Hendler! Do not leave, and, in God's name, do not be angry. I will never marry the Litvak, not if he were a thousand times richer and had millions! You, only you, must be my groom—I will certainly have no other.

REB GAVRIEL. (*Turns back to her and kisses her hand.*) Well that, you see, is a completely different story. Because I love you terribly, my beautiful Fräulein! If only you keep to that statement, that you want only me, everything will certainly turn out well.

FREYDE-ALTELE. Oh, yes, certainly, certainly, I will be true to my word. You must be my groom, you must become my husband—only do not get angry again, I beg of you.

REB GAVRIEL. No, no, I won't get angry any more, it had simply bothered me that such a wise, such a clever, and such a beautiful Fräulein as yourself should suddenly believe the type of foolishness that a scoundrel of a matchmaker had babbled to you. . . . (*Enter Yerakhmiel.*)

---

8. Litvak: Yiddish for a Lithuanian Jew. Litvaks tend to be seen as clever but cold, and their dialect is characterized by an absence of the *sh* sound. Where other Yiddish speakers say *shabbes* ("Sabbath"), for example, the Litvak says *sabbes*, and for *loshn* ("language"), the Litvak says *losn*. The Lithuanian Yiddish dialect thus earned the nickname *sabbes-losn*.

Scene 7

REB GAVRIEL. Are you back here again? What do you want?

YERAKHMIEL. The p-p-p-postman is driving me c-c-c-crazy; he wants me to drag y-y-you home.

REB GAVRIEL. Nu, go already, and to hell with you! (*To Freyde-Altele.*) Adieu, my beautiful Fräulein! Adieu, I must take my leave—it must be that I have some very important letters from Vienna and from Gdansk. I will return again today. Reb Yoykhenen will certainly arrive at your father's today. Just listen to whatever he has to say, and just keep to your promise—you understand what I'm getting at?

FREYDE-ALTELE. Don't worry; everything will remain as I wish.

REB GAVRIEL. (*Leaving.*) Adieu, my beautiful Fräulein! Adieu. . . .

FREYDE-ALTELE. (*Takes him by the hand.*) Wait a bit, why are you hurrying so? Would you like to go to the theatre?

REB GAVRIEL. Yes, my dear!

FREYDE-ALTELE. Then what is going on?

REB GAVRIEL. Like it always is—half past seven.[9]

FREYDE-ALTELE. (*Laughs.*) Ha ha ha, but what sort of a piece is being put on today?

REB GAVRIEL. Alina, or Lemberg of the Other World.

FREYDE-ALTELE. Do you mean that it's Alina or Lemberg which is of the other world?

REB GAVRIEL. It's all the same to me. Well, adieu, my beautiful Fräulein! Just keep your promise, for God's sake! I now have no more time, I have to go already. Adieu, be well!

FREYDE-ALTELE. Go in good health! (*Reb Gavriel and Yerakhmiel exit.*)

Scene 8

(*Freyde-Altele alone. She examines the bracelets and the material and fixes her hair in the mirror, then skips around the room and sings.*)

> Whoever from a life of sadness
> Seeks to find eternal joy
> Must flee herself, as if from madness,
> From love of any man or boy.
> Many women, just like you,
> In male arms solace hope to find
> But later they will come to rue
> The carefree life they've left behind.

---

9. Again, Gavriel is misunderstanding Freyde-Altele's somewhat mangled German.

(*Stands still and laughs.*) Ha ha ha. That is one song that I can let Shmelke the Litvak have—no, it'll be an entirely different story with me and my Hendler; I know, for I am convinced of his love. Look at what he has already sent me, since he came to us—ay, ay, ay! (*Quiet a moment, and then speaks gracefully.*) Ach! And my heart, my pure heart, speaks only of you—I would be a fool if I were to accept the Litvak and then, after the main event, go back on my promise like a Jew. (*Measures out the material on herself in the mirror along with the bracelets.*) Ach! This is perfect for me—and with that hat with the feathers that's arriving—oh, how pretty! How glorious I'll look! Yes, I must dress in the most modern German styles, and my Hendler must too! When we look like this, and go out together for a walk—no one would ever imagine that we were Jews, that's for certain. (*Quiet a moment.*) If only that damned matchmaker would come. And what is he going to say to Mother? (*Thinks a little more.*) He is very rich, that's certainly true, he's told me so himself several times. I think I'll be very happy with him; I'll be the envy of all the other girls. (*Silent for a moment, then suddenly slaps herself.*) Ach! I have completely forgotten the time! That Redlekh is driving me crazy with his lessons! If only Reb Yoykhenen would arrive already . . . If I can just put the lesson off until the afternoon, then I can take a good nap. (*Laughs and runs off.*)

Scene 9

HINDE. (*Comes through the door stage right, very upset.*) Oy! What doesn't one have to suffer, when one has no father and no mother! I may not stay in the room when Altele studies with Redlekh! Is it my fault that Redlekh says that I understand the lesson just from listening from a distance better than Friederika? God knows, soon it will be impossible for me to endure the daily suffering I get at the hands of both Frieda and my aunt. What can I do, they don't like me a bit. (*Calms down a bit.*) But maybe I am a little bit of a nuisance, as they say? After all, that's exactly what Redlekh has criticized me for and said, "This thing and that thing, my dear Hindele, are wrong; here's where you made a mistake, look at these errors and correct them." And if he even tells it to me once, then I certainly follow his instructions to the letter, but in the eyes of the others, I see that even good things, things that I did properly and that anyone else might do, I'm also not allowed to do! Why? Because it would upset Frieda if I were right! (*Silent for a moment.*) Oy! How my aunt used to love me, when I was still with my father, God rest his soul. As God is my witness, I love her as much as ever, and yet I can see how she hates me more and more every day. Oy! Today it will be four years since my dear father passed away! Even now he appears before my eyes, looking just the way he did when he was alive. Six years ago, before he went away from us, he took me by the hand and kissed me and cried over me. I remember—just as if it were yesterday—how he said that he would wait until Redlekh got out of school so that he could say good-bye to him. No, I will never forget as long as I live the kissing, the hugging, and the holding when Redlekh arrived, just as if he were his own son. Even total strangers, looking at us, lamented and cried. (*Wipes her eyes and cries.*) Good father! Sweet father! Did you already suspect that you would never return home again? That you would never see your child again? That it would be the last time? (*As she continues, she speaks more faintly and grows more preoccupied.*) Yes, yes, the last time! The last time? No, no. Beloved father! No . . . soon I won't be able to endure it any more. No, dear father! It was not the last time, not the last time you saw your child—we will soon, yes, soon, see each other again! (*Falls, completely drained, onto the sofa.*)

Scene 10

CHAVA. (*Entering, does not see Hinde.*) The apple doesn't fall far from the tree! Like mother, like daughter! Alte must have gotten up on the wrong side of the bed this morning, the way she's been fighting with me and with Hinde all day. Where is Hindele? I thought she was in here. (*Looks around and notices Hinde, goes and sits next to her on the sofa.*) Hinde my love! What are you doing lying there like that, my heart? Don't, I beg you, make a big deal of this. (*Takes her in her arms and kisses her.*) My dear! Don't get upset or suffer at all; you'll see that God will help you after all; you'll see that you will be happy once again. (*Cries and wipes the tears from her eyes.*) Don't cry, my dear! My heart! Don't cry, I beg of you!

HINDE. You're absolutely right, Chava, *nicht wahr*? I shouldn't cry, you say? Maybe you're right, Chava, but maybe you've forgotten what a completely dark day this is.

CHAVA. Believe me, I would forget my own name before I'd forget today's tragedy! I know full well that today is my master's *yortsayt*, but tell me, my dear: hasn't every day since the terrible letter came to your aunt been like Tisha B'Av?[10] Have I ever seen you have a single happy moment since then? I swear! It is no sin for you to forget a little bit, that's for sure—you must keep your health . . .

---

10. The ninth day of the Jewish month of Av. The saddest day of the Jewish calendar, it is a fast day commemorating the destruction of both Temples, as well as other tragedies of Jewish history.

HINDE. Chava! You're telling me this, you? (*Sits up.*) You can actually say such things? You, who were with us in our house, who were like one of the family? You, who know full well what sort of a father I had, you can say such a thing? You, who know full well how happy I used to be, you can now say that I should forget my poor, dear father? Just completely forget about him? Even on the day when his awful *yortsayt* falls, should I forget him then as well? *Nicht wahr,* Chava?

CHAVA. Oh, my love! I was wrong, you were right, you cannot forget—who could ever forget such a father? Just tell me, my love: if your father was really so good to you, why did he . . .

HINDE. (*Cuts her off.*) Might you be referring to the fact that he left his entire fortune to my aunt? Believe me, you can say what you want, but he must have known what he was doing, because the whole world knows what a brilliant man he was, and how much he loved me, his only child. You yourself always talk about how he used to cry and stay awake all night long if I felt the least bit unwell. So that's why I think that he must have had a good reason for what he did. And as for the other thing, would I really be any happier if I owned everything? He really is dead, for once and for all, and I have no father.

CHAVA. What would owning everything help? Hm! Would you have had to live with your aunt? Would you have had the troubles, the sorrow that you suffer at other people's hands? Would any old worm dare to say a word to you? And let's not kid ourselves—that's not to mention some other people who are not able to get anywhere near you—other people, you understand what I mean, who would also be happy around you.

HINDE. (*Looks Chava in the eye and examines her.*) I have no idea—other people? Who do you mean? Who are these other people? I don't know—do you mean, possibly, you?

CHAVA. Believe me, Hinde dear! I know what I'm talking about, believe you me! I've got it on the best authority—just answer me one question: just tell me what I've done to you that you've become so dead set against me. Tell me, please, let me know!

HINDE. Me dead set against you? Chava! You must be dreaming!

CHAVA. Sure I'm dreaming—as if I don't see myself that you're not the same Hindele to me that you once were.

HINDE. Tell me, Chava dear! (*She begs her.*) For God's sake . . . what are you talking about?

CHAVA. What am I talking about? Oy, oy, I'm no fool, that's for sure. I see everything that's going on perfectly well, but to tell you the truth, I thought all along that you would tell me yourself—because who loves you the way that I do? Why shouldn't you tell me everything, heh?

HINDE. (*Strokes Chava's cheek.*) I beg of you (*Kissing her.*), just tell me and don't torment me any longer!

CHAVA. (*Looks Hinde right in the eye.*) Just tell me, do you know somebody named Markus Redlekh, hm? (*They both remain silent a moment.*)

HINDE. (*Lowers her eyes and blushes, then clasps Chava with both hands and kisses her.*) Chava dear! You are absolutely correct! I know myself that I've acted badly toward you—I beg of you, my dear Chava, please forgive me—I'll tell you everything. (*She suddenly goes silent and blushes.*)

CHAVA. Well, tell me! What are you blushing like that for? What's making you so red? You little fool! Tell me everything—even though a blind man could see what's going on . . . Well, so you love him—but who doesn't love Redlekh? Isn't he worth loving? He's very good-looking, clever, wise, and he's certainly honest.

HINDE. Chava dear! How do you know what he is? There's no one in the world who's his equal! Wise, you said? The way he has behaved in my aunt's house for the past three years to each and every person, there's no one, even Frieda, who could possibly hate him—

CHAVA. (*Interrupting.*) And speaking of the mistress, she'd absolutely die for him—

HINDE. Good looking, you said? Just take a look at the beautiful face, the red lips, the lovely round cheeks, the high smooth forehead and the fiery eyes—he's pretty as a picture! What are you talking about, "if he's clever"?—his sweet little speeches, his honeyed words! He speaks just like a book. And who else his age is already in his third year of medical school? Soon he's going to be a full-fledged doctor!

CHAVA. You know, some time ago he spoke with the nobles who came to borrow money from the mistress in French and Latin—I swear! They might have been selling me off, and I would never have been able to tell— (*They hear Serkele's voice from offstage, calling "Hinde! Hinde!"*)

HINDE. I think my aunt is calling me.

CHAVA. Yes, yes, you'd better go before she starts screaming for you.

HINDE. (*Begins to leave, then looks back.*) Chava dear! There's just one more thing I have to ask you . . .

CHAVA. (*Interrupts her.*) I already know what you want to ask me: go already, go, I won't repeat what you've said for anything. (*We hear Serkele's voice once more: "Hinde! Hinde! Do I have the strength to say 'Hinde' a third time?—Hinde!" Hinde quickly runs off through the door, runs into Chaim, and, on the run, gives him a push into the main room.*)

Scene 11

CHAVA. (*Running to help him up.*) What is with you today? Are you drunk, or what?

CHAIM. Let Hinde go in already, she was making such a fuss.

CHAVA. Well, she's gone already. But show me: haven't you hurt yourself somewhere?

CHAIM. (*Angrily.*) Whether I've hurt myself or not, what do you care? Did I ask you anything?

CHAVA. My, you're so angry with me, Chaim! Weren't you just pushed?

CHAIM. Why are you talking to me so much, Chava! It's all over between us, finished!

CHAVA. (*Smiling.*) Doesn't that mean that there was something between us that started?

CHAIM. What? Nothing had started? Well, if that's how you want to play, so be it. (*He walks around the room and speaks, as if to himself.*) Do such things still happen? That a woman should allow a strange man to kiss her?

CHAVA. Who are you talking about?

CHAIM. (*Suddenly stopping in front of Chava.*) Who do I mean? (*Laughs angrily.*) It's you I mean, you!

CHAVA. (*Laughs.*) Ha ha ha, me? You mean me? I let myself get kissed?

CHAIM. Yes, yes, you think maybe I didn't see how Reb Gavriel came through the kitchen and gave you a kiss? That's how you've become, ever since you went off with the mistress in the spring. (*Chava laughs hysterically.*) But I always used to say that a man shouldn't take a bride that hasn't been out in the world a bit. (*Cries and wipes his eyes. Chava laughs even more loudly.*) No, no, I'm not going to put up with it any more! And all because of those blasted thermal baths! When I become a bridegroom, I'm going to have it put explicitly in the marriage contract that the bride is forbidden to go to the baths. (*Wipes his eyes and looks Chava in the eye.*) I don't know why you think so much of yourself. Maybe it's because you think that I'll make a fool of myself begging for you? Well, that's true; you've certainly hit the nail on the head there. It's all because my father convinced me that I should have only you, and, like a fool, I listened to him. But wait, just you wait—I'm going to go and tell him about the kind of hussy you become for just a bit of business. (*Chava holds her sides and laughs even louder.*) Well, go on, laugh; we'll see who'll have the last laugh, me or you. I'm going right now to my father and I'm going to tell him every last detail! (*He runs off angrily.*)

CHAVA. (*Laughs.*) Ha ha ha, what a fool! Like I'm going to fight with that good-for-nothing! He really is a bit of a fool! But he's a good and honest fool, that's for sure. It makes me sorry how I've caused him so much distress. But he'll get over it, even though he went away so angry. Later, he'll come crawling back to me and beg for forgiveness. I'm as sure of that as I am that we'll grow old together! (*Runs off.*)

The curtain falls.

Act II

The same room in Moyshe Dansker's house as in Act I.

Scene 1

(*Reb Moyshe Dansker, alone, sits at a table, his head cradled in his hands, deep in thought. He stands up, goes back and forth around the room a couple of times, and sighs. Then he sits down and thinks, as before. Suddenly he jumps to his feet and cries.*) It was just a dream! (*Calms down a little, then says a bit more quietly.*) Yes, but why did I never dream such a dream before in all my life? Today of all days! This very day . . . (*Looks around.*) I can say it here, no one's listening: this is the date when I tricked everyone into thinking that my brother Dovid died during his travels. Oy! It would have been better if I had died then; I'd probably be better off! Some evil wind had to bring me to get advice from that Shmuel Shrayber![11] But it's not his fault either: he just did as he was told—you dance to the tune that's played for you. Serke! It was you who destroyed me! (*Goes quiet for awhile, then as he starts to talk, he grows louder and louder.*) Last night—it must have been past midnight—I dreamt that I had gone to the world beyond, and I was sitting in a corner in a place where hundreds of candles were burning, just like on Yom Kippur in the synagogue, and many of the dead were walking around, all dressed in shrouds, but so quietly that you couldn't even hear them moving. (*Wipes the sweat from his brow.*) My hair stands on end when I think about it! Suddenly I heard a shofar blowing somewhere. It started to thunder and lightning very hard. I heard many voices, as if all the winds and blizzards in the world gathered together in one place and wanted to show who had the loudest voice. Then all the lights went out, it grew terribly dark, the ground started to shake beneath me. I was seized by fear and dread, and when I think of it now, I shake all over like a leaf, my stomach turns to ice, and it's as if I can still hear the trumpeting: very quiet at first, then louder and louder and louder, like the final blast of the shofar. (*Quiet for a moment.*) Suddenly, two enormous gates opened, and I noticed two extremely tall people with fiery wings on their backs. One was holding scales in its hands, the other a rod—they were frightful to behold![12] Then one of them suddenly started to cry out in a

---

11. Yiddish, "writer."

12. These objects are often associated with angelic figures in the world after death: the scales of judgment, and the rods for flagellation and punishment.

mournful voice, "Woe! Woe to him who has swindled widows and orphans! Woe to him who cannot bear the weight of judgment! Woe, woe to him! He has no remorse!" My head started swimming, and I stood there like a post. Next, the other one started to shout in a voice that could be heard from one end of the world to the other: "Wake up! Wake up for the resurrection of the dead!" And I saw with my own eyes how the earth and the sea coughed up heads, hands, feet, and guts, which came together again to form complete people, and they lived once more. Suddenly... (*Speaks louder and louder, pausing between each word.*) Oy! Suddenly I feel—as if someone—gives me—a slap—on the—shoulder. When I—look around—I notice—oy! I notice—my—my, my brother-in-law—Dovid—(*Shouts at the top of his voice.*) "Moyshe! Remember me?" (*Exhausted, he falls to the floor as if dazed.*)

Scene 2

REB YOYKHENEN. (*Who, having entered in time to hear Reb Moyshe shout, "Remember me?", goes to him.*) What do you mean, do I remember you? What kind of a question is that? Why, let me tell you something, we're practically from the same town! Your mother, Tsortl Zlates, may her memory be a blessing, came from around here! Ach! I knew her very well, and also knew your brother-in-law Dovid, may he rest in peace, very well, as if he were standing before me right now.

REB MOYSHE. (*Gets up suddenly.*) What? Oy! Where, where is he standing? Where? (*He grabs hold of Reb Yoykhenen.*) Where is he?

REB YOYKHENEN. What do you mean, where is he? Where should he be? He was a pious Jew, after all, a saintly man—of course he's sitting in Paradise with all the righteous ones. (*Stares Reb Moyshe in the face and says to himself.*) Oh boy! I didn't notice before—he must have some sort of disease in his head! I was surprised that he was so formal with me. (*Aloud to Reb Moyshe.*) Reb Moyshe! Tell me, it seems you aren't feeling well. What's the matter, ha? Do you feel sick?

REB MOYSHE. (*Returning to his senses.*) Ah, Reb Yoykhenen! Oy! Yes—yes—I'm a wreck.

REB YOYKHENEN. What's the matter, my dear Reb Moyshe?

REB MOYSHE. (*Beating his breast.*) Oy! Here, here is where the problem lies.

REB YOYKHENEN. Nu, let me tell you something, why don't you send for a doctor?

REB MOYSHE. (*Moaning.*) Oy! No, don't, don't, let it be, I'm perfectly healthy, nothing's wrong. (*Tries to get up but cannot.*) But—have you been in the room with me long? Oy! I'm shaking like a fish, aren't I? I'm sick, very sick, I can barely walk—my worries, worries don't let me rest.

REB YOYKHENEN. What? Worries? You have worries too? That's very fine! Let me tell you something, one person worries about a noodle pudding, another about an entire meal. But granted, I, I, I worry—nu, I am, as they say, a poor fellow! Sometimes I have food for the Sabbath and sometimes I don't—but you? You are, after all—may you avoid the evil eye—a wealthy man (may you live to a hundred and twenty), you have just one daughter, a very decent girl, good and pious and, if I may say so, pretty too. Let me tell you something: she comes from good stock, and with God's help, you'll surely make a good match for her—it's about time.

REB MOYSHE. (*Having come completely to his senses.*) Yes, you're right, my dear Reb Yoykhenen! The time has come. (*Scrutinizes him.*) Isn't that right? (*Stares at Reb Yoykhenen. Intently.*) Let me ask you—may you enjoy good health—have you been here in my house long? To be perfectly honest, I'm not feeling in the best of health; for the past couple of weeks, there's been something missing—I don't know what. I can't sleep at night, and I often say things that lack all rhyme and reason. (*Scrutinizes him further.*) I bet you heard such things here, ha?

REB YOYKHENEN. Yes, in fact, I did hear you ask me if I know you. Let me tell you something—may you live long—you've known me since I warmed a bench in the study house. Well, praise God for that. Now I'm a matchmaker, and arrange the biggest matches—good, I make a few rubles once in a while! And I swear I'm going to arrange a very good match for your Altele—I'm telling you, an exceptional match. You and your wife, may you both live long, know him very well.

REB MOYSHE. (*To himself.*) He heard nothing, thank God! (*Aloud.*) My dear Reb Yoykhenen! You know that I rarely get involved in such things. That's a matter for my wife, bless her; I rarely have any idea about them, so you should talk to her directly. If you'll excuse me and wait here a little, I'll send her in! (*Leaving, he runs into Serkele.*) And here she is in the flesh! (*To Serkele.*) Here, Reb Yoykhenen has something to discuss with you, my wife. (*Quickly exits.*)

Scene 3

REB YOYKHENEN. I hope you're well, Serkele!
SERKELE. Welcome, Reb Yoykhenen! What's new? Sit for a bit, sit. (*She sits.*)

REB YOYKHENEN. (*Sits.*) I've just come for a short visit. After all, we're neighbors now, Serkele. I've heard that your husband was under the weather, so I came by to pay a sick call.

SERKELE. Who? My Moyshe? My goodness, where did you get that idea? He's perfectly healthy, thank God! Who on Earth told you such lies—who?

REB YOYKHENEN. I've completely forgotten who came by today and told me that. (*He acts as if trying to remember.*) Sorry—I just can't remember.

SERKELE. May pain seize them when they speak. Oy, I feel faint! The lies one's enemies come up with! I just wish I were as healthy as he is.

REB YOYKHENEN. Well, let me tell you something, I wish you health and strength. May you enjoy wealth and honor in your old age, and may your child bring you all the glory and happiness you deserve.

SERKELE. Amen, dear God!

REB YOYKHENEN. Listen, I was just speaking to your husband about a match for your Altele, may she live long. Well, he likes the idea very much, I can tell you—I know he's gone out, but he said, "Whatever my dear wife wants to do, that's what we'll do!" I tell you, you're lucky to have such a husband. You're both master and mistress— your word is law.

SERKELE. (*Smiles.*) Aren't I lucky to have found him? And besides, don't I deserve it? Pardon my saying so, but he is—just between you and me—utterly helpless. Just look at him; there's not a person in the world who would pay ten kreuzer for him, body and soul. He's just useless—I tell you, absolutely useless. Who does everything? Who works like a dog? Who wears mourning clothes? Oy, I feel faint! Who works as hard as I do?

REB YOYKHENEN. You're absolutely right! You have a child to raise, and he leaves it entirely to you. God willing, you'll make the wedding arrangements without him as well.

SERKELE. That's the God's honest truth. But stop beating around the bush. Let's hear who the groom is—a student, perhaps?

REB YOYKHENEN. What? Would I bring you a student? Isn't that beneath a wealthy aristocrat like you? Go on—how could someone as clever as you think for a moment that I would match your perfect child to a student? (*Spits as if angry.*) Tfui! Let me tell you something: I didn't just hatch from the egg. I know that the innkeeper needs his wine and the weaver his flax—so would I bring your child a student? Look, I—I'm offering you a magnificent match. You can trust me on this: he has been sent from Heaven.

SERKELE. Nu, alright, but who is he? Does he come from a good family? Is he nice to look at? Oy, I feel faint! Does he have money, huh?

REB YOYKHENEN. Does he come from a good family? No less than the greatest of the age! The mother's side is first class: she's related to the great Rabbi Zalmen on one side, and the other side of her family is just dripping with important people. And as for his father's family: it's crawling with rabbis. In short, what can I say? Let me tell you: it's easier to talk the talk than to walk the walk, but he can trace his genealogy back to ancient times, all the way back to the High Priest Eli,[13] you understand?

SERKELE. (*Shakes her head in surprise.*) Really? Back to the holy High Priest?

REB YOYKHENEN. And money? Everyone should be so lucky! I wish I had what he spends in a year. Let me tell you something, show a dog your finger and it'll want the whole hand, but not me: I'd only like to earn what he spends in a month! He's a regular prince, lives like an aristocrat and is a wealthy merchant to boot—has dealings all over the world. (*Freyde-Altele opens the door very quietly so that they won't hear, and eavesdrops.*)

SERKELE. But tell me already, who is the groom? Perhaps I know him?

REB YOYKHENEN. You know him very well, he's a regular visitor. His name is—Reb Gavriel Hendler! Nu, what do you say? Do I know who to talk to, ha?

SERKELE. Reb Gavriel Hendler! Yes, I do know him well. He comes here almost every day—was just here, in fact.

REB YOYKHENEN. Nu, so how do you like him? Isn't that an excellent match? It seems to me that a better catch just doesn't exist.

SERKELE. Well, yes, I'll tell you the truth, it's not a bad match—oy, I feel faint! I even like him. He isn't bad, but—

REB YOYKHENEN. (*Interrupts her.*) Nu, what more do you want? If you like him, who else is there to ask? I tell you, your husband, long life to him, likes the match very much! The minute I brought it up, he was overjoyed! Believe me, he was simply beside himself!

FREYDE-ALTELE. (*Aside.*) May he live to be a hundred and twenty for that![14]

SERKELE. Yes, who knows what my only daughter will say to it—whether it will please my Altele?

FREYDE-ALTELE. (*Aside.*) What a question! (*She closes the door and opens it again, as if she had just come in, and runs to Serkele.*) Mommy! Have you taken the keys?

---

13. See 1 Samuel 1-2.

14. According to Jewish tradition, Moses lived to the age of 120, and it is a traditional Jewish blessing to wish someone the same long life span.

SERKELE. What's that, dear heart? They're hanging around your neck. You're always looking for things that are right under your nose.

REB YOYKHENEN. So this is your Altele, may she live long? (*He looks Altele over from head to foot.*) Nu, I tell you, she's become quite a fine young lady. Let me tell you something—the way children grow up! Nu, my child, do you want a husband?

FREYDE-ALTELE. (*Pretending to be embarrassed.*) Oh, let me be with your bridegrooms.

SERKELE. (*Laughs and winks at Reb Yoykhenen.*) Something's cooking there— just talk to her and she'll be yours.

REB YOYKHENEN. (*Smiles.*) Why are you so angry with me, my dear? Because I want to give you a handsome husband, heh? (*Freyde-Altele looks at Serkele and laughs.*)

SERKELE. Nu, why don't you answer? Have you gone mute, heh?

FREYDE-ALTELE. What do I need a bridegroom for? I do not need anyone.

REB YOYKHENEN. Don't talk like a child, my dear, because I hate it when people talk foolishness! What's with this "What do I need a bridegroom for?" Let me tell you something, you've already reached the age of . . .

SERKELE. Thirteen, may she live and be well.

REB YOYKHENEN. Nu, whatever you say. Listen, I have a very fine husband for you—you'll like him.

FREYDE-ALTELE. As long as he pleases my Mommy, I'll be happy too. (*She starts to run out.*)

REB YOYKHENEN. (*Grabs her by the hand.*) Nu, where are you running? Just come here; I'm not the one getting married. You see, when you talk like a smart girl, that's what I love. Believe me, I'm talking here about a husband who's very handsome, a good-looking creature, a big shot among big shots, has plenty of money of his own, is good and pious, behaves just as God commands—and, my child, you know him too.

FREYDE-ALTELE. I? I know him too?

SERKELE. Yes, you know him, dear heart! You know him very well—you know Reb Gavriel Hendler?

FREYDE-ALTELE. (*Acts embarrassed.*) *Ja, ich ken ihm, ich habe ihm hierbei amal gesehn.*[15]

REB YOYKHENEN. Nu, do you want him for a husband?

FREYDE-ALTELE. (*Laughs.*) *Ich habe ja schon einmal gesagt:*[16] if my Mommy likes him, then I'm happy too. (*She runs out.*)

---

15. German, "Yes, I know him, I've seen him here once."

16. German, "I've already said it once."

Scene 4

SERKELE. That's how it always goes. Everyone depends on me: my husband and my daughter, neither makes a move without me. Believe me, it's too heavy a burden to have all that weight on my shoulders.

REB YOYKHENEN. Nu, let me tell you something: who else can they depend on?

SERKELE. Eh! What do you know, my dear Reb Yoykhenen? All day long it's nothing but "Go to my wife, go to my *mamenyu*, go to my aunt, go to the mistress, go to Serkele!" I don't know—even someone made of iron couldn't stand it. Oy, I feel faint! But besides all that, every time another accursed Thursday rolls around, the paupers start streaming in. I tell you, the door gets no rest, and my mouth actually hurts from telling everyone individually: "Please don't be offended, and go in good health." His poor relatives are enough of a burden. I've got a big girl on my hands who's absolutely worthless, and eats me out of house and home, the devil knows why, just as if she were the breadwinner around here. Oy, vey, I feel faint!

REB YOYKHENEN. Who can you possibly mean?

SERKELE. What a question! Hinde, my Dovid's little daughter; what that girl costs me!

REB YOYKHENEN. And what she will cost you yet! Of course you're absolutely right. After all, let me tell you something—there's no such thing as a Jewish nunnery, so some day you'll have to make her a wedding.

SERKELE. Who, me? Ach, why is that? If I knew she would stay unmarried 'til her hair turns gray, it wouldn't bother me a bit. Oy, I feel faint! What's the matter, is she ill? Let her go get a job.

REB YOYKHENEN. Oy! What are you saying? You're a very wealthy lady, after all—may you live to be a hundred and twenty—and she's your brother's only daughter! I'm telling you, that's not how to do things; what will people say?

SERKELE. What, you think I have something to be ashamed of? May God strike me down in my youth if that bothers me at all. Well, let me just think: that can't do any harm to a match for my Altele, since I'm giving her a dowry of eight hundred silver rubles and jewelry and clothes, linens and bedding, on top of other stuff, and board, plus little presents and various other things. In other words, I'm offering a fortune. And I don't have to tell you what a fine family line she comes from, and who I am—oy, I feel faint. Nu, so tell me, may you be well, what harm could it do if the whole world knew that Hinde was somebody's servant?

REB YOYKHENEN. Maybe you're right. After all, different people reach different conclusions, and you don't know where the shoe pinches until you try it on. But tell me, Serkele, what's this? You're offering only eight hundred rubles?

SERKELE. What? Isn't that enough? I have to make ends meet, you know. It seems to me that I'm giving beyond my means. These days, who gives their child more than that?

REB YOYKHENEN. Oy, please don't be offended, but you ask who gives more? You know, you're as rich as Shifra Balban, and she is offering her daughter fifteen hundred rubles; and between you and me— even though I was the matchmaker—with whom did she make the match? With an ulcer.

SERKELE. Who? Shifra the Pauperess is offering fifteen hundred rubles? (*She pretends to laugh.*) Ha ha ha, it's so sad I'm laughing, oy, I feel faint! Will she pay up, though? You know, that's how people are: marry off their children, promise mountains of gold, sign ironclad papers, and when it comes time to pay, there's no one home.

REB YOYKHENEN. Eh, what are you saying? Shifra Balban is a very wealthy woman; she made a huge profit on a horse trade, and a week or two ago, her husband won sixteen thousand Rhenish dollars in the lottery.

SERKELE. (*Standing up.*) What? Shifra?! Sixteen thousand? That's how it is in this crazy world: the lousiest cur gets the best bone, oy, I feel faint! Sixteen thousand? The Devil take her father's bones.

REB YOYKHENEN. Well, it doesn't matter, what are we going on about eight hundred rubles for? You'll change the terms a little, you'll make it better; let's just take care of this.

SERKELE. How much does he have of his own, huh?

REB YOYKHENEN. Him? What a question! His entire fortune; he's very wealthy, you know. He earns, well, a lot more, although they say he's worth two thousand Rhenish dollars. I know all about it. I myself have seen a whole wad of banknotes at his house. I'm telling you, seeing that absolutely killed me. Not to mention his business skill. You think he's anything to sneeze at as a breadwinner? The transactions that man handles! May the evil eye not strike—that's what I call a good provider.

SERKELE. Believe me, my dear Reb Yoykhenen, the only things that matter to me are that my Altele, may she enjoy good health, won't have to live in her in-laws' house and won't have twenty people bossing her around. But those questions aside, I don't know that he's such a great bargain. I don't see that he's got any money lying around. Now and then when he's short of cash, I'm the first one he comes to for a loan.

REB YOYKHENEN. Nu, let me tell you something: what merchant isn't strapped for cash sometimes and is forced to borrow? But you can demand that he settle his debt to you before the marriage contract is signed.

SERKELE. Now that's a different story. Let him settle up at the contract signing—yes, I insist on that. And you know what? When the time comes to sign, maybe I'll also bend and throw in another two hundred rubles.

REB YOYKHENEN. Now you're talking! You say a thousand, I say twelve hundred. Let me tell you something: no match falls through because of money. A hundred rubles more, a hundred rubles less—it'll be alright. But there's just one thing I would like.

SERKELE. And what might that be?

REB YOYKHENEN. I would like to see to it that the future bride and groom get together at some point before the engagement is announced and get acquainted a little, have a chance to talk.

SERKELE. You know what? I'll send him an invitation to dinner today— in any case he comes here every day, and you can talk about anything over a meal; and we can sign the contract this very evening— I hate when things get dragged out for years on end.

REB YOYKHENEN. Of course you're absolutely right, because first of all, you can snap him up right away—he's being sought after for about twenty matches, so you can seal the deal—and besides, let me tell you, a person doesn't live forever.

SERKELE. Well, it's in His hands.

REB YOYKHENEN. I'll have my work cut out for me with that one, believe me; I'll have a few more gray hairs before I straighten everything out with him; but after all, as they say, that's why I'm a matchmaker. (*He gets up.*) Nu, let me tell you something: have a good day and be well.

SERKELE. Go in good health, and don't be a stranger. (*Exit Reb Yoykhenen. Serkele accompanies him to the door.*)

Scene 5

SERKELE. What do I know? Maybe that's the right way. You never know how something will turn out, but I'm starting to think this isn't so bad—he's rich, that's true; he has a few rubles. I just hope that Altele will have the sense to know what to do. She needs to take charge from the word go and not let him come to his senses, just like I did with my Moyshe, and then, God willing, she'll be successful with him. I've got to see that debt cleared, though; it has to be paid off. And he's certainly a nice-looking young man, and not old-fashioned either. (*Looks at herself in the mirror.*) Heh? What more do I need? (*Thinking quietly for a moment.*) I wish my Moyshe would travel to the spas. I just don't know what to do with him. He doesn't sleep at night, but walks around and talks to himself like a lunatic. I swear, it's a miracle that no one hears him. The Devil knows why he insists on dredging up ancient history! (*Quiet for a moment.*) The whole business, he says, is my fault! So tell me, who's asking him? If you can't stand the smell of gunpowder, then stay off the battlefield. (*Stamps her foot.*) Enough! Over and done with—who can ask me now where I got so much money? Even in a hundred years, who could figure out that the whole will was a fraud? Dead and buried. If I hadn't done it, someone else would have gotten the idea, and what would have happened then? I, and my husband and child, would have died of hunger, and would have had to look on while somebody else took advantage of my dear brother's hard-earned money, which the poor thing sweated and toiled for. And besides—who knows?—even if he had lived, then he wouldn't have gotten angry, God forbid, over the whole business, since could anyone possibly be closer to you than a sister? (*Thinks quietly.*) The only question is, is he dead? (*Quietly pensive; then she jumps.*) But why am I going over all this for nothing? Reb Shmuel Shrayber himself read in the newspaper at the time that the ship—I forget what it was called—that Dovid took to America had sunk. (*She sees Chaim approaching.*) Aha! Who's coming? Chaim! Another fool who's good for nothing—except sending to get the Angel of Death.

Scene 6

SERKELE. Well? What did Redlekh say? Will he come? Oy, I feel faint! Did you tell him that I'm ill?

CHAIM. Did I tell him?! What good does that do, though? When you really need the worm, he's suddenly too good for you.

SERKELE. What? He doesn't want to come?

CHAIM. He said that he can't cure your disease. What a doctor! Goes to school such a long time and still doesn't know anything.

SERKELE. But he's still going to come, *nicht wahr?*

CHAIM. Not a chance! He won't come. He said he doesn't want to come, and that I should go call on someone else. Look across the road there, my dear mistress: at Reb Fishl's place, that's where the old doctor lives—some people say he's a great expert. I stopped to see him on the way back and told him that you asked whether he would please come and pay you a visit—wait, don't say anything yet—he said that he'll be right over. Didn't I do good?

SERKELE. What? That old horse? You can both go to hell together—I don't know which of you is more useless! Who asked you to call on him, ha?

CHAIM. I don't know. I thought a doctor is a doctor—did I know you're in love with Redlekh?

SERKELE. What? I'm in love with Redlekh? You villain! May the evil spirits plague your father! I'm in love with Redlekh? You scoundrel! I swear, it's a good thing no one can hear my troubles! Just wait, you'll rue the day you were born, oy, I feel faint!

CHAIM. Did I say you're in love with him? It speaks for itself—if you don't want anyone but Redlekh, then . . .

SERKELE. (*Smacks him.*) There! How's that for love—may the evil spirits plague your father and your mother! Now go this minute and tell the old horse not to come. You and he both are a thousand times worthless! Go, I tell you!

CHAIM. (*Rubbing his cheek and crying as he goes.*) Does nothing the whole damn day but scream and smack. She's not too faint for that. (*Exits.*)

SERKELE. It's a good thing he told me beforehand that he called on the old man. (*Laughs hysterically.*) Ha ha ha! That would have been nice: for the doctor to come over, with me walking around as healthy as a giant! But how do you like that rogue, that Redlekh? He doesn't want to come? He can't cure me? He's such a scoundrel that he doesn't see how honored he should be that I call for him? (*Looks at herself in the mirror.*) Aren't I a pretty little wife, then? What's wrong with me, ha? (*She gets angry.*) I'll teach him some manners, that worm! He can't cure me! Wait, just wait, I'll teach you what curing is so you won't know what hit you! That pauper! That torn and tattered German! What's the matter? So he has a pretty face—that means he can order me to go call on someone else? Just wait, there are other fish in the sea, but I'll remember you. I'll show you who's boss. (*She yells.*) Chava! Chava! Oy, I feel faint!

Scene 7

SERKELE. I have to shout for her a hundred times before she moves, that slut! (*Chava enters.*) Go over to Reb Gavriel's and tell him that he is most warmly invited to breakfast today, you hear? Go and don't dilly dally, because you still have three other errands to do.

CHAVA. My dear mistress, I have no time at all—the soup will boil over while I'm out. Send Chaim instead.

SERKELE. That's how it is every time: I tell her to go, and she says, "Send Chaim." Why are you afraid to go? He'll bite off a piece of you? Just look at her, the royal pain—she thinks she really *is* royalty, the bitch!

CHAVA. Nu, okay, so I'm a bitch—don't marry me, then. But tell me something, please: if I'm such a bitch, why does he bother me with all sorts of things whenever he passes through the kitchen?

SERKELE. Look at the mouth on this scurvy girl! I just hope your mother will see you suffering—so who am I supposed to send for him? Oy, I feel faint! Is it possible to endure this? I swear, it's really true what they say: you mustn't give money to an ugly girl or you'll live to regret it. She thinks I have strength to spare, so I can squander my health on squabbling with her. Oy, I feel faint!

Scene 8

CHAIM. (*Stands by the door crying, and wipes his eyes with his sleeve.*)

SERKELE. Nu? Were you there?

CHAIM. Yes.

SERKELE. Nu? What was his answer?

CHAIM. What should his answer have been if he wasn't home?

SERKELE. So were you too sick to tell his servant?

CHAIM. But I did tell him; he even answered that the doctor was already on his way here.

SERKELE. What? He's on his way here? (*Wrings her hands and cries angrily.*) Oy, I'm cursed! What will I do now? Where do I begin? I hope you die an unnatural death! What on Earth am I supposed to do? (*Runs to the table, grabs a knife, and runs with it towards Chaim.*) Get out of my sight, you bastard, before I kill you!

CHAIM. (*Runs, hides behind Chava and screams.*) Help! Oh my God! Chava dear! Help!

CHAVA. (*Runs around the room with Chaim clinging to her skirt and running behind her, and Serkele pulling both of them.*)

Chaim and *Chava*. Help! Save us! Help! (*They trip over a chair and fall to the ground.*)

Scene 9

(*Reb Moyshe, Hinde, and Freyde-Altele come from the door on the right. The doctor enters from the door that goes to the street. When Serkele sees them entering, she pretends to swoon, falling to the floor in a faint. Everyone runs to her aid. Chava fans her with a handkerchief, while Chaim does so with his shirttails.*)

FREYDE-ALTELE (*Cries.*) Mommy! My dear Mommy!

DOCTOR. Just be calm; bring wine here, wine.

FREYDE-ALTELE. Right away, Herr Doktor! (*She charmingly curtseys to him.*) I shall bring it from the cellar straightaway.

DOCTOR. *Lassen sie,*[17] that will take too long. Just give her some cold water or a bit of vinegar. (*Hinde grabs a glass of water and sprinkles some in Serkele's face.*) *Recht so, mein kind.*[18] You have done well.

SERKELE. (*Pretends to come to a little and cries.*) Oy vey, I feel faint!

HINDE. Thank God! She's alive! She's alive!

REB MOYSHE. (*Aside.*) I always knew that she would come to a bad end. God, blessed be His name, knows what He is doing! (*Aloud to Chava.*) What on Earth happened here?

CHAVA. I have no idea. She was talking to Chaim, and then got angry as always, and ran to him with a knife, screaming that she was going to kill him. So he, poor thing, hid behind me, so she ran to *me* with the knife in her hand, and both of us tried to run away, and she suddenly got so angry that she fell into a faint.

CHAIM. Eh, my dear master! She doesn't know the story from the beginning. She sent me to get . . .

SERKELE. (*Suddenly screams very loud.*) Oy, vey! You scoundrels! Stop gabbing, or I'll faint again!

DOCTOR. (*Sits next to Serkele and takes her pulse. Says quietly to himself.*) This is a remarkable fainting spell: her pulse is completely regular. (*Aloud to Serkele.*) Well? How are you feeling now? *Ist es ihnen besser?*[19]

SERKELE. My dear Lord! Save me! Help! I am lost!

DOCTOR. There, there, do not worry, it will be alright. Bring her to bed; she must have had something terrible to eat or drink.

FREYDE-ALTELE. (*Says charmingly.*) *Nein, Herr Doktor!* She only had two cups of coffee and three buttered rolls for breakfast; other than that, she has not had a thing.

HINDE. (*To Freyde-Altele.*) Freyde-Alte-dear! Give me the keys; I'll give Auntie some eau de cologne.

FREYDE-ALTELE. (*Angrily whispers to Hinde.*) You're too sick to call me Friederika? (*Aloud.*) To tell you the truth, I have only a tiny bit, and I need that for myself today, since my bridegroom will be coming.

DOCTOR. (*Getting up out of his chair.*) Well, just bring her to bed, and please bring me a pen and paper. Everything will be fine. (*Hinde and Chava help Serkele sit up.*)

SERKELE. Oy vey! Oy vey! Oy vey, I feel faint! (*Hinde and Chava bring Serkele into her bedroom. Chaim looks for a pen and paper.*)

---

17. German, "Let it be."

18. German, "Good, my child."

19. German, "Are you feeling better?"

Scene 10

YERAKHMIEL. (*Enters from the door leading to the street, carrying a jug. He removes his hat and says in a loud voice.*) My ma-ma-ma-ma-master! (*Everyone shushes him. Freyde-Altele goes to Yerakhmiel and whispers something in his ear. Chaim brings the doctor a pen and paper.*)

DOCTOR. Well? *Wo ist di dinte?*[20]

CHAIM. Milord only asked for pen and paper.

DOCTOR. Well bring me ink as well.

FREYDE-ALTELE. (*Looking at herself in the mirror.*) Oh, look at me! My curls are a mess! (*Fixes her curls in the mirror.*) I gave myself quite a fright.

CHAIM. (*Brings an inkpot with some sand.*) Here is some ink and sand for milord.

DOCTOR. Nu, nu, nu, very good. (*Sits down and writes.*)

REB MOYSHE. (*Sighs very loudly.*) Oy! I hope it will turn out alright!

DOCTOR. But why, my dear Herr Danziger, so downtrodden? Do not worry yourself, your wife is already better; it was just a little fit of hysteria. But can you tell me what the problem was before—why she had me summoned?

REB MOYSHE. There was nothing wrong with her—she's just very evil and very worthless. God knows what her bad behavior will bring her one day.

DOCTOR. There, there, calm yourself, *mein lieber Herr Danziger, es wird schon alles gut,*[21] it will be alright. Her physical condition is not bad, I assure you, she is strong enough.

CHAIM. Yes, lord Doctor! She gave me quite a smack before—I actually saw stars! (*Freyde-Altele pokes him to make him shut up.*)

DOCTOR. (*Gets up and gives Reb Moyshe the prescription.*) Send this to the apothecary, and he will send a bottle here. Give her two tablespoons from it every two hours. When the bottle is empty, send for me again. Above all, she should keep warm, stay in her room, eat nothing but soup, and stop getting worked up and shouting. Take me to her one more time; I shall tell her that myself. *Kommen sie.*[22] (*He goes with Reb Moyshe to Serkele's room.*)

CHAIM. (*Follows them, then points at one palm, then at the other.*) When hair starts growing here, that's the day she'll obey everything that old shoe says. Just wait 'til he leaves—then she'll be barking her orders again. (*Goes into the bedroom.*)

---

20. German, "Where is the ink?"

21. German, "My dear Herr Danziger, it will be alright."

22. German, "Come."

Scene 11

FREYDE-ALTELE. (*Runs toward Yerakhmiel.*) Now speak: what do you want?

YERAKHMIEL. Ma-ma-ma-my master se-se-sent me with a-a-a note.

FREYDE-ALTELE. For whom?

YERAKHMIEL. For whom? F-f-f-for you.

FREYDE-ALTELE. (*Pretends not to understand.*) For whom, did you say?

YERAKHMIEL. A-a-again for whom—f-f-f-for you.

FREYDE-ALTELE. (*Angrily.*) What a scoundrel you are! Well, so who am I? What's my name, then?

YERAKHMIEL. You're name is F-f-f-freyde-Alte.

FREYDE-ALTELE. No, my name is Fräulein Friederika Danziger.

YERAKHMIEL. Well, I don't ha-ha-have any n-n-note for you at all. My ma-master told me to g-g-give the note t-to Freyde-Alte. (*Starts to go.*)

FREYDE-ALTELE. (*Not letting him leave.*) But come here, the letter is indeed intended for me. Show it to me!

YERAKHMIEL. (*Hiding the note in his pocket.*) Why should I?

FREYDE-ALTELE. You just told me yourself that you have a letter for me. Nu, *so gib es hier.*[23]

YERAKHMIEL. (*Turns back around.*) Nu, t-t-tell me, what's your name?

FREYDE-ALTELE. Well I'm also called Freyde-Altele—what an idiot!

YERAKHMIEL. (*Pretending not to understand.*) What? Freyde-A-a-altele is an idiot? Th-that doesn't m-matter to me at all; I still have to g-give the letter to h-her.

FREYDE-ALTELE. Nu, *so gib schon einmal hier.*[24] I'm telling you that my name is Freyde-Altele, but I'm also called Fräulein Friederika Danziger.

YERAKHMIEL. She s-s-seems to have s-s-seven names, j-j-just like Jethro in the Bible.[25] (*He searches in his pocket.*) Yes, and n-n-nothing f-f-for my trouble?

FREYDE-ALTELE. (*Gives him money.*) There, now give me the letter.

YERAKHMIEL. (*First puts the money in his pocket, then gives her the letter.*) Th-th-there's the letter, and give me a-a-an answer right away.

FREYDE-ALTELE. (*Reads the letter silently, then says.*) Tell Herr Hendler . . .

YERAKHMIEL. (*Interrupting.*) Y-you mean my ma-ma-master?

FREYDE-ALTELE. Yes. Tell him that everything is fine, thank God. Reb Yoykhenen has been here, my mother gave him all the right answers,

---

23. German, "Give it here."

24. German, "Give it here already."

25. According to the midrash (commentary on the Bible), Jethro was known by seven different names. See Exodus Rabbah 27:8.

and tell him we also desire that he not go away, for my mother wishes to invite him to dinner, and this evening the desired event will be assured.

YERAKHMIEL. (*Hesitates a moment.*) It would be b-b-better if you gave me a-a-a note.

FREYDE-ALTELE. But it's impossible for me to write right now.

YERAKHMIEL. (*Laughs.*) Heh-heh-heh, and I kn-know why.

FREYDE-ALTELE. Tell me, why do you think?

YERAKHMIEL. (*Taking the money out of his pocket and showing her.*) Because you h-hold on to your money a l-little too tightly.

FREYDE-ALTELE. You impertinent thing! Well, just wait, and I will write. (*Sits down at the desk and writes.*)

YERAKHMIEL. (*Stands on tiptoe and watches her write; he makes fun of her.*) H-h-hoo-ha! My goodness, w-w-what skillful handwriting, all sticks and pokers!

FREYDE-ALTELE. (*Folds the letter and gives it to Yerakhmiel.*) Here you have my answer, and tell Herr Hendler that he dines with us today, he must not go away.

YERAKHMIEL. A-a-and I should s-s-stay home a-and ha-have nothing t-to eat?

FREYDE-ALTELE. Just take it and go; that is no concern of mine.

YERAKHMIEL. B-b-but it's a concern of m-mine, s-so I'm not t-taking th-the letter.

FREYDE-ALTELE. All right, come with your master as well, but just take it.

YERAKHMIEL. Attagirl, you're r-really a good girl, and I l-love you too. (*Takes the letter and exits.*)

FREYDE-ALTELE. What a good-for-nothing! After the wedding he must be sent packing, and I will have only Christian servants, not a single Jew! That one treated me as if we were slopping the hogs together! Ach, what a stupid fellow! I will complain about him to my bride-groom. And I will put this letter away with the other things that he has sent me. (*Gives the letter a kiss and runs out.*)

The curtain falls.

ACT III

The same room as in the first act.

Scene 1

REB GAVRIEL. (*Lies on the sofa half-dressed.*) I hope I can figure out how to pay off this debt. This opens up a whole new world for me. Reb Moyshe Danziger's son-in-law! Who would have ever believed it? I'm going to lead all of them around by the nose. True, the father-in-law is nothing but a common run-of-the-mill boor, who doesn't know his ass from his elbow—to him, I'll be the rabbi. And I'll run such rings around my mother-in-law that she won't know which way is up. And my bride, the Fräulein Freidrika, all I've got to do is tell her just once how pretty she is, and she's completely sold. Gavriel! You're on fire, you're well on your way to the top! (*Rests for a moment.*) Yes, everything's going perfectly, but what am I going to do about the damn payment? Where am I going to get a thousand big ones? And that wonderful woman insists that I settle my debt directly with her before anyone signs anything. What am I going to do now? (*Gets up from the sofa and walks up and down the room twice, thinking.*) Maybe I should tell her that I can't pay it off now, because all my money's tied up in business deals—no, Serkele's not one of those dime-a-dozen fools; she'll just say (*Imitating Serkele.*) "Oy, I feel faint! My Altele, she should live and be healthy, is only thirteen years old; she can stand to wait a little bit, until you collect your money"—and then what? I'm afraid she'll have to wait a pretty long time. (*Thinks a little more.*) Maybe I should let Alte in on the secret that I don't have any money? Well, then what? Once a fool throws a stone into a garden, even ten sages can't get it out. Altele will tell Mamaleh right away, and Mamaleh will tell Papaleh, and then Gavrieleh will be thrown out into the streeteleh! (*Thinks some more and then, with a cry.*) Wait, that's it! But what does that help? (*Thinks further, then suddenly he slaps himself on the head and speaks more quietly.*) Aha! If this will save me— what am I saying? This must save me—need shatters even iron, as they say. (*Walks around the room, gesturing with his hands as if he were explaining something. Afterwards says very slowly.*) Listen, Gavriel, this sounds good to you. I'm telling you, Gavriel, it's good—better than good! You're a fine young man! (*Rests a moment.*) I swear, if I could only reach, I'd give myself a big kiss on the cheek! (*Looks in all of the corners.*) If only I knew where they kept it! Everyone has gone off to take a nap after lunch. Now's the time to strike, that's for sure. (*He goes to the door stage right and listens; goes to the door leading out to the street and bolts it; then goes to the dresser and sees if it's locked.*) Damn, locked. (*Goes to the cupboard and tries it as well.*) Awful! Also locked! (*Points to Serkele's bedroom.*) If only I knew for sure that no one would arrive, I'd clean the place out for Passover.[26] Nothing ventured,

---

26. The extremely strict laws regulating what food can be eaten on Passover call for a thorough cleaning out of all leavened bread and other forbidden products before the holiday begins. On the night before the first Seder, the family checks every corner of the house for any remaining crumbs, which are collected and burned.

nothing gained . . . (*Starts toward the bedroom and listens.*) I think someone's coming. (*Gets angry and quickly throws himself down on the sofa.*) Damn it!

Scene 2

CHAIM. You're not sleeping, my dear Reb Gavriel.

REB GAVRIEL. (*Angrily.*) No, I can't sleep.

CHAIM. (*Smiling.*) It's the same with me; you're distracted by Frieda and I can't stop thinking about Chava.

REB GAVRIEL. Is that so, boy? You and Chava—I had no idea you were such a young stallion! I swear!

CHAIM. (*Proudly.*) Well, what did you expect?

REB GAVRIEL. So what does Chava have to say about it?

CHAIM. Don't ask. Sometimes she says one thing and other times another—it's like she's crazy. I'll tell you, just today we fought over some little thing, because she was in one of her crazy moods—I have no idea what's going on with her. She's screaming, all of a sudden I'm a fool, an idiot, a no-goodnik, even though I know—from personal experience—that none of that's true. The long and the short of it is, even though she likes me, she blames me for everything.

REB GAVRIEL. And you keep quiet, you fool?

CHAIM. The thing is, I'm not sure myself what's going on with me. I have this terrible character flaw—it won't let me get angry with her, even once. It must be some sort of spell. Maybe it's a spell. And then again, whenever it occurs to her, she finds me and comes over to me with all of her sweet talk, saying, "Chaim my dear! I want to ask you something since you're such a fine young man . . . do thus-and-such for me, since you know how much I love you." Nu, you can't even imagine how that paralyzes me. And who could describe how when she makes one of her little graceful gestures and strokes my cheek— oy, vey! It almost drives me crazy; I can't sleep and I toss and turn the whole night long, and even in my dreams it always seems to me as if Chava is talking to me, murmuring to me . . .

REB GAVRIEL. But tell me, what is it that you find so attractive about that ugly maid?

CHAIM. Who? Chava? Ay! What are you talking about? Chava ugly? You'll have to pardon me for saying so, but you have no taste. Chava ugly?? Just look at her with my eyes. I think she's even prettier than . . . well, I mean, let me just put it this way, there isn't anyone prettier than Chava. But what I wanted to tell you in the first place is that you don't know her as well as I do—that's clear from what you said.

REB GAVRIEL. What on Earth has come over you, that you think Chava is so pretty? Well, I guess that's one way to get yourself a pretty wife. What difference do all these stories make? If she really doesn't like you, then she'll find someone else quickly enough, and you'll be twisting in the wind.

CHAIM. (*Clutching his head in both hands.*) Oy, vey! God should protect and preserve me! Chava with someone else? No, it can't be—it mustn't be! I would rather go on the road to find work, I'd rather go begging from door to door—anything, but I'll never let her do that.

REB GAVRIEL. Well, what sort of advice do you want then, Chaim?

CHAIM. Look, my dear, Reb Gavriel . . . (*He scratches himself behind the ear and says.*) I actually came here to ask you—well, I can see that you are going to become our young master, and I know that whatever you—God should grant you long life—whatever you say, the master, the mistress, and Altele—may they all stay strong and healthy—will second with a healthy "Amen"—so because of that I wanted to ask you . . . (*Kisses his hand.*) You see, I am, as you can see, a poor young man—and so I wanted to ask you if you would keep me, a poor young man, in mind . . . I know that you are a good man, and so I wanted to ask you if you would make the match between me and Chava—you'll see that I'll never forget it as long as I live.

REB GAVRIEL. So, young man! That's what you were getting at? If only you had just told me what you meant. Have no fear, it'll all work out just fine. (*He claps him on the shoulder.*) Don't worry, Chaim! Let us just get married, and then you'll see what I can do. Just leave it all to me, and I tell you, Chava is already your bride, so sleep soundly.

CHAIM. (*Cries and kisses Reb Gavriel's hand.*) Oy, my dearest Reb Gavriel! You've made me a new man, better than God Himself could have! I don't know how I can possibly repay you! God, blessed be He, will surely pay you back double for what you've done for me, a poor young man.

REB GAVRIEL. Nu, nu, stop crying already, it's not right for a bridegroom to cry. Go already, stop being foolish, just have faith in me and you'll see that everything is going to turn out well, and you'll get a very nice wedding present from me into the bargain.

CHAIM. Oy, you'll see how much faith I'll have in you—I'll listen to everything you say!

REB GAVRIEL. (*Suddenly gives himself a slap, as if he was just reminded of something.*) Yes, there was something I was going to say to you, that's right—yes, why is the mistress going around today without her kerchief?

CHAIM. You don't know? Today's the date her brother died.

REB GAVRIEL. The date her brother died? This is the first I've heard of it. Her brother's *yortsayt*? You hear about having *yortsayt* for a father or a mother, but suddenly to have a *yortsayt* for a brother? And also, just because you have *yortsayt* you go around without a kerchief?

CHAIM. I'll explain everything. She only had one brother. He was very rich, and a fine person to boot. She loved him as much as she loved life. Well, in the meantime it happened that he died on a trip somewhere, and he left his entire property to her. So she took an oath that on the day of his *yortsayt* she would go without her kerchief and not wear a single piece of jewelry.

REB GAVRIEL. And she must have quite a bit of jewelry, *nicht wahr*?

CHAIM. Oy, oy, oy! Does she have a lot of jewelry! You know—she has a full, and I do mean full, little trunk with pearls, diamonds, necklaces, medallions, brooches, and besides her own jewelry she has a lot that people have pawned to her.

REB GAVRIEL. I don't understand—how can someone hide so much jewelry?

CHAIM. Oh, I should explain, the trunk is actually quite small, but it's very full, and she always keeps it right by her in her bedroom at the head of her bed, and she always has the key with her and doesn't trust anyone in the world with it.

REB GAVRIEL. Very wise of her, I must say! She truly is a great mistress. She's afraid of a thief, you see. Oh, I forgot the main thing I was going to ask—what time is it? Is it two o'clock already?

CHAIM. Ah, what are you talking about? The town clock struck three long ago.

REB GAVRIEL. What, it's already three? Ah! What should I do now? They're all still sleeping, and I really need to run and catch the mail coach, but I don't like to leave without saying goodbye. Now I'm the one who needs advice. What should I do now?

CHAIM. You know what, I'm not afraid of the mistress. Maybe I could run and try to catch the mail coach.

REB GAVRIEL. Oy, you really are a fine young man. You could do that for me.

CHAIM. But what will the mistress say about it?

REB GAVRIEL. Go on, fool! Since I'm sending you, she won't say a word about it, that's for sure.

CHAIM. It's not her words I'm afraid of; it's her . . . (*Illustrates how Serkele hits him.*)

REB GAVRIEL. Her blows? Go, already, go—if I'm sending you, you can go. I'll be responsible for you, don't you worry.

CHAIM. I'm asking you this way because you know her already: when she gets angry, she starts with the orders . . . (*Makes the same motions as before.*)

REB GAVRIEL. Nu, go already, go, it's getting late. *(Chaim puts on his shoes and exits. Reb Gavriel looks after him. Then:)* Thank God, I'm finally free of him again. But I've just learned something new—that you can learn things from a fool as well. It always used to puzzle me: why did God put fools on His earth? But now I see how right He was. God created fools so that wise men could do what they wanted with them. If the world were simply full of wise young men, I do believe they'd all die of hunger—and you, Gavriel, among them. It was beautiful how I squeezed a cure out of him for what ails me. *(Points out Serkele's bedroom.)* That's where the sleeping dog lies . . . *(Looks closer.)* Yep, the dog's there all right. *(Chaim returns and looks in all of the corners of the room, apparently searching for something.)* Well, what did you come back for? And what are you looking for? Why don't you go? It's getting late.

CHAIM. *(Walking around the room, searching as he speaks.)* Yes, I'll go right away, but just tell me this: what should I do when I get to the mail coach? Huh?

REB GAVRIEL. Look, in my hurry I completely forgot: you should ask them there if there's any mail for me.

CHAIM. *(Keeps searching and speaking.)* Yes, but who should I ask there? Heh?

REB GAVRIEL. What does that mean? You'll go to the postmaster, you'll take off your hat, and you'll ask if there is a letter for Gavriel Hendler. He will then tell you, right away, either yes or no. He's a perfectly nice man, don't worry. So go already, go quickly, because it's getting late.

CHAIM. *(Goes, talking quietly to himself.)* She's not in the front room. Not in the kitchen either. I really thought that she must have come in here. *(He exits through the middle door.)*

Scene 3

REB GAVRIEL. There's something I don't like about that guy, with his coming back and looking all around the room—could he have guessed something? Ah, who knows what the idiot was looking for. And even if he does arrive, it's also not such a big deal. I've just promised him Chava for a bride. Okay, Gavriel, get down to business. First, though, I should check to see if the family is still asleep. *(He goes over to the door stage right and listens.)* Like the dead! Now, if only my ancestors' merits stand me in good stead, everything will turn out all right. *(Very quickly, on tiptoe, he enters Serkele's bedroom but returns quickly.)* I think someone coughed. *(He listens again.)* Yep, they're sleeping like after a wedding—no catnaps there! Sleep on, sleep well—I'll be the one making the wedding. (*He enters the bedroom once more and spends several minutes there. He returns with the small trunk tucked under his arm.*) Here's the payment. I've got the last laugh. You've done good, Gavriel; you read the situation perfectly. (*He dresses himself very quickly, and tucks the trunk under his overcoat.*) Now—home! It's going to be something to see here when Serkele realizes that she's missing her little head pillow. "Oy!" she'll cry. (*He imitates Serkele.*) "Oy, vey, I feel faint!" But this time she'll have a reason to faint. (*He goes once more to the door stage right to see if they are sleeping, and then exits through the middle door.*)

Scene 4

REDLEKH. (*Enters through the middle door and looks around to all sides.*) No one here? What is that? Where is everyone? (*He looks through the door stage right.*) Sleeping? Well, that's certainly careless—the room empty, the doors open—it's simple for anyone who wants to come in and steal whatever they wish, while the house is sound asleep. Where is Hindele, then? It seems that I'll finally be able to surprise her because of the carelessness in the housekeeping. (*He goes up and down the room.*) Should I go in there and call for her? But then who'll stay here? No, it's better for me to stay here, and then when she arrives, I'll be waiting to give her a talking-to. (*He thinks a bit more.*) But no; the talking-to can wait; why should I make her archenemy Friederika happy? Yes, that woman is diligence herself! In the morning she doesn't feel like a lesson, so she decrees that I come here in the afternoon—and now she's in the middle of an afternoon nap! (*He laughs.*) Ha ha ha! Her mother is very diligent when it comes to her business affairs. She sent for me today, calling yet again because she was sick, terribly sick, and she wants me to come to her bedroom only at night and cure her, that is, fix her up some medicine. Yes, yes, I understand your schemes, you good-for-nothing woman, I know you too well, you disgrace to humanity, you're making a big mistake if you think I'm going to break my back for you. Aha! You're far off the mark, my dear Danziger! You haven't calculated correctly, and it won't work! (*He stays quiet a moment.*) Unfortunately I know all too well that this so-called saint will revenge herself on me—on my one and only lesson, my last means of support which alleviates my extraordinary need. I also feel strongly that I should no longer see my beloved Hindele. But better to go to an early grave always yearning for my heart's beloved, than succumb for a single minute to the base demands of a fallen woman. But wait! Someone's coming! Aha—my dear Hindele!

Scene 5

HINDE. See here, Herr Redlekh! Where is the new groom? Chaim just told me that he was here.

REDLEKH. I arrived not long ago to find the door open and no one in the room. Who is the fresh-baked bridegroom that you supposed would be here?

HINDE. Don't you know that our friend Friederika has been freshly baked today?

REDLEKH. Baked? Today? By whom, may I ask?

HINDE. With Reb Gavriel Hendler.

REDLEKH. So! With Reb Gavriel Hendler? I wish her well, if she's satisfied with that.

HINDE. Ah! She is eminently satisfied, since she has managed to get her parents to support her own desires in the matter.

REDLEKH. So? She loved him before? Well then, that is true happiness for her, for there are many, especially among our people, who find their parents' choice for them utterly distasteful, but in the end either shame or obedience leads them to marry a good-for-nothing of their parents' choosing, whether or not he has money.

HINDE. Wait a moment, Herr Redlekh! The case is difficult to apply to our Friederika, since the Almighty has provided her with good, loving parents.

REDLEKH. (*Laughs.*) Ha ha ha! Truly good loving parents?—oh, yes! Anyone who has ever entered this house and had the opportunity to conduct any business here can see that right away. (*Laughs.*) Ha ha ha! Truly good and loving parents—I've never heard anything less true.

HINDE. You laugh? If you'll excuse me, appearances usually deceive.

REDLEKH. Deceive? No, no, if they deceive, then my senses have completely deceived me—*nicht wahr*, dear Hindele? Your aunt is a good person? Does she treat you the way a good person would?

HINDE. I don't believe that I have anything to complain about as far as my aunt is concerned. Tell me, Herr Redlekh, have you ever heard me say a word against her?

REDLEKH. No, you've never complained. Fine, that is very noble on your part, but it's not as if it does you any good. On the contrary, it may even be making your situation much worse. Ah, I have often seen how they begrudge you even the little bit of food they give you for all your hard work, how contemptuously they treat you, and the dreadful sight has broken my heart.

HINDE. I thank you for your heartfelt concern, but I must ask you not to express your feelings about my beloved aunt in front of other people, because by doing so, you could cast not only her, but also me and yourself, in a bad light.

REDLEKH. Do not be the slightest bit worried, my dear Hindele! If you were going to be cast in a darker light, no matter how dark, it would all be dissipated by your glorious rays of light! As far as your aunt is concerned, people understand her character much better than you do! Ah, if you could only know everything that the people in the streets say, that this female Fury...

HINDE. (*Refuses to let him finish speaking and interrupts him. She covers her ears so that she cannot hear what Redlekh is saying.*) I don't wish to know about such things, I don't want to hear of them, my dear, good Herr Redlekh! I beg of you, approach me only with happy news, spare me these kinds of sentiments and allow me to think only good of my aunt, my second mother.

REDLEKH. (*Remains quiet for a moment and looks at Hinde with pity; afterward, he goes over to her and takes her by the hand.*) Godly maiden! Please forgive me if I have discomfited you; please believe me that it was only my love for you which has caused me to call attention to your lot. I see now how rude it was of me, who was so self-satisfied, to try and darken what is so good. (*Serkele slowly opens the door stage right and stealthily looks on.*) I beg of you, my dear Hindele, do not despise me. (*He kisses her hand.*) Here I await your pardon, like a poor servant.

HINDE. For heaven's sake, I beg of you (*Tries to extract her hand from his.*), let me go, I ask of you with my whole heart, let me go. (*To herself, quietly.*) I cannot bear it any longer! (*Aloud.*) Dear, good, precious Herr Redlekh! (*She gives him a kiss.*) Let me go! Allow me. (*She tears her hand away.*) I ask you from the bottom of my heart.

REDLEKH. Ah! Now my joy is boundless! Now let the whole world chase after diamonds, pearls, and whatever they call riches. (*He takes both of Hinde's hands.*) But if I have you, Hinde, then that is pearls, diamonds, and jewels enough!

Scene 6

(*Hinde and Redlekh separate with Serkele's entrance.*)

SERKELE. Well, well, this is something I never expected. Well done, Hindele! You're doing your dear departed father proud. Oh, nice!

Very nice! You've fallen so low that you pick the very day of Dovid's *yortsayt* to go fooling around with Germans.[27] Oy, I feel faint!

REDLEKH. (*Looking at Serkele as if she were joking.*) Don't get any more upset, my dear Frau Danziger—you are quite sick, very sick, and you can't bear it.

HINDE. (*Trying to prevent Redlekh from speaking any further.*) For heaven's sake, be silent, I beg of you.

SERKELE. (*With both hands clutching her sides.*) And who is this? You scoundrel! You villain! Do you think that I'm running some sort of meat market here? I'll teach you to respect your elders, you rascally German. What a scoundrel! The nerve he has, to come to visit me in my house and then incite the women in it to riot against me! (*Redlekh wants to respond, but Hinde pleadingly gestures to him to go. Serkele shouts loudly.*) Out of my house, you ragamuffin, you two-bit German! Out immediately, I say! If you ever dare to darken my door again, I'll rend you limb from limb, oy, I feel faint! (*Hinde takes Redlekh by the hand and guides him out through the middle door.*)

HINDE. If you want to please me, you'll go. (*Redlekh looks angrily at Serkele once more from the door and exits.*)

Scene 7

(*Hinde stands by the door, head bowed, and weeps.*)

SERKELE. Nu, nu, that I have lived to see this—who could have possibly expected that that *shlimazl* would cause me such embarrassment, such shame! You wait, just wait, I'm going to take care of you, believe me, you animal, may a blight plague you all your years and days. Oy, I feel faint! This is what I get for all the troubles, all the suffering, that I've had day and night for you! Ah, what does she have to worry about?—nu, and she wants a German, too . . .

HINDE. (*Crying.*) Auntie, auntie! I am . . . .

SERKELE. (*Interrupting her.*) Shut your trap, you wretch! While you still have a trap to shut! How much do you contribute to the household, huh? You're crying? You should be crying—you've had something to cry about for your whole life. Why were you ever brought into this world? Tell me, you, you disaster: how could you not have had God

---

27. "German" here refers not actually to someone from the German principalities, but a modernizing Jew, whose adoption of German modes of speech and dress led to that nickname by traditional Eastern European Jewry.

in your heart on this fine, bright day in my house, whose door gets no rest from all the strange men. To sit down with such a hooligan, such a good-for-nothing? God only knows what would have happened here, if something hadn't yanked me out of bed, oy, I feel faint! My ancestors were looking out for me!

HINDE. (*Goes to Serkele with a cry and tries to kiss her hand.*) Auntie! Wonderful auntie! Just hear me out . . . if only you'll listen . . . I'm . . . completely innocent.

SERKELE. (*Pushing Hinde away from her.*) Get away, you, you . . . Go kiss yourself in the you-know-where! (*She is so angry she can't speak.*)

HINDE. (*Falls on the ground and cries.*) Oy! May God forgive you for this!

Scene 8

(*Chava enters through the stage right door.*)

CHAVA. (*Running to Hinde.*) Oy vey iz mir, my sweet Hindele! (*She helps her up.*) Have you done something to yourself, my dear?

REB GAVRIEL. What's happened here?

SERKELE. Don't ask, everything's fine now. Everything's all better.

REB GAVRIEL. What's that? Did something happen?

SERKELE. Oy, I feel faint! Believe me, it's too much of a scandal and a shame even to repeat it! Just look at her—wouldn't you have sworn that she's pure as a baby's bottom? The hussy!

HINDE. Oy, Chava dear! Take me to my bed, I need to lie down, I'm completely overcome—oy!

CHAVA. (*Taking Hinde in her arms.*) God will make sure that all of this fighting turns out well. Everyone has to pick on the poor orphan.

SERKELE. Just look at the way she pretends to be so weak, the little bitch! Now she says she has no strength—just bring Redlekh back and she'll be strong enough. Oy, I feel faint!

CHAVA. (*Takes Hinde away very slowly and cries strongly.*) It's high time that God gets around to showing some of His mercy.

Scene 9

REB GAVRIEL. What happened here that has made you so angry? It's not like you to act like this. Just tell me—or is it too much of a secret to tell even me, ha?

SERKELE. A secret here, a secret there—why shouldn't I tell you so that you can have your share of heartbreak as well? Believe me, I have more than my share—but you're the only one; this is between us. You can't tell anyone else.

REB GAVRIEL. Don't worry about it for a minute, my mother-in-law-to-be. Who do I have tell? As far as I'm concerned, it's in one ear and out the other.

SERKELE. Listen up, then, and you'll hear quite a story. I was lying down earlier, sleeping—and it wasn't even a proper sleep, I was lying there and dozing, like someone in a daze, and there was something that wouldn't let me lie in one place, I'm telling you, it was like it uprooted me, and demanded that I go into the main room . . . but then I reminded myself that you were lying in here sleeping—

REB GAVRIEL. (*Standing as if he were slightly afraid; now he interrupts.*) Yes, you're right, I certainly was sleeping here, only I remembered that the mail coach was leaving here today at four o'clock, and I still needed to write a few letters, so I quickly ran away, it was my good luck that I remembered—so what happened then?

SERKELE. Meanwhile, I heard that good-for-nothing here, his nasty voice. And I'm telling you the truth, I was never able to stand him, and believe me, if he weren't teaching my dear Alte her French, I would never have let him inside this house, that's for sure. Oy, I feel faint!

REB GAVRIEL. You're talking about Redlekh? Aha! Aha! You must be correct. That sort of trickster can walk off with something of yours just like that, and all you can do is shout and moan.

SERKELE. Meanwhile I thought to myself, let me go see who he's talking to so seriously over there, and so I got up and went over to the door and very very quietly watched what was going on there. What can I tell you, my dear Reb Gavriel?—I thought I was going to sink right down into the earth. Just imagine that here (*She places Reb Gavriel where Redlekh was standing earlier.*) is where Reb Redlekh was standing and close to him was that animal (*She places herself near Reb Gavriel, where Hinde was standing earlier.*) and he is embracing her all the time and caressing her. (*She takes Reb Gavriel with both hands and caresses him.*) Afterward he even gives her a kiss—I just watch and keep quiet. (*She is silent a moment.*) He gives her another kiss—I watch, and keep quiet. (*She is quiet another moment.*) He gives her a third kiss then, you know what I'm saying? And she gives him one back. (*She is silent a moment and looks at Reb Gavriel. He turns away from Serkele and makes a face, as if he is disgusted by something.*) Well, I think that's the whole story! Now's the time for me to show myself, because I have, sad to say, seen that this was clearly leading up to bigger things. (*She claps a hand over her mouth.*) Oy, I feel faint! I come in suddenly—well, I made an end of him, he'll never darken my door again; she's still going around, that shameless bitch, and trying to persuade me that the whole thing—what I saw with my very own eyes—is all a lie, and wants to apologize for everything—

REB GAVRIEL. (*Interrupting her.*) So you went and smacked her—nu, so what? You didn't turn her into a thief just by hitting her. Besides, we have an old saying, written down by our sages in black and white: spare the rod and spoil the child.

SERKELE. Well, no, I haven't hit her, but it always drives me crazy the way she's always denying things I tell her; and also, why should my house, which has always had the reputation of being good and pious, become the topic of conversation among decent people because of such a worthless creature? So I barely touched her, and she fell down—so let her fall down; does she think that's going to bother me?

REB GAVRIEL. You know, my dearest mother-in-law, you should thank your lucky stars that he didn't take anything from you in the course of things, because I'll tell you the truth—I always used to marvel at how you let him and the troublemaker stay in the house by themselves. He used to march all over the place exactly like he owned it.

SERKELE. Who could have expected something like that all of a sudden from such a *shlimazl*?[28] He always used to drop by to visit my brother, may he rest in peace and may his merits intercede for us, and at first, when he began to drop by my place, he did act as if he were some sort of master. And I'll tell you the God's honest truth, I always thought that a young man like that could come in handy—that's why he taught French to Altele, may she live and be well.

REB GAVRIEL. Oh, I almost forgot the most important thing—is my bride around? I swear, a few hours away from her, and I'm already starting to yearn for her! I don't know how I'm ever going to be able to tear myself away from her!

SERKELE. Where do you need to go?

REB GAVRIEL. For the time being, nowhere, but being a merchant, you never know—today you're here, tomorrow there; wherever the business goes, you go.

SERKELE. Just wait, I'll be right in. (*She exits.*)

Scene 10

REB GAVRIEL. (*He looks after Serkele and makes fun of her.*) Serke-dear! Where's your kerchief, heh? (*Laughs heartily.*) Ha ha ha! She doesn't suspect a thing. The way it looks to me, Redlekh's going to be the one in hot water. It's a shame, that's for sure—he's not a bad kid. But what do

---

28. Yiddish, a luckless person.

I care? Whatever happens, happens. These days, it's every man for himself. Today I need to make a payment, and I have to think of something; it's true, the corpse is safely stowed away, but how to make sure I end up in the clear? . . . I'll have to make sure to hang the whole thing on the poor *shlimazl.* The jewels can't stay in the city once and for all, that's for sure. I won't wait too long to get rid of them, you can bet on that—because no matter how much I make on the deal, it'll pull me out of the poorhouse. (*Laughs.*) Ha ha ha! (*Grows quiet and thinks.*) I don't know what to make of this. I remember, once I studied in a *kheyder*[29] where the teacher used to hit me day and night; he really gave it to me, but only if I was asking for it. Nu, good, my dear rebbe, I'm sure asking for it now . . . Nowadays, everyone says, "Don't covet other people's things." Idiots! If it was mine already, what would I need to covet it for? (*Gestures sweepingly with his thumb, as if making a Talmudic argument.*) My Rebbe, Reb Treytl the Hunchback, certainly had the right idea when he said that one could only covet other people's things, and there's no need to think about it any further—because think all you want, I'm going to stay as deep in debt as I was before. The creditors are so obnoxious! Day and night, all you hear is their complaining. I wish they'd get tired of it for once! They're already running after me in the streets and are actually tearing the clothes off my back; that I should suddenly pay them back what I owed them—isn't that a scream? It's a paradox: if I had the money to pay them back, wouldn't I have given it back to them? And besides, if I had been careful with my money in the first place, I certainly would never have borrowed so heavily that no one would trust me enough to lend me any more money. (*Suddenly looks up and sees Freyde-Altele.*) Gavriel! Guard your tongue! (*Shuts his mouth with his hand and says quietly.*) Just look at the airs she puts on!

Scene 11

REB GAVRIEL. (*Crosses to Freyde-Altele and kisses her hand.*) Did your dear mother tell you I was longing for you?

FREYDE-ALTELE. Yes, she told me so—God be thanked that we have come so far.

REB GAVRIEL. Praise be to God! It should only go so far that we have nothing to worry about!

---

29. A traditional school for young Jewish boys, where only religious subjects were taught. Maskilic literature often depicts the *kheyder* as a benighted place where corporal punishment was common and unjustified.

FREYDE-ALTELE. Will you always love me the way you love me now?

REB GAVRIEL. (*Gives Freyde-Altele a kiss.*) What kind of a question are you asking me? You're my golden Altenyu!

FREYDE-ALTELE. I beg you, my dear bridegroom—do not call me by that diminutive Yiddish name any more! Pfui! How old do you think I am?

REB GAVRIEL. All I know is that you're still a youngish sort of girl, and since you are very delicate and tender, you're called "Altele," so that you should grow up big and strong, because there is good luck in the name.

FREYDE-ALTELE. I know quite well that I have been very delicately brought up, but I would still rather be called "Friederika," and you should always refer to me by that name.

REB GAVRIEL. (*Quietly, to himself.*) As far as I'm concerned, she can call herself Nouveau-rike! (*Aloud.*) Nu, my love, from now on I will always refer to you as my beloved, majestic Frieredike, alright?

FREYDE-ALTELE. But not Frieredike, Friederika, and you, you yourself must also have a proper German name, like, for example—(*She remains silent for a moment; they look at each other and think.*)

REB GAVRIEL. Maybe—Chapriel?

FREYDE-ALTELE. Ah, feh! That's not at all pretty!

REB GAVRIEL. Nu, no, no. (*They look at each other once more and think.*) Maybe . . . Havrilo?

FREYDE-ALTELE. Ah, no, that sounds like a name for our coal man. No, no, let me just think a little bit more, by myself. (*Thinks some more; he wraps himself in her shawl and laughs while she is quiet and makes fun of her; she whacks herself on the head, happily.*) Guess what! You know what would be good—Gabriele! That's a very nice name. Yes, yes, that's what it's got to be, Gabriele is what you'll be called! I saw that beautiful name in a book once. (*Takes his hand.*) My dear Gabriele Hendler!

REB GAVRIEL. (*Quietly.*) And a mazl tov to you on the name! (*He takes her hand.*) My golden Frire- no- Friederikenyu!

Scene 12

REB GAVRIEL. (*Runs across the stage to Yerakhmiel.*) What is it you want this time?

YERAKHMIEL. C-c-c-ome home with me f-f-f-f-for once! I-i-i-i-if you graft y-y-y-y-yourself onto something, i-i-it will be impossible for y-y-y-you to tear y-y-y-y-ourself away.

REB GAVRIEL. Nu, talk already. What do you want?

YERAKHMIEL. Rabbi Shmuel Se-se-se-secondhand is looking for y-y-y-y-you again.

REB GAVRIEL. Nu, for what? Has he brought me back my two hundred rubles? (*He motions to Yerakhmiel to say "Yes."*)

YERAKHMIEL. Ay, ay, just the opposite; he s-s-said that if y-y-you don't pay him the two hu-hu-hundred rubles today that y-y-you owe him, that he's going to g-g-g-go to the p-p-p-p . . .

REB GAVRIEL. (*Not letting him finish, and frantically gesturing to him to keep quiet.*) Go, go, I know already, I know already!

YERAKHMIEL. . . . . p-p-p-police and will f-f-f-force it out of y-y-y-you. (*Freyde-Altele laughs loudly.*)

REB GAVRIEL. (*Taking Yerakhmiel by the hand and throwing him out of the center door.*) Go to hell! (*Yerakhmiel exits.*)

Scene 13

REB GAVRIEL. That's the price of having servants—they get everything backward. Like here, poor Rabbi Shmuel had to come begging to me; he came to ask me not to call in the police if he wasn't able to pay me back the two hundred rubles today.

FREYDE-ALTELE. (*Laughs.*) Ha ha ha! I certainly love to listen to the funny way your servant talks. (*She imitates him.*) "To the p-p-p-police." Ha ha ha ha!

REB GAVRIEL. (*To himself.*) I'm going to have to find some way to shut that trap of hers right away—the fool could babble everything to her mother. (*Aloud.*) My golden Friederikenyu! I've brought you a gift, which I think you will enjoy greatly.

FREYDE-ALTELE. Ah, give it to me, I beg you.

REB GAVRIEL. (*Takes out a ring from his overcoat and gives it to her.*) Just give me your golden hand, and I will put it on myself. (*Freyde-Altele gives Reb Gavriel her hand, and he puts the ring on her finger.*) Oy, vey! How beautiful! Just look at how that ring sits there like that! Oy, vey! How magnificent!

FREYDE-ALTELE. (*Happily.*) Thank you. My dear Gabriele, what are these four stones?

REB GAVRIEL. Ah? Those—those are very precious stones. Really, aren't they pretty? Just look. That one—that one's a topaz. And those two there are carbuncles, and the others are pure abellines and premethysts! (*He leans away from Freyde-Altele, makes fun of her, and laughs.*)

FREYDE-ALTELE. My dear Gabriele, now you wait here, because I have something that I wish to give you as a present. (*She begins to leave.*)

REB GAVRIEL. (*Holds her and does not let her go.*) What's the hurry? There'll be plenty of time later for me to see it. I believe you; I'm sure it's beautiful.

FREYDE-ALTELE. Just wait here one minute, I'm just going to call my mother. (*Screams at the top of her lungs.*) Mamenyu! Mamenyu! Mamenyu!

Scene 14

SERKELE. What are you screaming like that for, my dear? What do you want, my sweet?

FREYDE-ALTELE. Just look, Mamenyu, at what my bridegroom has given to me! (*She shows her the ring.*) Now, Mamenyu! I ask you, show him what you have purchased for him.

SERKELE. (*Examines the ring and then gives it back to Freyde-Altele.*) Why do I have to go and look for it right now? It's all packed away with the jewelry. Oy, I feel faint!

FREYDE-ALTELE. (*Kisses Serkele on the hand.*) I beg you, Mamenyu, show him, show it to him right now!

REB GAVRIEL. (*A little bit confused.*) Ah, there's no need to bother my mother-in-law right now! I'll have plenty of time to see it later as well. Let it go for now; I know that there's no way that it could possibly disappoint me.

FREYDE-ALTELE. No, no, Mamenyu! Golden Mamenyu! Go, go, get it for him right away! (*She takes her in her arms and kisses her.*)

SERKELE. Nu, nu, I'm going already. (*She goes into her bedroom.*)

REB GAVRIEL. Damn! (*He remains still, confused and distracted.*)

FREYDE-ALTELE. Now you're going to see something beautiful, you won't be disappointed—I'm telling you, it's magnificent.

REB GAVRIEL. (*To himself.*) Bad news, Gavriel! But stiff upper lip!

SERKELE. (*Enters running from the bedroom, wringing her hands and screaming.*) Oy, vey! Gevald! I'm dying! Gevald!

FREYDE-ALTELE. (*Running to Serkele.*) What is it? (*She screams.*) Gevald!

REB GAVRIEL. (*Simultaneously; screams even louder.*) Mother in-law! What is it? What is it?

SERKELE. (*Screaming loudest of all.*) Help! Somebody's robbed me while I was gone! Oy, vey iz mir! Where should I start? What should I do? (*She screams even louder and begins to hit her head with both fists.*) Oy, vey, my things! All my hard work! Moyshe! Moyshe! We've been left complete paupers! Help! Help! My jewels! My jewels! Help!

REB GAVRIEL. For God's sake, just tell me, what are you missing? Did you fall? Don't scream like that! The jewelry—you're saying—it must be here, just look, search everywhere!

SERKELE. (*Rakes her face with both her hands; wrings her hands and hits herself on the head, runs about the room and screams, finally throwing herself onto the sofa.*) Everything's going black! The whole chest with all my jewelry is gone! Oy, my life is over! I'm dying! Oy! Search, children! Search! Oy, gevald! Come on, come on, it was over there, in the bedroom, in my bed, at the head! Come on, come on, let's look! Help! (*They all run into the bedroom.*)

The curtain falls.

Act 4

Scene 1

At night, in the same room as in act 1. A candle is burning on the table. Serkele and Reb Gavriel are seated at the table.

SERKELE. This city is for the dogs! Such a big city, and there's not a single person who can give me some advice!

REB GAVRIEL. Believe me, my dear in-law, if I know you, you don't need anyone's advice. Because in a matter like this, it's best to keep your own counsel. Because you—may you be well—know better than anyone where you kept the chest, and you know everyone in your household and all your visitors. It seems to me that with your good sense, you'll accomplish more than the rest of us put together.

SERKELE. Oy, I feel faint! You know, I was feeling anxious before, as if I am completely lost. Listen, my dear Reb Gavriel! I was thinking something completely different. My idea was that you should have a little chat with Redlekh. But understand: so clever, really clever, that he won't suspect a thing. That's right. But I don't have to teach you. And I'll go to Hinde myself, and find out a little more from her. And I'm telling you, my heart tells me that with God's help, we'll find out everything from them.

REB GAVRIEL. Now you see, my dear in-law—please don't be insulted— you're talking like a child. What do you think: Redlekh is some kind of fool? Redlekh won't immediately guess what I'm up to as soon as I tell him what I've come to him about? And above all, if he is a thief, won't he watch every word he says? Because of all that, I have a very different suggestion: for now you should let it be and not let people know that something is missing, and I assure you that in a little while, everything will turn out just fine. Because the thief will definitely sell the jewels to someone. And tell me, who around here doesn't know your jewelry? They'll bring everything back to you just when you least expect it.

SERKELE. Well, yes, maybe you're right, but do you think I'll be able to contain myself until then? Will I get a moment's rest? Will I survive it? Won't that be an enormous strain to keep such anguish to myself? The holidays are coming soon—and how will I be able to go to synagogue? I won't even be able to show my face in the street, oy, I feel faint!

REB GAVRIEL. I just don't understand. Was all your jewelry stolen? How could that be? There must be something left!

SERKELE. What do you mean? How could there be anything left, when I kept all my jewelry in one chest and the thief took it all—so how could there be anything left? And to top it off, fate has dealt me such a heavy blow that this had to happen on the day Dovid died. And the thief managed to do it because he knew that on this day, I don't wear a single piece of jewelry! Oy, it's very grim! I'm practically going out of my mind! And the worst part of it is that no one can give me any advice on what to do, oy, I feel faint! It's really true what they say: when the wheels are too heavy, the wagon gets stuck.

REB GAVRIEL. Absolutely. What sort of advice can I give you? I have no idea.

SERKELE. I beg you, do what I tell you just this once, and talk to Redlekh. What are you afraid of? He won't hit you, you know. God knows I can't look that thief in the eye.

REB GAVRIEL. You know what, my dear in-law? I'll do that for you, so that afterward you don't start second-guessing me. But I'll ask you just this one thing: you do something for me too.

SERKELE. Well, tell me, what is it?

REB GAVRIEL. If you'll beg my pardon and send for Reb Yoykhenen to help me a little, you can be sure that we'll question the boy together, and we'll get to the bottom of it, no matter how deep we have to dig. Two heads are better than one.

SERKELE. Yes, that's true, but when can that happen?

REB GAVRIEL. As far as I'm concerned, today if you want.

SERKELE. Good, I'll send for Reb Yoykhenen right away. And you can both sit down and have him called in. I don't even want to be there. (*She gets up to leave.*)

REB GAVRIEL. Where is the boy, then? He's probably at home! Who knows whether he'll want to come here?

SERKELE. Eh, what are you saying! He's already here at my house, the rascal! I was afraid that he wouldn't come, so I tricked him into coming here by telling him that my Moyshe wants him. And once he came here, I wouldn't let him go home. So he's sitting in there, in the kitchen, and two beadles are watching him.

REB GAVRIEL. You've done very well. But now don't delay any more and send for Reb Yoykhenen right away, since it's getting late. And let him know why, and prepare something to drink to get him here sooner, since he won't say no to that.

SERKELE. I'll send everything in. (*Starts to go.*)

REB GAVRIEL. I almost forgot, come back for a minute, I forgot to ask you something.

SERKELE. (*Turns around.*) What is it?

REB GAVRIEL. What happens if Redlekh is a smart boy and keeps his mouth shut? What will you do if he doesn't confess to the truth, ha?

SERKELE. Don't you worry about that! If he doesn't confess here, he'll do it somewhere else! Just do what you need to and don't worry about me; I'll do what I have to. (*She goes.*)

Scene 2

REB GAVRIEL. Whatever she finds out from him, she can keep it. And at the same time, Redlekh came here to play around with Hinde! Nothing will help here; once she's decided that Redlekh robbed her, that's it. Even if the Grand Rabbi of Babylon were to come along, he couldn't talk her out of it. I pity him, I swear! She'll make mincemeat out of him. The poor guy will rue the day he was born! A real kangaroo court! But for all that, I want to do him a favor. I have to ask her not to press criminal charges. I have no idea how to begin with him, but it will be a nice little party! She thinks I had a drink prepared for Reb Yoykhenen's sake. No, no, it's for poor me; I need it! Gavriel, take heart!

Scene 3

(*Enter Reb Yoykhenen with Chaim, who is carrying a lantern, a bottle, and two glasses.*)

REB YOYKHENEN. A good evening to you, Reb Gavriel!

REB GAVRIEL. A good evening, a good year, welcome, Reb Yoykhenen!

REB YOYKHENEN. (*To Chaim.*) Go call him in, and don't tell him who wants him, you hear?

CHAIM. (*Going.*) Right.

REB YOYKHENEN. It seems that I have you to thank you for the negotiation—you suggested that they send for me.

REB GAVRIEL. Who, me? Not at all! I know nothing—Serke called for me, and when I got here, she told me that she had sent for you too: that the two of us should interrogate Redlekh together to see whether he took the box of jewels. Besides, what do you care? There's plenty of ale.

REB YOYKHENEN. Yes, that's true. (*Sits down and fills both glasses.*) But what good does it do me? I'll tell you the truth, the whole town will be upset that an honest young man is accused of being a thief. Let me tell you something, I also go to the houses of wealthy people here, and I've heard several people praise him as an honest student. Even Reb Dovid, may he rest in peace, once mentioned that he wanted the boy to be his son-in-law. At the time, I expected to collect a handsome fee for the match.

REB GAVRIEL. Well, that's a lost cause now. Believe me, I find the whole business distasteful myself. And I really regret having promised to intercede. But we're already involved, and there's nothing we can do to make it better. (*Drinks.*) L'chaim, Reb Yoykhenen—to life!

REB YOYKHENEN. To life and happiness! (*Drinks.*) A glass of ale—that's alright.

Scene 4

(*Redlekh is brought in by two Beadles.*)

REDLEKH. What do you want from me? Where are you taking me?

REB YOYKHENEN. Don't be afraid. We won't do anything to you. (*To the Beadles.*) You can go back in now. We'll call you if we need you. (*The Beadles exit.*)

REB GAVRIEL. (*To Redlekh.*) Have a seat. (*To Reb Yoykhenen.*) How do you like that stupid servant! He only brought two glasses! (*He finishes his glass of ale, then pours another glass and gives it to Redlekh.*) Have a nice glass of ale!

REDLEKH. I thank you, but I do not drink any spirits.

REB GAVRIEL. Don't worry, drink, drink! You study medicine; it must say in your books that a little alcohol is good for you.

REB YOYKHENEN. Why are you forcing him? Let me tell you something, ask the patient, not the doctor. For me, ale is really good for my hemorrhoids. But I still hate it when people force me to drink. (*He drinks.*)

REB GAVRIEL. (*Aside.*) Beats me if I know how to get started here. (*He drinks.*)

REB YOYKHENEN. I think I saw you once up at Reb Yitskhok Roytfeld's?

REDLEKH. Perhaps.

REB YOYKHENEN. Did you used to go there often?

REDLEKH. Whenever time permitted.

Reb Yoykhenen. You had to tutor someone there?

Redlekh. No.

Reb Yoykhenen. So how come you were a regular guest there?

Redlekh. He came from my home town, and was my best friend as well.

Reb Yoykhenen. Your friend? Get out! Yitskhok Roytfeld—your friend? How could you be his friend? You're talking nonsense! He's a wealthy man and from a good family too, even though he dresses like a German! So what brought the two of you together?

Redlekh. He and my father, blessed be he, were the most intimate of friends, and so it is with me.

Reb Yoykhenen. Your father's name was Blessed-be-he?

Redlekh. My father was Reb Zalmen Redlekh from Prague.

Reb Yoykhenen. Reb Zalmen Redlekh from Prague. I spent Passover once with a Zalmen Redlekh. But let me tell you, that's an amazing coincidence![30] There must have been two Reb Zalmen Redlekhs. Because the one I spent Passover with was a very wealthy man, a big tycoon, and a very pious Jew to boot, even though he dressed like a German. I had a wonderful holiday with him! The food, the drink! Everything was delicious, and was all served in silver dishes! I remember like it was yesterday how on the second day of Passover, they served a carrot stew, a *tsimes*—or as they pronounce it in Germany, a *tsomas*. I swear to you that I can still taste it. And that's not to mention what happened after the meal, when the man poured forth with words of learning. Let me tell you, I can't remember all of it, but I tell you, I was astonished—it was as sweet as honey! (*Drinks.*)

Reb Gavriel. (*Aside.*) The taste of the *tsomas* is still in his mouth and he can't remember the sermon!

Reb Yoykhenen. And after the holiday, when I was leaving, I was given a terrific package of food for the journey. I tell you, I was treated so well by that Reb Zalmen, that I can't tell you enough about it. Anyway, if you're from Prague, you must know him? His wife's name was Leah. The name suited her, because she was so modest, such a pious woman you just don't come across. Did you know them?

Redlekh. (*Cries and wipes his eyes.*) Oh, alas, both of them have gone.

Reb Yoykhenen. Really? They've left Prague? I'm really surprised; to have such an estate in a big city like Prague, and suddenly leave just like that? Where do they live now?

---

30. Literally, "There is such a thing as a red heifer," a reference to the animal (Hebrew *parah adumah*) whose ashes were used to purify people and objects defiled by a corpse. In colloquial Yiddish, though, a red heifer simply represents an extremely rare occurrence (see *Mishna Parah* 3:5).

REDLEKH. (*Crying very hard and pointing skyward.*) There, where all distinction ends. There where everyone takes his place according to his merit. There where every person must go, leaving behind their worldly goods.

REB YOYKHENEN. What? Reb Zalmen is dead? Blessed is the true Judge![31] Oh, what a shame, what a shame, I swear! He was a pious Jew. And Leah too? How terrible—may God have mercy on us! (*Thinks for a moment.*) So tell me, I beg of you, I think there must have been a son who survived them? Let me tell you, I remember as if it were today how I saw a very nice-looking boy sitting at the table . . . what became of him, poor thing?

REDLEKH. (*Wiping his eyes.*) Oh, that boy lost not only his good, dear parents, but also, through various misfortunes, everything they left behind as well. And now he's in a situation where he may also lose *sein guter ruf*—his good name.

REB YOYKHENEN. What? He lost his entire fortune? I can't stand it, such wealth! Such goods there were in that house! Oh, I could faint from the grief! (*He drinks.*) Anyway, tell me—may you be healthy—where was that good roof that you said the boy was going to lose?

REDLEKH. I was not talking about a roof, but rather about a *guter ruf*— that is, that young Redlekh may lose his good name.

REB YOYKHENEN. His good name? But tell me, I beg of you: how can someone lose his good name? (*He drinks.*)

REB GAVRIEL. (*Drinks too.*) In any case, you needn't cry like that, Reb Redlekh, for even when a wealthy or pious Jew dies in this city, no one moans so loudly.

REDLEKH. Listen to me first, and then you can say what you think. That Zalmen Redlekh, along with his wife Leah, were ill for two years, and then died in the same month. While they were still alive, the most famous doctors and apothecaries inherited half their estate, and the attorneys took care of the other half after they died. Their son was forced to rely upon the benevolence of a stranger by the name of Reb Dovid Gutherz,[32] who was an old acquaintance of his parents. This Reb Dovid took the boy in and became like a father to him. But the cup of sorrows was not yet filled to overflowing, so it pleased Divine Providence to add to it the most precious of the boy's rare solaces; that is, the same Reb Dovid Gutherz suddenly died on his way to America, and had made his sister Serkele the sole heir to his

---

31. The traditional formula recited upon hearing of someone's death.

32. German/Yiddish, "good heart."

entire fortune. For that reason, that only son of Reb Zalmen Redlekh had to work hard to earn his crust of bread by tutoring. One of his tutorials was at the house of the aforementioned Serkele. (*He suddenly stands up.*) He now stands before you, accused by the same Serkele of an ugly theft. (*He cries. The others sit mutely for a moment.*)

REB GAVRIEL. Well, so you are Reb Zalmen's son.

REB YOYKHENEN. What, you are Reb Zalmen's only son?

REDLEKH. Unfortunately, I am the very same. (*He cries, and covers his face with a handkerchief. The others are again silent for a couple of minutes.*)

REB GAVRIEL. (*Aside.*) Gavriel! Think of yourself, for God's sake, take heart! (*Drinks.*) This ale is very good. Drink, Reb Yoykhenen!

REB YOYKHENEN. (*Drinks; to Redlekh.*) L'chaim, Reb Zalmen's son! (*Drinks the rest, fills it again, and gives it to Redlekh.*) Have a glass of ale! Drink, drink, you'll enjoy it! This ale is delicious. Drink, I beg of you!

REDLEKH. I thank you, but I really do not partake of spirits.

REB YOYKHENEN. Nu, let me tell you something, it's always really good to have a little chat. But tell me now, since you are Reb Zalmen's son and I knew your father and your mother—how could you do such an awful thing? Remember, you must have studied Torah at some point, so you know that it says in our holy Torah, "Thou shalt not steal."[33] Let me tell you, that's no way to behave. And if a person goes through some tough times, does he have to become a thief?

REB GAVRIEL. That's absolutely true. Isn't that beneath a young man like you?

REDLEKH. Listen, my dear Gavriel! I would rather leave your question unanswered, feeling that anything I say would fall on deaf ears, since you consider every student capable of doing every wrong—every crime, even—without a pang of conscience. So I would rather not waste my breath. But the realization that one can stand before almighty God with a clean conscience is enough to convince even a myopic person of one's innocence. And isn't it every person's duty to justify his actions, and to defend himself as far as possible? Therefore, my dear Reb Yoykhenen, that duty forces me to demonstrate my innocence with a sacred oath, either in front of everyone in the holy synagogue, or under the auspices of the local rabbi.

REB GAVRIEL. An oath? Bah! That doesn't mean anything to Serkele.

REB YOYKHENEN. (*To Reb Gavriel.*) Please don't be offended, but why not? An oath is an oath. But let me tell you something . . . (*To Redlekh.*) Reb Gavriel just means, is Serkele such a fool that she'll believe your oath?

---

33. Exodus 20:12.

REDLEKH. (*His head in his hands.*) If even the first oath that I have ever sworn in my entire life does not have the power to save me in this difficult moment (*Raises his hands skyward.*), then You, all-knowing God, save your innocent creation from this shameful rumor! (*He cries.*)

REB GAVRIEL. (*To himself.*) I deserve a good lashing for this.

REB YOYKHENEN. Still, there's no need to cry like that. Let me tell you, Serkele is not an unjust person. Everyone's possessions are precious to them. But the simplest thing to do would be to tell the truth, because I've got to tell you that Serkele certainly won't keep quiet. And I'm really afraid that she'll have your hide.

REB GAVRIEL. And I'm also telling you, my dear Reb Redlekh, that I have the same fear. You have no idea what sort of a person this Serkele is.

REDLEKH. (*No longer crying, but speaking with strength.*) Believe me, my dear Reb Gavriel, I know this Serkele very well—perhaps better than anyone else. Nevertheless, I am not afraid of her at all, despite her belligerent character. For God, the Judge of all worlds, knows that my conscience is clean, and will undoubtedly guide the heart of my judge to make his verdict compatible with my innocence.

REB GAVRIEL. (*To Reb Yoykhenen.*) What's the use? Put an end to this; I can see that we won't get anywhere with him today. We've done our part; that's enough. End it!

REB YOYKHENEN. (*Fills both glasses and empties out the bottle.*) The end is the end! Let me tell you, we've done what we could. (*He drinks.*) And that's that!

REB GAVRIEL. (*Shouts.*) Beadles, come in! (*The Beadles enter.*)

REB YOYKHENEN. (*To Redlekh.*) Now go with them, back where you came from! (*To the Beadles.*) And while you're going, tell Serkele to come in.

BEADLES. Good, very well.

REDLEKH. *Gute Nacht, meine Herren.*[34]

REB GAVRIEL and REB YOYKHENEN. (*Simultaneously.*) Good night, a good year! (*Redlekh and the Beadles exit.*)

Scene 5

REB GAVRIEL. (*To himself.*) Thank God that's over!

REB YOYKHENEN. (*Pours from the bottle.*) Why did you have them bring so little ale?

REB GAVRIEL. And if I had asked for more, would Serke have listened?

---

34. German, "Good night, gentlemen."

REB YOYKHENEN. Eh, what can I say? Let me tell you something: she'd be quite happy if people worked for her for nothing, but not me.

Scene 6

SERKELE. (*Comes running in.*) Nu? Did he confess?

REB GAVRIEL. Bah! Something like that, something like that... We couldn't get it out of him.

REB YOYKHENEN. Why should I go on and on about it? I'd rather give you the short version and not drag it out: we questioned him plenty, here and there, one of us on one side of him and the other on the other side; in short, let me tell you something, we both—I as a good friend and Reb Gavriel as your daughter's groom, gave him a good talking to—sometimes gentle, sometimes rough. Because let me tell you something, if you want to do someone a favor, you have to go at it from every angle. I spoke to him separately and your bridegroom, long life to him, didn't spare any effort, we worked him over and made him plenty scared, and then we pleaded with nice words, because, let me tell you something...

SERKELE. (*Very impatient, interrupts him.*) Let me tell you something here, let me tell you something there, and I still have no idea what he said. Just answer this one question: did he confess or not?

REB YOYKHENEN. Confessed, that's what he, to tell the truth, didn't do, but he says that he wants to go to synagogue in his white robe and prayer shawl, and swear that he knows nothing about it.

SERKELE. (*Smiles angrily and mocks him.*) Really?! Look, this isn't a joke! Redlekh wants to take an oath! Oh! (*To Reb Gavriel.*) I don't understand why you're so quiet, Reb Gavriel? Do you also think I'm such a fool as to believe that scoundrel's vows?

REB GAVRIEL. That's just what I said to Reb Yoykhenen.

SERKELE. Alright, so where does this talking get me? I've just thought of a completely different idea. I know what to do with him. Don't worry, Serke isn't dead yet. He did his homework, but I'll make one more try and ask Hinde some questions; maybe I'll get further with her than you did with him. I can see that if you want to get something done, you have to do it yourself.

REB GAVRIEL. I beg of you, my dear mother-in-law, why are you so suspicious of us? We did all we could, of course; he just stuck to his story. I think even the hangman wouldn't help in this case.

REB YOYKHENEN. Nu, go ahead, we'll see what you can do; we'll see if you learn anything more from Hinde. And believe me, I wish with all my heart that you have more success than we did, but (*Shrugs.*) I think you're wasting your time.

REB GAVRIEL. Ay, how come? I agree with my in-law: that if she threatens Hinde just a little, maybe the girl will confess.

SERKELE. And if she won't confess, then there's still a criminal running loose in the world, oy, I feel faint!

REB YOYKHENEN. It must be getting late. (*Gets up.*) I'd better be getting home. And Serkele, please don't rush things with the criminal. Because let me tell you, it's better sweet than sour.

REB GAVRIEL. Reb Yoykhenen is absolutely right. Because a thing like this can drag out sometimes, and take a hundred years to come to an end, and in the meantime, it costs money. Meanwhile, here comes my father-in-law, may he be well. Go through the whole story with him one more time before you do anything drastic.

SERKELE. Oh, sure, that's just the person to tell, oy, I feel faint! (*She signals to them not to tell Reb Moyshe.*)

Scene 7

(*Reb Moyshe enters very quietly, preoccupied and sad, and not looking at anyone.*)

REB YOYKHENEN. Good evening, Reb Moyshe!

REB MOYSHE. (*Looks around.*) A good evening, a good year, Reb Yoykhenen! Welcome! How come you're here so late?

REB YOYKHENEN. I heard about your burglary, so I came to find out what's happening—whether you've found out anything or not. What do you think, my dear Reb Moyshe: who could have done it?

REB MOYSHE. I think it's very simple: she lost it the same way that she got it! Just ask her; I always used to . . .

SERKELE. (*Cuts him off.*) Why are you talking to him? The things he comes up with! What does he think: I gave it away myself? Didn't I put my headband with two kinds of pearls in the trunk early this morning with my own hands and lock the trunk with the key, and didn't I turn the key two times, and bury the trunk in the straw at the head of my bed?! If someone had ten heads, he would never have guessed there was a trunk there, oy, I feel faint! Isn't something strange going on? Has there ever been a punishment in the world like what's happened to me?

REB MOYSHE. Ay, I always knew it would end this way. I always said, "Serke, that money won't bring you any blessings." Oy, don't ask, Serke—we've brought this on ourselves! I just hope it will be alright in the end.

SERKELE. (*To Reb Yoykhenen and Reb Gavriel.*) What do we need his crazy talk for? Does he even know what he's saying himself? Nu, it's late already, that's enough for today. May you go in good health. But tomorrow, God willing, please come back here again just in case I need you, oy, I feel faint!

REB GAVRIEL. Nu, nu, I'll certainly be back at the crack of dawn; I won't be able to sleep a wink tonight anyway.

REB YOYKHENEN. I'll also come, of course. But I beg of you once more, Serkele: bear in mind what I asked you before. Because let me tell you, don't do it for him, but for his dead father's sake—I knew him very well, he was a pious Jew.

SERKELE. Nu, nu, I'll do it for your sake. Good night, good night, go in good health!

REB YOYKHENEN and REB GAVRIEL. (*Simultaneously.*) Good night! Good night, Reb Moyshe! (*They go.*)

Scene 8

SERKELE. Moyshe, Moyshe, you want to drive me into an early grave? Tell me, what do you want? What do you want from me? You talk like that with strangers in the house? Tell me, should I send for the rabbi so you can confess? Oy vey, Moyshe, Moyshe! What happened to your common sense? I swear, I'm amazed that you don't stand in the middle of the street and shout out everything you know! My father, may he rest in peace, spoke the truth when he said that a Jew is good for nothing but going to synagogue. He just doesn't care that I'm sick from all my troubles, oy, I feel faint! (*She cries.*) Will I sleep at all tonight? He doesn't care: so what if someone robbed him!

REB MOYSHE. Oy vey, what do you want from me? Nu, what can I do for you? I ask you, do I know who the thief is?

SERKELE. What are you saying? It was none but that thief, that Redlekh! And if the whole world says otherwise, it still was no one but him, that swindler, that thief!

REB MOYSHE. Oy, I don't know what you'll come up with next! Next you'll be saying there's a man in the moon! Is there a more honest young man than Redlekh? Suddenly, to you he's become a thief! Tell me, why do you want to spare the real criminal? Don't you have enough sins of your own? Oy, I, I've had enough.

SERKELE. Oy, I feel faint! Look at what a *shlimazl* you are—just listen to yourself! When I woke up this afternoon, there was no one in the house except that thief, that murderer, with that *shlimazl* Hinde. And she herself confessed that he was the only person she saw when she came home. Whatever he did, she hasn't yet told the truth about. And maybe he'll deny it to me too? Didn't I hear him tell her how happy he is, that now he has plenty of pearls and diamonds? Ask him, let him say to my face that it's a lie, the thief! Where did he get them, the murdering scoundrel? Where did he get pearls and diamonds? What, maybe an angel tossed them down from heaven? May he be so lucky!

REB MOYSHE. You can say it to me 'til tomorrow, but he still didn't do it. He wouldn't do such a thing!

SERKELE. Nu, good, okay, you and I didn't do it. Altele either. Chaim hasn't got the brains to do it. As for Chava, she's scum, but I'll swear she's not a thief. Because she's gone through the house on her own ever since she's been with us, and not so much as a hair has ever been missing. As for Reb Gavriel, you yourself know that you can leave countless rubles lying around with him. And besides, he was out at the post office at the time. There was not another human being in the house. If you brought two little children here, they wouldn't reach any other conclusion but that an insider did this, and that it was Redlekh. Oy, oy, I feel faint! I'm cursed to have you for a husband, when all you can say is, "He wouldn't do such a thing!"

REB MOYSHE. Yes, yes, and I'll say it again, he wouldn't commit such a sin.

SERKELE. Of course he doesn't sin, the hooligan! Have you ever seen him kiss the mezuzah? Have you ever heard him say the blessing after the meal, or before bed? Does he pray? Does he put on tefilin? Does he kiss the fringes of his prayer shawl, like you're supposed to? Does he know how to celebrate *Shabbes* or holidays properly? You've seen it: when he sees women, girls, he comes to life, the rascal! Then he's in heaven, the lecher! But just you wait, I'll bury him! Let's bring in the police, give him thirty lashes, and the bastard will confess soon enough!

REB MOYSHE. Nu, go and do what you wish; I wash my hands of the whole matter! I don't want to know about it. I've had enough. By all means, let's see how you proceed with your speculations. (*Starts to leave.*)

SERKELE. Where are you going? Shmuel's coming soon! Don't you know that we have to file a police report early tomorrow morning? I sent for him!

REB MOYSHE. Write and say what you want—you know how to take care of such things. (*He again starts to leave.*)

SERKELE. At least send Hinde to me.

REB MOYSHE. (*Stands by the door and glares at Serkele furiously.*) Tell me, what more do you want from that poor swindled orphan? Isn't she already halfway in the grave?

SERKELE. What are you so afraid of? I won't bite her! I won't do anything to her. I just want her to sew something on for me. Why are you making such a fuss over her?

REB MOYSHE. Just listen, Serkele! I'll send her in to you, but God forbid if you do anything to her—as you're inclined to—just remember that I'm in the next room! (*He exits through the right-hand door.*)

Scene 9

SERKELE. I'll start off by chatting nicely to her, in case that's the way to get her to confess. But if she stonewalls me, I wouldn't want to be in her skin! If she wants to marry that Redlekh, I'll give them a ball and chain for a present. He'll regret that he didn't want to come. I'll tear them both to pieces!

Scene 10

(*Hinde enters and remains standing by the door, hanging her head and crying.*)

SERKELE. Come here, Hindele! Come here . . . Closer . . . Closer . . . That's it . . . Sit down next to me on the sofa, my dear . . . (*Hinde moves fearfully this whole time, gradually nearer, and sits.*) Did you already have your bit of coffee, dear heart? You know, I forgot to put sugar in it . . . (*Hinde cries loudly and kisses Serkele's hand. Serkele fakes a laugh.*) Heh heh heh, nu, please, stop crying! I know that you're very concerned that something terrible happened to me. Still, you don't have to cry like that. You might make yourself sick, Heaven forbid. And we can't have that—it's not as if I have lots of nieces, do I? Oy, I feel faint! . . . There's just one thing that I really miss . . . the diamond earrings and the little pearls with the clasp. The ones that I always said that when you become a bride, God willing, I would give them to you! . . . Just the day before yesterday, I put them in the chest too, oy, I feel faint! (*Looks at Hinde intently. A long silence.*)

HINDE. My dear aunt! Did you have me come in to sew something? What should I sew?

SERKELE. There's always time for that tomorrow. Just listen, my child. To tell you the truth, I decided a long time ago, dear heart, that I would have a little chat with you. Of course you know that besides losing your mother so young, poor dear, you're without a father as well. (*She wipes her eyes.*) And if I hadn't taken you into my house, who knows what might have happened to you . . . Oy, I feel faint! . . . I

mean, on top of all that, I love you like my own child. And I don't
think you yourself could say that any harm has ever come to you in
my house . . . Ay, what, so I get mad at you sometimes? That, my dear,
I think you yourself will recognize, I do only for your sake. You're no
fool, and you might ask, what do I care when someone else's child
does something foolish? Why? It reminds me of the old story: "Don't
look at me, Rebbe, it's your cow." (*Hinde cries and kisses Serkele's hand.*)
Anyway, you can see for yourself that although I don't show it, deep
in my heart you mean very much to me—I love you like I love
myself. I just want you to be good and pious, just as our dear and
holy God commanded, oy, I feel faint! What do I want from you
then, my dear, ha? I'm not asking, God forbid, that you leap over the
roof . . . I only want you to tell me every tiny little thing that you
know about him . . . about Redlekh, I mean. And believe me, may I
be struck down in my young years if it brings the slightest harm to
you or even to him! Because what do you think, I'm a fool? If someone makes a little mistake once in a while, do you think that really
matters? No! People are not angels . . . It's okay, my dear, it won't
shock me . . . You can tell me everything.

HINDE. My wonderful auntie, don't be angry, I'll tell you everything. I'm
sure that when you hear me out, you'll forgive me. (*She kisses Serkele's
hand.*) You're my dear father's sister, after all. I know that I've done
a terrible thing, which I haven't told anyone up to now.

SERKELE. Nu, nu, don't be afraid. Tell me everything, but only the truth.
The truth, my dear, is what God loves. You'll see, my child, that you
won't regret it. Oy, I feel faint!

HINDE. It was about two years ago, when you were at the spas, remember? You remember? . . . I was, as you know, very ill. You weren't
here, and Uncle, may he live long, had also gone away somewhere.
Meanwhile, I kept getting sicker, to the point where I didn't even
have the strength to walk around the house. But Redlekh used to . . . I
beg you, Auntie, don't get angry . . .

SERKELE. Just tell me, tell me more . . . Nu? I promise I won't get angry.
You're so silly. If I swear? You know how precious an oath is to me.
Just tell me: but Redlekh used to . . .

HINDE. But Redlekh used to sit with me day and night. One time he told
me that I should let him call for a doctor. "I," he said, "am very
worried, Hindele, that you are seriously ill." But I was very ashamed
to tell him that I had no money to pay the doctor. But when he saw
that I was getting worse as each day went by, he went and brought
a doctor. After that I lay in bed and had no idea what was happening
to me. Only when I began to return to my senses a little, did Chaim
start to tell me how I talked nonsense, and that I had been in bed

for twelve days, and that one time I was doing so badly that Redlekh cried out loud, and called in three doctors, and that I was given all sorts of medicines from the pharmacy . . . In short, it was no joke. I had cost so much! Afterwards, thank God, I got better, and only then did I find out that it was all with Redlekh's money. He went whole nights without sleep on my account, and he sold all his clothes and things, even his watch. Several times I told him that little by little, I would pay him back what I had cost him . . .

SERKELE. (*Interrupting her.*) Nu, and then? Health is the most important thing to all of us. Nu, what then, my dear: you told him to take the chest of jewels, is that right, my child?

HINDE. (*Staring at Serkele.*) What? God forbid! I sold the earrings that I got from my mother, may she rest in peace. He didn't want to take a single kreuzer from me. But he did say that he would give his life for me, and that I deeply insulted him by offering to repay him. And from then on . . . (*She suddenly becomes silent and embarrassed.*)

SERKELE. Nu? From then on, what?

HINDE. And from then on, I began to see how much he loves me. (*Looks straight at Serkele.*)

SERKELE. Nu, yes, that's true. What did you do this afternoon though, ha?

HINDE. My dearest Auntie! I'll tell you the whole truth: he was here and said he pitied me for suffering so much from you, that you even begrudge me the bit of food I eat. I told him that that was a total lie, that he was quite mistaken. Of course, you're very good to me. He tried to make up with me for what he said and he . . . gave me a kiss. But I was afraid that someone would suddenly come in, so I asked him to leave me alone. He didn't want to. I asked him again. I don't know how it happened . . . but I kissed him back . . . (*She becomes quiet and embarrassed.*)

SERKELE. All true. (*Becoming somewhat angry.*) I forgive you. But what did he say, that he has more than enough pearls and diamonds? Is it then that he took the jewel chest, ha?

HINDE. What? Where did you get that idea? He would take your jewel chest all of a sudden? He? Him?! He has no idea about all that. He only said that if I loved him, the whole world could have all the pearls and diamonds it wanted . . . If he had me, he'd have more than enough pearls and diamonds!

SERKELE. So where is my jewel chest?

HINDE. Why are you asking me? How should I know?

SERKELE. (*Suddenly stands up in anger.*) What? You don't know? You don't know that Redlekh stole my jewels? Who are you trying to fool, you nasty girl?! . . . Maybe you think that because I've been talking nicely to you up to now, that you can trick me? Well, I'll show you, or my name isn't Serke! (*Louder and louder, in a rage.*) Just wait, I'll have him bound hand and foot 'til he tells the truth! Let them give him a few hundred lashes until his boiling blood flows like water, and he'll say where my jewels are! I'll have him skinned alive, bit by bit! And you, you thief, you'll have to stand by and scream until your voice reaches the heavens! I'll let him rot in prison! And you, you little outcast, will have to scrape the worms off him by the heap! No, I won't rest, I won't take pity! I'll take no prisoners! I'll sacrifice everything else, but he'll have to give me back what's mine!

HINDE. (*Extremely frightened, she hides her face in her hands. Suddenly she runs to Serkele and falls to the ground in front of her.*) Auntie, my wonderful Auntie! No . . . no . . . no . . . I can't . . . stand it . . . any longer . . . no, Auntie!

SERKELE. (*Screams very loudly, in a rage.*) Just tell me where my jewels are!!! Where did Redlekh put them? Tell me, where is my stuff?! Where are my possessions?

HINDE. (*Stands up, trembling.*) No . . . no . . . Redlekh . . . is . . . not . . . a . . . thief!

SERKELE. (*Runs to Hinde and raises both hands to strike her. Meanwhile, the right-hand door opens, Moyshe runs in. He throws Serkele onto the sofa, takes Hinde by the hand, and runs with her out of the door through which he entered. Serkele screams miserably.*) Oy vey, oy vey, I feel faint!

The curtain falls.

Act 5

The next morning. One can see a small street through the open doors and the windows of Reb Shmelke Troyniks's guesthouse. A window shutter bears a picture of the Jewish spies carrying a gigantic cluster of grapes on a stick,[35] and written beneath the picture, in large letters, is "Shmelke Troyniks." A large bench stands in front of the door.

Scene 1

THE STRANGER. (*Sitting alone on the bench, half-undressed and half-dressed in German clothing, like a traveler.*) I am extraordinarily tired. That was a trip indeed! Day and night, by land and by sea, without a place to

---

35. See Numbers 13:23 for the original source of this image, where the spies sent out by Moses to investigate the promised land return with a bunch of grapes so large it is suspended between two poles.

stop and to rest. May God be thanked, I have returned again to my homeland, after six long years. It seems to me that everything here has changed, improved—indeed, become more beautiful: the streets— so clean; the houses—how charming and beautiful! God! Do the interiors match the façades? How strange! How truly strange, that after so many years of suffering, after these extraordinary yearnings and longings for the favorite of my heart, I am unable to learn the least bit of news about her circumstances. (*He thinks silently for a moment.*) Dearest child! Whatever was it like for you during the time of my absence? Have your health and my fortunes kept pace? Be- loved daughter of mine! What do you look like now? Has the deli- cate little sprout grown here on the tree of hopelessness? Have you, as your father who loves you so much has wished, come to resemble my never forgotten, deceased Rokhl? (*He remains sitting, overcome by sadness, lost in thought. Subsequently, he starts.*) No, no, away with these hellish thoughts! Ah, Ever-Beneficent Creator, You who have so often stood by me in my time of need, Heavenly Father who knows all! Take back Your blessings, take my health, my life, take everything from me, everything, but not this love, this beautiful child of mine! (*He is quiet for a moment.*)

Scene 2

REB SHMELKE. (*Enters from the street with a stick in his hand and is about to go in the door; he remains still when he sees the Stranger.*) Aha! Good. Praise the Lord, Who has sent me a guest! (*He takes off his fur hat and bows deeply to the Stranger.*) My deepest greetings to ya', sir; how fares His Excellency?

STRANGER. (*Still not seeing Reb Shmelke and continuing to talk to himself.*) What is my life, my happiness worth, without the child?

REB SHMELKE. (*To himself.*) Aha! He's a German!

STRANGER. (*Looks around and notices Reb Shmelke.*) Are you perhaps the proprietor of this house?

REB SHMELKE. (*He draws closer to the Stranger and bows to him again, as he did earlier; he remains standing in front of the Stranger and speaks to him very softly.*) Yes indeedy, my good sir! Please accept my very warmest welcome, Your Grace! What can we do, what does Your Grace com- mand? A beautiful, gorgeous, painted, light-filled room? A magnifi- cent stable? Fresh hay? A good sack of oats? A hearty meal and lots to drink? Whatever Your Grace could possibly wish: some good ol'- fashioned mead, a dry glass o' wine, from the very best sort of grapes. Just snap your fingers, Your Grace! I'm Your Grace's to command!

Immediately, instantly, I'll take to my heels and bring you a cup o' tea, o' coffee, a glass o' strong punch, a liquor, a Swiss cheese, a piece o' meat—anythin', anythin' Your Grace desires can be obtained by your humble servant Shmelke Troyniks, and for just a teensy weensy bit o' money, Your Grace! Just say the word!

THE STRANGER. (*To himself, quietly.*) It pleases me mightily that this man here doesn't recognize me in the slightest! (*Aloud, to Reb Shmelke.*) You mistake yourself, Reb Shmelke! I am a Jew.

REB SHMELKE. (*Quickly puts his hat back on.*) A Jew! (*To himself, quietly.*) My very worst dreams should fall flat on his head; I thought he was a nobleman! (*He sits down near the Stranger and gives him his hand.*) Sholem aleykhem!³⁶ Where ya' from? Where ya' headin'?

STRANGER. Aleykhem sholem! I'm originally from right around h—

REB SHMELKE. Don't you have bristles, fats, anise, cowhides or groceries to sell?

STRANGER. No, I don't have anything to sell.

REB SHMELKE. Maybe you wanna buy from us? Piecework, haberdashery, cloth, maybe even straw? No? Just tell me, I'll go with ya', I'll show ya', you'll get everything half-price, no question. Just tell me, tell me, what stuff of ours do you want to trade in Lemberg? I'm a great expert in all kindsa commerce.

STRANGER. I have nothing to buy now; I only beg of you, don't you have some sort of separate lodgings for me?

REB SHMELKE. For you? Nope, nuttin'. (*He begins to leave.*)

STRANGER. If the answer is yes, I'll pay you well, I swear.

REB SHMELKE. No, no, nuttin'. You musta made a big mistake.

STRANGER. Didn't you yourself just say that you indeed have a beautifully painted room?

REB SHMELKE. Yeah, I've got a very beautiful painted room, but it's only for traveling noblemen. Sorry—today's the day I gotta take care of some contracts. (*He is about to go and then makes a joke at the Stranger's expense.*) But don't worry, my dear sir: you can leave your thousands of rubles here in the inn—no one's gonna steal 'em here, that's for sure! (*He laughs.*)

STRANGER. Don't go away; come here, please, I simply want to tell you something. Just a word, I beg of you!

REB SHMELKE. (*Comes back.*) Well, what is it?

STRANGER. Why are you running away? Just sit down here next to me for a moment.

---

36. Literally Hebrew/Yiddish "Peace be unto you," a generalized greeting, responded to by "Aleykhem sholem."

REB SHMELKE. (*Angrily.*) So, tell me already, whaddya want? I don't have all day to sit around with you. On a day like today, every minute's like an hour, every hour like a day—and every day is worth a few rubles.

STRANGER. I will be absolutely honest with you: I have arrived here after a very long journey; I have traveled day and night, and I am now exhausted, and all I would like is to rest somewhere. I beg of you, my dear Reb Shmelke, give me a room of my own—anywhere you wish to put me is fine—but just somewhere for me to rest. I will pay you very well, possibly better than a nobleman would. In short—I will pay you any price you ask.

REB SHMELKE. Yeah, I know how Jews pay; how much would you gimme for a twenty-four-hour stay? And how long d'ya think you'll stay? Tell me, tell me!

STRANGER. (*Aside.*) A little lie must serve in this time of need. (*Aloud, to Reb Shmelke.*) I cannot tell you precisely, because I must wait for a count who has ordered me here. He will arrive today or tomorrow, and will bring a large retinue. I am certain that you will make a large profit from him, since he is very rich.

REB SHMELKE. So . . . Nu, a Jew may do anything out of need, as the Berdichever Rebbe, may he rest in peace, useta say.[37] Nu, I'll give you a room; it's a little close to the stable, but for a Jew it's a nice enough room. All I'm asking is eight Rhenish thalers a week; I'm practically giving it away to you, but I'll do it since we're both Jews. What won't one do for a Jew on the road?

STRANGER. (*To himself, quietly.*) If he calls this "giving it away," what could he possibly call "charging?"

REB SHMELKE. So? Didja think it over? Is there a problem? (*He begins to leave.*) Nu, go, find somewhere cheaper and maybe *he*'ll give you a room for free—go to the communal hostel if you want; the synagogue sexton has the keys . . .

STRANGER. (*Grabs him by the hand and doesn't let him leave.*) Listen, I'll give you eight Rhenish thalers; just take my things over to the room.

REB SHMELKE. Nu, nu, there'll be plenty of time to take the things; let's see the cash first.

STRANGER. (*Takes off a moneybelt filled with money, takes out a ducat, and gives it to Reb Shmelke.*) There! Here's a ducat for you, and you can hold on to the change as a reserve.

REB SHMELKE. (*Gestures delightedly.*) Aha! A ducat! (*He grabs the ducat.*) Nu, nu, excellent! (*He weighs the ducat in his hand and shouts out the window.*) Berl! Carry in the German merchant's things and put 'em

---

37. Rabbi Levi Yitskhok of Berdichev (c. 1740–1810), a noted Hasidic rabbi well known for his sympathies for the needs of the Jewish people.

in the nice painted room. (*To the Stranger.*) May your days and years be long! What's your name?

STRANGER. My name is . . . (*He thinks for a moment.*) My name is Solomon Gutherz.

REB SHMELKE. Gutherz! Gutherz! Are you by any chance related to Reb Dovid Gutherz, who's been away from here for the past few years?

STRANGER. I can't tell you whether I am or I'm not, but I've forgotten the most important thing—you mentioned earlier that you had an excellent house wine?

REB SHMELKE. Oy, vey, such a wine! Such a wine! I'm telling you, so dry, so sweet, so strong, such a picker-upper! And, I promise you, it's pretty good, too; the Savranier rebbe, may he have long life, was once here, and he wouldn't drink any other wine but mine, I swear; I made quite a bit of money off that holy man. You can get all sortsa vintages here: red, white, two-thaler bottles, four-thaler bottles, and even eight-thaler bottles.

STRANGER. Nu, tell them to bring a bottle of four-thaler wine here—with two glasses.

REB SHMELKE. With two glasses? Immediately, right this minute, right away! (*He shouts out the window.*) Berl! Bring a bottla wine here quickly—the good stuff, with two glasses, ya' hear? (*He sits down near the Stranger.*) I'm tellin' ya', my dear Reb Solomon, times ain't what they useta be. People ain't what they useta be. I remember very well, how several years ago, when the time came for the contract signings, this place was bursting with noblemen; you couldn't even find a spot on the ground to fit a needle. Every noble had three coaches and six horses, who were just like lions, and maybe twelve servants—I'm tellin' ya', the place was swimmin' with princes, and the money was flowin' from one pocket to the other! It was such a pleasure; and when one of those princes useta drive in, we made a pretty penny out of 'im. These days, though, if a nobleman comes once in a blue moon, he drives me absolutely nuts! Oh sure, he rumbles and grumbles, just like he useta; he tosses his hair around like always; he screams and shouts that he wants somethin', just like he useta. But when the time comes for settling up the bill, everything changes; he gets so shy, so quiet, so calm—you don't hear a peep outta him, except for a little "Wait a bit, my dear Shmelkenyu, I'm a little short right now, I'll give you some grain instead." So what do I need his grain for? I need the money, the money!

STRANGER. But do you know why this happened, my dear Reb Shmelke? Because previously, a noble used to take very little care of his estates; he used to just travel around the region carousing and running up debts, until he had drunk up the whole estate and in the end had nothing left. If the nobles who had taken care of their estates and don't come around here any more did come to visit, they would be a lot richer in land and in cash.

REB SHMELKE. What?! I beg your pardon, but you don't know what you're talking about; I'll tell you what's caused all of this. In the past, it seems to me, there was a great blessing on the country, and no one knew anything about these modern new-fangled machines for plowing, sowing, and threshing, so there useta be very little grain and lots o' profit. If someone had a little wheat or corn, it was worth its weight in gold. It was an absolute pleasure, and both the noble and your humble servant Shmelke had plenty; but now, since the machines have come along, there's plenty o' grain everywhere. And what's more—the noble knows very well how to calculate now.

STRANGER. (*To himself, quietly.*) Unfortunately, swindlers like this give more broadminded Jews a bad name. (*Berl enters through the main door, bringing a bottle of wine with two glasses and putting them down on the bench. He pours the wine, then exits through the same door.*)

REB SHMELKE. (*Taking a glass of wine and drinking.*) L'chaim! This certainly tastes good. May the Holy One, blessed be He, strike me down if you can find me another wine like this in the whole of Lemberg. It's a real picker-upper, taste this!

STRANGER. (*Drinks.*) L'chaim! No, I'm not sure it's so good. It seems a bit watered down to me.

REB SHMELKE. What? Watered down? Believe you me, on my honor, in my entire cellar you won't find a single drop of wine that's watered down, I assure you. No kiddin', I'm not braggin'. Ask anywhere in Lemberg, anyone'll tell you that the best wine is to be found at the simple Lithuanian's. I'm not like one o' those guys who has to send to the tavern keeper if a guest of mine wants a glass o' wine; at my place, you see (*He shows him the sign on the shutter.*), at The Spies, I gotta a wonderful cellar fulla wine. And 'causa this, with the help of the Lord, I'm able to make my living, l'chaim! (*He drinks.*)

STRANGER. So apparently, you're not doing too badly here?

REB SHMELKE. I scrape by. (*He drinks.*)

STRANGER. And how goes it with this Reb Moyshe? . . .

REB SHMELKE. (*Interrupting him.*) Good, everything's good. (*He drinks.*) Just dandy.

STRANGER. So which Reb Moyshe do you mean, then?

REB SHMELKE. Do I know? Which one do you mean? Are you gonna drink something, or not?

STRANGER. (*Smiling tolerantly.*) Don't worry, I'll drink. I mean the Reb Moyshe known as Reb Moyshe the miller, because his wife sits among the grain and the meal.

REB SHMELKE. Reb Moyshe the Mill Jew? Aha! Now I know—his wife's called Serkele, right?

STRANGER. Yes, yes, Serkele, Serkele, that's who I mean, exactly!

REB SHMELKE. That's who you mean? Ha ha! Where has Serke gone to! She's no longer sittin' with the meal and the grain! (*Drinks.*) Ha ha!

STRANGER. (*Frightened.*) What? Has Serke died?

REB SHMELKE. What? What're ya' talkin' about dyin' for? The angel of death's got no power over evil, that's for sure! (*He drains his glass of wine, refills the Stranger's glass, and pours himself another.*)

STRANGER. Then what on earth do you mean? Tell me, my dear Reb Shmelke! (*Very impatiently.*) Is she perhaps ill, God forbid?

REB SHMELKE. What're ya' talking about? Every Jew should have her health and wealth—may she be punished from above! What does she need grain for? Don't you know that Serke's got something like twelve thousand rubles of her own—maybe even more?

STRANGER. (*Very quietly.*) She is a wealthy woman? Excellent, that is something quite different.

REB SHMELKE. What? A rich woman, you say? It's simply impossible to get close to her now. She's become so high and mighty, the Devil take her. And why and how it all happened the Devil also knows. You think it's 'cause she has money? Fat chance! She can't hide every little stain. The wheel hasn't come full circle yet, that's for sure.

STRANGER. I beg your pardon, my dear Reb Shmelke. You know that I am a complete stranger here, and this Serkele does not concern me at all, but I'm curious to know: why are you so angry at her?

REB SHMELKE. Since I see you're a wise fella, I'll tell you the whole story—briefly, of course. (*Drinks.*) I call myself Reb Shmelke, from my German name, Shmelke Troyniks. But the locals—my enemies, for the most part—call me "The Litvak." And why? 'Cause I happen to be from Lithuania, born in Vilna. Vilna—a holy place! No doubt you've been there?

STRANGER. Once, once.

REB SHMELKE. What did you think of the great chandeliers and the courtyards of the houses of study? Beautiful, eh? I swear, what a jewel! My father's fathers were rich big shots there; my righteous father—may he rest in peace, may his merits stand in our favor—always useta take his business to Lemberg: sometimes cowhides, sometimes with milk, and sometimes anise. Once he traveled here with bristles, and he settled down here and at the same time arranged me a marriage with the daughter of a local householder who always useta put him up. (*Drinks.*) In short, I got married, and the Holy One, Blessed be He, sent me His blessings. I became a powerful man, I got myself a nice guesthouse, a nice little wine cellar, a little silver, and plenty o' money. But God sent me a great trouble last year: my young wife Feygele suddenly fell down an entire flight of stairs and died. I cried for her, wept and wailed, but what does that get you? Dead people stay dead, and I'm all by myself and there's nothin' I can do about it. (*He drinks.*) She left me a nice bit o' jewelry, and in short, I don't want to babble on too long, I became a very rich man . . .

STRANGER. (*Impatiently.*) Get to the point.

REB SHMELKE. All right, to the point, I won't drag it out. (*He drains his glass and refills it.*) For the past few weeks, I've been sending a matchmaker, a Reb Shmerele—a fine Jew—to this Serkele; she has a young girl, a beautiful girl, you could say. True, she's a bit of a Frenchwoman and one of these modern types as well—but in society, 'specially the circles I move in, you need a woman like that. I know very well how to talk with a nobleman and how to receive him with honor—and also how to stand up to him and shout at him. You certainly know how to conduct yourself in the circles I move in.

STRANGER. (*Impatiently.*) Nu, nu, get on with it, get to the point!

REB SHMELKE. The point is—I won't go on too long—you must be tired from your trip, I'm sure! Yeah! That's right! Ha!—Ya' see, I've forgotten one thing after another. The main thing is, why did I send the man to Serkele? 'Cause I've heard from the mouth of a reliable witness that she's gonna give the girl about fourteen hundred rubles cash, not including all sorts of other goodies, and she's an only child to boot! The point is, Serkele knows that a few years ago she was a miller's wife, and her father was no great scholar— nu, so what, he had a good head on his shoulders, everyone says, and what's more, I myself have seen how lots of learned Jews have come begging to that house!

STRANGER. Unfortunately, this is the truth. Nu, go on, the point.

REB SHMELKE. Yeah, the point, in short . . . (*Drains his glass and refills it.*) Should I have another bottle brought out?

STRANGER. Go on, go on!

REB SHMELKE. Right away, right away. (*He shouts out the window.*) Berl! Another bottle!

STRANGER. (*Aside.*) Look how well he serves me now, he doesn't even wait for my command. (*Aloud.*) Nu, the point, keep it short . . .

REB SHMELKE. Certainly, the point—in short, what sort of family does the bitch have? It's true that her brother might have become a somebody, but he had to leave town a few years ago over some incident and no one's seen him since. Anyway, can such a nuisance, such a Serkele, order me around? Me, a rich man? (*Strokes his belly.*) A wealthy man, I swear! She sent Reb Shmerele to tell me, "My only daughter must first learn how to measure the oats and to speak in the Lithuanian style, and then it will be possible for her to become Reb Shmelke's bride." That's the kind of order that such a common grain-woman can give me! I'm embarrassed for the matchmaker, for Reb Shmerele; nu, what differerence does it make how I speak? Here in Lemberg they make fun of how we Litvaks talk, and in Vilna we make fun of the Lemberg accent. I'm telling you, I wasn't the one who invented all these accents. (*Berl brings in another bottle of wine and exits.*) So there, my dear Reb Solomon, I didn't drag out the story one bit. But why aren't you drinking? It's really good! (*He drains his glass of wine with one gulp.*)

STRANGER. Don't concern yourself; you drink, I'll join you in a little while. (*Drinks.*) So, Reb Shmelke, do you actually have a reason for being so angry?

REB SHMELKE. (*Filling the the Stranger's glass as well as his own again.*) L'chaim! (*Drinks.*) Do I have a reason! A good reason, even!

STRANGER. I know this Serkele from a long time ago; her husband is an extremely honest Jew, is he not?

REB SHMELKE. Who, Reb Moyshe? Yeah, he's just a bit of a fool, unfortunately, and goes his own way—but what good's the very best of drinks if it's in the hands of an evil innkeeper? Sure, the drink's good, but the innkeeper destroys it. That's the story, here's its meaning: Serkele tells Reb Moyshe what's what; she's got him wrapped around her little finger. (*He drinks.*)

Scene 3

(*Reb Gavriel begins to enter from the street, goes back and forth a few times past the Stranger and looks him over. He plays with a little stick in his hand and quietly sings a little tune to himself. In his other hand he carries a small box, wrapped up very well in a tablecloth.*)

REB SHMELKE. So you do know Serkele? So you must've been here in Lemberg in the past, eh?

STRANGER. Once, but it was a very long time ago.

REB GAVRIEL. (*Suddenly stands still in front of the Stranger and asks Reb Shmelke*): This gentleman seems familiar to me—he's from Brody, ha? *Nicht wahr?*

REB SHMELKE. (*Already a little sleepy.*) Right, yeah, I don't know...

STRANGER. (*To Reb Gavriel.*) No, I'm not from Brody.

REB GAVRIEL. But you're certainly no local, right? (*He puts down the wrapped-up box on the bench and offers his hand to the Stranger.*) Sholem aleykhem!

STRANGER. (*Shakes hands with Reb Gavriel.*) Aleykhem sholem!

REB SHMELKE. (*Rouses himself from his stupor and drinks.*) But my dear Reb Solomon! You're not drinking anything! (*He falls asleep sitting on the bench and holding the bottle of wine.*)

REB GAVRIEL. (*To the Stranger.*) So what's the news from your corner of the world?

STRANGER. No news.

REB GAVRIEL. Are you going to do any trading here? Or might you be buying something? I'm sorry for asking you, but, as you can see, I'm a local merchant, and, as it happens, quite a speculator. I have business all over the world; my name is known everywhere. Any place you can think of, everyone knows me there; I'm always getting letters from all of the biggest cities! Tell me, do you do any business with the Woltzman brothers in Moscow?

STRANGER. No.

REB GAVRIEL. No? That's a surprise! I didn't think there was anyone who didn't know them! Here, I'll show you a letter (*He searches in his pockets.*) that I just got from them the day before yesterday, about a little commission of twelve thousand bales of cotton . . . It's too bad, I don't seem to have the letter on me . . . but . . . do you perhaps know the Kitoyev House in Berlin?

STRANGER. No, I don't know any of these gentlemen; I've never even heard of them.

REB GAVRIEL. (*To himself, quietly.*) Me either! (*Aloud.*) What? You don't know of the Kitoyev House? You must be joking! How can you not know such huge speculators? They must be the biggest speculators in all of Holland!

STRANGER. In all of Prussia, you mean; Berlin is the capital of Prussia.

REB GAVRIEL. That has nothing to do with it; I get letters from them all of the time, that's the point. When was it, hm? . . . I think it was the eleventh, yes, that they sent me a whole box full of jewelry, pearls and diamonds—are you an expert on these kinds of things?

STRANGER. I used to be a great expert in the diamond trade; now, I don't know—I haven't been in the business for a long time.

REB GAVRIEL. You really seem very familiar to me, may you live to be a hundred and twenty; have you ever been to Breslau?

STRANGER. I just traveled through Breslau on my way here; I had never been there before that.

REB GAVRIEL. (*Aside.*) Me either. (*Aloud.*) And you've never heard of me? I'm fairly surprised, to be honest, that you don't know of me; I'm known far and wide as an honest man, God be praised. Just ask your host. (*Turns to Reb Shmelke.*) Reb Shmelke! Do you know me? Aha! He's fast asleep! (*Shouts.*) Reb Shmelke! Reb Shmelke!

REB SHMELKE. (*Starting.*) Ha? What? Right away!

REB GAVRIEL. Do you know me? Reb Shmelke!

REB SHMELKE. Good, it's very good, it's been in my cellar for eight years already, a real picker-upper! (*Drains the bottle and puts it down again on the bench.*) Yes, a real picker-upper! (*Falls asleep again.*)

STRANGER. (*Laughing.*) Let him be, he's had a bit too much to drink.

REB GAVRIEL. Yes, he certainly doesn't mind a drop; that's been his nature for a long time. So tell me, my dear fellow Jew, now that we've had the chance to become a little bit better acquainted, would you grant me the good fortune to make a profit on some pearls, diamonds, earrings, beautiful rings? I'm telling you, it's a good investment. Or let me trade for something; I'll certainly treat you honestly. You'll have to admit that you're getting it from me at a steal. Just buy it, buy. You'll thank me later.

STRANGER. I'll tell you the truth; I've completely gotten out of the trading business.

REB GAVRIEL. I'm telling you though, such a find, you're sure to make three times your money back, or—you know what?—buy something to bring home to your wife and kiddies, they should have long life! Honestly, I'm going to sell you these things dirt cheap, even below cost, since I need the cash. Make me a good opening offer.

STRANGER. How can I? Let me see the merchandise; maybe there's something that will catch my eye. Do you have it here with you?

REB GAVRIEL. I have just a little bit here with me, because I've just come from the Countess Strelkovska's—she ordered me to bring her a few pearls and diamonds today, but I didn't find her at home just now; now I see that it's your good fortune. If you like, I'll show you the merchandise. (*Looks around in all directions, to make sure that no one else is watching.*)

STRANGER. Just let me see.

REB GAVRIEL. (*Unpacking the little box while he speaks.*) Certainly, what harm can it do for you to look at it, you're not going to pay me before you see it. (*Looks around in all directions once more.*)

STRANGER. Why are you always looking around like that? Are you afraid of something?

REB GAVRIEL. You're not a local, so if you'll excuse me, you don't know anything; in Lemberg you have to be worried about any business transaction and particularly in diamonds, because, first of all, thieves are more common here than anywhere else. And second, I'm very afraid of the evil eye. (*He opens up the small box.*) Look how dazzling! (*He takes out a miniature surrounded by diamonds.*) How do you like this diamond-rimmed miniature? This must be a portrait of Queen Esther. (*He closes the small box and covers it with the tablecloth and gives the miniature to the Stranger. During the time that Reb Gavriel is involved with the little box, the Stranger stands lost in thought; now he takes the miniature from Reb Gavriel and examines it; suddenly he falls to the earth near Reb Shmelke, overcome, and cries.*)

STRANGER. Oh, God! My Rokhele! (*He drags Reb Gavriel down by his belt. Reb Gavriel falls down on top of the Stranger, tries to get up but is unable to. With his other hand, he pushes the little box under the bench and covers it up. Reb Shmelke starts awake from his sleep, greatly frightened, falls over Reb Gavriel, hits him, and shouts loudly.*)

REB SHMELKE. Berl! Feivel! Hershel! Velvl! Danger! Save us! Save us! Quickly! Oy, vey! Quickly, quickly, the rich merchant has fainted!

Scene 4

(*Berl and several Youths come running out of the door.*)

BERL and the YOUTHS. (*Help Reb Shmelke to his feet, shouting.*) Help! What's going on?

REB SHMELKE. (*Shouting.*) Grab him, hold him, that murderer! Berl! Save the rich merchant, quickly, quickly, and grab the wine, rub his temples! (*Berl grabs the bottle of wine and spills it on the Stranger and rubs his temples and his wrists. The Youths drag Reb Gavriel to his feet, hold him, and shout.*)

YOUTHS. Hold him, the thief, the robber!

REB SHMELKE. (*Shouts loudly in both directions.*) Help! Over here! Help! Save us, save us!

Scene 5

(*Policemen and three Beadles come from the street, leading Redlekh and Hinde, who are tied together with a rope. Chava and Chaim follow, in tears.*)

BEADLES. (*Shouting.*) What's this? What's this? What's all the shouting about?

REB SHMELKE. Come, come here! We've caught a thief.

BEADLES. Good, good, give him to us! We've already got two. Give us one more, and we'll have three of them dead to rights.

REB SHMELKE. (*Points to Reb Gavriel.*) Here—take 'im! (*To Berl.*) Give 'im a good shake.

BEADLES. (*Taking Reb Gavriel.*) Come on, buddy!

REB GAVRIEL. (*Pointing to Hinde and Redlekh.*) Let me go; these people know me. What do you want from me? I'm a local merchant. Get away from me, get away, let me go! Go ahead, ask these people whether I'm an honest man! (*He tries in vain to pull away from the Beadles*).

REDLEKH. (*To the Beadles.*) Let him be, it is true. We know him, he is a local merchant.

HINDE. Yes, yes, I know him very well—as well as I know myself.

REB SHMELKE. Yeah, yeah, I know you do. You're all the same: he's a thief, and so are you. (*Shouts to the Beadles.*) Send 'em back to kindergarten!

BEADLES. (*Shouting.*) Take him, the dog! (*They start to go with Redlekh, Hinde, and Reb Gavriel.*)

CHAVA. (*Suddenly falls to the ground next to the Stranger.*) Oh no, my master! Help, do something!! Hindele, help, help! It's your father! Your father! Oy, vey, my dear master . . . help him!

BEADLES. (*Stopping.*) What is it this time? (*Hinde and Redlekh run to the Stranger and shout simultaneously.*)

HINDE. My father? Where? Where is he? Help! (*She tugs at him.*)

REDLEKH. Herr Gutherz? For God's sake! Help him! (*Takes a bottle out of his pocket and holds it under the Stranger's nose.*)

STRANGER. (*Slowly coming to.*) Who . . . What . . . My Hinde? Where? Where? My child!

ALL. (*Shouting simultaneously.*) He's alive! He's alive!

REB SHMELKE. (*To Berl.*) Bring two or three bottles of wine right away! The rich merchant's alive . . . Quick, quick! But wait, wait, write it down first, that'll be good enough. . . . But hurry, hurry! (*The Stranger remains very still, unable to remember anything.*)

CHAVA. (*Stands to one side of the Stranger, fanning him with her handkerchief.*) Help! Save my dear master!

CHAIM. (*Stands on the other side of the Stranger, fanning him with his shirttails and crying.*) Help, my Chava, my love!

STRANGER. (*Rubbing his eyes.*) God! Is this real, or just a dream?

HINDE. (*Kisses the Stranger and helps him to his feet.*) No, my dear father! It is not a dream. I, Hinde, am at your side. I am your daughter. Just remember, Father! You are here with your child.

STRANGER. (*Goes to embrace Hinde, but when he sees that she is tied up, he stops, takes her head in his hands, and cries.*) Ach! What is this? My daughter tied up? No, no, this is not my daughter! It's just a dream! (*He buries his face in his hands.*)

HINDE. (*Also covering her face, she sobs loudly.*) God, let me die now . . .

REDLEKH. But my dear Herr Gutherz! Get a hold of yourself, for God's sake! Just listen to us for one minute: a horrible slander has put us in these chains!

HINDE. Daddy! We're innocent! (*She cries and moans loudly.*)

CHAVA. Praise God, my dear master, as you are alive! Just hear me out: I'll tell you. This is the story: someone walked off with all your sister Serkele's jewelry; so she up and accused these two. I'm ready to swear that it's a lie, that it's . . .

STRANGER. (*Cuts her off.*) What? My sister? Serkele? Her jewelry . . . stolen? (*To Reb Shmelke.*) Reb Shmelke! Where did that merchant go? Where is the young man who wanted to sell me jewelry? Where is the chest? God! Where is the picture of my blessed Rokhele? (*He finds the portrait on the ground, picks it up and kisses it, then picks up the chest from under the bench.*) Oh, divine Providence! How miraculous are your works!

CHAVA and CHAIM. (*Shout simultaneously.*) Oy vey, those are the mistress's jewels!

REB SHMELKE. The boy's here! (*To the Beadles.*) Just bring that pious Jew over here, yeah, yeah, some fine merchant he is! He buys everything with his kosher little hands. Just bring 'im over here!

BEADLES. (*Leading Reb Gavriel to the Stranger.*) Here he is.

STRANGER. (*Shows him the jewels.*) Don't try anything fancy; tell the truth, it will go better for you. Where did you get the jewels from? Tell us, are these yours or not?

REB GAVRIEL. I beg your pardon not one time, but a thousand times. I'll tell you the truth. But I beg of you, please have them untie me. Have pity, as you are a Jew! You are making me indescribably unhappy.

CHAVA. Aha, is that you, Reb Gavriel? Now I understand the whole story. How are things, Reb Gavriel? I think congratulations are in order? (*She takes Chaim by the hand.*) Come on, Chaim, let's go run to the mistress and tell her what's going on here! (*They both run out.*)

STRANGER. (*To the Beadles.*) Let go of his hands. He will not run away.

BEADLES. (*Release Reb Gavriel's hands.*) Don't worry, no one runs away from us so quickly.

REB GAVRIEL. (*Falls to the ground before the Stranger and kisses his feet.*) My good man! Have God in your heart! Have pity on my tender years! I'll confess everything to you—both of them are completely innocent. (*He gets up.*) Do what you want with me. I'm responsible, I'm the only guilty one. They knew nothing about it. I did it myself. Have mercy!

REB SHMELKE. (*Slaps Reb Gavriel.*) There's mercy for ya'. A curse on your whole family, you thief! (*Shouts to the Beadles.*) Send him back to kindergarten!

POLICEMEN. (*Shouting and laughing, in a singsong.*) Nyah, nyah, nya-nyah nyah!

BEADLES. (*Taking Reb Gavriel.*) Come!

STRANGER. Let him go, don't take him until my sister comes. Just keep an eye on him.

BEADLES. (*Obeying.*) Okay, okay, we'll watch him, don't you worry.

STRANGER. (*Untying Hinde and Redlekh.*) Yes, you are innocent, my child! (*He hugs and kisses her.*) God be praised! He has given me back my golden child! (*Covers her face with kisses.*) The very picture of my Rokhele. (*Kisses her.*) I have you back, my daughter, my Hinde! (*He lifts her up high and kisses her*).

HINDE. (*Embraces the Stranger, kissing him and crying.*) My dear, wonderful father!

STRANGER. (*To Redlekh.*) How horrible! You were tied up too? (*Embraces and kisses him.*) Don't you worry, I am here with you again! (*He looks at Redlekh and Hinde.*) My dear children!

REDLEKH. (*Kisses the Stranger's hand.*) My benefactor! My guardian angel!

Scene 6

(*Reb Moyshe's voice is heard in the distance.*)

REB MOYSHE. My Dovid! Oy, where is he, my brother-in-law? (*Comes running in without his hat or belt, his coat hanging open. He embraces and kisses the Stranger.*) You're here, my Dovid, my dear brother-in-law, my salvation! Thank God, you're back, you're alive! (*He kisses and pats him the way one does a little child.*) Yes, my joy, my glory, you are here. (*Speaks as if somewhat confused.*) Yes, I know that God sent you to us. Yes, yes, I know, you come from very far away. I know it all. I saw you. I've known for a long, long time that you would come. I remember, oy, I remember so well how you asked me, "Do you know me?" (*Kisses the Stranger.*) And now you're here. Now I've lived long enough. Now I can die. (*Gives the Stranger a bear hug.*) No, now I'll never let you go, no, no! (*Pats him and cries.*) I beg of you, my Dovid, my heart, don't go away from me again. Don't leave me alone! Or no—take me with you, because without you I've become a thief, a murderer. Yes, yes, your child's murderer! (*Falls to the ground, exhausted, next to the Stranger.*)

STRANGER. (*Picking him up.*) Moyshe, Moyshe, what's happening to you? Calm yourself!

REB MOYSHE. Oy, my dear Dovid! Pardon me, pardon me! I've done you much wrong. Or, no, no, don't pardon me, no, punish me, it's only right! Punish me however you can, I deserve it. Yes, yes, have me thrown in jail, have me whipped, beaten, stabbed, roasted, burned! Oy, I've certainly earned it.

STRANGER. Moyshe, are you mad? Why, what for? Calm down, for God's sake! Get a hold of yourself. Why should I punish you? Just settle down, be calm.

REB MOYSHE. (*A bit more quietly and calmly.*) Nu, yes . . . okay . . . whatever you say . . . yes, I'll calm down, I am calm . . . Whatever you say . . . yes, I'll do what you say . . . I'll do anything you say, my dear brother-in-law, as long as you punish me . . .

STRANGER. Okay, whatever you say, but just calm down first. Just sit down for a while. (*To Redlekh.*) Herr Redlekh! Please be so kind as to assist him, seat him on the bench.

REB MOYSHE. (*Sees Redlekh and Hinde and suddenly falls to the ground in front of them.*) Oy, vey iz mir! Can you ever forgive me?

HINDE. Uncle dear! You've done nothing wrong!

REDLEKH. Herr Danziger! *Bleiben sie nur ruhig!*[38] (*They help him to his feet and sit him down on the bench.*)

REB SHMELKE. (*Aside.*) Real nice, I tell ya'. A whole family o' thieves.

Scene 7

(*Enter Serkele, Altele, and Reb Yoykhenen. We hear Serkele long before we see her.*)

SERKELE. Why do you keep talking about it? Oy, I feel faint! I have to scream my heart out a thousand times before anyone listens to me once! Nu, go already, take them to jail, the thieves! And you, my dear Reb Yoykhenen, don't waste your time pleading for them, because it won't work with me.

REB SHMELKE. (*Runs quickly to Serkele.*) Come greet your guest, Serkele! Your brother Dovid's here! (*He indicates the Stranger.*)

SERKELE. (*Runs to Reb Dovid and tries to embrace him.*) Oy, vey iz mir! I am thunderstruck! My dear Dovid! I am absolutely bowled over! My beloved brother, oy vey, you're alive!?

STRANGER. (*Pushing her away.*) Away, you beast! Get away from me—you are not my sister!

POLICEMEN. (*Shouting.*) Nyah nyah nya-nyaaah nyaah! (*Serkele stands with her head bowed and arms limp, and cries. Complete silence for a moment.*)

STRANGER. You're crying? Yes, at crying and screaming you're a great expert. That's easy for you, but behaving honestly—that you find very hard! To act that way to my child, my only, innocent child, your own niece! Tell me, you wicked snake: can a person with any sort of conscience treat someone else like that? Just look at yourself, the way you stand there now . . . did you need it? You, I thought, will bring

---

38. German, "Just keep calm!"

up my child, teach her, console her, protect her from misfortune. That was some consolation to me while I was away, thinking that my own sister will look after my daughter. How happy I was whenever I imagined the moment that I would come home! How you would bring my Hinde to me, healthy and strong, honest and educated! I would often get so lost in my thoughts that I would forget myself, stretch out my hands, and in my mind take you in my arms and kiss you and hug you. But this I never imagined. This never entered my mind: that you would treat my child so horribly! To make your own niece feel such shame and disgrace! To treat her like a thief, to tie her up and take her off to jail! No, I never dreamed of such a thing. And on top of that, I hear that God did not abandon you either, that you've become a very wealthy woman. You hardly needed my money— God gave you plenty of your own . . . Nu, when you enjoy success, do you have to treat others so badly?

REB MOYSHE. (*Interrupting him.*) What are you saying, my dear brother-in-law? God willed it for her? God blessed her? For what? For her goodness, maybe? Maybe for her piety? No, God, blessed is He and blessed is His Name, rewards only the good, the honest, the pious . . . but her? Why? What for? Oy, my dear Dovid! Poor thing, you know nothing of how she ruined me, and you, and all of us! Oy, it will never make any sense.

REB GAVRIEL. (*Aside.*) Now's the time, now it must all come out. I've buried myself—I may as well bring her down with me! (*To the Stranger.*) A hundred pardons, my dear Reb Dovid, if you look in the chest, you'll find something much more precious than jewels. You'll be very happy, you'll find out everything . . .

STRANGER. (*Opens the chest and looks inside.*) There's nothing else here, just jewels.

REB GAVRIEL. Look carefully! There's a piece of paper underneath!

STRANGER. A piece of paper? (*Looks through the chest.*) Yes, it is here. What sort of a paper is this?

REB GAVRIEL. Just read it, you'll see . . .

STRANGER. (*Takes a piece of paper out of the chest, opens it, and reads it to himself, then exclaims.*) Almighty God in heaven! This is how far Your pure creation, made in Your image, can go astray! Oh, this is extraordinary . . . a false will!

REB GAVRIEL. Yes, just yesterday was the anniversary of your death, my dear Reb Dovid!

SERKELE. (*Suddenly throws herself at the Stranger's feet.*) Oy, do with me as you wish! I'm completely in your hands! (*She sobs forcefully.*)

REB MOYSHE. (*Very happy.*) Now that's nice. That's the way it should be. You see, Serke, that makes me happy!

STRANGER. (*Embraces Hinde and kisses her.*) You, my only child, I disinherited you? You, my life, you my soul? (*To Serkele.*) Feh, shame on you! You can still look me in the eye? It's no surprise that strangers could have done me wrong, when you, my own sister, treated me like that! (*To Hinde.*) Oy, now I understand how you must have suffered here, you poor girl.

HINDE. (*Kisses the Stranger.*) No, no, Daddy! Not as much as you think. I *have* suffered . . . that is true . . . but I have not suffered alone. (*Takes Redlekh by the hand and leads him to the Stranger.*) This man here befriended me in my suffering. He was my partner, my teacher, my pillar in my time of need!

STRANGER. (*Embraces and kisses Redlekh.*) *Ich danke ihnen, mein teuerer!*[39] I thank you; may God reward you with more, but I can repay your worthy actions only with this, the dearest thing I have. (*Places Redlekh's hand in Hinde's and kisses both of them.*) Always strive to deserve God's goodness, and He, the Almighty Father, will never forsake you! (*He places his hands on their heads and blesses them.*) Live happily together, my children! (*Hinde and Redlekh embrace and kiss the Stranger.*)

REB YOYKHENEN. (*Shaking the Stranger's hand.*) *Sholem aleykhem*, Reb Dovid! Praise God, I find you in good health. I tell you, a very good match. It occurred to me when the two of them were tied together. But let me tell you something, the words "birds of a feather flock together" are written in our holy Torah.[40] You, my dear Reb Dovid, are matchmaking in the modern fashion. But do you know with whom you're making the match? Who your in-laws were? That you have to ask me, Reb Yoykhenen the Matchmaker. I've known that little German over there ever since he was a little pisher. I knew his pious father, may he rest in peace, and also his modest mother. He is none other than the son of Reb Zalmen of Prague . . . that's right, the eminent genius . . . so I'll tell you up front, my fee will be very, very large.

STRANGER. Alright, alright, we'll take care of it.

HINDE. (*Takes the Stranger by the hand and asks.*) Daddy! I have just one request.

STRANGER. Tell me, my sweet, what would you like? I'll do anything you ask—just name it.

HINDE. (*Kissing his hand.*) My dear father! Please forgive my aunt. She'll reform. I beg of you, dear father, forgive her!

---

39. German, "I thank you, my dear!"

40. Literally "Each raven according to its species"; see Lev. 11:15 and Deut. 14:14.

STRANGER. Forgive who, Serkele? No, no, she doesn't deserve it. No, I want nothing to do with her. (*He thinks for a moment.*) But I must do it for your sake, my child . . . It's no use, I promised. Alright, for your sake, my child. Come here, Serke!

SERKELE. (*Who, up to this point, has been lying on the ground. Now she picks herself up and runs toward the Stranger with outstretched arms and a very loud cry.*) My dear brother! Remember, we come from the same parents! Have pity on me, on my Moyshe, on my only child! After all, we have no one else to turn to! Without you, we have no hope. My good, dear brother. (*She cries loudly.*) Oy, vey iz mir! We'll all starve to death if you don't have pity on us . . .

STRANGER. Well, what can one do—do I have a choice? You're my sister, after all. . . . Come here . . . I forgive you. But be a little better; it's high time. You're getting old, you're already forty-something. I shouldn't forgive you, but what can I do—a bad sister is still a sister. I'm not worried—you won't starve to death. God, blessed be He, gave me enough, and I hope He won't forsake me in the future.

REB GAVRIEL. It's amazing! Since yesterday she's lost ten thousand rubles and gained twenty years.

REB SHMELKE. That's nice, I tell ya'! I would make her pay, a sweet sister like that! (*He goes to Serkele.*) Serkele! Will you have some nice flour ready for Shabbes?[41]

FREYDE-ALTELE. (*Who, up to now, has been standing and crying very quietly. Now she goes up to the Stranger and talks to him very charmingly.*) Dear Herr Uncle! I give you my sincerest thanks for everything that you have had the decency to forgive my mother for, and for your tender heart, for which I have the utmost respect, and your excellent goodness does not let me rest until I ask of you that my betrothed, my beloved Gavriel Hendler, may be released.

REDLEKH. She is your sister's daughter and has been promised in marriage to Reb Gavriel Hendler. (*He indicates Reb Gavriel.*)

STRANGER. Come here, my child! Tell me, what do you want? Why don't you speak plainly? Tell me, what do you want? (*Freyde-Altele is silent and embarrassed, and hides behind a handkerchief.*)

HINDE. I'll tell you, Daddy: she was supposed to be married to Reb Gavriel Hendler; now she asks you to let him go.

STRANGER. No, my dear girl, you won't pursuade me to do that. I am your uncle and must have you provided for better than your mother would have. I cannot let him go. He'll serve out his sentence some-

---

41. The Sabbath.

where else, just as he deserves. (*To the Beadles.*) Is my old friend, Police Inspector Rechtzammer,[42] still alive?

BEADLES. Yes he is, may the good man live to a hundred and twenty.

STRANGER. Good, take him there. That upstanding man will know what to do with him.

BEADLES. Good, good, we'll take him there. (*As they start to go, Yerakhmiel comes running in, out of breath.*)

Scene 8

YERAKHMIEL. (*Runs up to Reb Gavriel.*) Ma-ma-ma-master! Clear out, r-r-right away . . . Reb Shmuel Se-se-secondhand came with p-p-p-policemen and already took your th-things away. Now they're looking for y-y-you, they really want to put y-y-you in j-j-jail.

REB SHMELKE. Go tell Reb Shmuel we saved him the trouble. We're taking him to the police, the thief.

YERAKHMIEL. What, y-y-y-you're taking him to the p-police? Where are my wages f-for the whole year, that I b-b-busted my back for? L-listen here: p-p-pay me m-my wages!

REB GAVRIEL. What are you shouting for? Your year isn't up yet. There are still six days to go. You know what? Come join me in my new place.

YERAKHMIEL. Go to hell w-with your pay, and with your place! (*He takes a watch out of his pocket and shows it to Reb Gavriel.*) Look here, y-y-you thief: this watch runs all b-by itself, but y-you have to be taken!

REB GAVRIEL. (*To the Beadles.*) Take that watch away from him, it's mine!

REB SHMELKE. (*To Reb Gavriel.*) You, thief! A curse on your ancestors! I'll stand up for him. Pay up; if not, he keeps the watch! I know him. He was my servant for five years, he's a very honest young man, and you're a thief, a criminal . . . Send him to kindergarten!

POLICEMEN. (*Shouting mockingly.*) Ha ha ha, nyah nyah nyah, ha ha ha!

BEADLES. (*Tie up Reb Gavriel with the rope.*) Come brother, it's time for kindergarten.

REB YOYKHENEN. (*Grabs Reb Gavriel by the hand.*) Nevertheless, let me tell you something. None of this changes anything. You still owe me my fee for trying to make you a match. I hate to forgive a debt, especially from a thief.

REB GAVRIEL. (*Pushing Reb Yoykhenen away.*) There's your fee for you!

---

42. Yiddish "justice encloser."

POLICEMEN. (*Shouting and laughing.*) Ha ha ha, nyah nyah nyah, ha ha ha, nyah nyah nyah!

YERAKHMIEL. You can t-t-tell from the wedding party what the g-g-groom is like! (*The Beadles take Reb Gavriel away, with several policemen running after them, shouting "Ha ha, nyah nyah!"*)

Scene 9

STRANGER. Well, that takes care of one person. Now let us continue. You, Reb Shmelke, you remember what you told me earlier about my sister Serke and Reb Shmerl the matchmaker?

REB SHMELKE. Some of it I remember, and some of it I don't.

STRANGER. (*Takes Freyde-Altele by the hand and brings her to Reb Shmelke.*) Do you have any objection to taking my sister's daughter for your bride?

REB SHMELKE. Well, Serkele the miller's girl says she won't have me. And why? 'Cause she's her only daughter and can't measure the oats and doesn't speak my language . . . Maybe she's right, what do I know?

STRANGER. Nu, nu, stop being angry. I assure you that in half a year, she'll speak your language and will obey you in everything. (*To Freyde-Altele.*) *Nicht wahr, mein Kind?*

FREYDE-ALTELE. (*Very charmingly.*) Ja. (*Catches herself.*) No . . . not "ja," "yeah," I should say.

STRANGER. (*Laughs and takes Reb Shmelke by the hand.*) Nu, Reb Shmelke, take her! She's starting to speak plainly. And I'm sure that you'll thank me again later. Your inn needs a woman like this. Take her!

REB SHMELKE. (*Scratching his head.*) Yeah . . . It's all true . . . but . . . you're forgetting something. I mean . . . you don't understand . . . remember . . . ya' see . . . I mean . . . just . . . the main thing . . .

STRANGER. Just take her. I'm telling you, I'll make sure that she doesn't take after her mother.

REB SHMELKE. Yeah, my dear Reb Solom . . . Reb Dovid, I mean. But I think, the main thing . . . you understand?

REB YOYKHENEN. Let me tell you something, every negotiation needs an arbitrator and every match a matchmaker! I'm telling you, my dear Reb Dovid, that although you're offering Reb Shmelke a very good match in terms of money, he's an aristocrat to boot, and you can tell that to anyone. I'm telling you, he comes from a distinguished family, and his ancestors were great scholars and rabbis, very holy men. When you talk to him again, take his family tree into account . . . But even then, what will come of it? Reb Shmelke is right. What does Serkele's daughter have in that department?

REB SHMELKE. Yeah, that's it, that's just what I mean. My dear Reb Shmer . . . Reb Yoykhenen, I mean, I love you for seeing just what I meant. What's the amount and who's paying it?

STRANGER. Is that it? That's what you mean by the main thing. (*Picks up the chest of jewels and gives it to Reb Shmelke.*) Have that appraised, and whatever they tell you it's worth, I'll pay you.

REB SHMELKE. (*Opens the chest and looks inside.*) Oy vey! Quite a bundle! (*Very happy, he takes the Stranger's hand and agrees to the arrangement.*) Mazl tov! You see, my dear Reb Dovidl, that's another story! Yeah, that's good. (*He takes Freyde-Altele by the hand.*) Don't be silly or ashamed of how I talk. Be a good wife. Don't be afraid. You won't have to measure the oats; I have more than enough servants for that.

REB YOYKHENEN. Nu, I've made another successful match! Let me tell you something, it's really a match made in heaven. (*He shouts.*) Mazel tov!

POLICEMEN. (*Shouting.*) Mazel tov!

SERKELE. (*Embraces reb dovid, cries, and kisses him.*) My golden, wonderful brother! I don't deserve everything you're doing for me and my daughter. May God reward you for it.

STRANGER. God has already rewarded me a thousand times over. I'm doing what it's my duty to do, nothing more. You see how nice it is to do good? If you behave from now on, I'll forget everything that you've done. I'll also do right by you for as long as God allows me.

CHAVA. But my dear master, you've completely forgotten about me. Don't you remember your servant Chava? You remember those delicious poppy cakes I used to make you?

STRANGER. Aha, Chava! How are you? Who do you work for now?

HINDE. She's always been faithful to me. True, she got no great joy from it, but she never abandoned me. She works for Auntie.

STRANGER. (*To Chava.*) Well, pick out a nice groom, and you won't have suffered in vain. I'll pay your dowry.

CHAVA. (*Takes Chaim by the hand and leads him to Reb Dovid.*) My dear master, I'll ask what you asked Reb Shmelke . . . Would Chaim object to being my husband? He's an honest young man, and not at all bad at his work.

STRANGER. So have you asked him if he objects?

CHAIM. Oy oy oy, do I object?! But she has to promise me this one thing: that she'll never go off to the spas again.

REB YOYKHENEN. (*To Chaim and Chava.*) You see, my children, that's a good match . . . Let me tell you something, every pot finds its lid. But I get a fee, because on my word of honor, I thought of this match three weeks ago.

STRANGER. Nu, nu, I'll reward you for everything. Now come, children! Let's go into Reb Shmelke's, and tonight we'll sign all three betrothals!

REB MOYSHE. (*Until now, has been sitting contemplatively. Now he approaches Reb Dovid and says very calmly.*) Nu, my dear Dovid, you've put everything right, now make an end of me and punish me like I deserve. Do what you want with me, have me taken away too . . .

STRANGER. (*Cutting him off.*) Come, I'll take you myself! (*Embraces and kisses Reb Moyshe.*) Come, come, Moyshe! Come into the house with me. There you'll be proud and happy, my dear brother-in-law!

REB MOYSHE. (*Embraces the Stranger, sobs very loudly, and kisses him. He tries to speak several times, gesturing that he is unable to say anything.*)

STRANGER. (*Wiping his eyes and kissing Reb Moyshe.*) I understand you, my dear brother! Just come, come! Come, children, come—with God's help, everything will turn out right.

REB YOYKHENEN. (*Shouting.*) Shout, children: mazl tov!

POLICEMEN. (*Shouting.*) Mazl tov! Mazl tov!

YERAKHMIEL. M-m-m-m-mazl tov! (*All go in pairs into Reb Shmelke's house.*)

The curtain falls.

A final word

If all of my words—
The ones you just heard—
Were not any good, were so very poor,
Then swear to me this: you'll read them no more.

But if anyone in so reading,
Thought to *her* my words were leading,
Then she should read it no more,
And I will not cry, that's for sure.

End of the entire play.

The Two Kuni-Lemls

by Avrom Goldfaden

Cast of Characters

REB PINKHESL. *A respectable Jew, a merchant dressed in Hasidic fashion.*
In the first and third acts he wears a robe and a yarmulke;
in act 4, a gaberdine with a shtrayml—*a fur hat*
worn by Hasidim. Speaks slowly.

RIVKE. *His wife, forty years old. Wears a red wig,*
but she is more worldly than he.

KHAYELE. *Their daughter, a young woman of seventeen.*

REB SHLOYMENYU. *A Galician Jew from Cracow, a well-respected man.*
Wears a long coat and a top hat.

KUNI-LEML. *His stepson. A twenty-year-old Hasid—blind in one eye,*
lame in one foot, and with a stutter. Wears a kapelyush, *a round black hat.*

KALMEN MATCHMAKER. *Speaks quickly but clearly, and frequently pinches snuff.*

LIBENYU. *His daughter, 19 years old and stupid as a cow.*

MAX. *A university student—a young man of 22.*

Hasidim, students, ghosts, guests, youngsters

The second half of act 2 takes place in Cracow, the rest of the action
in Odessa.

Act 1

Act 2

Act 3

Act 4

Act 1

Scene 1

We see Reb Pinkhesl's room—simply furnished, but by no means poor. Around a long table that stands center stage, and which has been laid with bottles of whiskey, glasses, plates, spoons, forks, knives, and challahs, many Hasidim are sitting and singing. They bang their forks against their glasses to the beat. Reb Pinkhesl sits at the head of the table, rolling his eyes the entire time.

---

1. Celebrated on the seventh day of the holiday of Sukkot, the Feast of Tabernacles, Hoshana Rabba is best known for the custom of beating the willow branches of the lulav, one of the ritual objects associated with the holiday, as well as being the day on which the book of judgment for the coming year is finally sealed.

ALL. We *yehudim*,[2]
Pious Hasidim,
Follow the Lord's good name.
The rebbe is our joy,
But those other men and boys,
Their pleasures just aren't the same.
Sabbath and holidays, they ruin absolutely.
"Who needs it?" they ask. "Where's the beauty?"
Oy, do we enjoy it!
Every minute,
There's a meal,
A flask and a cask,
A song, what a deal!
Oy, come eat, come drink, have a sip and a bite,
Everyone taste—what a delight!
Sing and dance, jump and prance,
For the love of God, tonight!

(*When they finish singing, they have something to eat. Afterward, they all get up and say to Reb Pinkhesl:*)

ALL. A good week to you, a good week, Reb Pinkhesl! May the Eternal Lord see to it that you'll soon be hosting an engagement party for your daughter!

PINKHESL. (*As they are leaving, he accompanies them and says:*) A good week, a good year! Go in good health! (*The Hasidim exit. Pinkhesl walks around the room several times, clapping his hands as he sings the same melody from a moment ago, with a pious expression on his face. He then stands still and says:*) Nu, thank God! We've celebrated the end of the Sabbath with the *melave malke* feast. Sure, why not? Once a week, we have the pleasure of *melave malke*, so it pays to enjoy ourselves. Yes, it's a pleasure, and the chance to hear a few words of Yiddish. And today I have my own personal joy, that's for sure, that's for sure. (*Pause.*) Now they've gone, and they wished me "a speedy engagement for your daughter." (*Thinking.*) Yes, an engagement for my daughter! (*Sighs.*) Oy, I hope I live to see the day, and that you, my fellow Jews, will join in the celebration! But when? When I can marry her to one of our own—that is, to a pious boy! (*In a talmudic singsong.*)[3] But what happens if she wants someone who's not pious?

---

2. Jews.

3. Traditionally, study of the Talmud—a highly verbal process, combining reading aloud and discussing meanings and questions with study partners—was associated with a vocalized singsong delivery.

(*Pause.*) Well, I'm not too concerned about what she wants, since I have my own opinion, and I am her father, may I live to a hundred and twenty.[4] It just galls me how her mother has spoiled her by sending her to that little teacher, the German[5] who wastes his time in school, and can do no wrong as far as she's concerned. What can I do? Shout to the skies, shout my lungs out, shout, shout, shout! (*He has not noticed Rivke's entrance, and continues talking.*)

Scene 2

(*Rivke enters from the left-hand door, where she stays for several seconds watching Pinkhesl, and as he says the words, "Shout, shout," approaches him. Pinkhesl acts startled, and backs away from her.*)

RIVKE. Shouting again, Pinkhesl?

PINKHESL. No, no, I'm done shouting. You're here now, so I'll let you take over. You're better at it than I am, may you continue shouting until you're a hundred and twenty.

RIVKE. Yes, I will shout, in fact, and why not? You can see that there's something wrong with our child, and it doesn't bother you a bit, dear Father in Heaven!

PINKHESL. (*Ironic.*) Is that so? Something's wrong with our daughter? So why don't you send for Maxie, the little teacher who tutors her. That will cure her completely . . .

RIVKE. (*Also ironic.*) Just take a look at him, my pious Hasidic husband.

PINKHESL. (*More serious.*) Listen here, Rivke. I wouldn't want to be your partner in the world to come. You know what they'll do to you there? And it's all because you yourself have spoiled her; you've raised her in your own manner, and because of you she's become a hussy!

RIVKE. (*Mimicking him.*) A hussy? (*Bursts out laughing.*) You're out of your mind, you crazy Hasid!

PINKHESL. I ask you then, Rivke, doesn't it make her a hussy if she already knows how to play love games? And with who? With the doctor's brat! A fine family: one doctor after another!

RIVKE. (*With an ironic smile.*) Aha, so that's what's gnawing at you. Well, and that's beneath you?

PINKHESL. No, Rivke. (*Pounds one hand into the other.*) As long as I live, I will not let my child play love games. (*A pause, after which he seems to come to, and suddenly says:*) Just tell me this, my dear wife: before we

---

4. Goldfaden playfully has Reb Pinkhesl extend himself the blessing traditionally bestowed on others: "May you (or he, or she) live to be a hundred and twenty."

5. As was the case in *Serkele* (act 3, scene 4), "German" here refers not actually to someone from the German principalities, but a modernizing Jew.

got married, did we also play at—what do they call it?—at these love
games? May God protect and defend me! I'm telling you, I didn't
love you then, and I don't love you now either. So has that done me
any harm? Aren't I, thank God, a good Jew and a wealthy man
without this love-shmove, huh? I'd really like to know what good
these silly things are, I mean—what are they called?—these love
games? Really, what can they be used for? To sell?—can you make
something from them? Can you charge interest on them, or what?

RIVKE. Go to the devil, you crazy Hasid, you think that if you can't sell
something it's worthless. If you don't make a profit on it, it has no
purpose. And yet there are times when you give away your money for
nothing, and so happily too—for example, to that rebbe of yours . . .

PINKHESL. (*Practically starts shaking with rage, and shouts.*) Rivke! Don't
even mention the rebbe with your unkosher lips. How can you understand what a rebbe means; after all, you're a sinful beast . . .

RIVKE. Of course I'm a beast if I have to teach sense to an old horse like
you . . .

PINKHESL. (*Somewhat calmer.*) Really? That's the respect I get from you?
Of all people you call me a horse?—I, who am known throughout
the city as such an eminent . . .

RIVKE. (*Finishing first.*) Ox!

PINKHESL. Don't interrupt, Rivke. As such an eminently wealthy man, I
was going to say. And don't forget, I was the rebbe's assistant, and
around me there used to dance so many . . .

RIVKE. Horses!

PINKHESL. No, Hasidim! There's no talking to her! To her it's all the
same, Hasidim and horses! (*Regards her angrily.*) But why argue with
you? I know what you're up to, but you listen to me, Rivke: whatever
you insist on doing, whatever you manage to do, doesn't bother me
a bit. But choosing a groom for our daughter, that's . . .

RIVKE. My job . . .

PINKHESL. No, that's my job, let me talk, don't interrupt! I'll give her a
groom who will be the envy of heaven and earth. Kalmen the Matchmaker told me that he's coming here today, and has a groom for me.
Rivke, I'm telling you, you yourself will be thrilled. Imagine, a son of an
elder of Shakhrayevke! I'm telling you, a groom who's an absolute . . .

RIVKE. Eyesore.

PINKHESL. No, an absolute gem. Listen, Rivke, you know . . .

RIVKE. You can keep to yourself, and you know that I always get my way.
(*Throughout her speech, Pinkhesl gestures that he doesn't want to hear, and
shouts, "Don't interrupt, Rivke, let me speak!" Rivke ignores him and keeps
talking.*) I want to give our daughter a groom she'll like, not someone you'll like, and probably whoever pleases her will please me too,
and I'm sure you'll say you won't be pleased, but . . .

PINKHESL. But that will definitely not happen, because the final say belongs to . . .

RIVKE. Me, only to me! (*Shouting this, she exits to the room to the left.*)

PINKHESL. (*Accompanies her to the door, and yells after her.*) No, to me, to me! . . . (*Stands and looks at the door through which she exited, then spits.*) Tfui! (*Walks around the room several times.*) So what is there to say to my wife? She's taken over and then run away. (*Pause.*) What can I do with her? Terrible! I know all too well that when she gets an idea in her head, that's it, but what, I'm going to listen to her? I'm supposed to let my family be tarnished with that doctor's brat who will soon be taking a pulse; no, any son of mine will do better to take good notes. When Kalmen Matchmaker comes, I'll just ask him if my bridegroom's father is really going to become the rabbi's assistant. If so, I won't ask too many questions, and we'll soon be drinking a toast!

⁂

Scene 3

(*Kalmen Matchmaker enters through the middle door and kisses the mezuzah.*)[6]

KALMEN. Yes, yes, a toast, hold your horses!

PINKHESL. (*Did not initially notice Kalmen entering. Looks around and sees Kalmen.*) Oh, welcome, welcome, Reb Kalmen. It's a good thing you've come, I was just talking about you! I'm talking to myself and thinking that . . .

KALMEN. (*Cuts him off.*) That what, hold your horses, that probably if Kalmen Matchmaker is involved, that's a good thing. Because Kalmen Matchmaker doesn't arrange matches between nobodies; I only do business with Hasidim and rabbis, but because you're Reb Pinkhesl—hold your horses—I've looked for a groom for you—hold your horses—I'm telling you, one in a million. Don't forget, a young man who knows nothing but God and prayer shawls and the rebbe, hold your horses, and doesn't set foot outside the rebbe's court all day long, hold your horses, because what does he know about making money? God should only bless all Hasidim with such children, hold your horses!

---

6. The commandment to write the words of God on the *mezuzot* (presumably "doorposts") of one's home and gate appears as early as Deut. 6:9 and 11:20. By the period of the Second Temple, these Biblical passages, along with other verses, were written on parchment, placed in containers, and affixed to the doorposts themselves. Often, particularly in the medieval era, the mezuzah was believed to have efficacy in ensuring God's protection of the home against dangers. Traditional Jews have the custom of kissing the mezuzah or touching it and then kissing the fingers that have done so (see BT Avoda Zara 11a and Maharil ad loc).

PINKHESL. I'll tell you, Reb Kalmen, you know that my daughter Khayele is . . .

KALMEN. An only child, hold your horses.

PINKHESL. And I'm giving her a thousand . . .

KALMEN. A thousand rubles' dowry, hold your horses.

PINKHESL. And you yourself won't come out too badly, you'll also get . . .

KALMEN. A nice commission, hold your horses.

PINKHESL. Lord Almighty, hold your horses and hold your horses, and you let your own horses stampede all over me.

KALMEN. You yourself say that I'll get a nice commission if I give you what you want, and I know . . .

PINKHESL. (*With a smile.*) Oh, oh, oh!

KALMEN. Ho ho ho! Hold your horses, I'm telling you that there is one Kuni-Leml in this world, and it's your destiny to snap up this wonderful bargain. But really, hold your horses a minute, he's not very handsome, I realize he has a few tiny flawlets, but I'm sure you know that people throw away the rind as long as the fruit is good. Because, I swear, who pays any attention to such nonsense? And don't forget who his father is—what is Reb Shloymenyu, a nobody?! Firstly, he is the rebbe's assistant, hold your horses! Secondly, he is the town alderman,[7] hold your horses! And thirdly, he's the third party brought in to settle every dispute, and soon, when he becomes the synagogue warden . . .[8]

PINKHESL. Oh, oh, oh! . . .

KALMEN. Oh oh oh! Hold your horses!

PINKHESL. You hold your horses—by the way, you've made my head spin so much that I've forgotten what I wanted to ask you. (*Puts his hand to his forehead and thinks.*) Yes, what did you say before, flaws?

KALMEN. Hold your horses! Listen up: when you interrupt me like that and don't let me finish speaking, you don't hear me. So who said anything about flaws, God forbid? I said he has a few tiny flawlets, like he doesn't see with his left eye—that means that with his right eye he sees much better, so that's fine, hold your horses. He also limps a little on one leg, and speaks with a bit of a stutter—that means he speaks slowly and doesn't interrupt. And that's the whole thing, and what's more, he's a Kuni-Leml, all Hasidim should be so lucky. Plus he's swarthy, but don't forget, Reb Pinkhesl, Reb Shloymenyu's son . . .

PINKHESL. Indeed, Reb Shloymenyu's son, but . . .

---

7. Literally "parnes-khoydesh," a local leader of the community chosen for a temporary term.

8. In Yiddish, *gabay,* a respected position of responsibility in the synagogue.

KALMEN. But what? Hold your horses! Don't forget that you are Reb Pinkhesl, are you going to make a big stew out of such small potatoes? What's the matter? So he can't see through one eye and can't walk on one leg; so show me, Reb Pinkhesl, where is it written in our holy books that a Jew has to see with both eyes, or walk equally well on both legs? So he speaks a little haltingly, so do our religious texts say that a Jew must speak perfectly? A Jew must know that he's a Jew—besides that, nothing matters. I tell you, Reb Pinkhesl—hold your horses! Don't dillydally and hold on to this gem so you don't find someone else holding him first, hold your horses!

PINKHESL. All right, I'm convinced, I don't care about such nonsense. The main thing is that he is an honest Jew from a good family; that's enough for me. But what do we do about my wife and daughter? They're certain to . . .

KALMEN. Scream and shout, hold your horses! This is what we'll do: I'll send off a letter to Reb Shloymenyu to have his son Kuni-Leml come to me first, and you'll welcome him at my house. But we must see to it that this thing is done slowly, because no good will come if it's done in haste. Have a good day, and be well, and hold your horses!

PINKHESL. Go in good health, and you hold your horses. (*Kalmen exits. Pinkhesl walks around the room again, muttering to himself.*) That will be the right thing to do. That's what I thought, and that's how it will be!

Scene 4

(*Rivke and Carolina enter through the left-hand door, Carolina in a coat and hat as if for going for a walk.*)

RIVKE. Go, my daughter, go and stroll a little on the boulevard; you'll get a bit of fresh air. But come home soon; don't be late.

PINKHESL. (*Stands off to the side, mimicking them.*) Aha, "fresh air," get some air! Look here, my daughter, just don't get any fresh ideas there . . .

RIVKE. Let her go, I have a bone to pick with you.

PINKHESL. Aha, you have a bone to pick with me. So let's go to another room. I know you can't say two words to me without nagging me to death, so at least let's not let strangers hear how you treat me. It's enough that I have to hear it. (*Both exit left. As Pinkhesl is leaving, he keeps his eyes on Carolina, mimicking her with the words, "air, air." Carolina watches him until he is gone, and sadly shakes her head.*)

CAROLINA (*Sings.*)

Imagine someone in a darkened room,
Sealed into a life of eternal gloom.
From his earliest days all is hidden away,
And he never sees the light of day.
Suddenly the doors are opened wide,
And he can see the sun's brilliant rays.
He feels new sensations stirring inside—
New life that brings promise of brighter days.
Suddenly, though, that world's closed off to him anew.
"The light is bright," they say, "but not for you."

I was raised in a gloomy tower
Born to fanatics, in an evil hour.
Every minute was dark for me
But I got used to it, thought, "Let it be."
Then I went out into the garden so sweet,
Of learning began to taste a small share,
From the tree of knowledge I started to eat.
My soul was revived by the breath of air.
Let it fill me through and through!
"The air is fresh," they say, "but not for you."

Among the Hasidim I've been raised,
They go around blind all their days.
I am a child, what do I know? I try to tell myself
That everyone should be that way.
So why am I suddenly ashamed
To see a well-educated man
With his noble mind and well-made frame?
He offers me all the love he can;
I love that man, and want him too.
"Oh, he is fine," they say, "but not for you."

Scene 5

(*A garden, various people strolling around, students walking arm in arm and singing.*)

STUDENTS.   Now let's relax,
              We're done with our tasks,
              Now we start everything over again.
              Together we crammed

For all our exams—
We've been most successful and feel like new men.

A STUDENT.   Remember: our professors deserve thanks,
They're the ones who showed us the light.
They've filled our heads, which used to be blanks,
And now we are erudite. (*Repeat last line.*)

STUDENTS.   Now let's relax . . .

2ⁿᵈ STUDENT.   So many nights without rest or repast,
Study and study until you're drained.
But now all that toil is in the past;
And a wealth of knowledge remains. (*Repeat last line.*)

(*One of the Students turns to Max, who paces back and forth, deep in thought.*)

STUDENT. So, Max, still head over heels in love?

MAX. I am truly in a pickle. That a girl as wonderful as Carolina should live under the roof of a rich Hasid like Reb Pinkhesl! You know, my friends, that they've cancelled her lessons with me? I'm not allowed to go there any more.

STUDENTS. What a shame!

MAX. I don't care about losing the lessons, but it is a shame about the girl. We've already read all the classics together: how well she understands, how nicely she grasps everything! And how much she loves me, and I her!

A STUDENT. So tell me, have you met your rival?

MAX. What rival? There are plenty of other mountains to climb before I reach that summit. Fortunately her mother is on our side; she's no fool, and she likes me. But with him, with her father, it's not so simple—he's a born Hasid, and runs a mile from anything modern! (*All laugh.*) So what hope can I have of ever being his son-in-law? The idea is so remote! (*He falls deep in thought, while the Students' expressions show their empathy.*)

Scene 6

(*From behind the curtains we hear Carolina's voice singing "Cuckoo! Cuckoo!" Max starts, listens to her voice, and says.*)

MAX. (*To the Students.*) Ha ha! I hear her coming, that's her signal. She promised to come here. Go stroll in the alleys, boys, and let me be alone with her—we have important things to discuss. (*All the Students exit to the side alleys. Max turns in the direction of Carolina's voice.*)

CAROLINA. My hunter has been waiting for an hour,
        If no one else is there, I'm in your power.
        You can catch me here and now,
        I'm in the trees, between the boughs.
        Cuckoo!
MAX.   Who's singing there between the boughs?
        It seems I know that voice somehow . . .
CAROLINA. Cuckoo!
        I sing, I do,
        Catch me, one-two,
        I'm a bird, I'll fly away,
        But listen, do,
        To the melody—
        Haven't you sung it today?
        Cuckoo, cuckoo . . .

(*She leaps out from behind the trees and runs to Max. They embrace.*)

MAX. How are you, my dear Carolina? I'm sure you have news for me.

CAROLINA. Yes, I've brought you important news—I hope you'll congratulate me. (*Max regards her curiously.*) Kalmen the Matchmaker has proposed a match to my father, from Shakhrayevke, the son of the alderman there.

MAX. Wait, wait! (*Thinks for a few seconds.*) All right, go on.

CAROLINA. And from what I overheard from their conversation, he seems to be serious competition, since you'll never have the qualities he possesses—and may God protect you from them. He is blind in one eye, lame on one leg, and . . .

MAX. Wait, wait—and I bet he stutters too?

CAROLINA. Oh, yes! How did you know that? Do you know him?

MAX. You ask how I know? Wait, I'll tell you in a moment. But first, tell me: when the matchmaker spoke to your father, did he say that the groom's father's name is Reb Shloymenyu?

CAROLINA. Yes, that sounds right, but so what?

MAX. If so, the groom is closer to me than to you. Do you know who he is? He's my uncle Reb Sholem's stepson, his second wife's son by her first husband. And do you know who Reb Shloymenyu is? No less than my father's own brother.

CAROLINA. What are you saying? Brothers! But your father's a doctor and he's a Hasid!

MAX. My uncle isn't the sort of Hasid your father thinks he is. He's as much of a freethinker as my father, but since he is the elder brother, he didn't have the opportunity to study. He plays the role of a pious man and leads the rebbe and his Hasidim by the nose—as you can see by your father being so impressed by his family connections.

CAROLINA. Yes, but that's no excuse for what my father is doing. He's made up his mind, and that's how it will have to be. Even my mother, who usually gets the last word, is having trouble contradicting him.

MAX. Nu, if it's hard for your mother, it will be easy for me. (*Thinking.*) I've thought of a beautiful plan. Yes, when you can't succeed either by being nice or by getting rough, you have to rely on desire.

CAROLINA. What do you mean? Don't forget, the matchmaker already wrote a letter inviting the groom to come to him first, and he'll bring the young man to us . . .

MAX. Very good! Listen to my plan. I'll get dressed up as this Kuni-Leml, I'll limp like him, speak like him, and make myself blind like him. And I'll pay a visit to Kalmen the Matchmaker, where I have a bit of business to tend to, and then you'll see me at your house, dressed as the real Kuni-Leml, and the rest you'll see for yourself.

CAROLINA. (*Smiling.*) Really! Will you really be able to disguise yourself so well?

MAX. So well that you yourself won't recognize me.

CAROLINA. (*Looks at him lovingly.*) Adieu, lieber[9] Max! May God give your plan success! *Adieu*, my Kuni-Leml-to-be! (*She backs away, throwing him kisses until she disappears into the distance.*)

MAX. (*Turns to the other side of the alley, and calls out.*) Comrades! (*They enter.*) I have a plan for getting married to Carolina, but I need your help to carry it out. Can you give me your word of honor that you will help me?

STUDENTS. Oh, you can be sure that we'll help you in any way we can! (*They all shake his hand as a sign that they are ready to serve him. He thanks them. All sing.*)

STUDENTS.   Now let's relax,
                We're done with our tasks,
                Now we start everything over again.
                Together we crammed
                For all our exams—
                We've been most successful and feel like new men.

MAX.   Let's give heartfelt thanks, remember,
                To him who loves us as he does himself:
                Our dear, beloved, loyal emperor,[10]
                May God grant him joy and good health! (*Repeat.*)

---

9. German/Yiddish, "dear."

10. The reference here is presumably to the current emperor of Russia, Alexander II (1818–1881, reigned 1855–1881), conventionally understood by proponents of Enlightenment to be sympathetic to their cause.

STUDENTS. (*Raise their hats into the air.*)
        Now let's relax, etc . . .
        Hurrah, hurrah, hurrah, long live our emperor,
        Hurrah, hurrah, hurrah! . . .

The curtain falls quickly.

Act II

Scene 1

(*Kalmen Matchmaker's room: a simple, ordinary room. Libele, his daughter, sits near a small table that is standing in the middle of the room. She sews and sings.*)

LIBE.   Every girl has got her mate,
        Though she may not be fair,
        And for my match I sit and wait,
        But there is no one there.
        One's man digs in ditches,
        Another's lives in riches.
        One girl really hit the jackpot—
        Her man's no Mister Right.
        Me, I wouldn't pass up even that crackpot
        But how would I sleep through the night?

        A journeyman my friend once did see,
        Listen, what a romance,
        He knew he liked Hannah, believe you me,
        From the very first glance.
        The gossip about her's mounting,
        She's twice divorced and counting.
        I couldn't carry on that way
        Holding marriage vows so slight.
        Divorces happen every day,
        But how would I sleep through the night?

        I should be jealous of my friend,
        All the neighbors mutter.
        So what—she has a husband then?
        But she loves another.
        To keep your husband clueless

Is sinful for a Jewess.
But being saintly isn't easy
When freedom's a delight.
It could be fun to be that sleazy
But how would I sleep through the night?

Before the wedding life's all gloom,
After is a pleasure.
Your married bliss fills every room—
The fighting's what you treasure.
The wife, she starts to riot,
The husband just stays quiet.
All you need are sharpened nails,
To win each time you fight.
I'd scratch his eyes out without fail
But how would I sleep through the night?

Once there grieved a wife so young
His age tore them asunder.
The old man didn't last her long,
He went quickly six feet under.
So, what if he did, though?
She became a wealthy widow,
Such a simple way to make her pile,
Isn't that all right?
I'd bury my old man in style,
But how would I sleep through the night?

Scene 2

(*Kalmen Matchmaker enters. He kisses the mezuzah, and quickly runs over to Libe.*)

KALMEN. Well, daughter of mine, have you already cleaned up the house? You know that today's the day that Reb Kuni-Leml—Shloymenyu's son—is coming. Nu quickly, quickly, clean up already, hold your horses!

LIBE. (*Grumbling and whining.*) Yes, yes, I cleaned up already. But? (*Sighs deeply.*) Oy!

KALMEN. What is it, my child, why are you so upset? Tell me, nu, quickly, hold your horses!

LIBE. Why shouldn't I be so upset, when I see how all of these other women get taken as brides, but there's no one who wants to take me?

KALMEN. What do you mean, "all of these other women get taken"? I *give* them away, hold your horses!

LIBE. So, what are you doing giving away the whole world, but not me?

KALMEN. Hold your horses!! If I had the money, I'd give you away too.

LIBE. So I should just wait until you manage to get some money for once, and in the meantime stay single, thanks to you, until my hair turns gray?

KALMEN. Nu, what do you want me to do for you, my child? That's the way the world is now, hold our horses! In the old days, our forefather Jacob was a slave for seven years before he was able to take Rachel as his wife.[11] Only afterward was he able to branch out on his own and become a master. These days, though, hold your horses! People are their own masters long before they get married, but right after the wedding, they're sold to their wives for eternal servitude! It's true that no one becomes a slave for nothing, certainly, certainly, you have to have a little bit of cash, if you want to get a husband, hold your horses! But if I manage to pull off this match for Reb Pinkhesl, I'll get a nice commission, hold your horses! And we'll probably also be able to find a husband for you!

Scene 3

(*Max enters, dressed as Kuni-Leml. He limps over to Kalmen and says.*)

MAX. Have I f-found Reb K-Kalmen Matchmaker here?

KALMEN. Yes, yes, you must be Reb Shloymenyu's son? Sholem aleykhem! (*He gives him his hand.*) Sit down, make yourself comfortable, just like in your own home, hold your horses!

MAX. I'm holding my h-horses; my father will be a-arriving after Hoshana Rabbah, because they are choosing him as the sexton.

LIBE. So? That's the bundle of joy that Reb Pinkhesl's daughter has in store for her? No, I'd never consider such a person, not even if he paid me to.

MAX. (*To Kalmen.*) Reb K-kalmen, who is the girl?

KALMEN. Hold your horses, that's my little daughter, may she live long, a good young woman, a wise young woman, an honest young woman, a fine young woman, hold your horses!

---

11. See Genesis 29:18–30. Kalmen seems to be eliding that because of Laban's trickery, Jacob actually served another seven years immediately after the wedding.

MAX. (*With a smile.*) Nu, and did you forget a "p-pretty young woman"?

LIBE. Just look at the stutterer. With that one eye of his he was still able to see that I'm pretty, he certainly has love on the brain!

MAX. (*To Kalmen.*) Reb Kalmen, is my b-bride also as pretty as your daughter is?

KALMEN. Hold your horses, you'll soon see for yourself, but I don't understand how it comes to pass that you, Reb Shloymenyu's son, are looking right at women like that? I happen to know that when a young Hasidic man meets a woman on the street, he closes his eyes.

MAX. On the s-street, yes, but behind closed doors, we Hasidim l-look very differently.

KALMEN. (*To himself.*) Ah, it's a fine jewel that Reb Pinkhesl is getting for his house! But what do I care, as long as I get my matchmakers' fee? After that, he can choke on him. (*To Max.*) You know, Reb Kuni-Leml, that in your father-in-law's house you're not going to be able to get away with saying those kinds of things. I mean, it doesn't matter to me, but if you're going to say things like that there, hold your horses, you could make all my matchmaking efforts be in vain! (*He exits through the center door.*)

MAX. (*To himself.*) Just look at how everyone only thinks about their own interests. After his speech, it's clear how violently he wants to make Reb Kuni-Leml Reb Pinkhesl's son-in-law. No matter how grotesquely I impersonated him, it's all fine with Reb Kalmen, as long as he collects his matchmaker's fee. Now I'm going to have to try another approach. (*To Libe.*) You heard what your father told you, that you should make sure that I don't need anything.

LIBE. Ah, very good. Just tell me what you want. Maybe you're hungry? Tell me, tell me what you want!

MAX. (*Romantically.*) What do I want? Oh no, it's not my stomach that's hungry—it's my heart! It burns with love!

LIBE. (*Looks at him wonderingly.*) What does that mean? You're going to become a bridegroom (*She mimics the way that he limped.*) and here you are starting up with me? Ah, ah, it's a fine piece of business, this is, a nice way to act, and you should have enough sense to know that.

MAX. What does sense have to do with it? It's the heart, the heart! I've gone mad, completely out of my senses from love of you! Your name is Libele,[12] and you were born for love! (*He falls to his knees in front of her and says ironically.*) Here I fall at your feet and I beg you, love me; if not (*To himself.*), if not, I'll hate you!

LIBE. (*Starts, as if afraid, and looks around at the door.*) Woe is me! Stand up, my father could come in. (*Max stands up.*) What's more, first you

---

12. Yiddish, "little love."

were stuttering and limping, and at one stroke you've been completely healed: you walk normally and talk normally! Tell me, I'm begging you, who are you? And what has happened to you?

MAX. Only to you can I show my true appearance. Do you see it? (*He removes the sideburns and the beard, as well as the black patch from his eye.*) I disguised myself as that Kuni-Leml so that I could get to you. I've loved you for a long time now, but until now, I had no other way of meeting you. Now that I've come, we can run off together into the wide world.

LIBE. Well, it's high time (*Happily.*) that such a beautiful young man is crazy about me, even though I don't have a penny to my name. You can't look a gift horse like this in the mouth! (*She takes Max by the hand.*) Come on, let's go get hitched!

MAX. Wait, wait. Nu, you're just going to run away without letting your father know? Hold your horses!

LIBE. Naturally. I'm yours now. Now I don't have to listen to anyone except for you.

MAX. (*To himself.*) She certainly was ready for me quick enough.

LIBE. Just tell me what I'm going to be able to call you later. What's your name?

MAX. You're the only one that I'm going to tell my true name. And only on the condition that no one will know it, not even your own father, until I carry out my plan. My name is—my name is . . . (*To himself.*) I should only know as much pain and anger as I know what name I should tell her. (*To her.*) Nu, let it be Shmerl.

LIBE. (*Happily.*) Shmerl! When I'll be able to call my Shmerlke, "Look!"— they'll say—"There goes Shmerlke"; "Speak of the devil! Shmerlke!" "What's going on with you, Shmer—"

MAX. Well, enough with the shmerling, let's say our good-byes, since I have to go and carry out my plan. But listen: in case we meet again as strangers, I'm going to give you a sign by which you'll be able to recognize me. I'm going to teach you a little song, and that'll be our sign, so sing after me.

> I am me, cuckoo,
> Catch me, one-two,
> I'm a bird, I'll fly away,
> But listen, do,
> To the melody,
> Haven't you sung it today?
> Cuckoo, cuckoo . . .

(*She sings it back to him after every verse, until finally, after the last verse, "Cuckoo," he ironically bows towards her and goes out through the center door. Libe looks after him lovingly.*)

LIBE. (*While he is exiting, she repeats to herself, happily.*) "Shmerlke!" "Speak of the devil! Shmerlke!" "Where are you going, Shmerlke?" (*Saying this sort of thing, she exits right.*)

Scene 4

(*A street. On the left, Reb Shloymenyu's house, which has a balcony. Far upstage is the façade of a small shul. Reb Shloymenyu stands on the balcony and looks down. Beneath him stands a crowd of assorted people with paper lanterns in their hands. They quarrel—singing.*)

ALL.   Just don't shout, just stay still,
     All in turn will speak their pleasure,
     Shush! Enough to make you ill,
     You're making noise beyond all measure.
     No, no, no, we cannot allow it,
     No, no, no, we cannot avow it,
     For them, out of sight,
     Is out of mind, right,
     We'll choose who we desire,
     Whoever we admire.
     Yes, that's what we say! (*The last seven lines are repeated.*)
FIRST PARTY. Here's what I think—listen, hear me out!
     Vote for the old sexton.
SECOND PARTY. Here's what I think—listen, hear me out!
     Vote for the new sexton.
ALL. Yes, it should be the new sexton,
     Yes, it should be the new sexton,
     Come to shul through the little gate
     We'll all cast lots to seal our fate
     Let all end well!
     Yes, yes, yes, let all end well!

(*They all begin to enter the synagogue through the little gate stage right; several turn to Shloymenyu.*)

ALL. Reb Shloymenyu, just wait out here a little bit longer, and then we'll go in and count the ballots, and it's more than certain that you'll end up being sexton. (*They all exit right.*)
SHLOYMENYU. (*Calling after them.*) Go, go, as long as you don't addle my head; I have things to do anyway. (*Descends from the balcony onto the stage.*) Have you ever heard such mind-addling nonsense? The only

reason that they want me for sexton is that they haven't been able to find anybody else. They've addled my head so much that I haven't even had time to read this letter that I've received here. I don't even know where a letter could have come to me from. (*Opens it and looks at the signature.*) Ah, the letter is from Kalmen the Matchmaker. Let's see what he writes. (*Reads.*) "To The Rabbi, The Genius, The All-Knowing Sage, The Pious, The Sharp, The Renowned, The Brilliant, The Central Pillar, The Mighty Hammer, The Light of the Jews, The Repository of the Holy Writings, hold your horses!"[13] (*Stands still and looks around, astonished. Reads further.*) "The grandson of the rabbi Reb Kalonymus, may his honored name be blessed, Our Teacher, the Rabbi Rabbi Sholem, may his Light burn Eternally." (*To himself.*) A grand title. (*Reads further.*) "As we have heard of your name, since you are very well known, and of your sterling lineage, hold your horses . . ." (*Again looks around, astonished. Reads further.*) "And as Reb Pinkhesl of Krakow is also a great scholar, an honest Jew, hold your horses! . . . It would be a great honor for him, if he would be able to make a match with you." (*To himself.*) With whom could he possibly want to make a match? (*It becomes clear.*) Aha! It must be with my prized stepson. (*Reads further.*) "I have heard, it's true, that your young man has a few small faults, but lineage trumps everything. Reb Pinkhesl will give him his girl, hold your horses! . . . With a thousand ruble dowry. You should send your young man over to me as soon as possible. We'll talk about my commission later. We're already set to discuss the fine print on the marriage contract. From me, Kalmen Matchmaker, with the permission of Reb Pinkhesl of Krakow. Hold your horses!" (*Folds up the letter, tucks it into his pocket, and says to himself.*) Nu, nu, just take a look at this letter, hold your horses and hold your horses! It certainly seems that my stepson has met up with a fine bit of business. And it all comes down to lineage. Yes, I know this Reb Pinkhesl quite well; he's certainly a rich man, a fine Jew, but I don't know this girl of his; she must be some sort of monster if he's offering to take that stepson of mine. What's more, it's possible that it'll be a real match, and if that's the case I'll be delighted, since I'd love to get him out of the house once and for all. Yes, a real jewel that mother of his brought into this house of mine when I married her. But maybe now the time has come. (*From backstage, Kuni-Leml's voice can be heard, crying, "Daddy! Daddy!"*) Aha, here comes the jewel!

---

13. There is a convention in traditional Jewish epistolary writing to greet the addressee with a number of high-flown titles, generally in Hebrew.

Scene 5

(*Kuni-Leml enters, holding a flag in his hand.*)

KUNI-LEML. D-daddy, come to s-shul. I've got a f-flag with a little candle, come on!

SHLOYMENYU. Stay here, and listen up a little. You do know that I'm going to become the sexton and you're going to become a groom?

KUNI-LEML. (*Laughs, embarrassed.*) A g-groom? Get out of here, you're lying, trying to trick me!

SHLOYMENYU. I've just received a letter from Kalmen the Matchmaker, and he's written to me that Reb Pinkhesl the rich man wants to arrange a match with me.

KUNI-LEML. Aha! You see, you were trying to trick m-me with a lie. If R-reb Pinkhesl the rich man wants to make a match w-with you, then you're the one who's going to be a g-groom, not me. (*Smiles.*)

SHLOYMENYU. Get out of here, silly. You didn't understand me. I mean that he asked me—he has a girl, and wants you to take her for a bride.

KUNI-LEML. (*As if ashamed of himself.*) I should take her as a b-bride? (*He smiles.*) Get out of here, you're lying, you're trying to trick me!

SHLOYMENYU. (*To himself.*) It's simply unbelievable to him that someone would be willing to accept him. (*To him.*) I'm telling you, it's true. Nu, just look, I've even got the letter. (*He shows him the letter. Kuni-Leml opens it and looks at it. He wants to start reading, but he begins to stutter very strongly. He gives the letter angrily back and says.*)

KUNI-LEML. It's some sort of nasty writing, when y-you can't even start r-reading it!

SHLOYMENYU. But now do you believe me already?

KUNI-LEML. Yes, now I b-believe you, yes.

SHLOYMENYU. Yes, but what is he going to want with you, since you're such a helpless cripple?

KUNI-LEML. What? I'm a c-cripple? I c-can run better than you can! Do you want to see? (*Runs across the stage and falls. While lying on the ground.*) Oh, no, no, I'm all wrapped up in the f-flag. (*Gets up.*)

SHLOYMENYU. (*Smiling.*) Well, that was certainly a fine run. Anyway, let's let that be. Even so, what is anyone going to want with you, you're such a stutterer? You should get in the habit of stuttering less.

KUNI-LEML. Get a load of him—I stutter?

SHLOYMENYU. What, you don't? Let's say, for example, that you go to your father-in-law, you're going to have to say hello to him. Nu, let's hear how you can say "How do you do?" smoothly, without stuttering.

KUNI-LEML. What, you think I c-can't? You want to hear it? So, for example, you b-be the father-in-law, and I'll be K-Kuni-Leml. (*He crosses to the other side of the stage and shows how he would enter.*) I'll come in just like this, and I'll give a hearty sh-shout of H-H-H- (*He stutters, very strongly, and can't finish speaking. Shloymenyu bursts out laughing; Kuni-Leml becomes red with anger and says.*) L-look at how he's laughing. What are you laughing about, w-wise guy? It's a joke that I have a speech d-defect?

SHLOYMENYU. And in addition to all of your other virtues, you're blind too.

KUNI-LEML. Who's blind? Me? Oh, what a smart guy you are! I'm b-blind as a bat, he says, but I see you (*He points to the flag.*) and I see the flag. (*He points to Shloymenyu.*) And I'll b-be able to see my b-bride too.

SHLOYMENYU. (*To himself.*) So! If this one is right for her father, it's certainly fine with me. What can you say? Lineage covers up everything.

KUNI-LEML. Well, that's for sure, I certainly trump that lineage, since I'm bigger than it. I must not be a prize bridegroom, because you're my father and you haven't wanted to arrange a marriage for me even once, as long as I've lived.

SHLOYMENYU. Fine, fine already. Tomorrow I'll send you off there with Mikhoelke. And I'll even come there myself right after Hoshana Rabba. Right now I'm going to go into the synagogue, since the whole world's waiting for me there. (*A sort of shout is heard from a lot of people. Shloymenyu looks around and says.*) Aha, there they go already!

Scene 6

(*Many Jews exit the synagogue, accompanied by many children, who hold flags in their hands on top of which wax candles are burning, stuck into apples. A part of the crowd approaches Shloymenyu and shouts joyfully.*)

CROWD. Reb Shloymenyu! Mazl tov! You're still the sexton! Come in the synagogue! (*They take him into their midst and lead him by the arm around the stage several times, singing. Kuni-Leml lights his flag's candle and goes to the front of the procession. Throughout, he secretly takes bites out of the apple and, each time he does so, burns his face on the burning candle, jumps up in the air, and falls down.*)

ALL. Lead him quick, lead him quick,
Lead the sexton into shul,
Let's eat cakes and drink some wine!
Hoshana Rabba is a celebration,
Drink and carouse 'til you're uproarious.
Drink and sing to the sexton's elevation,
Spend all night on it, it's meritorious!
Lead him quick, etc. (*As they begin to enter the synagogue, still singing, the curtain slowly falls.*)

Act III

Scene 1

(*Reb Pinkhesl's house, doors on both sides, in the middle an archway through which we see an orchard. Rivke and Pinkhesl, in the middle of a conversation, enter from left.*)

RIVKE. (*Shouting.*) No, no, you won't convince me, I won't buy a pig in a poke. At the very least, you should have directed the bridegroom Kuni-Leml to go not to the matchmaker, but straight to us; if he really is such a monster, we could have disposed of him without anyone being the wiser.

PINKHESL. You silly cow! I had enough sense to do that without you. Just after I told Kalmen Matchmaker to write a letter to Reb Shloymenyu to have Kuni-Leml come to him and we would meet the boy there, I immediately wrote a letter to that very same Reb Shloymenyu, asking him to send his Kuni-Leml straight to us so we can welcome him here. But listen here, Rivke, I want you to get one thing straight. All right, so you're a pest—fine, be a pest, but don't turn our daughter into a mini-pest! Don't listen to me if you don't want to, but you should teach our child to respect and obey her father. This Kuni-Leml, you understand, will be arriving any minute, and I wanted to talk to our Khaykele about him first, and at a time like this, I don't want you to contradict me. On the contrary—you're a mother, after all; you should make sure that we're together on this, because two are stronger than one.

RIVKE. But I ask you, Pinkhesl, isn't it a sin to make her marry a creature like that?

PINKHESL. If she doesn't want to, I won't force her. Just do me a favor for the time being and don't contradict me. You know what? You can't restrain yourself. Don't interfere, just stand back and keep quiet, will you promise me that? (*Rivke doesn't answer.*) I'll call her in right now and discuss it with her. (*He goes to the left-hand door and shouts.*) Khayele, Khayele, my daughter!

Scene 2

(*Carolina enters, and he leads her to center stage.*)

CAROLINA. What is it, Father?

PINKHESL. Come here, daughter, to your dear father, I have something to discuss with you. Your mother has probably told you already what a golden boy, a treasure, I've found to be your husband, so that you'll be the envy of Heaven and Earth. I realize, however, that you have other ideas. I sense that you've got big wheels turning in that little brain of yours: little Max, the doctor's brat. Well, has your father guessed right? So tell me, my dear daughter, which is better: a coarse bolt of cloth like that, or a fine bit of silk? (*Rivke tugs at him from behind, he turns around to her, and they mime as if they are quarreling.*)

CAROLINA. (*Aside.*) Now it's time to play my part, just like Max taught me. (*Aloud to her father.*) You see, Father, even though we women know more about material like silk than you men do, I'll leave these goods up to you. After all, you're my father, may you live to a hundred and twenty. I'm sure you mean me no harm.

PINKHESL. (*Turns back to Rivke and says to her with a smile.*) You see, Rivke, what did I tell you? (*To Carolina.*) That's it, my daughter, I knew all along that when you thought it over, you would realize that your father wishes only the best for you. I promise you that soon after the wedding, I'll make him a rabbi in a little shtetl,[14] and you'll be a *rebetsin*,[15] and all the women will envy you . . .

RIVKE. (*Sarcastic.*) Oh boy, oh boy!

PINKHESL. (*Angrily to Rivke.*) You promised me something! (*To Carolina.*) Yes, daughter, your husband will guide you on the path of righteousness, he'll teach you what is written in the holy books: that a Jewish child must not chase after wordly pleasures. You'll learn from him that a twinkling eye, a lively leg, is all vanity of vanities,[16] Satan . . . (*Rivke tugs at him from behind, he turns around and gives her an evil look, and shouts out his last words.*) Satan, the devil's work!

RIVKE. (*Interrupting him.*) Oh, the Devil take you!

PINKHESL. (*Pushes her out of his way and continues to Carolina.*) Right, daughter? It's all frivolity; once you die, you just lie there . . . (*Rivke tugs at him, he turns around again, angry, and continues.*) We all end up six feet under, and the main thing is to make sure we enter the next world with a clean soul . . .

RIVKE. Are you crazy? Why are you burying her all of a sudden? We're still alive, you know.

PINKHESL. (*Angrily pushes her out of the way once again, and continues speaking to Carolina.*) Therefore, a Jewish girl must pay no attention to whether her groom is handsome and merry. As it says in the scriptures, don't look at the barrel, but at what's in it.

---

14. Yiddish, "little town."

15. Yiddish, "rabbi's wife."

16. Compare Ecclesiastes 1:2.

RIVKE. (*Angrily.*) Oy, merciful Father, may you be stuffed into a barrel!

PINKHESL. (*Angrily to Rivke.*) Rivke! Rivke, you promised me something. But let's ask her what she herself wants. (*He turns back to Carolina.*) So, what is your answer, daughter?

CAROLINA. (*With a pious expression.*) How else can I answer, Father? Isn't it all true, what you say? I'm sure it is!

PINKHESL. (*Happily, to Rivke.*) You see, Rivke? What do you say now? (*To Carolina.*) Oy, my sweet, pious daughter! (*He caresses her.*) Now I see from all this that you are Reb Pinkhesl's daughter. (*He sticks his left hand inside his belt, and with his right hand strokes his beard as he says contentedly.*) Now, daughter, imagine for example that your father brings you to a young man who has one leg whose growth is a little delayed compared to the other one, and your father says to you, "You see, Khayele, this is the young man you will take to be your husband." What would you think then?

CAROLINA. I would think that such a flaw doesn't keep him from walking in the path of God. (*Pinkhesl practically leaps for joy.*)

RIVKE. In other words, straight to the Devil!

PINKHESL. (*Shouts at her.*) Rivke! (*He gnashes his teeth and gestures to her to be quiet. Then he turns back to Carolina and says to her pleasantly.*) Oh, may you enjoy long life, my dear little daughter. . . . But tell me, my dear Khayele, what would you do if the Almighty afflicted him with another problem above and beyond what I mentioned before? For example, he doesn't see with one eye—that is, he therefore sees a lot better with the other one. He doesn't babble obscenely like hooligans do; that is, he speaks, how do you say it, with a bit of a stutter, a stammer. What would you say then?

CAROLINA. What a question! We have to have pity for such things. Is it the poor thing's fault if God has punished him like that?

PINKHESL. Oy, my pious, sweet daughter, you've made me very happy! I'm luckier having you than having all my wealth. (*He begins to run excitedly all over the room, joyfully clapping one hand in the other.*)

RIVKE. (*To Carolina.*) Think carefully, daughter, about what you're going to do. Make sure you won't regret it. It's better to look before you leap. (*While she speaks, Pinkhesl places himself between them, as if Carolina won't be able to hear Rivke if she can't see her. At that moment, we hear Kuni-Leml's voice outside.*)

KUNI-LEML. Does Reb P-pinkhesl live here?

PINKHESL. Sha, sha, that must be him. Rivke, I beg of you, be nice to him. And you, daughter, make sure you speak to him nicely, at least don't embarrass me. (*He runs to the left-hand door, opens it, and says.*) Yes, yes, this is Reb Pinkhesl's house, come in, come in.

Scene 3

KUNI-LEML. (*Enters, stands by the door, and looks around.*) Sh-sholem aleykhem,[17] Reb P-pinkhesl. (*He extends his hand.*)

PINKHESL. Welcome, Reb Shloymenyu's son, come in. I am your in-law Reb Pinkhesl, and this (*Indicating Rivke.*) is my wife, and this (*Indicating Carolina.*) is your bride.

CAROLINA. (*Aside.*) Oh, my Max has disguised himself brilliantly. It's impossible to recognize him. (*To Kuni-Leml.*) Allow me the honor of presenting myself to you—your bride Carolina!

KUNI-LEML. Why is she using such funny language?

CAROLINA. (*With a smile.*) I am your bride.

KUNI-LEML. My b-bride? Yes, I know.

CAROLINA. Yes, your bride Carolina.

KUNI-LEML. What's this C-crinolina?[18] (*To Pinkhesl, who has been gesturing to Rivke this entire time as if they are arguing.*) Reb P-pinkhesl, oy, is she a here-t-tic! Can a Jewish girl have an aristocratic name?

PINKHESL. (*Goes to Carolina and whispers in her ear.*) You should have said "Khayele" to him. (*To Kuni-Leml.*) Reb Kuni-Leml, you understand, a modern girl, and she's dabbled a bit in foreign languages. No matter—she's still a very decent child.

KUNI-LEML. (*Looking at Carolina the whole time.*) Oy is she a here-t-tic! She's reading foreign books? How much do you b-bet that she d-doesn't even know which ch-chapter of the Torah we're reading this week?[19]

CAROLINA. (*Aside.*) I could kiss him, he plays his part so naturally. (*To Kuni-Leml.*) It's a shame, but I don't.

KUNI-LEML. What's this "shame"? There's no Torah portion called "Shem."[20] Oy, is she a here-t-tic! What will you b-bet me that she doesn't even believe in d-demons and in spirits, and in wonder workers?

CAROLINA. Who believes in such foolishness these days?

---

17. Hebrew/Yiddish, literally "peace unto you," a traditional greeting.

18. A "crinoline" is not only a kind of stiff fabric (generally cotton or horsehair), but also a petticoat made of such fabric.

19. The word Kuni-Leml uses is *sedre*. In much of traditional Jewish society, a section of the Pentateuch is read weekly every Sabbath, allowing the entire work to be completed annually; each week's reading is referred to as a different portion, or *sedre*, often named after the first significant word in the reading.

20. In the original, Caroline uses the German/Yiddish word *leyder* (unfortunately), and Kuni-Leml mishears it as *ledoyr*, part of *l'dor vador*, biblical Hebrew for "generations and generations."

KUNI-LEML. Oy, is she a here-t-tic! The Talmud says that we m-must believe in d-demons, and in spirits, and in wonder workers.[21] A Jewish girl m-must obey what's wr-written in the Talmud!

PINKHESL (*To Rivke.*) You hear how well he knows the Talmud?

RIVKE. Yes, I hear. That's a lovely way for a groom to talk who's coming to see his bride for the first time. And take a look at the whole package, you horse! What do you say to that? (*As Pinkhesl and Rivke are talking, Carolina throws kisses to Kuni-Leml.*)

KUNI-LEML. (*To Pinkhesl.*) Reb P-pinkhes, what is she doing?

PINKHESL. (*Doesn't hear him, and continues speaking to Rivke.*) I'll tell you, Rivke, Talmud scholars like that are embarrassed to speak to a bride in front of her parents. Remember when we got engaged? We were too embarrassed to look each other in the eye. Come, let's go and leave them alone and let them have a proper conversation so they can get to know each other better. (*They start leaving through the left-hand door.*)

KUNI-LEML. (*Runs after them and shouts.*) Reb P-pinkhesl, where are you going? You're leaving me alone with an unmarried g-girl?! It's forbidden!

PINKHESL. It's alright, stay here, we'll be back soon.

RIVKE. (*As they exit.*) Good luck to both of you. (*They exit. Kuni-Leml tries to follow, but Carolina grabs him by his caftan and pulls him back into the room.*)

CAROLINA. Nu, enough, Max, stop now.

KUNI-LEML. Oy vey! What a here-t-tic! An unmarried girl should drag a strange man by the coat?

CAROLINA. (*Applauds.*) Bravo, Max! You've played your part well, like a true actor.

KUNI-LEML. What's she clapping for? She thinks it's the wedding already?

CAROLINA. Nu, enough already, *lieber* Max.

KUNI-LEML. What, now she's cursing me, calling me "Mocks"? (*He places his hands together.*) Well, I mock you right back!

CAROLINA. All right, enough already, you've played your part brilliantly. But let's talk about something important. How do you expect to carry out the rest of your plan? How will you jump the next hurdle?

KUNI-LEML. What's all this about t-turtles? Am I so slow? I came to g-get a thousand rubles' dowry, and y-you for my wife, and that's it!

---

21. The Talmud certainly accepts the presence of demons (see, among other places, BT Sukkot 28a, Pesakhim 110a–112b, and Berakhot 6a); belief in these spirits among the writers of the Babylonian Talmud, however, seems so widespread and natural that mandating belief would have been unnecessary.

CAROLINA. I am yours—I've known that for a long time. But how do you know that my father will agree?

KUNI-LEML. What do you mean? Your f-father wrote to m-me and told me to come take y-you as my wife, and now I'm here!

CAROLINA. Max! Stop torturing me with your disguise, or I'll think you're teasing me, sweet Max!

KUNI-LEML. What? Now it's become sweet Mocks? Listen, if you don't call me by my proper name, Kuni-Leml, I won't take you as my wife.

CAROLINA. (*Flustered.*) Eh, you want to leave me? You're taking your joke too far. (*Happier.*) You remember how you taught me "Cuckoo!"

KUNI-LEML. (*Amazed.*) What cuckoo? Now's she's playing cuckoo with me!

CAROLINA. (*More serious.*) Max! If you keep torturing me with your mask, I'll tear it off with a kiss!

KUNI-LEML. Oy, she is really a . . . I can't even say it. Kissing before the wedding? What, that's allowed?

CAROLINA. You've pushed me to the point where I can't hold back any longer. Max, dear Max! (*She tries to hug and kiss him, but he tears away and cries.*)

KUNI-LEML. Shma yisroel! Shma yisroel![22] (*He runs out to the left.*)

CAROLINA. (*Distressed.*) What's this? Max should behave like this with me? He, who swore he would give his life for me, carries on with his joke when we're alone, tears away from my kiss, and runs off without an explanation? (*Pause.*) Just wait, Max, this little scene will cost you dearly. When you come back again, or wherever we next meet, the roles will be reversed. Then I'll be as cold to you as you were with me just now. (*We hear the voices of Pinkhesl and Rivke from the left, preparing to come in. Carolina starts, and says.*) Oh! My father's coming. Despite what just happened, I must go back to playing my role.

Scene 4

(*Pinkhesl and Rivke enter; we hear his voice before we see him.*)

PINKHESL. Too late, too late. True! Now I see that everything that you complained about is in fact true, yes, yes, I realize how much I deluded myself about him. It is true that he's a jewel, a gem, a learned boy, from a prominent family, Reb Shloymenyu's son. But I have my doubts—just as you said—whether our child will be able

---

22. The essential doxology of the Jewish tradition, "Hear O Israel [the Lord is our God, the Lord is One]," Deut. 6:4, is also well known as an incantation against evil spirits, and as a response to terrifying situations. See as one example BT Berakhot 5a.

to live out her life with him. One thing about this is very bad: I gave my word, and one shouldn't go back on that. But if she says she doesn't want him, she may say so; in that case, I won't interfere.

RIVKE. Aha! Bless you, you old horse. You're so clever in all your affairs. I knew all along that you'd regret what you were doing, but now you can make amends. So do that, by all means.

PINKHESL. Yes, yes. But you know what, Rivke? Our daughter is a modern girl, and between you and me, it seems she rejected him already, because I saw him run out of there very angry. Wait, we'll ask her in a minute, and then we'll know. (*He approaches Carolina, who has been lost in thought the entire time.*) Khayele, Khayele! You're so preoccupied, daughter, that you don't even see who's standing next to you. (*She lifts her head and looks at him.*) You must be angry at your father for promising you to a boy like that?

CAROLINA. You know how I am, Father. It's just hard for me to decide, to say yes. But once I have said yes, that's all there is to it. I am content with the match—happy, even!

PINKHESL. (*Is silent for a few second, as if unable to find the words. He looks at Rivke in amazement, then back at Carolina, and then says suddenly.*) *Vey iz mir*! Rivke, you hear? She thinks that creature is a great catch. No, there's something wrong with the child's head. *Vey iz mir*, she's out of her mind. (*Runs around the room, wringing his hands.*) What have I done? What have I done?

RIVKE. (*To Carolina.*) My daughter, surely you're joking? You know that now is no time to fool around. Don't forget that your life, your happiness, hang on your answer. We both want you to tell us what you feel in your heart. You should know that your father himself regrets having let such a creature into our home. Just say you don't want him, and we won't argue.

CAROLINA. Mother, you hurt even more when you insult such a well-educated man. I've thought about it enough, and the more I speak to him, the more I see what an artist he is, what a noble spirit he has!

PINKHESL. (*Has stood by her side listening to what she says, and wringing his hands.*) *Vey iz mir*! With that cripple, with that stammerer, she's fallen in love? No, the child is simply out of her mind. (*Runs around the room smacking his head and shouts.*) It's all because of me, it's all my fault! Old fool that I am, I'm the one who talked her into it!

RIVKE. My child, maybe your little head is hurting? Are your eyes blurry? Does your heart ache?

PINKHESL. Maybe you're hungry, God forbid?

RIVKE. (*Pushing him away.*) Because I know that if you were in your right mind, you wouldn't talk like this. I mean, you were so devoted to Max . . .

PINKHESL. (*Runs up to her angrily.*) Aha, Max, Max! Again with Max!

RIVKE. (*Pushes him away and continues talking to Carolina.*) And in the end, for you to be so confused, so disoriented—such behavior! Why—may God not strike me down for saying this—he's simply hideous to look at! (*Pause.*) No, daughter, just tell me one thing and I'll know whether or not you're in your right mind. If Max were standing next to that creature (*On the word "Max," Pinkhesl grimaces.*) and someone said to you, "Choose, daughter, whichever of these two you want," how would you answer?

CAROLINA. (*Unhappy.*) Leave me alone, Mother.

PINKHESL. (*Runs up to Rivke angrily, and says with a shout.*) Again you start pestering her with your Max? I'm telling you, you'd better stop mentioning that name to me. She'll marry that schoolboy Max over my dead body—I'd sooner have her marry the cripple than the doctor's brat. (*He turns to Carolina and speaks to her sweetly.*) I swear to you, my dear daughter, just tell me the whole truth: what did he say to you that has made you so attached to him? No, that must be it: he must be some sort of hidden saint, a miracle worker! (*He puts his hand to his forehead, thinks, then suddenly starts and says happily to Rivke.*) Sha! Rivke, I've just thought of something. Unless I'm mistaken, that must be it. I know that in every generation there are *lamed-vovnikes*[23]—thirty-six righteous men, who can work great miracles. For example, they can make themselves invisible, they can change their appearance. One minute they're here, the next they're over there; now he's a man, and the next minute he's a beast! Maybe he's actually one of them, ha? Who knows? (*To Carolina.*) Just tell me, daughter, when he spoke to you just now, was he the same person as before, or was he transformed?

CAROLINA. (*With pretended innocence.*) No, Father, he became a completely different person, he astonished me so, that . . .

PINKHESL. (*Curious.*) That what, that what?

CAROLINA. That I actually wanted to kiss him . . .

PINKHESL. Well, well, and what happened next?

CAROLINA. He just disappeared.

PINKHESL. (*Amazed.*) Ha, disappeared? Flew away? You hear, Rivke, poof! (*He makes hand movements as if flying.*) Well, Rivke, isn't that what I said? He is not only a saint, but a *lamed-vovnik* too, yes, yes. That's clearly how it is. (*We hear someone entering from the right.*) Wait, I think that's him coming back.

---

23. According to Jewish tradition, there are thirty-six righteous men in every generation upon whom the continued existence of the world depends. *Lamed-vov* is the Hebrew alphabetical equivalent of the number thirty-six, and additionally significant because it is twice the number *khai* (the letters *khet-yud*), which means "life." The sacred identity of the *lamed-vovnik* is hidden from others, and sometimes even from himself.

Scene 5

(*Max enters dressed as Kuni-Leml.*)

PINKHESL. (*Dashes up to him and says respectfully.*) Why did you run away, and why have you come back? Did you forget something?

MAX. Yes, I forg-got to tell your daughter something. Leave us alone.

PINKHESL. Very well, very well. (*To Rivke.*) Come, Rivke. (*As they exit, he speaks to her quietly, and gestures to her to look at Max.*) Well, Rivke, what do you say now? You see that he's not the same person; before he was afraid to stay alone with her, and now he tells us to go himself. And his voice doesn't sound the same at all. It's just as I said. Come quickly, Rivke, let's go. (*They exit to the left. Max watches them until they leave.*)

CAROLINA. (*To herself.*) He probably realized his mistake and came back to explain himself.

MAX. (*Once Pinkhesl and Rivke have gone.*) Oh happy occasion! To be alone with you in your father's house and be afraid of no one! (*He races to her and tries to embrace her, but she pushes him away.*)

CAROLINA. Take your compliments elsewhere, you hard-hearted man!

MAX. (*Puzzled.*) I don't understand you at all. What have I done to you that you call me hard-hearted?

CAROLINA. You have to ask? Did you have to test me to see whether I truly love you?

MAX. I have no idea what you're talking about.

CAROLINA. You're still playing dumb? You have to disguise yourself from me too? Can you have the heart to drive me away when I'm so kind to you?

MAX. (*Astonished.*) When did I do that? What are you talking about? Have I ever failed to return your affections? What's gotten into your head all of a sudden?

CAROLINA. You really act as if you don't know? Have you forgotten how you mercilessly threw me out when I wanted to kiss you for playing your role so well?

MAX. You wanted to kiss me and I didn't want to? I'm telling you, you must be dreaming!

CAROLINA. If so, I don't know what to think. My parents say that I'm out of my mind, and you say that I'm dreaming. Soon I really will start to wonder whether I'm in my right mind.

MAX. Wait a minute. (*Thinks for a moment.*) Tell me, I beg of you, have we seen each other since we spoke in the garden?

CAROLINA. What do you mean? Weren't you in our house just a quarter of an hour ago, and I marvelled at how well you imitated him?

MAX. (*Thinks for a second more, then bursts out laughing.*) Ha ha ha! What have you done? You were too hasty; that was the real Kuni-Leml, and he's the one you tried to kiss! Ha ha ha!

CAROLINA. (*Covers her face as if ashamed.*) Ha ha ha! That was the real Kuni-Leml, and I tried to kiss him! Ha ha ha! You should have seen how that penguin tore himself away from me with a *Shma yisroel*! Ha ha ha! Really, I'm so embarrassed that I can hardly look you in the eye. Forgive me, my dear Max.

MAX. (*Lovingly.*) I forgive you, but on one condition: you have to give me the kiss that you wanted to give him.

CAROLINA. (*With an embarrassed smile.*) Alright, alright, we'll leave that for later. Now we have more important things to talk about. Tell me, what do you think we should do next? Kuni-Leml has gone, but he may be back any minute. What will happen if you run into each other here?

MAX. That's just what I'm wondering, because I heard that he's back. I must do everything I can to get in his way. But tell me something: what does your father think of him?

CAROLINA. My father? At first he regretted having brought him here, and begged me to reject him. But since I thought the whole time that he was you, I stood my ground and insisted on marrying him. Of course that seemed crazy, but my father had an idea. He decided that Kuni-Leml is one of the *lamed-vovnikes* who has supernatural powers, and that his secret magic powers were what drew me to him.

MAX. (*After thinking for a moment.*) Bravo! That will come in handy. Carolina, it will be all right. Quick, give me some paper, ink, and a pen. (*She shows him the desk where there are pen and ink; he sits down and writes.*) I've thought of another plan. Take this paper to my comrades who are waiting for me outside, because I arranged with them to be ready to help me if I need them. (*He finishes writing and gives her the folded paper.*) Alright, go give it to them. When they read it, they'll know what to do.

CAROLINA. (*Lovingly.*) Oh, my dear Max, your words have revived me. God grant your plan success! (*They embrace.*)

Scene 6

(*Enter Kuni-Leml. Seeing Max and Carolina embracing, he screams.*)

KUNI-LEML. Oh no! He's squeezing my f-fiancée! (*They are startled. Carolina runs off, embarrassed. Max takes several steps toward Kuni-Leml, who stays put as if frightened. He takes one look at himself, a second at Max, as if trying to figure out if Max is him or not. After several moments of their looking at each other, says.*) Oy vey! B-but just like me!

MAX. (*In the same voice as Kuni-Leml.*) B-but just like me! (*Kuni-Leml takes several limping steps closer to Max, who then does the same. Kuni-Leml grows even more astonished, and contemplates further.*)

KUNI-LEML. Wh-who are you?

MAX. Wh-who are you?

KUNI-LEML. Me? I'm K-kuni Leml, the son of Reb Sh-shloymenyu, the alderman of Sh-shakhrayevke.

MAX. L-liar! How can you p-pass yourself off as me, when *I* am K-kuni-Leml, the son of Reb Shloymenyu, the alderman of Sh-shakhrayevke?!

KUNI-LEML. (*Upset.*) Oy vey! My f-fiancée calls me "Mocks," and now he says he's K-kuni-Leml. Th-then who am I?

MAX. How can you prove to me that you are K-kuni-Leml?

KUNI-LEML. What do you mean how? The whole t-town knows that K-kuni Leml is blind in one eye, and lame, and talks with a s-stutter, oy! (*Shows how he walks lamely.*)

MAX. Well, I'm b-blind in one eye, and lame, and talk with a s-stutter, oy! (*He takes several limping steps.*)

KUNI-LEML. Oy, vey, really! If I d-didn't know that I'm me, I w-would think th-that he is me!

MAX. Yes, but you c-can walk, and s-see, and speak just like everybody else. You're j-just in disguise.

KUNI-LEML. I can swear on my f-father and m-mother that I was born b-blind and l-lame and with a s-stutter.

MAX. Q-quiet, you liar. You better tell me right now why you d-disguised yourself as me. What are you doing here?

KUNI-LEML. What am I d-doing here? Reb P-pinkhesl wrote me a l-letter that I should c-come and take the one thousand rubles' w—no, dowry, and take his girl for my w—oh, here's the letter. (*Takes a letter out of the breast pocket of his coat and shows Max.*)

MAX. (*Skims through the letter.*) Now I see what a s-schemer you are. This letter is c-counterfeit. You've just come to grab the thousand rubles, n-nothing more. How c-can you become her g-groom when y-you're in love with K-kalmen Matchmaker's daughter?

KUNI-LEML. W-what love? Which K-kalmen? W-what matchmaker? Which daughter? How c-can that be?

MAX. Y-you yourself s-swore to her that you love her.

KUNI-LEML. Who? I s-swore? In my whole l-life, I've n-never sworn more than once. J-just once, I swore that I would never eat p-prune jam with bread. That was because my dog snatched it away from me once, and t-took a bite out of me at the same time. But b-besides that, I've n-never sworn.

MAX. W-what do I care about such n-nonsense? I'm taking this letter to the p-police, and I'm g-going to show them what a s-swindler you are unless you bring a s-signature from home that this is you. (*Starts to go.*)

KUNI-LEML. (*Runs after him and stops him.*) Reb K-kuni Leml, come here. (*Pleading.*) What do you need the p-police for? I'll run home right n-now to get the proof in b-black and white. But is it f-fair for me to leave here without a name?

MAX. (*Grabs him by the lapels and speaks to him as if angry.*) No, no, y-you're a swindler. C-come with me to the police.

KUNI-LEML. (*Afraid.*) Oy, oy, Reb K-kuni-Lemele, may you enjoy g-good health, don't t-take me to the p-police. I'll run home right now without a name and bring proof in b-black and white that I am Ku— no, no, you are K-kuni-Leml! I am Mocks—no, no, that I am . . . that I am me! But I beg of you, Reb Kuni-Leml: until I c-come back, please don't squeeze my fiancée. (*Starts to go, looks Max over, says to himself.*) Apparently he really is K-kuni-Leml. (*Starts to go again, turns back.*) Reb Kuni-Leml?

MAX. W-what is it now?

KUNI-LEML. I m-meant to ask . . . For example, if I walk down the street and someone c-calls out to m-me, "Reb K-kuni- Leml! Reb K-kuni-Leml!" should I answer or not?

MAX. (*With an angry tone.*) No, you m-mustn't answer, since you're not K-kuni-Leml! Now r-run along home!

KUNI-LEML. So he r-really is Kuni-Leml, and I am . . . me. (*He exits right.*)

MAX. So that takes care of Kuni-Leml. As far as he is concerned, *I* am Kuni-Leml. But before he returns, I must see to it that Carolina will remain mine. Now for my final trick. Carolina told me that her father believes that Kuni-Leml is a *lamed-vovnik*—that he can work miracles, vanish into thin air, commune with angels, summon the dead. Let's make all of that serve my plan. I must show him how one speaks to the dead. That will certainly impress him. (*At this moment, we hear someone approaching from the left. Max turns and sees through the window that it is Pinkhesl. Max sits down at the table and pores over a religious book. He starts gesturing piously and speaking in the intonation for learning Talmud. Throughout this, he cries out, "Ha ha ha!"*)

Scene 7

PINKHESL. (*Enters fearfully, stands far behind him, and says aside.*) Ah, ah, he's absorbed in his craft, in his secrets! He must have a good mind, a sharp brain—I mustn't interrupt him.

MAX. (*Shouts with pretended enthusiasm.*) Ha, ha, ha!

PINKHESL. (*Frightened.*) Vey iz mir!

MAX. (*Starts wildly and lifts his head, and seems to direct his argument heavenward.*) Ha? What? Fine, fine. No? What, "no"?

PINKHESL. Oy, oy, this is a *lamed-vovnik*, a saint. He's speaking with some-one, and I, simple man, do not deserve to look upon him.

MAX. (*Pretends not to hear, and argues further.*) No! You must help me now. You, the holy soul of my great-grandfather Reb Kalonymus the miracle worker. And you, souls of my entire holy family, you yourself brought the news from heaven that Reb Pinkhesl's daughter is my mate. Now I ask you—answer me! May I carry out the match? Will I live happily with his daughter? Ha? Yes? Why are you silent? Why don't you answer? Ha? You want to speak with me when there's no one else in the room? Yes? There's a stranger in the room? Where? (*He turns around slowly and pretends to search the entire room until he finally finds Pinkhesl prostrate on the ground with fear, and speaks to him in a pious, friendly manner.*) Oh, Reb Pinkhesl, you must excuse me, my dear in-law. You must go out and leave me here alone, for these pure souls will not speak to me if there is someone else in the room.

PINKHESL. (*Washing his hands.*) Uh, uh, may I? (*He points to his mouth.*)

MAX. You may, you may speak.

PINKHESL. Fine, I see that you are not one of us sinful folk, but how is it, I'd like to ask, that you are completely transformed? You see, and walk, and speak, just like everyone else.

MAX. (*Proudly.*) What can we wise men not accomplish? What are we not able to do? Those are our secrets, we won't reveal them. We can change our form when we need to, we can summon the dead, dance with angels, we can speak with an ass just as with a person, but only when necessary. Oy, you don't want me to be your son-in-law.

PINKHESL. (*Interrupting him.*) God forbid, who doesn't want you? I wouldn't want a sage[24] like you?

MAX. If you don't want me, you may say so—I'll fly straight home! (*He prepares to "fly away" through the door. Pinkhesl grabs him from behind by his coat and stops him.*)

PINKHESL. Oy vey, don't fly away! God forbid, who wouldn't want you? All I want is you! And when they find out how you see, and walk, and speak like everyone else, my wife and daughter will surely want you too. So why do you want to fly away? (*Aside.*) It's a miracle that I stopped him. If not, he'd be flying over the mountains as I speak.

MAX. Well, give me your hand on it that your daughter will be mine.

PINKHESL. Ach, I'll give you both hands. (*Extends his hands.*)

MAX. No, we sages don't shake hands like that. First I have to summon forth all the souls from my sainted family to make sure you keep your word. After all, they're the ones who brought the news from heaven. They all wanted this, so they must be here.

PINKHESL. I'm agreed, but I'm afraid I'll be in the way, because I've never had the privilege to see the dead or to hear them speak before.

---

24. Reb Pinkhesl uses the word *tanna*, which literally refers to one of the rabbis of the Mishnaic period (c. 200 CE), but seems simply to be using the word to mean "a prodigious scholar and holy man."

MAX. If you stay with me you have nothing to fear. Just hold my hand and keep quiet. (*He takes hold of his hand and intones.*) Sweep down quickly, you soul of my great-grandfather Reb Kalmenyu, and you souls of my entire sainted family. Quick, everyone appear! (*We hear thunder, then see lightning, and far upstage appears a Dead Man in an old white shroud, speaking with a deadened, smothered voice. Pinkhesl, frightened, flops onto a sofa near the table, covers his face with his coat, and trembles.*)

DEAD MAN.   It is being shouted,
                    There's no doubt about it,
                    That Reb Pinkhesl's daughter
                    Is yours—how about it?
                    This is your fate, we're witnesses, mate.
                    The entire clan, woman and man.

(*Another flash of lightning, and many more Dead People appear.*)

CHORUS OF THE DEAD.   What do you want? What do you want?
                    What do you want, my dear?
                    Why do you haunt, why do you haunt
                    Our quiet tombs, my dear?
                    In our prayer shawls—so poor, don't be ashamed,
                    Arise, you dead,
                    From your watery graves . . . (*Repeat.*)
                    We have all—mazl tov,
                    Come to call—mazl tov,
                    Khosn-kale mazl tov,
                    We all wish you mazl tov,
                    Khosn-kale—groom and bride—a happy mazl tov!

(*As they sing, Pinkhesl looks around. He becomes frightened and grabs the fringes of his prayer shawl, then clutches a prayer book. Finally the song ends and the stage is lit with electric fire.[25] The curtain falls slowly.*)

Act IV

Scene 1

(*Reb Pinkhesl's room. Around the table, around which candles burn, sits Max, still dressed up as Kuni-Leml. Near him is Carolina, and behind them are Reb Pinkhesl, Rivke, a Cantor, who is writing the marriage contract, and other Relatives, male and female. All sing.*)

---

25. This refers to a theatrical innovation of the time: electric light.

ALL. We wait, we wait, there's nothing to do,
Oh why are we waiting, why?
We wait, we wait, there's nothing to do,
Let's go—time's flying by!

MAX. My father's blessing's not mine to distribute.
Just wait a bit longer—he'll come, you can trust him.
Let's seal the deal. Pinkhesl must contribute
Half the dowry, that's local custom.

ALL. Yes, that's the custom.
Yes, that's the custom.
That's how it has to be.
To make this real,
To make the deal,
Half the dowry—that's his fee.

PINKHESL AND RIVKE. Gentlemen, we've nothing to hide.
We're giving the dowry, right here, thus.
We're giving the groom my daughter, the bride,
May this be a blessing for us!

ALL. Nu, so quickly open that little mouth wide,
Say yes, bride, never take it back.
Mazl tov, our little bride,
For happiness may you never lack.

ALL. (*Turning to the bride and groom and to the in-laws, and shouting.*) Mazl tov! Mazl tov!

PINKHESL. Gentlemen, may you also enjoy good fortune. Come into the next room. We've covered the tables there, and that's where we're going to celebrate. (*To the Servant.*) Anshl, carry those tables over there. And take the benches as well, just in case there won't be enough. (*The Servant carries them offstage. The crowd all exit stage left into the other room, leaving Reb Pinkhesl last on stage. He is about to leave as well.*)

Scene 2

(*Kuni-Leml arrives, and when he sees that Reb Pinkhesl is about to go into the other room, runs over to him and strikes him a blow from behind. Pinkhesl looks at him and gets frightened.*)

KUNI-LEML. Aha! Now we'll see whether I'm a liar or not. I've b-brought s-signed proof from my city—in black and white—to show that *I* am Kuni-Leml.

PINKHESL. (*Astonished.*) Who are *you*? What sort of nerve have you got, to come to my house like this and to imitate my bridegroom's speech and make fun of him?

KUNI-LEML. M-make fun of him? But I have it in b-black and white! Is that what you call m-making fun?

PINKHESL. Just tell me, quickly: what is it that you want? What sort of devil has brought you here to spoil this happy occasion of mine?

KUNI-LEML. Just take a look at w-what sort of devil I am. (*He shows him a piece of paper.*)

PINKHESL. What kind of paper is this? You must have gotten lost and ended up here by mistake. Who *are* you?

KUNI-LEML. W-what, already you don't recognize me? You yourself j-just wrote me that I should c-come and take the thousand rubles' dowry, and your daughter a-as my wife, and so here I am.

PINKHESL. What, my daughter? What do you mean by my daughter? I have no idea where you're coming from.

KUNI-LEML. No, no, I just g-got here! Call your daughter in here, she herself will t-tell you how much she loves me—I'm ashamed e-even to say the words—can I say it? Yes, I'll say it—s-she herself wanted to give me a k— a kiss. (*He laughs ashamedly.*)

PINKHESL. (*Angrily.*) What is he babbling about?

KUNI-LEML. Yes, yes, call her in, she herself w-will t-tell you personally. (*He goes over to the door and shouts into it.*) Crinolina! Crinolina! C-come here, I won't run away any more.

PINKHESL. (*Tearing him away from the door.*) What is this, "Crinolina?" That's not my daughter's name—she's called Khayele!

KUNI-LEML. So let it be Khaye, Paye, Sh-shmaye; as long as she's a young woman, it's all the same to me.

PINKHESL. It may be all the same to you, but it's not all the same to me to give away my daughter's hand in marriage to some sort of swindler. Sha! You say that I wrote you a letter; so nu, show me the letter.

KUNI-LEML. I'll show it to you r-right away. (*He looks for the letter in all of his pockets, and can't find it anywhere. He stands still for several seconds lost in thought, and then all of a sudden shouts.*) Aha! I j-just remembered that the other K-kuni-Leml has the letter, yes, that's right!

PINKHESL. What do you mean, "the other Kuni-Leml"? What do you want? (*Angrily.*) Tfu, some kind of crazy person, there's no talking to him! (*He exits left into the second room, leaving Kuni-Leml by himself, flustered. He looks around in all directions, looks himself over, and says to himself.*)

KUNI-LEML. Woe is me, the whole world is out to get me; I—I'm completely confused. I don't even know if I'm K-Kuni-Leml or not . . . (*Pause.*) That one shouts that he's K-Kuni-Leml, and I shout that I am. (*In a Talmudic singsong.*) Nu, if I-I'm actually him, what if my b-bride calls me Mocks? Should I say that I-I'm the one at home, and that I'm really called K-Kuni-Leml, only I've p-passed away and have

been reincarnated as this M-Mocks? Yes? Why shouldn't I g-go around
in sh-shrouds? But apparently, I really haven't died, and I really am
called K-Kuni-Leml, since I have some proof: that just last week, when
they called m-me up to the Torah, they sh-shouted out, "May Reb K-
Kuni-Leml rise!"[26] Yes, but why should the f-father-in-law not b-believe
me, if I am him, and why is my b-bride calling me Mocks? Hm? It must
be, because I really am named Mocks. I-I really am this M-Mocks.

Scene 3

(*Kalmen Matchmaker enters stage right and, when he sees Kuni-Leml,
grabs him.*)

KALMEN. Aha! Here's the fine young man! Hold your horses! Sholem
aleykhem, Reb Kuni-Leml! (*Gives him his hand.*)
KUNI-LEML. So? Am I really called K-Kuni-Leml once more? Th-thank
God, that you have returned my holy name K-Kuni-Leml to me again!
KALMEN. Right. But it's really not very nice of you, hold your horses, to
slip out of my house like that without my knowing about it, hold
your horses!

Scene 4

(*Pinkhesl arrives from stage left; Kalmen turns to him.*)

KALMEN. Aha, Reb Pinkhesl, and it's not very nice of you either, to fool
the groom like that and to sign all the marriage papers without my
knowing it, and without my matchmaker's fee . . .
PINKHESL. As far as your matchmaker's fee . . .
KALMEN. Hold your horses, I don't have anything to worry about.
PINKHESL. In God's name, just let me get one word in edgewise, hold
your horses and hold your horses and go hold your horses yourself
as much as humanly possible. Just let me say one thing. Just tell me,
Reb Kalmen: you considered this young man for my bridegroom;
do you know the young man well? Did you know that the young
man is Kuni-Leml, the son of Reb Shloymenyu, the alderman of
Shakhrayevke?

---

26. As part of the Sabbath morning liturgy, a section from the Pentateuch is read. That
section is itself divided into seven readings, each of which is preceded by an individual
(in traditional society, always a man) who is called up by his Hebrew name and patronymic to recite a blessing before and after the reading.

KALMEN. Naturally! What, I shouldn't know him? He was in my own house with me! And you yourself told me to send him a letter to come, hold your horses, and stay with me, and that you would meet him there at my place, hold your horses. That's why I came just now to meet him, because he slipped out of my house without my knowing about it.

KUNI-LEML. (*Astonished.*) W-what sort of f-foolishness is this? This one says I-I was in his house. Listen, Reb P-Pinkhesl: may I break my other foot if I even r-recognize this man.

KALMEN. Hold your horses, if that's how it is, then you're a swindler, that's what you are, and you're lying right to my face.

PINKHESL. (*To Kuni-Leml.*) Now look here, what sort of a liar are you? You just want to trick me out of the dowry, and nothing more! (*To Kalmen.*) Listen, Reb Kalmen, the minute that you left me, I myself sent a letter to my new in-law, telling him that his son Kuni-Leml should come right to me, and he certainly came . . .

KUNI-LEML. Yes, yes, it's absolutely t-true!

PINKHESL. (*Angrily.*) Shut up, you liar! (*To Kalmen.*) At first I was even fairly frightened, when I saw what kind of cripple he was. But afterward, when he showed me how well he knew Talmud, and that he was one of the thirty-six righteous saints, it's no wonder to me that my daughter loves him as much as she does.

KUNI-LEML. That your daughter l-loves me—that I know. But that I know Talmud—that's news to me! Sha! Sha! Here she comes h-herself.

Scene 5

(*Carolina enters and whispers something in her father's ear.*)

KUNI-LEML. Perfect, I-I'll ask her right now. C-Carolina, show your father how much you love m-me, and how you w-wanted to give me a kiss . . .

CAROLINA. (*Angrily.*) Shameless! What sort of talk is that? Who are you? (*She moves away from him.*)

KUNI-LEML. W-who am I? She herself called me her M-Mocks earlier!

PINKHESL. What *is* your name, if one may ask?

KUNI-LEML. My name is Mo—no, my name is . . . How the devil should I know what my name is?

Scene 6

(*Libe enters stage right, and when she sees Kuni-Leml, she runs over to him and grabs him.*)

LIBE. Ah-ah! So you're here, you liar? I've caught you now!

KALMEN. What are you doing here, Libele? Hold your horses!

LIBE. I came to settle things with the liar here.

KUNI-LEML. Woe is me! Wh-what sort of misfortune is happening to me now? What does she w-want?

LIBE. What do I want? Tell me, why did you have to deceive me?

KUNI-LEML. G-get a load of her! Sh-she's acting like my pal already! Sh-she's so familiar with me; tell me, do we know each other, that you're s-so familiar?

LIBE. Do I know you? Sure, I know you very well.

KUNI-LEML. If you know me so well, then b-be my witness that my name is K-Kuni-Leml.

LIBE. Sure, I'll prove who you are right now. You're the one who came to our house in order to trick me. You told me that you loved me; I fell in love with you too, and then all of a sudden you ran away. Well, now I'm not letting you go so easily.

KUNI-LEML. (*With a smile.*) I n-never would have believed that so many women would l-love me this much. That one wants to k-kiss me, and now this one would rather skin m-me alive than let me g-get away.

LIBE. I'm not going to let you get away. You have to keep the promise you made me.

KUNI-LEML. What promise?

LIBE. Do you mean to say that you didn't get down on your knees in front of me?

KUNI-LEML. On my kn-knees? Like a Christian? Is that even allowed?[27]

LIBE. And don't you remember how you sang me "Cuckoo"?

KUNI-LEML. It's come to such a pass that a girl is playing Cuckoo with me.

LIBE. (*To Pinkhesl, who, this entire time has been arguing silently with Kalmen and been demonstrating with his hands how this groom of his was about to fly away, and how he had shown him miracles and other things.*) Listen, Reb Pinkhesl, you should know that this isn't Kuni-Leml. He's only trying to trick you, the same way he tricked me, because when he was alone with me, he was a completely different person. He spoke and walked normally, saw perfectly, like anybody else.

KUNI-LEML. I'd l-like to see that miracle for myself.

LIBE. He even put on a fake beard to make you think that he's the real Kuni-Leml in order to trick you out of the thousand rubles' dowry. That's one proof that I'll get rid of right away. (*She runs over to him with a shriek.*) Give me that beard! (*Kuni-Leml tears himself away and runs away from her.*)

KALMEN. Sha, sha, hold your horses! Here comes Reb Shloymenyu himself!

---

27. With certain very specific exceptions, bowing to (or kneeling in front of) someone else is strongly discouraged in traditional Judaism, as it smacks of idolatry.

Scene 7

(*Shloymenyu enters. Everyone greets him.*)

KUNI-LEML. Father, father! Th-thank God you've c-come. You'll be a witness that I'm your son K-Kuni-Leml.

SHLOYMENYU. So who's denied it?

KUNI-LEML. N-nobody . . . well, everybody.

PINKHESL. (*To Shloymenyu.*) You mean this is really your son, Reb Sholem?

SHLOYMENYU. No, he's my stepson.

KUNI-LEML. Yes, yes, I-I'm his very own stepson.

PINKHESL. So? And who's the other one?

KUNI-LEML. They mean the other K-Kuni-Leml.

SHLOYMENYU. (*After thinking a moment.*) Ha, ha! What Max told me must be absolutely true. (*To Pinkhesl.*) Understand me, Reb Pinkhes, this one is my stepson, and the other one is my brother's son, the doctor's son.

PINKHESL. (*Vaguely dissatisfied.*) What, your brother's a doctor? (*He makes a face.*)

SHLOYMENYU. Listen, Reb Pinkhesl, it's high time that you open your eyes. You should pardon me for talking like this, since I know you're older than I am, but just consider how unhappy you've been willing to make your own child. And for what? For status! I don't want to insult him, since he's family, but nevertheless I have to ask you: how can a father have the heart to sell off his own child to a cripple like this when there's absolutely no need for you to do so? You're rich, a fine citizen, an important figure in the city. So what? So you want status! Don't think, Reb Pinkhesl, that I'm the saint you take me for: more than once I've envied my brother, who's reached such a height and has turned his child into a real man. We still have to play the old roles, since we're men of the old world, but that doesn't mean the old ideas have to turn us into fools. I'm telling you, Reb Pinkhesl, if you want to make yourself happy and earn real honor, then take my brother's son as your son-in-law. He's probably just as religious as I am, and educated to boot: that is, about both religious and worldly affairs. Listen to me, Reb Pinkhesl: don't think about it. Just say the one word—yes—and may it be a happy occasion.

RIVKE. (*Who has arrived during the course of this conversation.*) Aha, husband, you see? Me and the rest of the world are in agreement.

PINKHESL. That's what I've said for a long time now; in fact, I've already given my word on it and have put down half the dowry to boot, and agreed on behalf of both our families. All right, but if that's the case, then tell me: who were all the dead people that he showed me?

SHLOYMENYU. Nu, Reb Pinkhesl, just look at how much smarter the younger folk are than we are. Who knows what he cooked up, with that sharp brain of his . . . sha, here they come now, we'll ask them. Come in, children, come in, you've got nothing to be afraid of any more.

Scene 8

(Max, dressed very elegantly, a top hat on his head, enters arm-in-arm with Carolina.)

PINKHESL. *(First looks quickly at him and doesn't recognize him; once he does, he then says to Rivke.)* This must be that Max that used to be her teacher! *(To Max.)* So you were the one who tricked me? Well, look, if you were able to lead me around by the nose like that, then you must really be the smart one, and I must be the fool.

KUNI-LEML. And I must be K-Kuni-Leml.

PINKHESL. Well, that can't be helped. But tell me, though, who were the dead people that you showed me?

MAX. There's a perfectly natural explanation. I'll show it to you right now.

KUNI-LEML. So then w-what are you? And who is really K-Kuni-Leml? I am! E-eh!

LIBE. *(To Max.)* So, you're the fine young man who played me for a fool?

MAX. It's true; I won't deny it. I allowed myself to play a little joke on you which helped me with my plans. But truthfully, I didn't trick you at all. In your words, when we were talking then, I heard how afraid you were that you would stay an old maid. All I promised you was that you wouldn't stay unmarried and that you'd have a wedding. But because I allowed myself to play a little joke on you, I'm going to give you half of my dowry.

KALMEN. Grab it, Libele, we're in business, hold your horses! A miracle like this doesn't happen every day.

MAX. But only on the condition that you take that young man as your bridegroom. *(He points to Kuni-Leml.)* Nu, and you, Reb Kuni-Leml, will you take this young woman? To you it's all the same, Khaye, Paye, Shmaye, as long as she's a young woman.

KUNI-LEML. *(Looks at Libe, first bashfully, then with a smile.)* Certainly, for my part! I don't want to have t-traveled here for n-nothing!

KALMEN. Hold your horses! May God look on this as a happy and blessed hour!

ALL. *(Shouting.)* Mazl tov, mazl tov!

MAX. Now I'll tell you who all the dead people were. They were my friends. I decided to pull that trick because I had heard that you believed that Kuni-Leml was one of the thirty-six righteous saints, that he could dance with angels, and speak with the dead. (*Everyone laughs.*) I took my friends and had them dress up as dead people, and had them stand under your window in order to scare you. If you want to see them again, come with me, I'll show them to you— they're in your garden right now.

ALL. (*Laughing.*) Come on, come on. Let's go see the dead, the living dead. (*All exit stage left.*)

KUNI-LEML. (*As he leaves, he says happily.*) But I really am K-Kuni-Leml!

Scene 9

(*Reb Pinkhesl's garden. Everyone enters together, and stand along both sides of the garden. Music begins to play from behind the trees. From deep in the garden, Students emerge, dressed as dead people, and they sing the same song as earlier. Pinkhesl acts as if he wants to look at them, but he is too frightened and has to run away. Kuni-Leml does the same.*)

STUDENTS.　　What do you want? What do you want?
　　　　　　　What do you want, my dear?
　　　　　　　Why do you haunt, why do you haunt
　　　　　　　Our quiet tombs, my dear?
　　　　　　　In our prayer shawls—so poor, don't be ashamed,
　　　　　　　Arise, you dead,
　　　　　　　From your watery graves . . . (*They throw off their white
　　　　　　　　shrouds to reveal their student clothes.*)

ALL. (*Bursting out laughing.*) Ah, such handsome corpses!

KUNI-LEML. Oy, vey, just look, dead heretics!

STUDENTS.　　We all wish you mazl tov,
　　　　　　　Khosn-kale mazl tov,
　　　　　　　We have all, mazl tov,
　　　　　　　Come to call, mazl tov,
　　　　　　　Khosn-kale—groom and bride—a happy mazl tov!
　　　　　　　　(*The stanza is repeated.*)

Scene 10

(*The Hasidim run in from stage left, run over to Reb Pinkhesl and the others and sing.*)

HASIDIM.　　Mazl tov, mazl tov, be of good cheer,
　　　　　　　For the betrothal,
　　　　　　　Once and for all,
　　　　　　　Everybody's here.

(The Students run over and drive them out.)

STUDENTS.   Away, away, away, away!
            You disgusting creatures.
            We're all fed up—so we say—
            With your horrid features.
(The Hasidim reenter, and run over to Reb Pinkhesl.)

HASIDIM. What's going on, Reb Pinkhesl? Heretics throw pious Jews like us out of your house, and you just watch and don't say anything? What's going on?

PINKHESL. I'll tell you. As long as I thought highly of you, you were honored guests of mine, but now you can take my new son-in-law who I've taken into my home as proof that I've split with you for good. Now I see clearly that they are the wise ones and that the only thing that you know is how to drink brandy. Go in good health!

HASIDIM. We're going to tell the rebbe everything . . . *(The Students run over and don't let them finish speaking. They throw them out. Everyone laughs. The Hasidim exit.)*

MAX. *(Sings, to Pinkhesl.)* So that's all through,
            How good of you!
            Now you can see, how disgusting they can be,
            And especially,
            Reality:
            The only lineage that counts is of the man of the world.
(Everyone begins to pair off, singing and dancing. The Students begin to form a circle, and also dance.)

CHORUS.   We are all, mazl tov, etc.
MAX.   I thank you, my dear fellows!
CHORUS.   We all wish you mazl tov, etc. . . .
KUNI-LEML. I th-thank you all, my d-dear fellows!
CHORUS.   We have all, mazl tov, etc . . . .
(Fireworks begin to go off, and the stage is electrically illuminated. As the song ends, the curtain is quickly lowered.)

The End

Appendix

KUNILEMEL

Words and Music by A. GOLDFADEN

For Piano Arranged by J. M. RUMSHISKY

A. GOLDFADEN

PUBLISHED BY

HEBREW PUBLISHING CO.

50-52 ELDRIDGE STR., NEW YORK

Opereta Kuny Lemel.

Chasidim Chor.

Arr. by J. M. RUMSHISKY

Violin 8

Lied Karoline

Alle meidlach hoben chasanim

Studenten

Duett Kuku

Violin 8

Nein dem alten Gabai! Nein dem neuen Gabai!

Firt dem gabai in shil arein

Choɪ Toidte - und Masel Tow

Gesang Ensemble

Finale

Miriam

by Peretz Hirschbein

Cast of Characters

SHIMEN, *a shoemaker, 50*

DVOYRE, *his wife*

LEAH, *their daughter, 23*

YOYSEFL, *their son*

JONAH, *Leah's fiancé, 26*

MIRIAM, *18, lives at Shimen's*

MOYSHE, *an old porter, lives at Shimen's*

DVOSHE, *his wife*

ZILBERMAN,[1] *20, a son of Shimen's landlord*

GRUNYE, *25*

NATALKE, *24, a Gentile* } *fallen women*

CHILDREN

---

1. Yiddish, "silver man."

Act 1

A large, four-sided room in a basement, the walls dark yellow from dampness. The vaulted ceiling is dirty. Left: two windows recessed into the wall look out onto sidewalk level, their panes spattered with dirt. Right: Moyshe's room, patched together with boards. Left, not far from the wall, a large oven. Next to that stands a bench, and next to that, a cradle suspended from ropes. To the left of the oven hangs a flowered curtain, from behind which can be seen two broken-down beds. Between the windows stands a large table, and next to it, a low stool which serves as a cobbler's workbench.

It is evening, the end of the Sabbath. Shimen and Jonah sit at the workbench mending shoes. On their little table burns a lamp with a piece of dark paper placed over its glass as a lampshade. Not far from them, at the large table, sits Miriam. She knits stockings on a machine. Dvoyre washes the dishes. Yoysefl sits on the ground next to the oven, warming himself. From time to time we hear the footsteps of passersby walking along the sidewalk outside the window.

Long pause.

MIRIAM. (*Tying the thread, which has broken. Sings.*)
> I am lonely as a stone;
> I've been abandoned, all alone—
> Please take pity, gentle friends,
> Don't let me meet an early end.

(*To Dvoyre.*) Once I start singing that song, I forget all about the machine; then the thread goes and breaks on me.

DVOYRE. What sort of fool dreamed up that song? Even if I knew I was going to kick the bucket, I wouldn't go complaining about it in public. Do you really think there are good people like that in the world?

MIRIAM. Here it's a blind orphan girl complaining. Probably came up with the song herself. (*Long pause.*) There are still plenty of good people.

JONAH. (*Not raising his head from his work.*) Ech, what a little goat! In your shtetl[2] you had plenty of beans and noodles. Here you won't eat so well; the red in your cheeks will disappear, and your lips—fyu-fyu! Then, ketsele,[3] you'll find out if there are any good people.

MIRIAM. (*Interrupts him.*) He's mouthing off again! Reb Shimen, stuff a shoe in that mouth of his. (*Shimen is completely preoccupied with removing the last from a shoe.*)

---

2. Yiddish, "small town."

3. Yiddish, "kitten."

JONAH. Mirele, Mirenke, Mirtshele.[4]

MIRIAM. What's up?

JONAH. Want some beans and noodles?

MIRIAM. (*Smiles.*) And if I do, then what?

JONAH. Then nothing. What else could you possibly need?

DVOYRE. What are you laughing at? That's why they're so healthy in the little *shtetlekh*.[5] What was I like before I got married? Each hand an iron rod . . . And my cheeks? . . . We're rotting here in the basement; your eyes go dark and you sink into the ground.

MIRIAM. It's true, the basement will be the death of us. Have you noticed I'm a little hoarse?

JONAH. And you probably thought you'd get a job as cantor. What a shame!

SHIMEN. (*To Dvoyre.*) Why didn't you to rent the attic?

YOYSEFL. Ha, up there! I'd be there in one jump! I can climb five or ten steps at a time! . . . Why didn't you want to, Mama?

DVOYRE. Your father wanted to be upstairs. A lot he cares for your mother. I should have to *shlep* his water up ten flights of stairs. God in Heaven knows the pains I have just getting down these few steps . . . What will be, will be. I won't be around much longer anyway. If it weren't for the children—

SHIMEN. Enough—she's at it again! Women always have something bothering them—and they're always complaining. Better I should have been made out of brass . . . Just see to it that there's something to eat. Our girl will be hungry when she comes home. (*Pause.*)

MIRIAM. (*Takes a finished stocking from under the machine, stretches it.*) Jonah, you know what I'm thinking about now?

JONAH. A handsome guy!

MIRIAM. Pssh! Big deal! I'm thinking about something completely different . . . magnificent! If I had lots of money, I would . . . I would . . .

JONAH. What would you do? Would you give me a loan—a couple of rubles? . . .

MIRIAM. (*Drawing a new thread through the needles.*) I'm not thinking about rubles at all—not even thousands of them. If I had lots of money— really loads, like millions—then I'd go all over the world proclaiming, "Whoever can't find work to support his wife and children, come to me; whoever doesn't have a dowry for his daughter: to me!" And when everyone gathers around me, I'll say, "A handful of money

---

4. All diminutives of Miriam.

5. Plural of *shtetl.*

for you, and a handful for you—now go home!" People wouldn't live in basements any more. And I wouldn't let them live in attics either...

JONAH. Ha ha ha! Every pauper loves to give handouts! Listen to her: she'd turn the whole world upside down.

SHIMEN. Maybe you'll choose a doctor for a husband—a fine profession, I'm telling you.

JONAH. She's going to choose me for her husband... ha ha ha ha! Look how much she likes the idea: look how red she's turning... Bravo, bravo, ha ha ha! (*He gets up.*) Come on, *ketsele*, I'll give you a kiss and seal the deal.

MIRIAM. Don't even try it; I'll poke your eyes out with this needle.

JONAH. Oho—look how she defends those cheeks of hers! For whose sake, I'd like to know?

MIRIAM. More of that crude talk of his... (*Works the machine quickly.*) I'm not laughing. If I had a few million, there wouldn't be any poor people in the world. (*Sings.*)
> I am lonely as a stone,
> I've been abandoned, all alone...

DVOYRE. A person should think only about himself, 'cause no one else will worry about you. Does anyone out there know how I'm wasting my life away in this basement?

SHIMEN. (*As if to himself.*) The world is like a wedding. Whoever jumps in there gets the food.

DVOYRE. Whoever jumps in there gets the food... yes, yes. (*The baby in the cradle starts to cry. She breastfeeds it.*) Oh, how my heart aches. (*The baby cries.*) What do you want, what? (*Rocks the baby and sings.*)
> Baby's cradle rocks to and fro,
> There's a goat there white as snow.
> The goat's gone to the fair—
> Trading raisins and almonds beyond compare....[6]

(*Long pause.*)

JONAH. (*To Miriam.*) Millionairess! For the time being, give me two rubles, and we'll send for tea. Brr, so cold! There are still a couple of sugar cubes left.

MIRIAM. Why aren't I cold? Shame on him: he served in the army and is afraid of the cold. I'm wearing this thin blouse and I'm warm.

JONAH. I've known for a long time you're a warm-blooded girl—your cheeks prove it... (*To Shimen.*) You see, in-law: what cheeks!

---

6. This is a part of a well-known Yiddish folk song called "Unter yankeles vigele" ("Under Jacob's crib"); however, the song became much more famous as the chorus to Abraham Goldfaden's "Rozhinkes mit mandlen" ("Raisins and Almonds"), written as part of his 1880 operetta *Shulamis*.

MIRIAM. Someone do me a favor: tell him to be quiet for a while.

JONAH. My dear lady, my first fiancée was like this too—that's why I sent back the marriage contract... Nu, all kidding aside, give me two rubles... I'm sitting by the window—the damn thing is drafty...

MIRIAM. I don't have so much as a plug nickel. Take a look. (*She turns her purse inside out.*) Empty! Tomorrow I'll have plenty of money; I've knitted maybe a dozen extra pieces today. (*The baby cries.*)

DVOYRE. The Devil knows what he wants from me today. If he'd only close his eyes for a minute... (*Sings.*)

> Learning Torah is your lot,
> I'll cook you kasha in a pot,
> There'll be butter on your bread—

(*Footsteps are heard outside the door.*) There, Leah's coming! (*The door opens and Moyshe enters. He is dressed in rags, with a rope holding up his trousers, and is carrying wood chips under his arm. Leah enters behind him.*)

MOYSHE. Good evening! Ach, it's so cold out there on the street! (*He tosses the wood chips next to the oven.*)

LEAH. We met on the steps. I heard someone fumbling out there in the dark. Didn't recognize Reb Moyshe—a sign that you're gonna get rich[7]... Ha, so cold! It's gotten into my heart; it feels like I have needles under my fingernails. (*Looks in the oven.*) Ha, potatoes are cooking! I'm so hungry!

DVOYRE. We'll have dinner soon, when the baby falls asleep.

MOYSHE. (*Trying to tie the rope around his waist. Goes to Jonah.*) Ho—oh— oh, here, tie the rope, Jonah. My fingers are frozen solid. (*Jonah ties the rope.*) How come you're working so late?... Got up and stood out in the cold since morning, and not so much as a dog showed up. It was already pitch dark when someone came, a nobleman or some-thing, and told me to carry some wood up to him on the third floor. Gave me forty kopecks and took a little wood.

SHIMEN. (*Standing by the wall, says the evening prayers. Jonah and Leah whisper to each other, laughing. Miriam looks on with interest.*)

MOYSHE. They say it was maybe twenty degrees today. (*Goes to throw the wood chips into the oven.*) This should liven things up in here.

DVOYRE. There's no need, Reb Moyshe. Better to leave it 'til tomorrow. At night it's okay as it is. We can curl up under the the rags and sleep. I'm on my feet all day, and at night I sleep like a stone.

SHIMEN. The other night the baby was screaming maybe two hours. No one heard. (*Pause. Moyshe goes to his bedroom. We can hear him saying his evening prayers.*)

---

7. A well-known Russian folk belief.

MIRIAM. You know what, Leah? Today I knitted about a dozen extra stockings.

LEAH. You'll be rich for sure. It's rough on your hands, though; later on they won't work so well . . . (*To Jonah.*) Maybe you'll sleep here with us tonight? I can make up a bed up for you on the table—there'll be enough room for you . . . Oy, Mama, I'm dying of hunger!

DVOYRE. You didn't have to stay out there so late, it's maybe ten o'clock already.

LEAH. We had to get a wedding dress ready for tomorrow . . . Nu, let's eat already.

DVOYRE. In a minute. There are all sorts of good things here: bread, potatoes. Too bad the kids fell asleep. The little one barely keeps body and soul together. (*She strains the water from the potatoes.*)

MIRIAM. I've got an idea—ah, this is great! Let's put the big table by the oven—it'll be heaven! What do you think?

LEAH. A brilliant idea! We should've thought of this sooner. Come on, Jonah, let's take the table and the lamp . . . put the baby's cradle on the floor. (*Starts to drag the table.*)

MIRIAM. You'll break my machine. (*Unscrews the machine.*)

DVOYRE. Just don't wake the baby. (*She pours the potatoes into a bowl. Jonah and Leah carry the table to the oven. Miriam takes the cradle off of its hooks and lays it next to the bed. Dvoyre brings the potatoes to the table. Calls.*) Reb Moyshe! Reb Moyshe! Where are you hiding? I cooked this with you in mind.

MOYSHE. (*From his room.*) Thank you very much, but I'm finishing my prayers. They're decent folk—they won't eat my food. (*The others eat without spoons, blowing on their food.*)

SHIMEN. (*Sits across from the oven.*) Look how chilled they are!

MIRIAM. Reb Moyshe, I'm eating your food!

MOYSHE. Just a second, I'm coming.

JONAH. He's praying to God that his Dvoshe will come back. He misses Dvoshe, right, Reb Moyshe?

MOYSHE. (*Going to the table.*) Of course I miss her. What else—waste my whole life without a wife like you good-for-nothings?

LEAH. (*Glancing at Jonah.*) Jonah isn't a good-for-nothing. If he had moved too fast, he wouldn't have me now. He's no dummy!

DVOYRE. Every shopkeeper praises his own goods.

MOYSHE. We'll dance at your wedding, God willing. The ground will shake! (*Sits at the table and reaches gingerly for a potato.*)

MIRIAM. Will you dance with me, Reb Moyshe?

JONAH. You see how she's decided that his wife has gone for good? From me she runs away . . .

MOYSHE. Enough foolishness. What do you really think about my wife—will she come back tomorrow? It's just wrong, to abandon your house for two whole weeks.

DVOYRE. What makes you think you've lost her? Everything'll be alright. I wish I could break away from this hell for one week. I bet the kids didn't give her a minute's rest.

SHIMEN. I think this week was her *yortsayt*.[8] She probably went to visit her parents' graves. (*Pause.*)

DVOYRE. Oh, people are so foolish. Why visit graves and bother the dead?—they've got enough to deal with. Let them rest there . . . Nu, why aren't you eating? There's plenty in the pot. (*She brings the pot to the table and pours its contents into a bowl.*)

MOYSHE. (*Pensively.*) That's true, I'm telling you. What can the dead do for you? But that's the way of the world: you have a good cry and your heart feels lighter. How does the saying go? A drowning man grasps at straws . . . I had a grandfather, a blacksmith, a decent Jew. He always used to say: "Give—God will give to you too." And, may he forgive me, he died a pauper—there wasn't even enough money to bury him. He loved me very much; my mother was his only daughter. I was sixteen years old when he died. That was before I married my first wife, may she rest in peace. The day before he died he called me over to his bed—this was at our house—he could barely speak, and said to me: "Moyshele," (he says), "I love you . . . I won't forget you . . . I'll plead for you up there at God's throne. If I manage to get there—not everyone manages to . . . " When I told my mother—may she rest in peace— she said to me, with her eyes full of tears, "You're lucky, my child. With God's help, life will be good to you . . . " Since he died it's been . . . (*Looks toward the ceiling.*) It's been thirty-nine years . . . And you can see how rich I am! They say they don't keep even the worst villains in hell for more than a year[9] . . . and here—thirty-nine years!

JONAH. Maybe it's your own fault—you're such a sinner that he can't do anything for you.

MOYSHE. Thanks a lot! The young folks make fun . . . Maybe you're right. All I know is this: I'm a porter. Go argue with the Creator of the Universe.

DVOYRE. Sinful-shminful—what sort of sin would a Jew like Reb Moyshe commit? What chance does he ever get?

SHIMEN. You don't know what you're babbling about. A man, if he's healthy, can carry loads on his shoulders, that's enough. Maybe that was his grandfather's promise. What else? A man—if he's healthy, that's enough.

---

8. The anniversary of a loved one's death.

9. See BT Rosh Hashanah 17a.

MOYSHE. That's absolutely right! I'm telling you, I hate to think too much. But when I'm walking in the middle of the street with a heavy trunk on my shoulders, I think deep down, I'm happy! An old man! Lots of guys at my age are either lying six feet under or sitting by the fire.

JONAH. (*Emphatically.*) But why doesn't a guy like you think, dragging himself along with a trunk on his back, Why should I have to be bent in half in my old age when there are people as healthy as horses who are too lazy even to fetch themselves a glass of water?

LEAH. (*Approaching Miriam.*) And why shouldn't a girl like you think, sitting hunched over her machine, Why should I have to suffer in a basement at my machine while other girls like me sit in their salons and live it up?

MIRIAM. I'm content as I am. We should look down, not up.

MOYSHE. That's absolutely right! That's smart. You shouldn't think too much.

JONAH. A horse has a big head and doesn't think either.

MOYSHE. I know all your arguments already. Such ideas will get you a whipping down below. . . . You, my daughter, should be well rid of such nonsense. God gave you hands—what more do you need? Only good-for-nothings talk like that—you understand?

YOYSEFL. (*Crying from his bed.*) Mama, Mama, I can't sleep, I want to eat.

DVOYRE. Stay there, stay. I'll bring it to you. (*She brings the bowl to his bed.*)

MOYSHE. Eh, nonsense! . . . Listen here: you fed me, so I'm going to treat you to tea. (*Searches through his pockets.*) Come here, Mirele. There's a kopeck; go get us a pot of tea.

MIRIAM. Gladly! I wanted to go out earlier. (*Takes a teapot from on top of the oven.*)

LEAH. Wait, I'll come too. (*To Jonah.*) Sleep here tonight; I want to tell you something.

JONAH. No, I'm going too. I promised my mother I'd go to her place. (*Takes his coat.*)

DVOYRE. Where are you shlepping in this cold? Stay here.

JONAH. No, I have to go.

MIRIAM. What's taking so long? (*Pushes them out the door.*) Brr . . . we're going to be so cold! (*They go.*)

MOYSHE. (*Calling after them.*) Make sure they put enough tea in the pot. I can't stand watery tea! (*To Dvoyre.*) A wonderful girl, that Miriam. Straightforward, just the way I like. What good is thinking too much? Let everyone live their own lives. Jealousy's for other people! Whoever has, can eat meat. Whoever doesn't, can eat bread. Shame on Jonah for saying such things around her . . . no good can come of it.

DVOYRE. Young people—they see things, they feel things . . . (*Pause.*)

ZILBERMAN. (*Enters. A healthy young man, 20 years old. Dressed in a short winter coat. In boots. Looks around.*) Good evening! It's dark on your stairs. Someone could trip and break their neck . . .

DVOYRE. (*With a forced smile.*) Your father is pinching pennies; the rich folks' places are well lit. . . . But then who ever comes to us?

ZILBERMAN. I'm here. Aren't I a guest?

DVOYRE. (*Offers him a chair.*) Sit, of course you're a guest.

ZILBERMAN. Thank you. I'll see to it myself that your stairs are lighted.

DVOYRE. Thank you very much! We didn't dare to bother anyone about a little thing like that.

SHIMEN. The gentleman must have come for his ice skate. I've fixed it already—was thinking of bringing it up to you myself. Sit by the oven, it's warmer. (*He looks around his work station.*) I've fixed it once and for all! You see? First stitched it up and then put on a little patch up here . . . why don't you sit?

ZILBERMAN. (*He takes the shoe, but doesn't yet look at it.*) Danke, danke,[10] I really should go. (*He is silent for a while; looks around.*) This evening in the courtyard I met the young lady who lives with you—and made a mistake. I thought she was your daughter. I stopped her and asked her to bring me the ice skate, but then thought better of it. A pretty girl. Where is she from?

MOYSHE. From a small shtetl, a very fine girl.

DVOYRE. Came here to make some money. Darns stockings.

ZILBERMAN. That's what I gathered. I like small-town girls very much. Our maid turns red whenever you talk to her.

DVOYRE. She has to get a little more used to being around people.

MOYSHE. (*Looks carefully at the ice skate.*) How did the gentleman tear such a strong shoe?

ZILBERMAN. (*Animated.*) Aha, that was quite a tear, an embarrassing story. I go out ice skating—I'm considered an excellent skater. On the ice there are all these schoolboys whirling around, falling every minute. (*Laughs.*) I also fell many times when I started . . . So there I am going straight as an arrow when a schoolboy pops up beneath me, gets tripped up in my feet and falls . . . and I got caught in a tree and the skate was broken.

MOYSHE. (*Diffidently. With a smile.*) When I was a boy, in *kheyder*,[11] I used to skate with my friends, and the rebbe[12] beat us . . . (*Miriam and*

---

10. Zilberman responds in German rather than Yiddish, which underscores his social superiority (intentionally or not).

11. A religious school for young Jewish boys.

12. Here, the teacher of the *kheyder*.

Leah boldly burst into the room, but stop dead in their tracks with amazement when they see Zilberman. Miriam puts the teapot on the table.)

ZILBERMAN (*To Leah and Miriam.*) Good evening! (*He offers them his hand. They respond reluctantly.*) I saw you walking from a distance. I thought you were their daughter.

MIRIAM. (*Laughs.*) I carried the teapot under my shawl—it kept me warm.

ZILBERMAN. A brilliant idea! You don't need a coat that way. (*Pause.*)

SHIMEN. If the gentleman likes, I'll bring the skate up to you tomorrow.

ZILBERMAN. I'll take it myself. You folks think I'm quite the nobleman. You've got it all wrong! I love to work, I chop wood every day myself. Physical work is very healthy. (*He pauses for a moment.*) I beg your pardon! I'm disturbing you. You want to drink your tea. I'll send you the money tomorrow. I'll also order some shoes from you soon . . .

MOYSHE. (*Takes a glass to the table.*) Absolutely. If only the gentleman would order a couple hundred.

ZILBERMAN. (*Extends his hand to Miriam and Leah.*) Good night! Thank you—tomorrow I'll be able to skate again—good night!

DVOYRE. Take the lamp, children, and throw a little light on the steps.

ZILBERMAN. Tomorrow you'll have lights on the stairs. (*He exits. Miriam lights the way for him and returns right away.*)

DVOYRE. (*Bringing two glasses to the table.*) He really wanted to come himself. (*Moyshe and Shimen drink tea.*)

LEAH. A charlatan . . . . He knows what he's doing.

MIRIAM. He met me in the courtyard today—he said he thought I was Leah . . . . He asked me where I'm from. He said he's been to loads of little *shtetlekh* . . . . He can tell shtetl girls, he said, by their cheeks . . . . He asked me how I'm doing here. Funny! He said he would come—look how he's kept his word. (*Laughs happily.*)

DVOYRE. He doesn't walk like other people—he leaps.

LEAH. It's because of you, Miriam, that we had such a distinguished guest today. Don't get too close to him. I know very well what kind of guy he is.

MIRIAM. (*Insulted.*) He came on my account, did he? . . . Did I invite him, then? Why should I be afraid of him? Can he do something to me? What am I, a little child? I don't know what to say; I go out in the courtyard, I hear someone call me . . .

LEAH. I didn't mean anything by it. I'm just saying that you have to watch yourself around people like that. (*Pause.*)

MOYSHE. Nu, I'm done with my glass. Anyone who wants, can drink. Oho, a great legacy awaits him—I've looked out for you. You won't die of hunger.

DVOYRE. (*After a long silence.*) If you've struck someone's fancy, that's fine. Especially if you're poor. But you have to watch out. You can sink so deep that you'll be in over your head. Leah. Miriam's offended. She thinks Mama means her.

MIRIAM. I don't know who you mean. (*A heavy silence. Miriam goes to the window, covers her face.*)

LEAH. (*Goes to Miriam.*) You're such a fool—if that's how it is—no one was talking about you . . . On the contrary . . . I'm an expert in things like this.

DVOYRE. It's not enough that the poor man is at the bottom of the heap; everyone has to trample on him too.

LEAH. (*Suddenly.*) Come here, Miriam, let's learn how to dance . . . You'll dance at my wedding, right? (*Miriam says nothing.*) It's bothering you, what we said.

MIRIAM. Nothing's bothering me.

LEAH. Then what's with you?

DVOYRE. Maybe it's what I said? I swear to God, I meant nothing by it . . . Just talking.

LEAH. Come dance with me!

SHIMEN. You're happy today, my daughter.

LEAH. What do I have to complain about? Had dinner—what else do I need? And now I'll enjoy myself. (*Starts to dance a round dance, dragging Miriam with her. Miriam follows half-heartedly.*)

Curtain.

Act 2

The same room as in Act 1. A warm, beautiful summer's day. The windows are open. Jonah sits at work. Across from him, on a bench, sits Zilberman. Miriam stands at the big table and mends some clothes.

ZILBERMAN. (*Holding an awl.*) If I spent just one hour each day watching you sew, I'd be a full-fledged shoemaker already.

JONAH. As if you really needed to do that—you can just pay for it, and that's that! So you don't need any great skill.

MIRIAM. I think Zilberman doesn't love money as much as you think.

ZILBERMAN. To hell with it! Believe me, Jonah, there's many a time I envy a simple workingman.

JONAH. Talk's cheap. You're all jealous of the workingman—and I've never once seen any of you guys give up his comforts and become a shoemaker. . . . You wouldn't want to get your hands dirty . . . you can manage fine without it.

MIRIAM. You don't know Zilberman.

ZILBERMAN. You're mocking me, and I'm serious.

JONAH. It's easy to watch others sweat. When it's you, though . . . nu, Reb Shoemaker, here's a shoe with a needle—already threaded—let's see what you can do! (*He hands Zilberman a shoe.*)

ZILBERMAN. You'll see . . . you'll see, soon enough . . . . (*Wipes his hands and takes a close look at the shoe.*) My hands were made for this sort of thing. (*He measures the shoe against his left hand.*)

JONAH. Ha ha ha! Give me that shoe. He wants to be a shoemaker— ridiculous. You're afraid of the shoe! Why are you so scared of sticking your hand in there? This is how it's done. (*With particular pleasure, he puts his hand in the shoe.*)

ZILBERMAN. It's just that you grabbed it away from me. (*Miriam laughs.*)

JONAH. And there's another thing you should know: a shoemaker has to live in wet basements, and you won't want to do that.

ZILBERMAN. (*Looking at his hands.*) It's just that my hands are so delicate.

MIRIAM. I'm pretty sure that my hands are just a little more delicate and petite than yours. (*She looks at her hands.*) They're not even half the size of yours.

ZILBERMAN. Let's measure them!

MIRIAM. Nu, let's! (*Zilberman goes over to Miriam to measure their hands.*)

MIRIAM. (*Very happy.*) Look, just look, Jonah! My hand is completely hidden in his. Even the thumb is much smaller. It'll be awhile before any man's hands are as delicate as mine.

JONAH. You're all real princesses; and still you've got ugly guys hanging all over you. All the goons have beautiful wives. (*He smoothes out his mustache.*) Look at what a handsome guy I am—and what a wife I got myself.

MIRIAM. If I were Leah, I wouldn't have even looked at you. I'm going to choose myself a groom you wouldn't be ashamed to see on display at the fair! (*Smiles at Zilberman.*) He'll have dark eyes, dark hair, snow-white cheeks with a tint of red in them . . . and red lips . . . Nu, what do you think?

ZILBERMAN. Very nice!

JONAH. (*Not taking his eyes off his work.*) In the winter she dreams of millions, and in the summer of handsome boys . . . You may be able to get yourself a beautiful boy with delicate hands, but forget about those millions, my dear friend . . . pickpockets have delicate hands, too.

MIRIAM. I *will* find him! And if I don't, what do I need to get married for? What do you say, Zilberman?

ZILBERMAN. Certainly, certainly! (*He approaches her and takes her by the jaw.*) Take a look, Jonah, she's a real . . .

MIRIAM. Don't laugh at me, I beg you.

ZILBERMAN. I'm not laughing. (*He kisses her hand unobtrusively, so that Jonah doesn't notice. Suddenly.*) I have the key to the apartment. I don't want my father to know that I'm here anymore—when he opens his mouth, he sometimes forgets to close it again. I'll come back soon. (*He exits the apartment.*)

(*Pause.*)

JONAH. (*As if to himself.*) So he wants to turn himself into a shoemaker . . . a real gem, that one. You'll be angry if I say anything—better to keep quiet.

MIRIAM. (*A bit confused.*) Say it, say it.

JONAH. It's easier to keep quiet. And besides, it's even worse if you speak up and no one listens.

MIRIAM. I already know what you're going to say . . . Dvoyre's been driving me crazy with her speeches.

JONAH. So why do you have to pay attention to what strangers tell you?

MIRIAM. (*Angrily.*) I can't just kick him out of the apartment when he comes here! He gives you work, too!

JONAH. Work is one thing—and this is something else again.

MIRIAM. Dvoyre's always reading me the riot act, and now you want to browbeat me for my behavior . . . . "You can't go around talking with men"—like you and Leah are saints.

JONAH. But what about what you said in the winter?

MIRIAM. In the winter, I was a fool, and now I've wised up. I thought the happiest thing in life was to knit another dozen stockings . . . but now I don't want anyone to get on my nerves.

JONAH. (*Slowly.*) You're talking like a child. You think you live a year in the big city and now you know everything . . . . Thank God, I've already finished serving the Tsar, and believe me, I've seen everything. I like to keep an eye out . . . . Not that I mean anything by this, God forbid . . . . I do have a wife, you know, and—I love her . . . you understand? A soldier likes to talk to girls. And the girls used to come to the barracks at night . . . . A soldier's a soldier: here today, there tomorrow . . . . What, you think I'm lying? But you need to have a head on your shoulders, to know where you stand . . . . That's what I wanted to tell you.

MIRIAM. (*Embarrassed. Turning red.*) And you were such a saint . . .

JONAH. You don't understand. You and Zilberman—quite a pair!

MIRIAM. Do I ask him to come here?

JONAH. (*Looks her straight in the eyes.*) And you didn't go walking with him outside of town? You see, I know everything . . .

MIRIAM. (*With tears in her eyes.*) He just ran into me there.

JONAH. I'm not going to give you the third degree . . . I don't want to talk any more, anyway.

MIRIAM. That's a good idea. You and Dvoyre always forget that I'm a complete stranger here among you, and I can leave any time.

JONAH. If you're a fool, that's your own fault . . . . (*Zilberman boldly enters.*)

ZILBERMAN. Here I am again. (*He notices Miriam's distressed expression.*) I'm dying for a drink . . . . Jonah, be a good fellow? Go get a couple of beers, and we'll all have a drink. Where are the Mr. and Mrs?

JONAH. Outside.

ZILBERMAN. Nu?

JONAH. Maybe this time you want to stick with water?

ZILBERMAN. What do you have to lose? Three minutes!

JONAH. I have to finish up this work and start on your shoes—after all, you hate to look less than your best.

ZILBERMAN. If it's my shoes you're worried about, they can wait 'til the day after tomorrow—you know what a good fellow Zilberman is, after all . . . . (*He gives him money.*) Here's some change, now get going . . . we'll all have a drink together.

JONAH. (*Reluctantly removing his apron.*) I won't be drinking, anyway . . . . What sort of beer should I get?

ZILBERMAN. There's a good fellow. Zilberman'll take care of you.

JONAH. You'll have to wait awhile, though. While I'm out, I'm going to go see my wife.

ZILBERMAN. Look how stubborn he's being.

JONAH. (*Exiting.*) Maybe you want to finish up my work?

ZILBERMAN. It'll all be fine. (*He sits down in Jonah's place. Miriam goes out to the street and quickly returns.*)

ZILBERMAN. I'm a genius! Look how the guy fell for it . . . . Ha ha ha! Led the fool right by the nose. (*Long pause. Miriam lowers her eyes to her work. Zilberman approaches her.*)

ZILBERMAN. Why so sad, Miriam? You won't even look at me. (*He strokes her hair.*) Maybe you're not feeling well?

MIRIAM. I'm fine.

ZILBERMAN. So what's wrong? Hmm, Miriam?

MIRIAM. I tried to find a time to speak to you on Sunday . . . . I have so much to talk to you about, but . . . (*In tears.*) You're making me miserable!

ZILBERMAN (*Confused.*) Me? What are you talking about? Miriam . . .

MIRIAM. But not any more, not any more . . . (*She tears herself away from him, sits on the stool, and covers her face.*)

ZILBERMAN. I don't understand you. Do you want to tell me something? Or maybe you're just teasing? (*He tries to raise her head.*) Tell me, are you making fun of me, Miriam?

MIRIAM. (*Raising her head.*) I won't any more, enough . . . I was always happy, and you . . .

ZILBERMAN. Miriam . . . What are you talking about? When I saw you for the first time, right after the winter, I liked you right away. . . . You yourself said—

MIRIAM. Nothing, that's what I said. What could I say? I was thinking like a little child . . . . I want to stay an honest woman. I don't want to be like . . .

ZILBERMAN. (*Sitting down close to her.*) You said it yourself: we're both young; we're both—Look, I'm not ignoring anything. I come here, to Shimen the shoemaker's, down in the basement . . . all for you, Miriam, all for you!

MIRIAM. (*Wiping away tears.*) I always think: I shouldn't let myself get so close to you. Here in the basement they're always giving me a hard time—and they're right . . . I'm a poor girl, a small-town girl, and you—you couldn't possibly love me. I'm—I'm an orphan . . .

ZILBERMAN. Nonsense, nonsense! And if I'm rich, so what? What difference does that make to us? Look; I wanted to get to know you, and I didn't pay attention to anything; just the way you are, that's how I like you. (*Kisses her.*) To hell with wealth! I understand: here in the basement they're telling you what to do. Are they your parents? Hm? Are you a small child? Hm? Look, we're both so young . . . so young; who can give us advice? Nobody! You were happy; you won't be alone any more; you won't be alone any more. I love you! (*Kisses her.*) I love you—

(*Pause.*)

MIRIAM. (*Childlike.*) And a year from now will you still love me?

ZILBERMAN. Why wouldn't I?

MIRIAM. And three years from now?

ZILBERMAN. I have no idea why you're asking me these things.

MIRIAM. And will you marry me?

ZILBERMAN. Of course! I love you so much . . . If my father won't give me any money—then it'll be just fine without it! You don't care if I'm rich anyway. (*He clasps her to him.*) So you see, my little fool. (*Miriam begins to cry.*) Nu, what is it now?

MIRIAM. I'm afraid of my mother . . .

ZILBERMAN. But you said your mother's been dead for ten years.

MIRIAM. But I'm still afraid of her; she comes to me every night in my dreams. I never wanted to tell anyone about it . . . . Yes, it's been ten years since she died. I loved her so much! I cried so much when she died! I didn't have any more strength . . . maybe for two years straight I didn't stop crying at night, lying in bed, constantly thinking: maybe God will make a miracle, and she'll come back to life . . . . I always wanted to see her in my dreams and she never came. But now, since we met, she doesn't give me any peace.

ZILBERMAN. Dreams—nonsense!

MIRIAM. Believe me, Boris—I'm going to call you "Boris"—believe me, there's something to this . . . (*She pulls away from him.*) I want to wash my face, so no one can tell I was crying. (*She washes her face.*) I get a chill in my bones when I remember my last dream. Just listen to this.

ZILBERMAN. Don't tell me, you don't have to!

MIRIAM. You have to hear it. . . . In our shtetl, there was a little river flowing right by the town; and near the river there was a path where everyone from the shtetl used to go walking. . . . I always used to go walking there with my girlfriends. (*She shudders.*)

ZILBERMAN. Better not to tell this.

MIRIAM. Who should I tell it to, if not to you? I can't tell Dvoyre or Leah . . . . After the two of us had gone walking in the woods . . . that night I couldn't get to sleep. I didn't even shut my eyes . . . Suddenly, it seemed to me, I was walking all alone near the river of our shtetl. At first, there were lots of people walking around; but as soon as I got near them, they disappeared one by one . . . . I look at the river and something looks different than usual: the water is black as pitch . . . . I want to run away, but I can't. I can't budge. I can't move my feet an inch . . . . I want to scream—but it sticks in my throat and I can't. And suddenly I see: the trees and the reeds that grow on the riverbank, they're getting larger, growing, growing . . . and I stand and I look, the trees are already so tall, that I can't see their tops . . . and the water flowers peeked out of the water, also began to grow; now they're already the height of a small child; now they're like a large man . . . . I want to run away . . . to scream—but I can't. And suddenly—my mother! She's peeking through the water flowers . . . . I shut my eyes tight so I can't see her—no use! I see her through my eyelids . . . . I recognized her: she had a round birth-mark on her face. And she looks at me and says nothing. Her glances were so sharp . . . they looked right into my heart. I felt like she knew everything that was going on in my heart. . . . She didn't say any-thing, she didn't even move a muscle . . . and she looks at me sharply. Judging me for my behavior . . . . I wanted to cry, beg her to forgive me, I'd behave better . . . . Suddenly, I hear Shimen's voice, waking me: "Miriam! Miriam!"

ZILBERMAN. (*Applauds.*) Ha ha ha, I could die laughing! Have you ever heard such a dream? The trees growing; the water flowers grow-ing . . . I bet you were growing too . . . you must have been as big as Goliath.[13] It's a pity I didn't get to see you . . . Little fool, when you're

---

13. The simile he uses in the Yiddish is "as big as Og, king of Bashan," known in the Bible and later Jewish legend for his enormous size; see Numbers 21:33 and Deut. 3:11, where his large bed is described.

lying in bed in the middle of the night, you imagine things: thieves, robbers lurking . . . so add your mother to the mix!

MIRIAM. So then why didn't I imagine any robbers lurking? . . . Only my mother came.

ZILBERMAN. Nonsense! Just ask me what I saw in my dreams . . . Once I wake up—pfft! That's it for the dreams.

MIRIAM. (*Kissing him on the forehead.*) You mean I shouldn't be scared?

ZILBERMAN. Haven't I already told you that?

MIRIAM. (*Quietly.*) Do you love me?

ZILBERMAN. Again with this?

MIRIAM. And you'll never abandon me?

ZILBERMAN. Am I a child or something? (*Pause. He takes her hand.*)

MIRIAM. Ah, she looked so scary!

ZILBERMAN. Enough . . . enough.

MIRIAM. But I'm still frightened . . . some sort of terrible thought gnawing at my heart, gnawing . . . (*She remains silent a moment.*) Do you remember, Boris, that first evening? . . . You were so good . . . I was so ashamed, when I went into the woods . . . you weren't there yet . . . I did all of it unconsciously: why was I going into the woods? I didn't know myself. Unconsciously I put down my work, gathered together the stockings, and unconsciously went out of the basement. I went, I went . . . all the while unconsciously . . . (*Pause.*) Can you hear how my heart is pounding? Ba-boom, ba-boom, ba-boom! . . . You won't be angry?

ZILBERMAN. Why would I be?

MIRIAM. I want to ask you something.

ZILBERMAN. So ask.

MIRIAM. But you won't be angry?

ZILBERMAN. You already know how nice a guy Boris is.

MIRIAM. (*Childlike.*) Can you hear how my heart is pounding? Ba-boom, ba-boom, ba-boom!

ZILBERMAN. Why don't you just ask?

MIRIAM. And if you find someone else, someone prettier than me, richer than me?

ZILBERMAN. Since I love you, why should I go looking for anyone else?

MIRIAM. Here in the basement they all say—I should keep my distance from you . . . you're only going to make me miserable, they say . . .

ZILBERMAN. (*Angry. He pulls away from her.*) Ha ha! Now I understand everything!

MIRIAM. Yesterday, when you left, Dvoyre talked and talked . . . Jonah makes fun of me, and sometimes I believe them. You sit by yourself at home and I'm here in the basement; I want to see you so much and I can't . . .

ZILBERMAN. Once and for all—you have to get out of here.

MIRIAM. They're always asking, "Where are you always getting money from, Miriam?"

ZILBERMAN. (*Giving her several gold coins.*) Here's some money; now get yourself out of there.

MIRIAM. And if they ask me where I'm going?

ZILBERMAN. Ha ha ha! Are they your parents? I don't pay much attention to what my father says, either.

MIRIAM. Dvoyre I respect. She's like a mother to me. . . . I bet this evening she's going to keep talking again, talking . . .

ZILBERMAN. Well, if this is how it's going to be, then enough already! You won't see me any more. (*He kisses her.*) Take the money, twenty rubles. You'll have enough for now. Throw out those stockings . . .

MIRIAM. (*Taking the money.*) What do I need so much money for?

ZILBERMAN. You won't be darning any more stockings, understand?

MIRIAM. (*Kisses him.*) How good you are! . . . Someone's coming! Dvoyre, I think. Go sit in your place and pretend you're working. (*They return to their places.*)

ZILBERMAN. Nobody's coming . . . . Come here, little fool, come—

MIRIAM. Enough, enough . . . they'll be here soon enough. I really am a little fool—what right do they have to give me advice?—but this is just how I am . . . (*Long pause. She sings.*)

> I am lonely as a stone,
> I've been abandoned, all alone . . .

ZILBERMAN. If you don't want to come to me, I won't stand on ceremony; I'll come to you. (*He goes to her and kisses her.*) Where did you hear that song of yours? You're always singing it.

MIRIAM. It's perfect for me . . . I'm also an orphan, a lonely orphan . . .

ZILBERMAN. Somebody's coming! (*He hurries back to his place.*) Mirele, today you're getting out of here—you'll find yourself a nice attic room—I'll pay.

MIRIAM. (*Quickly.*) You should come to the woods today . . . you'll be there? I have something else to tell you . . . (*Knits.*)

ZILBERMAN. I'll be there. (*He starts to leave. Enter Dvoyre and Jonah.*)

JONAH. (*Puts two bottles of beer on the table.*) I'm the man you want to send to get the taxman. My wife held me up.

ZILBERMAN. I learned how to make shoes and Fräulein Miriam has told me her dreams. Jonah, come take your place.

DVOYRE. Get a glass, Mirele.

ZILBERMAN. Bring a couple of glasses. Everybody'll drink.

DVOYRE. Thank you; I don't drink beer.

MIRIAM. I simply can't understand how a person can drink something so bitter. (*She brings the glasses.*)

ZILBERMAN. (*Opens the bottle. Pours two glasses.*) Well, Jonah, drink up; I'm not saying a word to the women. (*He drinks.*) Oh, that's good!

JONAH. (*Drinks.*) It's good to have a beer after a big lunch . . . . In the service I used to drink more often . . . good beer!

ZILBERMAN. Another glass?

JONAH. No more. It'll be hard to work.

ZILBERMAN. If that's the case, then no more for me either. You can drink the other bottle all by yourself. (*A child shouts through the window.*)

CHILDREN. Mommy, give us something to eat!

DVOYRE. Come into the basement.

CHILDREN. We want to play outside. (*Dvoyre hands some bread to the children through the window.*)

ZILBERMAN. Well, Jonah, will I have my new shoes tomorrow?

JONAH. You're not keeping your word. You yourself said the day after tomorrow.

ZILBERMAN. Well, then that's when it'll be. Adieu! (*Exits.*)

JONAH. You see, Miriam, I'm not such a bad guy. (*He gets back to his work.*)

MIRIAM. What do you mean?

JONAH. You saw . . . I got out of here.

MIRIAM. And how was that doing me any favors?

JONAH. (*To Dvoyre.*) A real pity, Mother, that Miriam isn't your daughter.

DVOYRE. (*Smiling.*) And why is that?

MIRIAM. (*Angry.*) And here he is starting in with the preaching already!

JONAH. You would have had yourself a rich society girl!

MIRIAM. Pfui!

DVOYRE. Leave her be, Jonah.

JONAH. What are you so angry about, *ketsele*? Just give me a nice matchmaker's fee, and Zilberman is all yours . . . . Look, mother: she's laughing, she's happy. (*Miriam is quiet.*)

JONAH. (*Looking at her.*) Look, now she's crying!—Because he went away!

DVOYRE. I'm begging you, Jonah, be quiet. (*She picks up the bottle of beer.*) I'll put this under the stairs. It's cooler there. (*Exits.*)

JONAH. (*Joking.*) Don't cry, I promise you I'll get him for you . . .

MIRIAM. (*Tearfully.*) What do you want from me? You're strangers to me, nothing more!

JONAH. Sha sha sha . . .

MIRIAM. I'm not a little child. Make fun of anyone you want—just not me!

DVOYRE. (*Runs in.*) What's going on here? Jonah, I'm asking you nicely, please stop. He's laughing and she's wailing like a child . . . what happened here?

JONAH. I'm not kidding. I want my matchmaker's fee. You told me yourself that you'd marry him with pleasure.

DVOYRE. What business is that of yours? Everybody should do as they please. I've said it once and that's enough.

MIRIAM. You shouldn't even have to say it once.

DVOYRE. You're talking like a child. You would think that you're a complete stranger to me . . . with or without the money you pay me. A person needs a guide every once in a while.

MIRIAM. I don't need any guide.

JONAH. You've made a big mistake, Mother. You think of Miriam as a little child and she's been wanting a husband five years already. But Jonah's not such a bad guy; I'll find you a husband, and he'll be a real . . . (*Kisses the tips of his fingers.*)

DVOYRE. (*Laughs.*) I asked you to be quiet. (*Miriam throws down her work, and quickly puts a scarf on her head.*)

JONAH. Look, she's running away. Come on, I'll boost you through the window, it'll be faster.

DVOYRE. (*Astonished.*) Where are you running off to?

JONAH. Come here, I'll say a prayer for your trip.

DVOYRE. (*Angrily, to Jonah.*) Stop it, I'm asking you! Tell me, Miriam, where are you running off to? Look, you're going to run off with your eyes all red like that? (*She takes her by the hand.*)

JONAH. She's going to go tattle to Zilberman.

MIRIAM. Let me go, let me go. (*She frees herself from Dvoyre.*) I want to escape from this dark basement of yours! . . . I want to live, and you're not letting me . . . you're strangers, and I don't need your permission! (*She exits.*)

JONAH. (*Bitter.*) Ha ha! She wants to live—but how? And with what?

Curtain.

Act 3

The same room as in the previous acts. The night following the Fast of Esther.[14] *Shimen and Jonah sit across the table from Leah, who is holding a small child. They are eating. Dvoyre prepares some herring. On the bench next to the oven, two children are sleeping side by side.*

LEAH. Is there something else to drink? My breast is dry; he's sucking the marrow out of my bones.

---

14. The Fast of Esther is a fast day commemorating Esther's fast (along with that of the Jews of Shushan) before her visit to Ahasuerus asking him to attend the banquets that will be Haman's undoing; see Esther 4:16. The fast is celebrated on the day before the holiday of Purim.

DVOYRE. Ech, that's enough. He's full, bless him. Put him to bed—he should have sweet dreams.

JONAH. Listen, who asked you to fast? If you're nursing, you don't fast.

DVOYRE. We fast enough the rest of the year, praise God.

SHIMEN. No harm can come from fasting on a winter's day.

LEAH. As if Father would know if it's healthy to fast while you're nursing; I'm completely drained.

JONAH. Still talking, O wise one? As if the Creator of the Universe really cares about poor men's fasts.

DVOYRE. (*Brings herring to the table.*) If you don't have luck . . . If you're born under a bad sign, you're better off never being born at all.

SHIMEN. It's Purim and they're sitting around spouting stuff and nonsense.

DVOYRE. So what if it's Purim?

SHIMEN. So buy some flour and bake something.

LEAH. Oy, *mameshi*, give me something to drink already. He's sticking to me like a leech. With his little hands . . . (*To the child.*) My little treasure! Look how he grabs, Mama.

DVOYRE. (*Going to them.*) Bless your little head!

SHIMEN. What a winter! If only this cold snap would break. Last year by Purim there wasn't even a trace of snow. This time last year we already had a few rubles put away for Passover. . . . The rent was paid up.

DVOYRE. And don't forget, we married off these two gems last year.

JONAH. A lot of good that did!

DVOYRE. You yourself were itching to do it. You could barely last 'til Purim.

LEAH. I asked him why he was chomping at the bit. What would I care if I still wasn't married?

JONAH. I was afraid you'd have second thoughts; you'd find some other guy and show me the door.

LEAH. Naturally! I had better prospects throwing themselves at my feet, and I . . .

JONAH. (*Laughs.*) Nu, so why didn't you marry someone else?

LEAH. Because I loved you. If you hadn't chosen me—I might not have been able to bear it.

JONAH. She's teasing, but I'll tell you what she said to me before the wedding. Once, when we were alone . . .

LEAH. (*Cuts him off.*) When, when?

JONAH. Back when Moyshe moved out.

LEAH. No, I don't remember at all, and I've never been anyone's fool.

JONAH. I'll remind you right now.

LEAH. Nu, nu . . . quiet already, quiet. Daddy, will you shut him up?

SHIMEN. (*Lightly.*) I can't listen to your stories now. I've got something else on my mind.

DVOYRE. Neither of you has anything to be ashamed of.

LEAH. He tricked me.

JONAH. Now I have to tell it.

LEAH. You win, you win—just be quiet. (*Everyone laughs.*)

DVOYRE. What more could you want—you have a wonderful baby.

LEAH. Jonah didn't do me any favors. Before I had a stomach ache and now it's just a headache . . .

SHIMEN. The One above will look out for the child.

LEAH. Of course; we can see how well He looked out for your children.

DVOYRE. What do you mean, daughter? Children came along, new mouths to feed, but no one died of hunger, God forbid.

LEAH. Lucky us! We had potatoes to fill our bellies, but the heart wants more.

SHIMEN. What, marzipan? Just pretend—then you can have all you want.

LEAH. (*Carries the baby to the cradle, puts it to bed.*) If he'll only sleep tonight . . . My little treasure! I never believed I would love my own child so much . . . (*Pause.*)

DVOYRE. You'll never guess who I ran into in the street today. I completely forgot to tell you.

LEAH. Who?

DVOYRE. Miriam. May anyone who wishes me ill come to such a pass.

SHIMEN. Ha, how's she doing, that tramp?

LEAH. There you go! Why does she deserve a name like that? (*To Dvoyre.*) What's she up to? . . . How is she? Why doesn't she come over?

JONAH. He dumped her six months ago.

DVOYRE. Apparently she's darning stockings again. If you could only see her. (*Tearfully.*) Her face is so pale and drawn.

LEAH. She was so pretty, so young.

SHIMEN. Whose fault is it? She got what she deserved.

DVOYRE. When she saw me, she started to cry. (*Wipes her eyes.*) She couldn't say a word. Wrapped in a coarse shawl.

LEAH. Why hasn't she shown her face here all this time?

DVOYRE. She threw her arms around my neck. It looks like pretty soon she'll . . . (*Doesn't finish the sentence.*)

SHIMEN. (*Spits angrily.*) Tfu!

LEAH. Seriously? You know that for sure? . . . So unfortunate! So alone! I had this feeling . . . How can she work in that condition? (*Jonah walks around the room, agitated.*)

DVOYRE. (*With a lump in her throat.*) I don't know why I got so attached to that girl. I wanted her to stay here in the house with me. I was afraid something would happen . . . . It was hard for me to see her sitting bent over her machine until late at night.

LEAH. You remember how she looked when she first came to us?

JONAH. I knew this was how it would turn out. Oh, that pretty little face of hers!

LEAH. How did you know that?

JONAH. I've seen and heard plenty of stories like this. You have no idea what big cities are like . . . I know what becomes of girls like Miriam.

DVOYRE. When her mother died, she should have taken a rope and hanged herself.

JONAH. How many times did I have to tell her! (*Seething.*) You know, more than once I was ready to take a stick and show him the door . . . . I never told you that that clown once asked me—even wanted to give me money—to help him get Miriam.

SHIMEN. What's the point of all this talk? I don't want to know her. She paid up, moved out, and went where she wanted. She made her bed, now she can lie in it.

LEAH. I know, you couldn't care less.

SHIMEN. A slut . . . That—thing . . . She didn't have to go crawling to him.

LEAH. Listen, I know she's not completely blameless . . .

DVOYRE. It's better not to talk to him.

JONAH. (*Ironic.*) If Miriam has a boy, father in-law will have the honor of being the godfather.

SHIMEN. Tfu! Go to Hell! (*Goes to the oven.*)

LEAH. Papa called her "that thing" . . . I remember when I was working in a factory. The pillars of society—to hell with them! At any minute, if I had lost my head . . . I'm sure she thought he would marry her . . . (*Pause.*)

DVOYRE. It was no skin off his nose, damn him.

JONAH. I'm sure he's gotten someone else in trouble by now. (*They all sit quietly thinking.*)

DVOYRE. Go to the table, children, there's thick millet sprinkled with ground sugar. (*Brings the food to the table.*)

JONAH. I've had enough already. (*Shimen goes to the table. Eats.*)

LEAH. I can't eat anything else either.

DVOYRE. What's with you?

LEAH. I just don't feel like eating.

DVOYRE. Eat children, eat, you just fasted. Jonah, Leah, what's with you? If we want, we can say what your father says: it was no one else's fault . . . Eat.

SHIMEN. Mm—mm—mm—

JONAH. (*Takes a spoonful of millet.*) I'm a simple guy; not learned, a shoemaker. Served in the army, made friends with peasants—but when I hear stories like this, I'm ready to do I don't know what. (*Throws down the spoon.*) I swear to God, I could stick a knife through his heart . . . An orphan, alone in the world—what a scoundrel! . . .

DVOYRE. And if she delivers in secret . . .

JONAH. And then what—she'll become a virgin again? (*A cry is heard outside.*)

DVOYRE. Quiet—what is that?

LEAH. It's a fight! On the back steps . . .

JONAH. They're fighting . . . A woman's voice—you hear? (*The shouting continues.*)

SHIMEN. On Purim yet . . . (*Leah opens the door slightly. A woman's miserable voice is heard: "No, kill me. Do what you want with me . . . I won't go!"*)

JONAH. Miriam's voice! Let me go. (*Leah closes the door in front of him.*) Let me out!

LEAH. Don't you dare go. (*The shouting gets nearer; the same woman's voice: "Kill me on the spot!" . . . It grows quiet for awhile. Everyone listens . . . someone knocks at the door. We hear a woman crying softly. Leah opens the door.*) Miriam! It's Miriam—

MIRIAM. (*Falls into the doorway. Red from crying. Agitated, wrapped in a shawl. She throws her arms around Deborah's neck. Trembling, pleads.*) Dvoyrele, save me . . . have pity on me.

LEAH. What happened? What was that?

JONAH. Someone hit you—say the word, I'll break their heads. (*Miriam sobs like a baby on Dvoyre's shoulder.*)

DVOYRE. But tell us, what happened? Who did this to you?

MIRIAM. (*Her face hidden.*) Save me . . . I'm out of luck, lost . . . I'm going to die . . .

DVOYRE. For God's sake, what happened here?

JONAH. What were you doing by the door? (*The children by the oven get up and look on with great interest.*)

MIRIAM. Dear people, good people . . . save me . . . they threw me down the stairs . . . right here at Zilberman's . . . I went . . . I felt . . .

DVOYRE. (*Brings her to the table.*) Tell us, tell us what happened . . . Who hurt you?

JONAH. (*Suddenly.*) Tell me who hit you—Zilberman? Huh, Zilberman? I'll break his head open! Where's that iron rod? (*He looks for it.*) I'll take care of him once and for all.

LEAH. (*Grabs him with both hands, kisses him.*) Don't go, Jonah, I'm begging you, don't go, they'll arrest you . . .

JONAH. (*Trying to break away.*) Once and for all—I'm going to settle things with him!

MIRIAM. Don't go, Jonah . . . Don't go, I'm begging you . . . (*Coughs.*)

SHIMEN. Don't go, I'm telling you—you want to get in trouble?

DVOYRE. Tell me, where did they hit you . . . Where, tell me . . . Maybe we should . . .

MIRIAM. (*Trembles.*) Forgive me . . . Dvoyre, I have . . .

SHIMEN. We should call the doctor.

LEAH. (*Leads Jonah to a chair and sits him down.*) Sit right there, take pity on me too . . .

MIRIAM. (*Sinks to the ground at Dvoyre's feet.*) Forgive me, Dvoyre . . . Don't hold it against me . . . Oh, I'm dying . . . It's tearing me apart! . . .

DVOYRE. (*Afraid.*) She's having the baby . . . Miriam . . . What should we do? . . . What should I do? . . . (*Leah props Miriam up.*)

MIRIAM. I'm dying . . . I'm dying . . . Mama, where are you?

DVOYRE. Leah, get your bed ready, quick! (*Leah runs to her room behind the curtain. Dvoyre supports Miriam under her arms.*) Calm yourself, my child . . . I'll take you to Leah's room . . . Straighten up . . . Come, Jonah, let's bring her in.

MIRIAM. Leave me . . . (*Shimen leaves the house.*)

LEAH. (*Emerges quickly.*) It's ready. Come lie down on my bed, Mirele.

MIRIAM. Take me to my grave . . . Bury me alive . . . (*They lead her into the bedroom.*)

DVOYRE. No one wishes you any harm. (*We hear them talking behind the curtain.*) Lie down, just like that . . . Give her another pillow, Leah . . . . Jonah, get another pillow from my bed. (*Jonah hurries and gets a pillow.*) Calm yourself, my daughter, it's a good thing you came to us. We won't let you come to harm . . . calm yourself. . . . Jonah, my child, go call for Dvoshe . . . or just bang on the wall. (*Jonah bangs on the wall, and leaves a moment later.*)

MIRIAM. (*Her voice heard from behind the curtain.*) Have mercy on me, don't call Dvoshe . . . Let me die . . . Bring me poison! Mama, take your child . . . come take your child . . . (*We hear her sobbing.*)

DVOYRE. (*Pours water in a pot and puts it in the oven.*) Calm yourself, I'm coming, my daughter . . . . Who would have known it would come to this? Who would have known? . . . (*Miriam's cries interrupt her.*)

LEAH. Don't cry like that . . . Don't cry . . .

DVOYRE. I should have thrown boiling water on him when he came into the house. How many times did I say . . . beg . . .

LEAH. Mama, cut the sermon . . . (*Dvoshe's voice is heard outside.*)

DVOSHE. (*Enters. A fat woman wrapped in a shawl. We can see her nose poking out even from the doorway. Kisses the mezuzah.*[15]) Her mother must be spinning in her grave!

LEAH. Please, not now . . . (*Miriam coughs.*)

DVOSHE. The devil won't get his due today. Decent women kick the bucket in childbirth . . . But this one—worse than a bitch! . . .

---

15. See note 6 to *The Two Kuni-Lemls.*

LEAH. Dvoshe, I beg you, do me a favor, don't say anything else . . .

DVOSHE. (*Stands in the doorway to Leah's room.*) Nu, Mirele, is it good and painful? And the—

LEAH. (*Interrupts, patting her.*) Maybe you're right, but for now . . .

DVOSHE. (*Angry.*) What now? What about now? They should die—them and their children together! They shouldn't get any mercy . . . I've never heard of such a thing . . . A girl with no parents, a pauper, should get herself into a mess like this! Woe to parents in this world with such children, and a curse on the ones in the world to come . . . What was I dragged here for? . . . It would have gone fine without me too . . . You'd be better off sending someone to the shul to say Psalms and the prayer for a woman in labor.[16]

MIRIAM. (*Wretchedly.*) Dvoyre! Leah . . . Have pity on me—let me die . . . Mama! Take me . . . (*Weaker.*) Let me die . . . My dear Mama! My dear Mama . . . My dear Mama . . .

DVOSHE. (*Calmly shaking her head.*) You won't die, you won't die. Decent women will die in childbirth before their time because of you, but you . . . you won't die. (*Miriam's cries cut her off.*)

Curtain.

Act 4

At Grunye and Natalke's. Evening. An attic room somewhere on the edge of the city. Low ceiling. In the middle of the room stands a round table covered with a thin tablecloth; four chairs around it. A door in the background. At right, two wide windows, curtained. At left, a neatly made bed. Across from it, a second bed, in disarray. On the walls, unframed pictures. A lamp burns on the table, with a pink lampshade. Near the lamp an alarm clock, which ticks unceasingly. Miriam, Grunye, and Natalke sit at the table squeezed onto two chairs and are drinking. Near them, a bottle of liquor on the table, black bread, chocolate, pickles, etc.

NATALKE. (*A healthy country girl with a round face, dressed very neatly, half fills a teacup with liquor and offers it to Miriam.*) Drink, Mirke, drink!

MIRIAM. I don't want any.

NATALKE. (*Grabs Miriam with both hands.*) Grunye! Pour the liquor in her mouth. I'll hold her—you pour, Gruntshe.

GRUNYE. Good! (*She tries to force the liquor into Miriam's mouth.*)

---

16. Traditional Jews would frequently recite psalms in moments of crisis.

MIRIAM. (*Defending herself.*) Let me go, I want to tell you something . . . just one thing.

NATALYE. Pour! Pour!

MIRIAM. I want to—

GRUNYE. No excuses. You drink or I pour.

MIRIAM. I have to go home already. It's late. I'm going to catch it from my "madam." (*A knock at the door.*)

GRUNYE. *Kto tam?*[17]

VOICE. (*Behind the door.*) Open up, open up.

GRUNYE, NATALKE. Not today. We can't.

NATALKE. Can't have guests. (*Long pause.*) Should've let him in.

GRUNYE. He can go to hell!

NATALKE. Might have been a big fish.

GRUNYE. *Vsyo ravno!*[18] Even if it's the top dog himself—he gets a stick across the head; today's a holiday for me. You get it? That's how I want it.

MIRIAM. I need to get home.

GRUNYE. And we won't let you. You're spending the night with us. (*A knock at the door.*)

NATALKE. (*Without turning her head.*) Who's knocking? (*More knocking.*)

GRUNYE. And we're not letting you go home. The winter's plenty long. You'll have more than enough time for that. (*She coquettishly takes a drink of liquor, gets up, and takes Miriam by the arm.*) Come, Mirele, let's dance a polka.

MIRIAM. I have to go home.

GRUNYE. Forget it!

MIRIAM. You don't know my madam.

GRUNYE. I've known 'em five years already. But I never acted like you do. If you let 'em—they'll skin you alive. You'll have a thousand johns a night . . . With me it was different. (*She puts away the glass.*) What's mine—I told her—is mine . . . and what's yours—is yours . . . and if not—bad luck to you—I said—go take a long walk off a short pier! A-a, they trembled at the sight of me . . . Miriam! Stay here tonight— I (*She bangs her chest.*)—I'll teach you how to live.

NATALKE. (*Shaking her fist.*) And I tell her: I smash your teeth to bits— and she clams up—not a word!

GRUNYE. You think I'm her servant—well, up yours! She's the servant! I was always the favorite; all the johns—they were going out of their

---

17. Russian, "Who's there?"

18. Russian, "Just so!"

heads for me . . . They used to ask, "Is Grundele here?" Boy, did I set the world on fire! (*She looks in the little mirror that hangs on the wall.*) I haven't looked like that for four years. Not even for two years. (*She pinches her cheeks, goes over to the table, drinks.*) *L'chayim!* Today I'm gonna drink 'til . . . *L'chayim!* Today you're going to stay with us, ha?

NATALKE. (*Kisses Miriam.*) Stay the night, stay the night . . . You didn't open the door. A john?

GRUNYE. Walk the streets all night if you want, just not here in the room.

NATALKE. I need money.

GRUNYE. Money, money . . . (*She throws her purse at Natalke.*) Take the money, as much as you want . . . money, money—I won't sell my soul! . . . Drink, Miriam!

MIRIAM. (*Drinks a little.*) If I'm not going to my madam, then I'm going to go check on my baby.

GRUNYE. (*Astonished.*) You have a kid?

MIRIAM. Six months old already. With a wet-nurse.

GRUNYE. You have a kid? Ha ha ha!

MIRIAM. Why are you so surprised?

GRUNYE. Ha ha ha! Little fool . . . you should have strangled it.

NATALKE. (*Putting her hands together, as if she were strangling someone.*) Look, this is how you do it . . . just like this . . . and *pfft!*

MIRIAM. (*Covering her face.*) Go away, I can't look . . . my little darling— you have to see him, he's such a doll . . . the way he looks at me, when I come to see him. He looks me right in the eyes.

GRUNYE. Ha ha ha!

MIRIAM. If you had a baby like that, you'd love him too. (*Pause.*)

GRUNYE. Better to give it away to the police.

MIRIAM. And who do I have besides him? No father, no mother, lonely as a stone.

GRUNYE. Parents, hmm . . . they'd just be on my back . . .

MIRIAM. If my mother and father were still alive, I wouldn't be in this situation now.

GRUNYE. Ah, forget it! (*Smokes a cigarette.*)

MIRIAM. Ah, mommy, daddy . . .

GRUNYE. Now my mother and father, ah, them I'll never forget.

MIRIAM. Are they still living?

GRUNYE. Dead.

MIRIAM. (*To Natalke.*) And are yours still living?

NATALKE. I send them money.

MIRIAM. They're not mad at you?

NATALKE. Why you sitting like this, moaning? Grunye! Mirke! Come, dance. (*Dances, pulls Grunye by the sleeve. Sings.*)

GRUNYE. You're a lightweight . . . you can't hold your liquor.

NATALKE. (*Looks at her dully.*) "Not hold liquor," you say. Natasha, show 'em what you can do . . . (*Pours a teacup of liquor and drinks it down in one gulp.*) Atta girl, Natasha! Come, you, Mirke, I kiss you. (*Gets down on her knees and kisses Miriam's hands.*) Hee hee hee, Natasha . . .

MIRIAM. (*To Natalke.*) Have you ever had a baby?

NATALKE. Ah ah!

MIRIAM. Have you?

GRUNYE. She's had ten.

NATALKE. Lies, lies, lies! Two!

MIRIAM. Where are they?

NATALKE. Foy, children! I no need children.

GRUNYE. She's a fine one. She lives only for herself. Mother, father . . . no mercy on them, either. The whole world—can go hang! (*Drinks. Clinks the glass.*) Now this, this is my friend . . . like walking on hot stones . . . Drink, Mirele.

NATALKE. (*Stands up and falls back onto her chair.*) Gimme, I drink . . . (*She barely manages to get to the bed and then falls down.*)

GRUNYE. (*To Miriam.*) What are you crying about, silly? Me? Still crying? *Vsyo ravno!* (*Miriam drinks.*) Drink, there you go . . . Forget everything! Take my advice, forget everything . . . Couldn't you have found someone nice to take your kid?

MIRIAM. The police had him; I took him back myself.

GRUNYE. What do you mean?

MIRIAM. Back there in the basement.

GRUNYE. And you think . . . (*A knock at the door.*) I can't today!

NATALKE. Can . . . can.

GRUNYE. (*Angrily.*) And I can't, I say! I'm sick! (*Points to the door.*) Well, and whose fault is that, tell me that? (*She goes to the door, shaking her fist.*) They stomp all over you . . . they spit and they stomp on you . . . spit and stomp and skin you alive . . . (*A moment later.*) So how did the policeman find him?

MIRIAM. I was living in the shoemaker's basement. I told you once— where it is—and that's where I had the baby . . . There are still good people in this world, Grunye. When I think of Dvoyre, the shoemaker's wife, I want to cry so . . . If it weren't for her . . . even at the last minute, when I was so guilty . . .

GRUNYE. (*Interrupts, banging the table.*) What guilty? Who's guilty? No guilty here! Listen up: I'm twenty-five years old—in the life five years . . . A door everybody gets to walk through . . . I've done it all. On the bottom, on the top . . .[19] No mercy! It's a lie! You hear?

---

19. Literally "under the bench, over the bench."

NATALKE. (*Barely able to drag herself over to Grunye. Hugs her.*) What you shouting for? Poor me, poor me . . . you talk, I no understand . . . two johns came, she sends away . . . more vodka . . . poor me, poor—ah, my heart . . . my heart . . . (*She sings.*) Ekh muzhtshini vy skatini . . . [20] (*She slides down to the ground.*)

GRUNYE. I'm telling you, I've been on top and I've been on the bottom . . . Loved . . . lots of times—tfui! Miriam, listen—no use in crying—lost!

MIRIAM. I'm not a lost cause yet. I can still claw my way out . . . He was a good person in spite of everything . . . you're laughing at me . . . I caused him such shame . . . he got so sick—that's what they said.

GRUNYE. What sort of shame? (*She looks in the mirror.*)

MIRIAM. I lived all by myself in an attic room. He used to visit me all the time, but afterward, he stopped. He still sent me money. I lived alone . . . darned stockings. He came one more time when I was in my fourth month. And then never again . . . Soon I started thinking he was going to throw me over. He used to come, sit a little bit, work the sewing machine . . . As soon as I left the shoemaker's I started to feel miserable . . . As soon as I left. Everyone suddenly became strangers . . . I was still in my fourth month. People still couldn't notice anything, but I was already ashamed . . . I even used to be ashamed in my room, at the machine . . . . It felt to me like—the machine was staring at me . . . scolding me . . . and why? What did I do wrong?

GRUNYE. (*Drinks. It's hard for her to stand up straight. She grabs Miriam by the hand.*) Give me your hand, Miriam . . . I hate talking . . . hate it . . . but now . . . you have a heart, Miriam. (*Kisses her.*) You feel . . . I don't feel, I talk . . . a heart . . . you understand? Up there in high society you don't think the same things happen? Even more so . . . they're allowed! They have bastards . . . they're allowed . . .

NATALKE. In bed . . . (*Miriam and Grunye drag her to the bed and lay her down.*)

MIRIAM. (*Stays sitting near Natalke.*) I don't think I did anything wrong . . . but this idea worked its way into my head . . . that I was the worst . . . I felt like there was this black stain on my face, and everyone was looking at me. I went to the storekeeper to get some thread for darning; and the way the girls looked at me . . . and whispered . . . I was still in my fifth month . . . you couldn't tell anything . . . and they were whispering.

---

20. Russian, "Ach, men, you are swine."

GRUNYE. Whispering . . .

MIRIAM. Afterward I started to hate them as well . . . I didn't go there looking for work any more. I still had money . . . my belly kept getting bigger, bigger . . . but I still didn't believe that I was going to give birth . . . that there was another person inside of me . . . I jumped off the chair, off the table—but it didn't die . . . and my mother— every night—visited me in my dreams . . . every night . . .

GRUNYE. (*Grits her teeth.*) Ah, my mama! She turned me into what I am today. (*She sits on the ground.*) My father died afterward. We lived in the cemetery. My father was a gravedigger.

MIRIAM. You weren't afraid?

GRUNYE. I used to hide among the graves . . . at night . . . boys used to come, waiting among the graves . . . one time we did it in an open grave . . . no one knew . . .

MIRIAM. (*Shocked.*) You weren't scared at all?

GRUNYE. My mother figured it out soon enough . . . she saw it in my face, that I was pregnant . . . she beat me with a stick . . . How did they find it out in the city? . . . I really hurt them . . . The hell with them . . . and then my father—he beat me like a madman. (*A long pause.*)

MIRIAM. No one hit me. I ran off all by myself . . . ran straight to hell . . .

GRUNYE. When I found out I was pregnant, I wanted to run away. They wanted to kick my father out . . . since he wasn't able to bury the dead any more, once his daughter became an unwed mother . . . [21] "Ah, your daughter—your daughter . . . "—it stabbed him right through the heart . . . and he would hit, he would whip . . . So the rabbi passed away . . . It was right before Passover. The whole shtetl came out for the funeral . . . Everybody streamed into our house . . . and I started going into labor. (*Wildly.*) Ha ha ha! My mother started to faint . . . I tried to control myself . . . I controlled myself, but screamed anyway . . . shouted . . . anyway . . . my father died soon after . . . My mother didn't want to feed me . . . she hit me . . . "I'll get some food"—I said—"Shame on you!"—I said—"You're a mother and you don't have any mercy"—I said—"But who needs it! Forget it! (*Stands up.*) I'll have no mercy!" Let 'em come . . . with these feet, I'll stomp all over 'em . . . (*Drinks.*) Drink, Miriam! A year from now, you'll be saying, "Gruntshe was right."

MIRIAM. I'm going to break free again . . . you'll see.

GRUNYE. Drink; there's no way out for us . . . none!

---

21. Despite the seemingly low status of a gravedigger, he was an employee of the traditional Jewish community, which expected those who worked for it, and their families, to hold to certain standards of morality and behavior.

MIRIAM. (*Drinks a little.*) When I felt the baby coming, I thought I would go crazy . . . I picked myself up and ran to him.

GRUNYE. To who?

MIRIAM. To Zilberman . . . they threw me down the steps . . . then I went to the shoemaker's in the basement and gave birth . . . and Jonah went to beat him up with an iron rod.

GRUNYE. And who's this Jonah?

MIRIAM. The shoemaker's son-in-law. They arrested him. I cried so much . . . (*She cries.*)

GRUNYE. Cut it out, silly . . .

MIRIAM. They shouldn't have laughed at me. Once I got out of bed . . . everyone started talking . . . I couldn't stay in the basement. There was this Dvoshe there, and she made my life a living hell. I sold the sewing machine. The money dried up . . . and my hands became useless . . . as if I had lost them . . . by day I was ashamed to go out, but at night I went out and wandered the streets . . . Whatever would happen would happen . . . I wandered . . . starved . . . Some guy comes by . . . says something to me quietly . . . I didn't understand . . . but I followed him anyway . . . I didn't speak . . . In his room, he didn't speak to me either . . . He gave me a ruble and something to eat . . . He gave me a cigarette . . . and my head starts to spin . . . I almost fainted. (*She sits down at the table.*)

GRUNYE. Curse, if you can . . . with fiery curses.

MIRIAM. He told me to come again tomorrow. I went to him again . . . And in the basement they chide me, because I'm not working—but I can't . . . my hands are useless . . . when I went to him a third time, I met a woman there . . . That was my current madam.

GRUNYE. (*Drinks down the last bit of liquor and hurls the glass at the door. The glass shatters. She laughs wildly. Miriam is startled.*) That's it, ha ha ha! Ha ha ha! That's it. (*She gathers together the pieces of glass and then throws them back on the ground.*) That's it! That's it!

MIRIAM. Grunye!

GRUNYE. I'm going to smash the table to smithereens in a minute, too!

MIRIAM. What for?

(*Grunye hugs Miriam firmly and kisses her passionately.*)

MIRIAM. (*Struggling to get free.*) Grunye!

GRUNYE. (*Calms herself.*) I'm furious . . . d'you see? At the whole world . . . I want to get revenge . . . poke out everyone's eyes, murder them . . . everyone . . . mangy dogs! Who can I lash out at? Who? (*Lets Miriam go.*) Who can we lay into? (*She beats her breast.*) Flames are burning there . . . cry for me, Miriam . . . cry, Miriam . . . I want to feel . . . cry, you're a good girl . . .

MIRIAM. (*With a trembling voice.*) You've never cried?

GRUNYE. Never!

MIRIAM. Not even the first time?

GRUNYE. I was drunk! (*Long pause.*) Come here, Mirele, sit right here, sit on the chair. (*She sits next to Miriam.*)

MIRIAM. What's going to happen?

GRUNYE. (*Kisses her. Buries her head in Miriam's breast.*) That's it . . . your breast . . . that's it . . . (*Raises her head.*) Give me the bottle.

MIRIAM. What for?

GRUNYE. Give it to me. (*Sticks out her hand.*)

MIRIAM. What for?

GRUNYE. I want to smash it!

MIRIAM. You don't need to.

GRUNYE. Smash it to pieces!

MIRIAM. You don't have to.

GRUNYE. I have to! I need to! For revenge . . . (*She beats her breast.*) Flames are burning here! Press my head more strongly . . . to your breast . . . cry, Miriam . . . wail . . . I want to feel . . . I can't . . . (*Miriam presses Grunye's head to her breast.*) That's it . . . that's it . . . I feel . . . cry, Mirele . . . I can't . . . Natalke can't either . . . press harder . . . that's it . . . harder . . . harder . . . harder . . . (*Pause.*)

MIRIAM. (*Sings with a trembling voice.*)

> I am lonely as a stone,
> I've been abandoned, all alone . . .

Curtain.

The Duke

by Alter Kacyzne

Cast of Characters[1]

OLD DUKE

YOUNG DUKE, *his son*

MOYSHE, *a Jewish tavernkeeper*

PESSIE, *Moyshe's wife*

NEKHAMELE, *their daughter*

ZADOK, *Moyshe's father*

DVOYRE

YOSHKE, *a tailor*

CLOWN, *servant to the Old Duke*

BISHOP

RABBI

HUNCHBACK, *a pious Jew*

CRIPPLE, *a pious Jew*

HERALD

Noblemen, merchants, yeshiva students, Christian hermits, other Jewish and Christian townspeople

---

1. The published version of Kacyzne's play lacks a cast of characters.

About *The Duke*

I have used the legend of the *Ger Zedek*, the Righteous Convert of Vilna,[2] not as a theme for a drama, but rather as a tapestry on which I have embroidered my own flower. And in the process I have undoubtedly transgressed against the reverence for a folk tale about whose every detail the Vilna Jew, among others, is passionate.

From the tale itself, as it has been told and retold, it would actually be impossible to make more than a heart-rending melodrama—one in which we Jews should be portrayed as the bearers of the Holy Torah and of all good attributes. And how? The prince himself converted, and they, the non-Jews, showed themselves for who they were, when they had the newly converted prince burned at the stake.

Of course, this interpretation, which is closest to the spirit of the legend, is the furthest possible from my own spirit.

The tale of the Righteous Convert inspired me not as a legend born of the Jewish imagination but rather as a plausible event that is psychologically extraordinary.

Extraordinary because of the social abyss that divided two such separate worlds—those of the Jews and of the aristocracy. With such a perspective on the matter, the dramatic emphasis naturally also changed. The Righteous Convert with his aristocratic fantasy of becoming a Jew interested me only to the degree that it allowed me to illuminate the background of the Jewish community. And, once illuminated, that background would cease to remain in the background. It approaches the footlights and becomes a dramatic hero in its own right.

I have here, for the most part, aimed at a social Jewish drama, rather than the personal drama of the convert. To what degree I have succeeded I cannot judge.

But in freely reworking the legend and even avoiding the given names of the duke and of his friend (see "Kraszewski," by I. M. Dik),[3] I have taken care to maintain the name of Yoshke the Tailor, because this

---

2. Valentine Potocki (d. 1749), a Polish count who, according to legend, became interested in Judaism while studying in Paris and eventually converted. He was reported by a Jew to the Christian authorities and burned at the stake at the foot of the fortress of Vilna. On his grave, which became known as the grave of the Righteous Convert, a large tree grew that served as a pilgrimage site for many Jews on the Ninth of Av and various holy days. The grave was later destroyed by Polish vandals.

3. The noted and popular Yiddish writer Isaac Mayer Dik (1814–1893) published an account in Hebrew and Yiddish of the Ger Zedek, based on its first literary treatment in 1841 by the Polish writer J. Kraszewski, who in turn claimed to find the account in a Hebrew manuscript.

name has become a synonym for an informer (just as the name Moshek has become a synonym for a servile Jew). In the legend a woman is also mentioned who laughed when the prince was taken to the bonfire. As a result, says the legend, she has remained rooted to the spot. I have developed the figure of Nekhamele from this woman. I have also omitted the convert's blessing before his death.

This is everything that connects me to the legend.

And now a few words about the theatrical piece itself.

The dramatic form is not new to me. I wrote *The Spirit-King* and *Prometheus* in that form, and also published several fragments of *The Tower of Babel*.[4] This, however, was theatre of the writing table, theatre for the reader. I have had an antipathy for the stage. I have been unable to conform to theatrical conventions, because the theatre has for a long time been tedious to me. And not to me alone. All of the upheavals that have taken place in the theatre over the last several years, all of the searching and the directorial accomplishments, bear witness to the fact that the theatre has fundamentally needed refreshing. With my current work, *The Duke*, I have aimed above all to solve a purely theatrical problem: to truly advance, or even to shatter, age-old theatrical forms with the help of the text itself and through that to create something fresh, because I have no faith in the ingenious autocracy of the director, who thinks he can turn water into wine. Any means were justifiable: suspense, unexpectedness, a constant influx of fresh figures, a change of tone in the text itself, and, above all, well-written roles for the actors. However, these means lie in the author's hand, not the director's. The good director must make connections and distinctions; he must be a man of character—character he will stamp on his work. My dilemma is this: either the author needs theatre blood, or the director must become a writer. Otherwise, this is not reinvigorated theatre, but simply a new misunderstanding—one which leads to the loss of the axis around which the theatre revolves, to the loss of the actor and of the spectator.

Therein lies the whole outward confusion of *The Duke*. The fact that the characters play out their own dramas as if they were actual independent people, the fact that each succeeding act doesn't proceed easily and logically from the preceding one, and in tone even stands in contradiction to it—all this, for good or for ill, I tried to write from the perspective of my theoretical approach to the matter. I have struggled with the form and call on you for judgment.

---

4. See *Der gayst der meylekh* (Warsaw: self-published, 1919); *Prometeus* (Warsaw: Hendler, 1920); and *Der turem fun bovl* (published under the title *Meysim-tants*), fragments published in *Vayter-bukh* (Vilna, 1920).

I need to make one more point, concerning the transcription of the word *Dukus*—Dux. Among ourselves, we write *dukhs*. This is what the Hebrew form demands. The word, however, is a decrepit one, little in use. As a result, I have heard the word pronounced in many different ways: *dukus, duks, dukes, doykhes,* and even *dikhes.* An end needed to be put to such anarchy.

I write *dukus* with a *u,* which sounds the most correct to my ear. I do not see any violent sin against the tradition of Hebraicizing a Latin word in doing so.

In closing, I would like to express my heartfelt thanks to my friend Avrom Morevski[5] (who directed and acted in the play) for his pointed suggestions, which have in various places liberated the text from being overly weighty. With a few exceptions, I have taken his suggestions into account in the process of preparing the manuscript for print.

A. K.

Act I

A porch stage left, a little window. A tree at right. Under the tree a table on a wooden beam. Two solid old benches. In the background, a fence with an entrance in the middle. Behind the fence, an uphill slope.

Scene 1

(Moyshe the Innkeeper sits at the table, partially dressed in his Sabbath clothes. He is reading a holy book. Pessie sits nearer to the porch, hands on her hips. She looks right.)

PESSIE. (*Yells offstage.*) Kazik! Hey, Kazik! Get that saloonkeeper's horse out of those oats! What a pain! Every Friday I have her as my guest!

MOYSHE. She's just passing through . . . Don't make a scene, woman . . .

PESSIE. Sure, husband—as if people like that embarrass easily. Drive them out of the door, they'll come in through the window . . . what was I going to say, Moyshele? Maybe a little glass of milk, hm? Since Friday is a short day and you don't get to really eat.

---

5. Noted Yiddish actor and director (1886–1964); a member of the esteemed theatre company the Vilna Troupe, one of the organizers of the Yiddish State Theater of Belarus, and author of the book of essays *Shylock and Shakespeare* (originally published in Vilna in 1937), befitting his particular interest in Shakespearean characters.

MOYSHE. And have you already sent some milk to the old man in the woods? He sits there from morning prayers on, fainting away.

PESSIE. As if I could possibly forget! Once that man picks up his fiddle and heads off to the woods to welcome the holy Sabbath, it's like the world doesn't exist! No eating, no drinking—ridiculous!

MOYSHE. Aha! That's grandpa for you! We'll have to send Nekhamele to him . . .

PESSIE. Speaking of Nekhamele, Moyshele, we really need to talk about her . . . But near the bar, with the drunken peasants, is that the place to talk about this, Moyshe?

MOYSHE. (*Impatiently.*) What's been eating you this past week, woman? Coming, going . . . Nekhamele, Nekhamele . . . our child isn't tainted goods, God forbid. And her hair hasn't gone gray yet, either.

PESSIE. (*Noticing Dvoyre approaching from the porch.*) Shh . . . here she is, our uninvited guest. Don't say a word . . . God damn it! My daughter's beautiful work in those grubby hands of hers!

MOYSHE. Hush, woman!

Scene 2

(*Dvoyre the saloon keeper descends from the porch. A young widow with pretensions to coquettishness.*)

DVOYRE. Pessele, my little jewel, you are the most blessed of mothers! Golden hands that Nekhamele of yours has, no evil eye! I'll tell you the truth: you go into the finest houses these days, you see all the beautiful things they've got there—of course, they should all rot in hell for what they do to the Jews—you go to embroider all sorts of curtains, tapestries, all sorts of embroidered crinolines . . . you know, Pessele, everyone's wearing crinoline these days—it's a pleasure to see, I'm telling you . . . the flowers start here, in the front, and fall in row after row. Like real flower beds! Don't take it the wrong way, Reb Moyshe, all this silly women's talk . . . (*Moyshe waves his hand dismissively, picks up his book, and goes inside.*)

DVOYRE. Look here, Pessele, it's a whole world of its own. Just look at the peacocks, the little beads, the golden flower! (*She is delighted with the embroidery that she's holding. Pessie takes it out of her hands.*)

PESSIE. My daughter showed this to you herself?

DVOYRE. Who? Like she'd show it! I stumbled across it by chance. I was looking around for my cap—oh, it's so late! I'll never get home by the Sabbath! . . . So I'm looking around, and I see in the corner, on the table, a pretty little something. Really pretty! "Nekhamele, is this your work?" "Mine," she says. I liked it right off, and now I can't let it out of my hands . . .

PESSIE. She said that? I'm going to . . .

DVOYRE. You've got yourself a business, Pessele! A golden goose! But tell me, Pessele, my little jewel, I'm just a sinful woman, and, you know what they say: the truth will out. Are congratulations in order? Hm? Do I hear wedding bells?

PESSIE. Dvoyrele! If there's any news, God willing, you'll be the first to know.

DVOYRE. But I thought . . . well. May God send joyful tidings in good time, Pessele! I'll have my horses harnessed . . . may we all have a good Sabbath.

PESSIE. And a good Sabbath to all the Jewish people.

DVOYRE. And don't take my dropping in like this the wrong way. "Friday guest, host's oven don't rest." But what can you do, Pessele, when my livelihood demands it? I need to run to settle up accounts with the bishop . . . since my scholar has begun to get so ill, poor man . . .

PESSIE. Ay, Dvoyrele, don't mention it . . . we're thankful that you don't forget us. Go in good health. (*Dvoyre exits right.*) Go . . . to that bishop of yours. What are you doing bringing that brazen face of yours into a Jewish house? Have you ever heard such a thing? "Her scholar" . . . don't make me laugh! . . . Arele the drunk . . .

Scene 3

(*Nekhamele descends from the porch, holding a small pitcher of milk.*)

PESSIE. You're going to the woods to see Grandpa? Good girl.

NEKHAMELE. Daddy told me to.

PESSIE. And you didn't have the sense to do it yourself, child?

NEKHAMELE. When you don't see him around, you forget about him, like a shadow.

PESSIE. What sort of talk is that, child? And that Dvoyrele, may she never darken our door again—ripping that beautiful work right out of your hands!

NEKHAMELE. No, mama, it really wasn't work.

PESSIE. Why not, my child? Mind your mother. Take a needle and silk thread, and go to your grandfather in the woods. He'll be giving a concert there for the birds, and you'll sew them into the velvet with golden thread. It's holy work, child. You need to finish by the High Holidays.

NEKHAMELE. God knows if I'll be able to. . . .

PESSIE. *Oy, vey iz mir*! Tfu, tfu! Daughter! I don't want to hear that kind of talk from you! Drive that nonsense right out of your head!

NEKHAMELE. Mama, take the ark covering into the house. Maybe I'll get to it after the Sabbath.

PESSIE. Well, go, child. I'm not going to press you. But have mercy on your poor mother! (*Goes to the porch.*) *Oy, vey iz mir!*

NEKHAMELE. Nonsense . . . how do you know I'm talking nonsense, Mama? Have you been seeing my dreams?

Scene 4

(*Dvoyre, with a cap in her hand, enters from right.*)

DVOYRE. I looked for this all over the house—it was lying in the wagon . . .

NEKHAMELE. What?

DVOYRE. This cap. Nu, Nekhamele, my dear! The coach is ready. I have to go into the city before candle lighting. Everyone's going to be pointing at me: "Look at the sinner!" May they see as much bread in their houses as actual sins of mine. But Nekhamele, my dear, I can't move an inch from here. I have to know the whole story, from beginning to end, with all the details. Because if I don't, you're going to find me passed out in a ditch somewhere. (*She guides Nekhamele to a bench and sits her down, almost against her will.*) Nu, quickly, the Sabbath waits for no one and someone might still come by.

NEKHAMELE. Just look, your eyes have perked up like two squirrels: what are you making such a secret about all of this for? So he was here, the young duke, so what?

DVOYRE. Oy vey, I can't stand it. So what?!—The young duke? Do you have any idea who the young duke is?

NEKHAMELE. He's a goy, like all the other goyim.

DVOYRE. Oy, they're going to find me dead in a ditch! It's the duke, the greatest of the princes, a monarch!

NEKHAMELE. Good for him. What are you so excited about?

DVOYRE. My God, girl! Do you have any idea what you're saying? They have all the luck, those nobles! He must have come into the inn when your parents were away at the fair.

NEKHAMELE. Even Zlate the maid ran off somewhere in the heat of the moment. I thought I was going to die of shame. I even ran outside in my shift.

DVOYRE. Oh, wonderful, what a stroke of luck for the nobleman!

NEKHAMELE. And what was so lucky about it?

DVOYRE. Sometimes I'm not sure if you're a child or a mooncalf! If your parents had been here—you would have been locked up behind seven doors, hidden under seven curtains . . . in your shift!

NEKHAMELE. It was so embarrassing![6] It was so flimsy. I was even barefoot!

---

6. Literally "a kharpe un a shand," or "A shame and a disgrace."

Dvoyre. Tell me, Nekhamele, my dear, how did he look at you, the duke?

Nekhamele. Stared at me, like this. He smiled and twirled his mustache.

Dvoyre. Twirled his mustache?! And what does he look like? Is he handsome?

Nekhamele. Yes, very handsome.

Dvoyre. Really, truly?

Nekhamele. How should I know? You'd know better.

Dvoyre. Ay, I would know better, but who's ever gotten a look at him? He's just arrived from abroad, traveling through all the foreign lands. They say he knows every language under the sun. They even say that he learned Hebrew from the rabbis.

Nekhamele. Hebrew? A goy—Hebrew?

Dvoyre. And that's not all! They tell all sorts of incredible stories about him. Some people even think he converted.

Nekhamele. (*Still thinking.*) Yes, he's handsome. He's very handsome.

Dvoyre. Did you like him?

Nekhamele. Yes.

Dvoyre. Just take a look at the poor little thing! . . . And what sort of eyes did he have for you?

Nekhamele. (*Remembering.*) Naked.

Dvoyre. What sort?

Nekhamele. Naked.

Dvoyre. Shame on you! Where did you pick up that kind of talk? Naked eyes!

Nekhamele. What? It can't be? Look—a naked hand, a naked foot. Why can't you have naked eyes too?

Dvoyre. (*Shrugging.*) And how did the two of you meet?

Nekhamele. I was sitting by the trough, washing my feet. I heard some sort of commotion from the highway, horses riding, someone pulling up at the inn. Happens all the time, right? But then there was a shout: "Moshek!" And so scornful. I ran out.

Dvoyre. Did you see him?

Nekhamele. I saw a coach. Three horses in tandem. In the coach were two young nobles. And Stach the huntsman, with his red sideburns and his clean-shaven chin, was holding the reins himself. Oy. My blood froze! Listen to this, Dvoyrele! There was a monkey in a long red jacket standing on the back of the coach, rolling his eyes and grinding his white teeth!

Dvoyre. Lord preserve us!

Nekhamele. It looked like a real person. It made some strange sounds. It looked like the nobles understood monkey talk.

Dvoyre. Unbelievable! What happened next?

NEKHAMELE. Nothing happened! One of the nobles got angry that Moshek wasn't coming out with the bread and salt.[7]

DVOYRE. Well, naturally! He *was* a guest, after all.

NEKHAMELE. And I didn't understand that at all. I told him that if he needed bread and salt, then I could bring it out to him.

DVOYRE. You're killing me. Did he get even angrier?

NEKHAMELE. He burst out laughing. They all burst out laughing. Even the black monkey laughed so hard, his teeth almost fell out. I wanted to cry. And then it hit me: I was in my shift. How embarrassing! I wanted to run away. The young duke jumped down off the coach, tripped, and almost fell on his face. *I* burst out laughing.

DVOYRE. You're killing me!

NEKHAMELE. He grabbed me by the hand and asked my name. I told him. "Nekhamele"—he said—"you're a beautiful girl." He took a good look at me—such bright, naked eyes . . . like he had spread a blanket over me . . . what are you trembling for?

DVOYRE. A breeze must have blown through me. Nu, nu, nu?

NEKHAMELE. They went into the inn . . . ordered ale.

DVOYRE. Tell me, sweetheart, tell me all your secrets . . .

NEKHAMELE. What secrets? So he said, "I drink to your health."

DVOYRE. Really? And what did you answer?

NEKHAMELE. What do you think? That I don't know how to talk to people? I thanked him nicely and drank to his health. It was such strong ale. The old stuff, Castilian. Buried somewhere in the cellar. It went straight to my head . . .

DVOYRE. Why have you gotten so quiet?

NEKHAMELE. Ay, Dvoyre, this is just a joke to you. But something about it bothers me. The young duke grabbed me and gave me a kiss. Oy, I wanted . . . I don't know what I wanted: to cry or to laugh. God would have spat on me. I wanted to get out of there, to escape, but the black monkey appeared in the doorway. I got scared and clung to the duke.

DVOYRE. Nu, nu?

NEKHAMELE. He kissed my eyes, my lips, my cheeks. Maybe five, ten times. They left such fiery traces. Maybe more than ten times.

DVOYRE. So who's counting?

NEKHAMELE. And he went away. (*Dvoyre disappointed, Nekhamele—thoughtful.*)

DVOYRE. Now I understand why the ark covering isn't the first thing on your mind.

---

7. In Eastern Europe, traditional items of hospitality.

NEKHAMELE. Dvoyre? You must have some idea of what sort of people these are, these nobles? What sort of a world it is, of huntsmen and monkeys and pointed mustaches? What sort of a world it is, where people stare at you while getting drunk on old Castilian ale? Where you sit on a duke's lap?

DVOYRE. Oy, vey, it's late! I have to run already!

NEKHAMELE. (*Starts.*) Sit! I almost forgot the pitcher of milk for my grandfather!

DVOYRE. So come, Nekhamele, I'll take you in my coach, it's right on the way. What sort of people, you ask? What sort of world? A different world. Nekhamele, different people, a whole different way of life. Sometimes it seems strange. But once you get used to it, you can't live without it. By the way—about luck. My child, noblemen need luck too. Ay, luck, luck! A good thing, luck! (*Both exit right.*)

Scene 5

(*Yoshke the village tailor enters from the gate opposite. Dusty. Sweaty. A bundle on his shoulders, attached to a stick.*)

YOSHKE. Ay, luck, luck! It's good to be a prince, a real pleasure, a taste of paradise! The Sabbath smells are spreading through my bones . . . Fish, with pepper and onions . . . ah! A real prince of a Jew, Reb Moyshe! A bream's head with horseradish! Oy, oy, oy! (*Tightens his belt.*) Sabbath pleasures really are a little bit of heaven, there's no denying that.

PESSIE. (*On the porch.*) Who are you talking to, my good man?

YOSHKE. And a good Friday to you, Pessele! As I live and breathe, as I stand here and preach: lucky are the weary who arrive at your tents. They will not leave you empty-handed. I stand here before you a poor working man, a poor tailor, a poor orphan, who could eat Jonah's whale single-handed but hasn't had a morsel touch his lips since morning, except for some liquor and a cold knish.

PESSIE. Don't change the subject. This tailor of yours, why don't you have him sit down and tell him to wait. How's that mother of yours, Yoshke? She's a smart one, that woman!

YOSHKE. (*Sits, puts down his bundle.*) Ay, Pessele! What do brains matter if you don't have your health? When your time's up, there's nothing you can do. You know what they say: when you're old and sick, not even a magician can help you. (*Opening the bundle.*) Pessele, God save you! Have you heard the news?

PESSIE. What news?

YOSHKE. The news that's worth a bottle of whiskey.

PESSIE. (*Still from the porch.*) Get out of here.

YOSHKE. In the village they're saying the young duke has arrived from abroad. I wanted to ask Reb Moyshe about it. They say he studied in a yeshiva over there. Is that true?

PESSIE. Tfu! Tfu! You and your tailor thoughts! The man's already been back for a few weeks. He's been here for over a week already.

YOSHKE. You're kidding! So much for my bottle of whiskey! (*Exit Pessie.*) Ay, Yoshke, Yoshke, don't take chances, Yoshke! Don't risk something so precious! Your bottle of whiskey is lost! (*Heartbroken, he scrounges some pieces of bread from the bundle and stuffs them in his mouth.*) Oy, vey, you pauper! Unwashed? That is—a hick! You've become common. You don't wash. You're not so particular about what you scrounge, where you scrounge . . . oy, vey iz mir! (*He goes off right, apparently to the well. We hear his voice and Kazik's coarse laughter.*)

YOSHKE. (*Voice.*) Ah, Kazik! What's going on, Kazik? Ah, you're sewing? Shrouds, *mirtseshem bimheyre beyomeynu u'vizman korev.*[8] What? You don't understand? Well, no harm done. (*Pessie appears on the porch with food for the tailor. A distant shot is heard and Yoshke jumps back out on stage with his shirttails in his hand, half dead from fear, accompanied by Kazik's laughter.*)

PESSIE. Tfu, tfu, tfu! Who took a shot at you, Yoshke?

KAZIK. (*Voice.*) The young duke, ha ha ha, was hunting, ha ha ha! Yoshke ran away!

PESSIE. Come eat, my hero, and you'll soon recover.

YOSHKE. (*To Kazik's side of the stage.*) What are you braying about, you donkey? Pessele, you actually think I was scared? It was just a surprise, that shot! Nothing more than that—just so unexpected!

PESSIE. Well, have something to eat and hurry into town. Don't waste time.

YOSHKE. So who's wasting time?

PESSIE. So, are you bringing home some nice earnings for the Sabbath?

YOSHKE. (*Eating; takes his purse out of his belt.*) Hm . . . Pessele, may you live and prosper, seven gulden and fourteen groshen!

PESSIE. My dear boy! Well done! Your mother will be overjoyed. A smart woman, your mother.

YOSHKE. (*Chewing.*) Listen! That's just what I'm talking about. Why should I spend all my time on the Devil knows what, if with God's help I can do a little business on my own.

---

8. Hebrew, "With God's will, it should quickly come in our days and soon."

PESSIE. You're talking like a real man! I've always thought so highly of your mother . . .

YOSHKE. You're probably wondering why I'm not married—how long can you stand being a young widower? Here's what I'd answer— L'chaim! I've got my eye on someone. What next? May God only help me.

PESSIE. Tell me, who are you going to talk to?

YOSHKE. Better I should tell you who's going to talk to me. (*Pauses.*) If I were to tell you: Dvoyretshke the saloon keeper, would you believe me? Quite a lot to swallow, eh? May we all live so long! Heh, heh, not so crazy about it? That's what I thought.

PESSIE. I'll tell you the truth, Yoshke. If that's the choice you're making, you don't deserve any better. Such a strapping young man, no evil eye, a real breadwinner.

YOSHKE. That's just what I'm talking about. I'm an honest Jew, aren't I? And if I stop into a tavern every once in a while to wet my whistle— well, I'm a working man, too . . . Nu, she's already sending me match-makers.

PESSIE. And what have you told them, these matchmakers?

YOSHKE. I told them: they can wait awhile. I want to get the bishop's permission.

PESSIE. (*Bursts out laughing.*) Oy oy oy! Go on, then! That's what you told them? Eat, little brother, eat! Eat bread, eat challah . . .

YOSHKE. (*Chewing.*) Challah's better . . . Have you ever seen someone get drunk on challah and fish, Pesenyu? And at your place I get drunk, that's for sure, Yoshke isn't just anybody . . . Yoshke's managed to put aside a gulden or two . . . and luck, as they say, is in God's hands. Take your old man—Reb Zadok, I mean, may he live long—he used to be one of the greatest idlers. Nevertheless, when God willed it, the noblemen took a liking to him . . .

PESSIE. Quit while you're ahead, Yoshke . . .

YOSHKE. What, now? Why should I? I'm just getting started. You think it's so easy for me to open my trap? I've wanted to talk to you for such a long time . . . and now that I've found the words, you won't hear me out, Pesenyu!

PESSIE. So what are you holding it in for? Let's hear it!

YOSHKE. And hear it you will! Yoshke's eager to tell it! So listen up! Well, as sure as you're looking at him, Yoshke's ready to send a match-maker himself . . . can you guess to who, Pesenyu? To you! To you and Reb Moyshe. About Nekhamele, you understand . . . I've grown fond of her . . . What, you're getting angry? I'm a Jew, aren't I? Pessele, God be with you! You're getting upset? Why? What for? Nothing bad has happened . . . Pessie, lighten up . . . .

PESSIE. You! You—tailor! This is how you repay me for everything I've done for you? By courting my daughter? You! With my daughter! Oy, Moyshe, Moyshe? You should live so long! Look somewhere else!

YOSHKE. So what if I am? Aren't I a Jew? A good man? Don't I make good money by the sweat of my brow?

Scene 6

MOYSHE. (*On the porch, already dressed in his Sabbath clothing.*) Again with the shooting? Must be the young duke. What a racket! Sholem aleykhem to you, Yoshke. I was just about to have my holiday cloak mended.

PESSIE. What cloak? What holiday? Just listen to what this apprentice is saying, just listen! He wants to marry your daughter. How would you like being his father in-law? Nu, what have I told you? What have I complained about?

MOYSHE. Don't scream so much, woman! Yoshke, have you lost your mind? Have you ever seen such chutzpah in a tailor's apprentice? What's gotten into you?

YOSHKE. Reb Moyshe, you're a man, with you I can talk. It just came out. I didn't mean anything by it, God forbid.

PESSIE. *Oy, vey iz mir*! A nobody, a tailor's apprentice, who's ever heard of him?

YOSHKE. Who's a nobody? Aren't I just as honest a Jew as Reb Moyshe, even if I'm not a scholar or a prince?

MOYSHE. Don't shout, young man! Nobody's questioning your small-town honesty. But what does it have to do with me? And you, Pessie, what's gotten you so heated up? Nobody's carrying off your daughter by force. And if you're really so smart, Yoshke, then listen to what we're saying: take your pack and take your sack and go straight to hell! Don't show your face around here any more! There's never been anyone in this family who's worked with his hands, and there never will be, God forbid. I'll arrange things with a scholar, not a beggar like you!

YOSHKE. Good! Very nice! So this is how you dump on me! This is how you embarrass me!

MOYSHE. Who's embarrassing you? You're embarrassing us, you upstart!

YOSHKE. I'm going! I'm going! You don't need to kick me out, Reb Moyshe! So how much do I owe you? Here, take it, groschens, gulden, for the challah, for the fish, for the liquor . . .

PESSIE. Oy, Moyshele! I can't stand it! He's going to try to pay us! Gevald, it's like a knife through the heart!

MOYSHE. You lunatic, are you going to try to pay Moyshe the tavernkeeper, Moyshe the hospitable, Moyshe the scholar? (*Moyshe and Pessie shove Yoshke. He retreats backward and defends himself with his stick.*)

Scene 7

(*The Young Duke enters right with his friend. Both are dressed in hunting clothes, with rifles over their arms. They take in the scene of the departing Yoshke and burst out laughing.*)

YOUNG DUKE. "How goodly are your tents, O Jacob."

FRIEND. "And your dwelling places, Israel!"[9] (*Moyshe and Pessie stare at one another, astonished, and suddenly bow down before the nobles.*)

MOYSHE. (*Finally stepping forward, still bowing. Pessie follows him.*) My most wonderful Lordship! My most noble master! My lord of all lords! How overjoyed I am! How moved I am! How happy! His Lordship has descended upon us like an angel from heaven! And when did His Excellency arrive from abroad? And how were His Lordship's travels in all the far off lands? You were practically a child when you left, and you've returned a young man with a mustache, a lordly mustache! What a fine set of whiskers! Oh, how good it is, how fine it is, that our nobles do not forget their poor little Jews!

PESSIE. Ach ach ach!

YOUNG DUKE. And this is how you receive the duke himself? A few false words of flattery and nothing more? Decent people would have built some booths on the highway, decked them with branches, and adorned themselves with fancy headscarves and velvet yarmulkes. Decent people would have salted the highway and conveyed me in a sled—in the middle of summer! Where is the bread and salt on a silver platter covered with a flowered tablecloth? Have we done so little for your family, granting you the rights to this inn in perpetuity? Well, why don't you say something?

MOYSHE. (*After being stunned for a moment.*) Oy, vey, Pessie! His Excellency is absolutely right. I'm going, right away.

YOUNG DUKE. Stay! Where are you running to? You can forget about the bread and salt. Rather, tell me: are you pleased that I've come?

MOYSHE. Pleased? I'm delighted! Such a joy! Does His Excellency doubt me? Shall I cut my own heart out to prove it? Gevald, such happiness! I'm dancing for joy! Tell him, Pessie, tell him!

---

9. Together, the two complete Numbers 24:5. The verse is spoken by Balaam, a non-Jewish prophet who is sent by the king of Moab to curse Israel but instead blesses them.

PESSIE. Ach! Ach!

YOUNG DUKE. I'm still not seeing any dancing. If that rebbe of yours were to come, you'd be dancing for sure.

MOYSHE. Do you hear that, Pessie? Golden words! Pearls of wisdom! Nu, nu, Pessie, heh heh heh!

PESSIE. Nu, nu, Moyshe, hee hee hee! If he's happy, then I'm happy.

MOYSHE. Oy, Excellency, I'm overjoyed! Oy, dear man, I'm happy! (*Makes a dancing motion.*) Oy, it's so good! It's so great! Oy, I'm merry, merry and joyous! Oy, what happiness, what honor! . . . Pessie, hide the girl.

PESSIE. (*Joining in the dancing.*) Oy, an honor! Oy, a joy! Moyshe, I heard you!

YOUNG DUKE. Stay, Moshek—I mean stop dancing. How does Rashi put it in your *khumesh*? *Vayokhelu*—and they pretended to eat.[10]

MOYSHE. (*Surprised.*) Pessie! His Lordship knows the Holy Tongue!

YOUNG DUKE. If you learn it, you know it. If you had learned to dance, you'd know how to do that, too. But I'm going to teach you. Bring a fiddle! Bring a flute!

MOYSHE. Sainted lord! We can dance, we're just not musicians. Okay, my grandfather does play the fiddle. Does the lord remember Zadok?

YOUNG DUKE. The old man's still alive? Bring Zadok and his fiddle here!

MOYSHE. And how am I supposed to bring him here? He's gone off into the woods to play for the birds. Such a crazy habit, may it never happen to you, heh heh heh! But he's coming soon, he'll be here any minute. How about a glass of ale in the meantime? Some preserves? A little bit of gefilte fish—a real pleasure! Ha, ha! Such honored guests!

YOUNG DUKE. (*To the Friend.*) What do you say?

FRIEND. The Jew makes sense. My throat's bone dry after all that riding.

MOYSHE. Perhaps Your Lordships would like to go inside?

FRIEND. No, Moshke, the air is better out here. Where's that ale of yours? Give us some of that stuff your daughter was good enough to honor us with while you were at the fair, ha ha ha!

YOUNG DUKE. Ha ha ha!

MOYSHE. Ha ha ha! *Oy, vey iz mir*! Pessie! The Sabbath tablecloth! Pessie! Ha ha ha! (*Moyshe and Pessie exit via the porch.*)

---

10. The young duke is referring to the events of Genesis 18:8, where messengers (traditionally understood as angels pretending to be human messengers) visit Abraham and Sarah (a story referred to later in the play). The verse states that the angels, who are generally understood not to eat, ate from the meal that Abraham prepared for them; the famed twelfth-century biblical commentator Rashi (ad loc) explicates merely that they pretended to eat, teaching that a person should not deviate from what is customary. "Khumesh": Pentateuch or Five Books of Moses.

YOUNG DUKE. (*Laying down the rifle, he sits on the bench.*) What a people!

FRIEND. Wise.

YOUNG DUKE. Wicked.

FRIEND. Cowardly.

YOUNG DUKE. Impudent.

FRIEND. Cunning.

YOUNG DUKE. They're not going to outwit me—just dance for me!

FRIEND. The way I see it, you're turning your back on the way we felt about Judaism in Paris. What's with you? I hardly recognize you.

YOUNG DUKE. It's the homeland air, my friend, that's worked this change. All my earlier feelings washed away in a single moment. Here, I'm a lord and all around me slaves . . . And also, there's . . . there's a big gap between Judaism and Jews. You remember that old rabbi in Paris? Made of completely different stuff. His tone, his sermons, he had something of Buonarotti's Moses[11] about him, something that only a Christian aesthete could grasp. Ha ha ha! My father's right when he laughs at all my Jewish fantasies! Moshek, the bearer of absolute truth? Here he comes. Just take a look at him!

FRIEND. What are you laughing for? He's bearing something very important: drinks! Moshke's bringing vodka . . .

MOYSHE. (*Enters with a silver tray, silver goblets, and a jug of ale.*) My dear guests! My noble guests! My most excellent lords! Pessie will be bringing out the tablecloth momentarily.

YOUNG DUKE. "We will do and we will hear"![12] First the ale, then the tablecloth! Little Jew!

FRIEND. Listen up, Moshek, are you going to serve us yourself?

MOYSHE. And how could I do otherwise, my lords? When the angels came to Abraham, didn't he bring the water for them to wash their feet and serve them himself? How could I do otherwise?

FRIEND. If we were guests at his house, Moshek, we wouldn't have allowed it, because Abraham had himself a pretty little wife, by the name of Sarah.

MOYSHE. Heh heh heh? Then would Your Lordships prefer that my Pessie serve you?

FRIEND. I couldn't care less about Pessie, or about Sareh![13] You have a beautiful daughter, Moshek!

---

11. The duke is referring to Michelangelo's famous statue of Moses (c.1513–1516), known not only for its beauty but for its depiction of the patriarch with horns.

12. See Exodus 24:7. Notably, the Jews say that they will accept God's word at Sinai before they hear it.

13. The fact that the friend mispronounces "Sarah" here and "l'khayim" a moment later indicates his lesser familiarity with traditional Jewish culture.

MOYSHE. I have a beautiful daughter? Maybe she's beautiful to Your Lordships. To me, she's pure trouble. A young woman, ugly, and not too bright, either. When she waits on a table? She stumbles three times on the way there. Feh, a disgrace.

FRIEND. We'd like to see exactly how she stumbles.

MOYSHE. But lord, master! His Lordship wouldn't want to shame me. And anyway, the girl isn't here, she's gone off to the forest, to her grandfather.

YOUNG DUKE. (*To the Friend.*) Come on, let's go to the forest and find her.

MOYSHE. Oy, gevald! Where are you going, my lords? She'll come back here soon enough. This very minute, this second, as I'm a Jew!

YOUNG DUKE. "A Jew?" And what exactly is Jewishness?

FRIEND. Some kind of merchandise.

MOYSHE. Ha ha ha! Your Lordships are jesting. Your Lordships know very well what Jewishness is . . . (*Pessie runs in with the tablecloth; both serve.*)

PESSIE. May their excellent Lordships drink in good health and may they enjoy it deeply!

YOUNG DUKE. *Prozit!* This ale isn't bad!

FRIEND. *La-kha-yem,* Moshek!

MOYSHE. *L'khayim toyvim u'lesholem!*[14]

FRIEND. Let's get down to drinking that ale of yours.

MOYSHE. It's really astonishing. I didn't believe it. They told me that His Excellency knows every language under the sun. I didn't believe it.

YOUNG DUKE. Only King Solomon knew all seventy languages.[15]

FRIEND. The little Jew's feeling more at home.

MOYSHE. True enough, as I'm a Jew! I humbly ask His Excellency the duke: His Excellency has arrived here from the wide world, where he has certainly spoken with great men. What are they saying about us little Jews? I don't mean about just us here, God forbid, but about the "Red Jews" too, the Ten Lost Tribes, who live far away, past the Sambatyon river?[16]

---

14. Hebrew/Yiddish, "To a happy life and to peace!"

15. Though Solomon is certainly the paradigmatic wise man in Jewish culture, this statement of the Young Duke's seems to be inaccurate; Moses, Mordechai, Joseph, and members of the Sanhedrin that met in the Temple are all, at one point or another, characterized as knowing the seventy languages that in antiquity were believed to be the total number of human languages.

16. According to Jewish legend, ten of Israel's ten tribes, which were "lost" when the Northern Kingdom of Israel fell to the Assyrians in 722 BCE, were not actually lost, but in fact had formed their own kingdom behind the Sambatyon river, an unpassable river which threw stones up during the week and rested on the Sabbath (when traditional Jews would not ford it). The kingdom there was populated by "Red Jews," strong, empowered members of an autonomous Jewish nation. The river is mentioned in Jewish sources (Targum Pseudo-Jonathan to Ex. 34:10, BT Sanhedrin 65b, Genesis Rabbah 11:5), as well as in Pliny the Elder's *Natural History.*

YOUNG DUKE. What do you want, Moshek? You want people to talk about you? And what can they say about you?

MOYSHE. What I mean, my dear lord, is how long can this go on, and what does it all come to? . . . We're practically brothers and yet . . . In every doorway, a beggar—and your bread, begged for—and your sweat, from fear and shame—and your Torah learning and your serving God don't seem to accomplish a thing . . . and you, and your wife and child, and all you have are at everyone's mercy, everyone's! . . . Nu, nu, what does it all come to? And how long will it go on? What I mean is: has His Excellency heard nothing on his travels about the Messiah?

FRIEND. The Messiah?

MOYSHE. Nu, yes, the Messiah. If a Jew isn't waiting for the Messiah, how can he look himself in the mirror?

FRIEND. What do you think of him?

YOUNG DUKE. I think he's joking.

FRIEND. Aha! Here comes old Zadok with that fiddle of his—just in time.

Scene 8

(Enter old Zadok in his Sabbath jacket with his fur hat. He clutches a holy book to his chest, and a fiddle is tucked under his arm. He suddenly sees the noble-man, is surprised, and bows.)

REB ZADOK. All joy to His Excellent Lord! Joy to his friend! Old Zadok must make a blessing! A blessing that he has merited to see His Lordship at home once more. Does the Duke remember old Zadok? When Zadok used to come to the castle, the old Duke—your grand-father, Excellency, may he rest in peace—used to put aside all his other affairs and play a game of chess with Zadok. And you, Excellency, were still just a little child . . .

YOUNG DUKE. Those days are long past, old Zadok. Now everyone must know his place. Jews are Jews and nobles are nobles. We have been waiting for you and your fiddle, so you can make us merry. And you, Moshek, take your wife and dance for your lord, a Sabbath dance.[17] Nu, lively! A-one and a-two!

---

17. Literally a *ma-yofis* dance. The Sabbath hymn "Ma yofis" (How Beautiful), extolling the pleasures of keeping the Sabbath, became so popular that it became known by non-Jews as well. During drunken revelries, Polish noblemen would force Jews to sing or dance to traditional Jewish songs in a humiliating manner, and would sometimes mention "Ma yofis" by name in such situations. This interaction gave rise to the expression *tsu zingen ma-yofis* (literally "to sing 'Ma yofis'"), i.e. to cringe and be servile.

REB ZADOK. (*Shrinking.*) M-ma! When His Lordship commands, a Jew plays. You couldn't have said it quietly? Why so angry? I would have played myself in honor of His Excellency.

YOUNG DUKE. Moshke! Sureh! Dance for your lordship! Your Lordship wants to make merry! Your Lordship will be generous! Go! (*He throws his purse at them. Reb Zadok stands on the side of the porch, strumming the fiddle tunelessly. Moyshe and Pessie dance with feigned merriment. Pessie makes some nervous movements and indicates stage right, where Nekhamele has appeared.*)

Scene 9

(*The Friend points her out to the Duke.*)

YOUNG DUKE. Ah, my beautiful girl! Nekhamele! I've longed for you! Dance, Moshek! Play, Zadok! And you, beautiful girl, come here! Sit on my lap. If we're going to have fun, then let's really have fun. Your Lordship can pay for everything. (*Nekhamele takes a step toward the Duke. Moyshe and Pessie run to block her way.*)

PESSIE. No, my dear lord! That won't do! What are you staring at like a statue, ugly girl? Go in the house!! His Excellency is just making fun of you!

MOYSHE. My lord, do not shame me like this!

YOUNG DUKE. Play! Dance! Who is the duke here and who is the servant? Here, girl!

NEKHAMELE. (*Tearing herself away from between her parents.*) Let me go! I have a mind of my own! Don't tell me that I'm ugly, mama—it's a lie! I'm pretty! And you, papa, don't talk about shame. There's nothing to be ashamed of! If my parents are going to dance like bears for His Lordship, if my old grandfather plays the fiddle for him—then I can certainly go and sit on the duke's lap! (*Runs and sits on the Duke's lap.*) What next? Hugging? Kissing? How? Like this?

FRIEND. Ha ha ha! Clever! Remarkably clever! Moshek! What exactly is that Jewishness of yours?

NEKHAMELE. Have I done something wrong? Teach me! I'll do it better, harder. (*Moyshe and Pessie are astonished. Old Zadok lays down his fiddle and sticks his arms into his sleeves.*)

YOUNG DUKE. Play! Dance! I'm just getting warmed up. Let the ale flow like water! Moshek! Zadok!

REB ZADOK. (*Looking at the heavens.*) The Sabbath!

MOYSHE. (*Quickly coming to his senses.*) The Sabbath!

YOUNG DUKE. (*Jumps to his feet, pushing off Nekhamele. Pessie drags her away by the hand.*) Are you defying me?

REB ZADOK. We can't play music or dance on the Sabbath!

YOUNG DUKE. You will play music and you will dance. If not . . .

FRIEND. Is it worth getting all worked up over? You've had too much ale.

YOUNG DUKE. Leave me alone! Such nerve! I won't spare anyone. Back off, friend!

REB ZADOK. Do you think there's no God in heaven, duke? (*The Young Duke grabs his rifle and aims it at old Zadok. The old man, seeing this, pushes his fur hat down on his head, sticks his hands even deeper into his sleeves, and raises his head. Moyshe watches terrified, then runs over and shields the old man with his body.*)

MOYSHE. Sabbath . . . Sabbath . . . Sabbath . . .

FRIEND. Milord! What sort of foolishness is this? Are you in your right mind?

YOUNG DUKE. Get back, my good man!

FRIEND. And what if you're not? Get back, Jews! (*He runs over, pushes away the Duke's hand, and the gun discharges into the air.*) Damn you! Look what you could have done!

YOUNG DUKE. (*Shaking.*) Quiet . . . don't say anything . . .

FRIEND. Get out of here, Jews! (*Reb Zadok and Moyshe slowly exit via the porch. The Young Duke lowers himself onto the bench, and covers his face with his hands. A pause.*) Well, come on! You've been sitting here too long. It's tedious and harmful.

YOUNG DUKE. (*Mournfully.*) Terrifying . . .

FRIEND. Apparently, there's such a thing as too much joking around.

YOUNG DUKE. The joke's on me. I shot them.

FRIEND. You're talking nonsense!

YOUNG DUKE. No, I shot them. Or it's the same as if I did . . . it seems to me that the fresh air of home has completely cured me. I'm no longer a nobleman.

FRIEND. Look, friend, what's done is done. You were overreacting then, and you're overreacting now.

YOUNG DUKE. Call them out. I won't be able to go home.

FRIEND. (*Shrugging his shoulders, goes to the porch.*) *Panye*[18] Moshek! *Panye* Zadok! The Duke wishes to ask your pardon. (*The Jews appear in the window and in the door.*) You see, Duke, you can go home quietly now. They're all fine . . . they're still in one piece.

YOUNG DUKE. (*Jumps up, hysterically.*) Jews, please forgive me, if you possibly can.

REB ZADOK. If you are truly contrite, then God will forgive you.

---

18. A Polish term of respectful address, generally used to refer to non-Jews.

Moyshe. If it weren't for the rifle, lord, it wouldn't have come to that.

Young Duke. I swear to you, Jews, that from this day forward no rifle will ever touch my hands again!

Reb Zadok. God's miracles are great!

Young Duke. Quiet, Jews, don't say anything. One studies for years, and wisdom comes in a single, frightening moment. I'm cold, friend. Jews, a good Sabbath to you.

Zadok. And a good year to you. Calm yourself, my lord, this was meant to be.

Young Duke. Yes it was, but that's not why I need to calm myself. . . . I'm shaking in every limb . . . Reb Zadok, I now understand the meaning of the verse, *Kol atsmoysai te'amarnah*—"And all of my bones shall speak."[19] Give me your hand. The scales have fallen from my eyes.

Zadok. (*Leads Moyshe out onto the porch.*) Come, my son. We have a great God. Come, let us accompany our guest to the Sabbath boundary.[20] (*All exit right.*)

Scene 10

(*The stage remains empty. Nekhamele runs on from left, letting her hair down.*)

Nekhamele. Oy, they're not here! My dream has vanished! Who's gone crazy? They're the crazy ones! I want to go to the duke! My mistake, mama: to all the nobles! To sit on all of their laps! To hug and kiss them all! I want to run to that brilliant world, where people are beautiful and don't know about sinning, because everything there's a sin! (*She hides.*)

Scene 11

Pessie. (*Running from the porch.*) Where are you, daughter? *Vey iz mir*! Someone's put a spell on that girl! It's late! Stars . . . and we still haven't lit Sabbath candles . . . a tragedy![21] Daughter! I have to find

---

19. Psalms 35:10. The verse reads, "All of my bones shall speak: 'Lord, who is like You, who saves the poor from him that is too strong for him, the poor and the needy from him who despoils them?'"

20. Traditional Jews will not go beyond 2000 amot (about 3000 feet) from their habitations on the Sabbath.

21. Sunset is the traditional beginning of the Sabbath.

you—I want to tear your hair out. Where are you? Have you climbed up a tree? Daughter, it's the Sabbath already! (*She discovers her behind a tree, and drags her into the house.*)

NEKHAMELE. Drag me, mama, pull my hair—harder, harder!

PESSIE. You're our worst nightmare, mine and my husband's and all our friends—tramp!

NEKHAMELE. Hit me, mama! Hit your Jewish daughter! She's become impure. You can't hurt her anymore!

PESSIE. Oh, it'll hurt plenty!

NEKHAMELE. Oy, mama, just don't drag me into that Jewish house! Not into that dark house! I'll set it on fire! Let there be light in every crevice ... (*They both disappear into the house. Soft, muffled cries. The Sabbath candles are lit in the window. Pause. Darkness.*)

Scene 12

(*Reb Zadok and Moyshe, dressed in Sabbath clothes, enter slowly from right.*)

BOTH. (*Singing dreamily.*) "Sholem aleykhem, malakhey hasholem, malakhey elyon, mimelekh, malkhey ham'lokhim ...[22]

Curtain.

Act II

A room in the Duke's palace, decorated in Oriental fashion. Weapons mounted on the walls. Ancestral pictures. At left, a large window. Bottles of wine next to the wall. A bearskin rug on the floor. A taffeta. Pillows, an ottoman, and benches. A chessboard. The Clown, in cap and bells, is dusting the pictures on the walls with a featherduster.

Scene 1

CLOWN. (*Approaching the jug of wine on the chessboard.*) Wine ... When it comes to wine, I'm as much of a connoisseur as the duke himself, despite my lowly ancestry. Long live Dvoyre. She never abandons us.

---

22. Literally, "Peace be unto you, angels of peace, angels of the most high, from the king, the king of all kings." This is a traditional Sabbath hymn, sung Friday night after returning from synagogue.

It's just a shame that the duke doesn't entirely rely on my highly refined sensibilities. "You," he says, "have a higher calling: to suffer for the truth." And then he doles out slaps from his most excellent hand; for every truth I tell him—one right in the face: pow! A high calling for my humble position—but it hurts. (*Returning to the portraits.*) Nu, my good old friends, how's it hanging? I hope you're hanging in there! Noble knights! How are things in the other world? What's my grandfather up to—the one you beat to death? Is he serving you in Paradise, too? Nu, nu, excuse me, a bit close to the bone . . . and as for you, Whiskers, we're a little bit related. You sniffed around my mama right up to her wedding day. And you didn't hold back from exercising your rights on the wedding night . . . The poor folks wept, and fell at your feet . . . but the tears of the poor stink . . . wait, my lord. You see this little knife? Bit by bit I'm scraping you off the canvas. Nobody will suspect a thing. And then one fine morning—no more Whiskers! Just an empty canvas, ha ha ha! And you, my lady, you owe me one, breaking my rib like that. I have you to thank for my distinguished career, ha ha ha! "He walks just like a duck. Give him a cap and bells!"

BISHOP. (*Entering from left.*) Praise be!

CLOWN. Amen and amen! Oh, holy Father, you scared me half to death! Here I was, just standing and talking a little to myself: the world's gone mad, little Father!

BISHOP. For example, you scoundrel?

CLOWN. Well, the way our young duke has turned into a regular Psalmist. And he's wandering all over the place with mumbo-jumbo books. The other day he left one of those books in the garden—it was a horror.

BISHOP. Inconceivable! Still so melancholy? The things a Jewish girl can do!

CLOWN. He's a laughingstock at court. He's already gotten a nickname: "Half-a-Jew," hee hee hee! They say he wants to be a full Jew. That's what he wanted when he was abroad. So His Excellency ordered him back home. That's how God punishes a man. Listen, he's roaring now . . .

BISHOP. Who?

CLOWN. The bear. Didn't the little Father know? The old man captured a bear last night. And what a bear! They carried out five armed Hungarian soldiers from the forest, ground to a pulp. His Excellency ordered them to capture him in a net. So they wouldn't ruin the hide. And now it's roaring and running around and turning the stable upside down.

BISHOP. The whims of a nobleman. What does he need it for?

CLOWN. God be with you, little Father! There's a whole plan afoot. First they're going to teach the bear to march back and forth, like a soldier, and to shoot a rifle too. The world's gone mad, little Father! The young duke has turned into a regular Psalmist, the bear into a marksman, and the Hungarians are licking their wounds. The duke has already sent for Yoshke the tailor.

BISHOP. He's going to teach the bear to shoot?

CLOWN. Ha ha ha! An excellent joke, little Father! No, little Father, His Excellency's plan is to make the bear a pair of red trousers. They say that when His Excellency was abroad, he once saw a picture of a bear wearing red trousers, and shooting. Well, if the French have it on their walls, we need it in our halls.

BISHOP. Ha ha ha, you windbag! And I've been standing and listening to this. There isn't a grain of truth in this story of yours!

CLOWN. So the holy Father thought such a crazy idea was possible . . . ?

BISHOP. You good-for-nothing! I'm going to break another one of your ribs!

CLOWN. Nu, nu, little Father. I belong exclusively to His Excellency. You're not allowed to break any part of me.

Scene 2

(*Yoshke stumbles onstage left holding a pair of loosely stitched red trousers.*)

YOSHKE. Help! I'm going to complain to the duke! Why pick on me? They send for a craftsman just to mock him! Oy, dear God, how can I get out of this in one piece? Get this: trousers for a bear! I don't know what style they wear! And where do the buttons go?

BISHOP. (*Astonished.*) So it's really true?

YOSHKE. (*Delighted.*) Little Father, is that you? It's true, holy Father; if only it were a dream! Have you heard: trousers for a bear? And they have to fit like a glove. And those Hungarians are even worse than bears! They can drive a Jew right into his grave! Oy, little Father, save a Jew!

BISHOP. And you can't figure something out yourself?

YOSHKE. What do you mean, I can't? I'm a craftsman, with a Jewish head on my shoulders. I just go and stitch the cloth . . . just look, little Father, what beautiful material I'm ruining here! I swear to them, those Hungarians: you can try these on later—just make a mark with charcoal, with a little piece of charcoal, where to take it in, where to let it out . . . try measuring a bear, and he'll scream like a woman in labor.

BISHOP. (*Barely restraining his laughter.*) But how can you do it without measuring?

YOSHKE. May you live long, little Father, I'm using my head. If that devil nearly killed five Hungarians, couldn't he have finished off two of them? That is, the bear's twice as big as they are. So I measured two Hungarians for one pair of trousers. (*The Bishop and Clown finally burst out laughing.*) What's so funny? You think I don't get it? I'll err on the baggy side. (*Falls at the Bishop's feet.*) Oy, little Father, have mercy! Get His Lordship to set me free! I just can't do this job. And what does he care, I ask you, if the bear wears trousers or not? I'll take the blame! . . .

BISHOP. (*To the Clown.*) What are you laughing for, you good for nothing! Can't you see that this is the awful truth?

CLOWN. Ha ha ha! So why . . . why did the father not believe me earlier? Ha ha ha! If someone says something crazy—believe it! (*He runs off stage right.*)

BISHOP. Just tell me, Yoshke, do you want me to ask his Highness to grant your request?

YOSHKE. Oy, little Father, I will always remember your kindness! Little children . . . a sick mother . . . and I myself am an orphan to boot . . . Today I have to light a memorial candle. It completely slipped my mind. I have to go run to say the Kaddish . . .

BISHOP. Gevald, Yoshke, why are you such a coward? His Holiness will simply laugh at you!

YOSHKE. May he laugh in good health. I'll be delighted if he laughs . . . as long as I don't cry. The father should know how dangerous it is to start up with a bear!

BISHOP. You haven't even laid eyes on the bear!

YOSHKE. So imagine what I'll look like when I actually see him! What does the Father think, that a Jew's got two lives? Oh, and by the way—how does one become—it shouldn't happen to me, or to you—a bear's tailor?

BISHOP. You're right, heh heh heh! I'll definitely discuss it with the Duke. But remember, Yoshke, what we talked about recently!

YOSHKE. (*Straightening up.*) About Dvoyrele? But little Father, she's a widow!

BISHOP. And you're a widower; you're well matched. Is she or isn't she a child of Israel?

YOSHKE. You're asking me? Mm—ah . . . but what's in it for the holy Father?

BISHOP. I pity her.

YOSHKE. Hm . . . If the little Father is such a nice guy, then why doesn't he take pity on a poor tailor? Why do I have to be the rag with which . . . Oy, vey, is the Father getting angry? Sha, sha . . . I'm done talking.

BISHOP. You dog! I'll talk to him about doing right by you.

YOSHKE. Doing right costs dearly, though . . .

VOICE OF DUKE. (*From right.*) Right! Right! Rub harder! Scoundrel! A little to the left! By the shoulder blades, you good for nothing! Lower! Even lower!

BISHOP. Get back, Yoshke, the duke is coming!

YOSHKE. Good, little Father, good, it really is a nice thing for Dvoyrele. I'll think it over. Really a nice thing. So you see, little Father, Yoshke can be of some use after all . . . .

VOICE OF DUKE. Why are you stamping out the fire, scoundrel? Come here! The pipe! Get back! Come here! Open the door! Get back! Come here! Get back!

Scene 3

(*The Duke strides in with solid steps. A ruddy face. Gray hair, black mustache. A Turkish cloak. In his hand—a pipe.*)

BISHOP. Praise be!

DUKE. Ah! My dear sir! Amen and amen! It's good that you're here. My dear sir! I sent a knight especially for you. Two knights. Let's play chess.

BISHOP. And how did Your Excellency sleep?

DUKE. Ha ha ha! Snored for fourteen hours straight on one side, and woke up aching in every bone in my body. You think it's a joke, how that bear wore me out yesterday? But if you wanted to see a fine specimen today, my dear man, you came to the wrong place. And you, Yoshke, my good man, what are you doing here? Ah! Trousers? Trousers for the bear. Ha ha ha! Good, and if you finish the slacks— a purse full of gold coins! If not—then the whip. Ha ha ha! So tell me, have you ever sewn trousers for a bear before?

YOSHKE. (*In a boldness born of despair.*) So many bags of coins . . . What is His Excellency thinking, such a strange thing—trousers for a bear? . . .

DUKE. Ha ha ha! What do you say to the little Jew, my dear man? And the Clown swore that Yoshke practically died of fright. Hey, rascal! Where have you gotten to, my good man? Get over here! (*The Clown bounds in from stage right, bowing and scraping furiously.*)

DUKE. It's not going to help. Fifteen lashes!

CLOWN. (*Falling to his knees.*) Unclean, oh Excellency: my conscience will be unclean, unless I know what the beating means.

DUKE. You can take your whipping with an unclean conscience. You tell lies, scoundrel. Yoshke's not afraid of the bear.

CLOWN. Woe is me! They whip me if I tell the truth, they whip me for a lie! Excellency, I'm neutral. And since that's the case, I'm ready to get whipped for staying neutral, too.

DUKE. Isn't it true, Yoshke, that you're not afraid of bears?

YOSHKE. It's the God's truth, Excellency! What's there to be afraid of? As long as I'm behind an iron wall. That's all I ask: a cellar, or a little attic room, where I can sit and sew. Where I can't hear the bear roar. It makes me ill. (*Laughter.*)

CLOWN. Aha! So who's lying?

DUKE. Whip them both!

YOSHKE. Oy, gevald!

DUKE. Take him to an attic room, get him out of here. Move it! (*Yoshke and the Clown exit.*)

DUKE. Well have a seat, my good man! Hey, scoundrel! (*The Clown runs in.*) A chessboard! Wine! Did she bring any today? Dvoyre? You have to sample every bottle. (*The Clown prepares the wine and the chessboard.*) *Prozit!*

BISHOP. I don't quite follow this business with the bear, Excellency.

DUKE. Ah, that's good wine! If the wine is good, I have to make a blessing—that's the kind of man I am. So you don't quite follow, my good man? Yoshke doesn't either. Those long robes of yours are turning you into a woman. And where's the thrill of the game? Go . . . you take the black, I'll take white.

BISHOP. In my opinion, Your Excellency, we are not granted life solely for the sake of entertainment.

DUKE. I'm taking your pawn. What does a bishop need a pawn for? It depends on who you are, my good man, it depends on who you are . . . The peasant is afraid of everyone. You—you're afraid of God. But for me, a noble—well, for me life's a game.

BISHOP. Sinful words, Excellency, sinful words . . . you've left your queen open.

DUKE. Don't look where it isn't necessary . . . my queen is still perfectly safe . . . Hmm . . . hmm . . . But the game should be for higher stakes. Different stakes. (*The Clown waits expectantly.*) Go bring in the old book . . . the one in the bedroom, under the table. The one that smells of mold and tobacco. Remarkable, little Father, how a book preserves the odor of its surroundings. Yes, my good man, for you life is serious, and serious means fear, and fear means slavery. . . . Ha ha ha!

BISHOP. Sinful words, Excellency, sinful words! Oh, my castle?

DUKE. Ah, ah, my good man, no taking it back. A move is a move.

CLOWN. (*Entering with the book.*) It's written here, Excellency, that it's Yoshke that deserves a whipping, not me.

DUKE. (*Taking the book.*) It's written, it's written . . . You're right, but you still deserve a whipping. Just look, my good man, what sort of mumbo-jumbo is this? (*Glares at the Clown.*)

CLOWN. I'm going . . . I'm going . . . (*Exits.*)

DUKE. Now talk!

BISHOP. Excellency, I'm no expert in the Hebrew language myself.

DUKE. Ah, so this is Hebrew? (*Contemplates the book.*) Strange, the little squares and scratches . . . the work of Phoenicians, you know. Interesting, my good man, extraordinarily interesting. And you read it from right to left?

BISHOP. From right to left, Excellency, but . . .

DUKE. Heh . . . strange . . . And he understands all this, that son of mine, the young duke! Some head on his shoulders, some head, my good man. Have you ever seen a hen that hatched a duck? That's me and my son. Little Father, do you think there's some sort of old smell coming from the book?

BISHOP. The young duke was reading *this* book?

DUKE. Of course, who else? You mean you don't know what sort of book this is, little Father?

BISHOP. Unfortunately, I do know. There's a Latin title . . .

DUKE. Ah! A Latin title . . . a theological tractate, certainly? Why so quiet, little Father? Cat got your tongue?

BISHOP. (*Standing up.*) Highness! I cannot hide my distress and my pain. I must tell you that in another time, in another place, this book was burned, and the Courts of Inquisition sentenced people because of it. Has Your Excellency heard of Shlomo Molkho?[23]

DUKE. Shliama? Shliama? There's no Jew by that name in my lands.

BISHOP. No, Highness, this was a Spanish grandee. A young confidant of Queen Isabella's. And this very same grandee converted to Judaism.

DUKE. And so that's how you get a Spanish grandee named Shliama! Is the book about him?

BISHOP. No, Highness, these are sermons[24] he wrote.

---

23. Solomon Molcho (ca. 1500–1532), born Diogo Pires in Lisbon to Marrano parents—that is, they had been forcibly converted to Christianity, but secretly continued practicing Judaism. After meeting messianic pretender David Reuveni in Portugal in 1525, Pires circumcised himself and took a Hebrew name. Molcho soon left Portugal and wandered eastward, gathering a following in Greece and gaining further prominence in Italy, where he even was granted the protection of Pope Clement VII. He made powerful enemies as well, however, and was burned to the stake in Mantua in 1532. His remarkable life inspired a number of works of fiction and drama, including the Yiddish plays *Shloyme Molkho un Dovid Ruveyni* by Dovid Pinski and *Shloyme Molkho* by A. Leyeles.

24. This refers to Molcho's collection of sermons, *Derashot* (Salonika, 1529).

DUKE. Hmm. . . . interesting!

BISHOP. No, Highness. It's not interesting, it's tragic. This book must be burned.

DUKE. Well, well, why so serious? What's so tragic about it?

BISHOP. I'll tell you the plain truth, Excellency: it is my sacred duty. I'm not happy with the young duke.

DUKE. Must he be burned as well? Ha ha ha! I drink to the health of Shliama the Spanish grandee! His name was Shliama?

BISHOP. His Christian name was Diego Pires.

DUKE. Ah! That's different. That has a nice ring to it: Diego Pires . . .

BISHOP. And he was burned at the stake in Mantua, two hundred years ago.

DUKE. Damn it! You people are so severe, aren't you? It's a dangerous game with you. But interesting, my good man, very interesting!

BISHOP. This too is "interesting"? Excellency, don't take this the wrong way, but I'm losing the tranquility befitting a servant of God. I must tell you that the young duke is playing a dangerous game. Who is he befriending? Who is he learning from? He's already become half a Jew! What sort of behavior is this for a Christian? What sort of behavior is this for a nobleman?

DUKE. Little Father, little Father! You're crossing the line!

BISHOP. My sacred trust is to speak the truth. It is not I, but your son, Excellency, who is crossing the line. His great learning is taking him on a dangerous path, a path which may bring tragic consequences. And all for what? For whom? Yes, I'll say it openly: for a Jewish girl!

DUKE. Wh-what?

BISHOP. I might as well say it all: his whole friendship with the innkeeper, his whole interest in Jews and Judaism—who is it all for, if not the innkeeper's daughter? (*The Duke bursts out laughing. The Bishop waits expectantly.*)

DUKE. Oh, my good man, you've made me so happy! Oh, my good man, you are a joker, a regular jester in cap and bells! And talking about what? You're talking about a Jewish girl? Ha ha ha! (*He forces himself to take a serious tone.*) Good little Father, now I'm going to tell you something in earnest. I have no doubt that your dedication to God forces you to say such things. But remember: the young duke is his father's flesh and blood. He is a nobleman. Do you hear, my good man? A nobleman. And what is permitted to a nobleman is not permitted to ordinary mortals. The young duke may allow himself to cross the line. What is "crossing the line"? Doing what others don't because they're bound by the rules. And so, little Father, you may play your game. No, no, I will not get involved in your private matters, little Father, but understand me—the young noble is something else again. He knows how the game is played just as well as his father does. We both play with all our hearts. But he, the young duke—he understands the game differently. Who am I, then, to give him advice? Yes, little Father. What makes this game with the live bear, the game with the wild peasants, or this chess match with you, for that matter, any finer or more exalted than my son's game with a beard and sidecurls, with scholastic tractates, with a Shliama Molkho, or even with the Messiah? Ha ha . . . and even if there's a Jewish girl in the mix . . . No, little Father, I firmly believe that even if the way my son plays the game disturbs you, even if you see him as a danger to the church—then . . . my regard for my son . . . No, little Father, I'm no enemy of the church; I'm a tolerant man. But I have great respect for my son.

BISHOP. Will His Excellency tolerate this game against the church?

DUKE. I don't give advice to other nobles.

BISHOP. Even if your son speaks out against your Grace?

DUKE. Then we will compete as equals.

BISHOP. And until then?

DUKE. My good man! Do not make my life a misery while I still derive some small enjoyment from it. Until then, until then . . . until then I'll play my own games. Capturing bears, praising good wines, and thanking my Creator for every happy moment . . . your move, little Father. Enough arguing; defend your rook. You see, my queen is still protected . . .

BISHOP. Excellency! I'm so shaken that I couldn't possibly play any more. Permit me to take a break, Excellency. I shall minister to the injured Hungarians. (*A tumult in the court. The Clown runs in, breathless.*)

DUKE. What's happened?

CLOWN. Excellency, the bear!

DUKE. What about the bear? Has it hung itself? Is it wounded? Speak!

CLOWN. Broke out of the stable.

DUKE. Damn! (*He throws off his cloak, runs over to the large window, and thrusts his head out. The Bishop and Clown follow him. The tumult subsides. A shot is heard.*) Hey there! Don't shoot! I'll flay the skin from your bones! Chase him from the right, the right!

CLOWN. Right!

DUKE. Close the gate!

CLOWN. The gate!

DUKE. Surround him from all sides! Hey, scoundrel! No spears! No sharp weapons! You'll ruin his hide!

CLOWN. No weapons! Use your hands! And your caps!

DUKE. With poles! Only with poles!

CLOWN. Poles! Poles!

Bishop. Oh! He'll maim them, a giant like him!

Duke. Well, my good man, what do think of my bear, hm? One fine bear! Doesn't he deserve a pair of red trousers? Hey there! No sharp weapons! Don't provoke the beast!

Bishop. Highness, look who's standing in my courtyard. Moshek, Moshek the innkeeper.

Duke. Ha ha ha! That's all that was missing. What are we going to do with the Jew?

Clown. A Jew has to stick his nose into everything.

Bishop. Excellency, this game is out of control. Look, he's caught someone else now.

Duke. What are you thinking, little Father? It's not a real game without blood. Without bloodshed, people would go mad. Drive the dogs away, drive them away! I'm afraid that I'll have to shoot for the little Jew's sake.

Clown. A bold little Jew! His hat is all messed up, and he's looking the bear right in the mouth.

Bishop. He can't move—the bear's practically on top of him. Excellency, don't wait! Here's the rifle; shoot! Now's the moment!

Duke. Should I really shoot? It's a shame; such a bear! On the other hand, I can't let my Jews down . . . (*The Duke aims. The Bishop grabs his hand.*)

Bishop. Don't shoot—careful! Who's running toward them?

Duke. (*Directing the rifle away.*) What? My son? With a knife? With a dagger? Ho, noble. The beast is furious!

Clown. They're running away. The Jew has fallen under the bear—the duke has thrown himself on the bear!

Duke. (*The rifle trembling in his hands.*) Children, children, I . . . I can't shoot! Save the duke! (*The Clown runs out. The Duke covers his face. The Bishop starts to run to the courtyard, looks around, and instead runs to help the old Duke. He helps him to a seat, pours him a glass of wine. The tumult in the courtyard suddenly stops.*)

Duke. What has he done? And what did he do it for?

Bishop. Calm yourself, Excellency . . .

Clown. (*Running in.*) He killed him, wiped the floor with him . . .

Duke. Who?

Clown. The young duke . . . wiped the floor with the bear.

Duke. And how is he?

Clown. A trifle. A scratch on his left arm. The doctor's bandaging the wound.

Duke. (*Jumps up, looks around, grabs the goblet from the Bishop's hand, drains it, and throws it to the ground.*) Ha ha ha! Hurrah, duke! What did I tell you, my good man, what did I tell you? The young noble has played well! Ha ha ha! Still waters run deep! He risked that noble head of his for Moshek. And without a rifle, my good man, with nothing but a dagger, like his grandfather, like his great-grandfather. I have to admit, I never would have dared to do it. Ha ha ha! Hey, scoundrel! More wine! Stay, little Father, what's the rush? Come dance! I want to dance, jump around—I'm a bear myself! I've become a young cub!

BISHOP. Excellency, I understand your joy. But I cannot dance. Someone has been crushed by the beast. I must go to him.

DUKE. Go, little Father, go, go, good sir. Fulfill your Christian duty and come back quickly. (*Bishop exits left.*) Hey, Fool! I'm ecstatic right now! Still haven't been whipped? Well, I pardon you. Ha ha ha! Bring the cymbals here! No, wait, how did it happen? Like a dream. The bear stood on his hind legs and moved toward Moshek. Suddenly, there he was, the young pup with the dagger . . . stand here, Fool; you'll be the bear and I'll be the young duke. Bring me a dagger!

CLOWN. (*Falling to his knees.*) Excellency, I would rather be a live dog than a dead bear!

DUKE. Ha ha ha! That's what you are anyway. Let the game begin!

CLOWN. Right away, Excellency, right away! Careful with that dagger. His Excellency might mean it as a joke, but the dagger is serious. (*He crawls under the bearskin.*) Oy, I'm lost! Boo hoo!

YOSHKE. (*Enters with the finished pair of bear's trousers. Lost in thought.*) Up in the attic it's as quiet as a tomb; practically puts you to sleep. What an insult—trousers for a bear! . . . If only they'd let me . . . (*Sees the Duke.*) Finished, Excellency! They're ready to be tried on . . . ! (*The Duke looks at him, astonished. Yoshke holds out the trousers to him. The Clown, wrapped in the bearskin, sneaks up from behind and embraces Yoshke with the paws.*)

CLOWN. B-boo! Gimme—I'll try them on. (*Yoshke screams and runs off. The Duke and the Clown clutch their sides in laughter.*)

Scene 4

YOUNG DUKE (*Runs in, the arm of his shirt in tatters, his hair disheveled, the broken dagger in his hand.*) Esau's den![25] What are you two laughing about?

---

25. The Young Duke's remarks plays on the Jewish convention of referring to non-Jews as "Esau."

DUKE. Ah ah, noble youth! A bold blow. This is all that's left of the dagger? Interesting, my good man, let's take a look . . . ah ah ah!

YOUNG DUKE. What did you have against that poor Jew? What did you want with those unfortunate slaves? Barbarians! (*The Clown sneaks out, terrified.*)

DUKE. And here I was afraid my son had lost his knightly boldness! First he takes on a bear, and then he raises his voice to his own father. It seems there's never a glass of wine without a bitter drop. But what an idea, my good man: attacking that beast without a rifle?

YOUNG DUKE. What of it? I had sworn an oath: I would never pick up a rifle again. I feel nothing but disgust for the symbol of your knighthood, for weapons of any kind. I am breaking the shameful chain that binds me to all the noble knights—a nobility born of spilled blood, a nobility of unpunished crimes. This is my oath: I am none of theirs, they none of mine.

DUKE. But they are mine, young gentleman! Boldness is a fine virtue, but a knight should know that he will be called to account for too much boldness. You will not leave here without satisfaction, my good man. Nobleman, hear this: your father is a tolerant man. Your father has seen what you're up to, and has kept silent. That is your business. You have exchanged your knightly life for an ascetic one. Your gentlemanly amusements and studies for moldy scholasticism. Your intelligence, your conscience will answer for it. Here is your book. Take this moldy thing out of my chambers. I have been considerate of your aristocratic freedom. Yes, my good man. And now you come, dear gentleman, and break off the branch on which you perch! You are cutting yourself off from knighthood's noble legacy! A heavy blow for your father, who is no longer young, but I will bear it. But you have dared even further: you have called my house "Esau's den." And all of these noble knights, who look down upon us from these walls, whose names are recorded in the chronicles in golden letters—you have called them criminals. Are you aware, young man, that I, the last living branch of this noble tree, that I must intercede on behalf of the honor of my forefathers and cleanse it with blood? Stand and deliver, my good man, stand and deliver! (*He takes two Turkish scimitars down from the walls.*) The swords are sharp. Choose, gentleman, defend yourself. Here we will fight until first blood. I know not how Jacob does it—but in Esau's house the stain of shame is washed away with blood.

YOUNG DUKE. (*Takes the scimitar. Lays it down.*) No, dear father, let it be. This fight between father and son for the honor of deceased grandfathers seems childish to me. If father wishes to fight—let him do so with his equals. I am not one of those . . . would the noble care to fight with Zadok the innkeeper?

DUKE. Zadok?? That's going too far! The young noble may act as humble as Jacob, and play with little Moshkes and Yankels as he pleases. But the young noble has yet to take the sign of Jewishness upon himself, the sign of Abraham's covenant with Jehovah![26] So, my son, take the sword! One two, 'til first blood. If not . . . if not, I shall suspect the noble of Jacob's cowardice.

YOUNG DUKE. Father, do not awaken the Esau within me. He is not dead, he merely slumbers. I have struggled with a bear, like a savage. Now what do you want from me? Should I strike my own father?

DUKE. Who asked you to stand up for Moshek?

YOUNG DUKE. I was paying a debt.

DUKE. And you owe your father no debt? I claim a debt of honor. Take the sword! One two! (*He forces him to cross swords.*)

Scene 5

(*The Bishop leads Moyshe in from stage left. Moyshe's head is bound; he wears a tattered coat.*)

BISHOP. Deal with this as you see fit, Your Excellency; I've done my duty. (*To Moyshe.*) Here he is, the young duke himself. Turn to him, Moshek. Pour out your bitter heart to him.

MOYSHE. Oy, things are dark for me indeed! No, little Father, it's not the young lord I must speak to, but His Excellency himself. A great request, Your Lordship, a great request!

DUKE. (*To his son.*) Young man, we will finish this talk. (*To Moyshe.*) Where did you get the idea, Moshek, to come into the courtyard just as the bear was escaping? You must have thought someone would sell you its hide, eh?

YOUNG DUKE. Father!

MOYSHE. Excellency, how can you joke at such a difficult time? Look at me—I'm barely keeping myself together, after barely surviving that attack. Your Lordship, I've come to weep, lament, plead for mercy, fall at your feet. . . . Do not make me wretched. Your Lordship, return my daughter to me!

DUKE. What? Return your daughter? What makes you think your daughter is with me, and that it is in my power to return her?

MOYSHE. I don't know, Your Excellency. Have I said that I do know? I am a wretched father, a miserable Jew, and your servant. Do with me what you will, my lord, take all I have—it's thanks to you that I have it—take my life. But my honor, my poor Jewish honor! A daughter,

---

26. The reference is to circumcision; see Genesis 17 and commentaries ad loc.

a Jewish daughter—a curtain for the holy ark already sewn in her honor, her parents swelling with pride . . . She's run away from me, my daughter, run away from her Jewish parents!

DUKE. But why are you complaining to me, my dear sir? What have I done to you? Why must I return your daughter to you, if she herself ran away?

MOYSHE. I'm not saying—I'm not saying anything . . . After all, you're the all-powerful one, you can do anything. Give an order, dispatch riders, stand up for your servant, wash away his disgrace. Help me, my lord. A wretched father falls at your feet!

YOUNG DUKE. Reb Moyshe, what is this about?

BISHOP. I cannot be silent, I must not be silent. I will speak, come what may. Why is the young duke making the poor innkeeper so miserable? Who knows more about his daughter than he does? Where could she be if not in his hiding place? And why, Moshek, don't you ask the young duke directly? Do you think prevailing upon the father will make the young duke take pity on you?

YOUNG DUKE. Who? Me? I'm the guilty one here? I should take pity?

MOYSHE. No, little Father, that's not right. Don't involve the young lord. Why cause a fight between a father and his son? The young duke knows nothing of my misfortune. It only happened two days ago. (*To the Duke.*) Sir! All roads lead to you!

DUKE. So why do you come to me, Jew? Dare you to say that I have stolen your daughter away from you? And if she has run away for her own reasons, can I force her to return to her gloomy Jewish home?

MOYSHE. Out of your own mouth, my lord! You know where she is!

DUKE. And even if I did know? Have I ever tried to persuade you or anyone else to convert? I'm not God's Cossack. Did I ever warn my son, the young duke, to stay away from Jewish learning when it was brought to my attention? I don't preach to him. Why should I take your side all of a sudden, Moshek, and force your daughter to do something she finds unpleasant? I'm actually a freethinker, I won't persuade anyone to convert. But then it follows that I won't discourage anyone from doing so either.

MOYSHE. My lord, give it to me straight. Tell me she's already converted. I'll tear my garment and sit *shiva* for her. Help me, my lord: what's happened to my daughter?

DUKE. Don't make a scene, Moshek! If your daughter has converted, the holy Father would know. (*To the Bishop.*) Do you know something, my dear sir?

BISHOP. This is news to me, Excellency . . .

YOUNG DUKE. Father, I want to know . . .

DUKE. Young man! We haven't finished our business yet.

MOYSHE. Save me, Excellency, I throw myself at your feet!

DUKE. Hey, Moshek, you want your daughter? You know what? We'll play chess for her right now. Hey, scoundrel, where are you? (*Clown leaps onstage.*) Bring the chessboard here. Right here on the ground, next to Moshek. Don't drop it. I'll finish the game I started with the holy Father. Why are you all staring at me like that? Every ruler has his whims. If you play like your grandfather, Moshek, you're in luck. Old Zadok won his lease from my father, and you'll win your daughter from me. Why are you staring at me? The game's not fair? I've got nothing at stake? Old Zadok bet his beard and sidecurls; you—your daughter; and I—nothing? That's not the case, you hear? The duke has plenty at stake here—far more than you think . . . But that's his affair. Let the game begin!

MOYSHE. (*Astonished.*) My excellent Lordship, what do you want from me? I should wager my flesh and blood? Play—when my head is splitting?

DUKE. Hey, Moshek, all this time that you're talking, you could be winning. (*He kneels by the chessboard.*) Don't you want to play? (*Gestures as if he's about to overturn the board.*)

MOYSHE. (*Grabs him by the arm.*) Ay! My life is in your hands! I'm playing, I'm playing! (*They stare at each other for a long time and begin to play.*)

DUKE. There's my move.

MOYSHE. (*Grabs his head.*) *Oy vey iz mir!* If that's your move, then that's mine.

DUKE. Hey, hey! I'll attack you like that . . .

MOYSHE. Then we'll . . . we'll defend ourselves.

DUKE. (*Makes a quick move.*) Your turn, Moshek!

MOYSHE. Oy vey, lost! No, no, I haven't lost my daughter yet, my Nekhamele, the apple of my eye. Hee hee hee! Your Excellent Lordship! What are we doing here on the floor . . . two old men with a board between us . . .

DUKE. We're playing, my dear sir, we're playing a game of chess.

MOYSHE. Heh . . . is that what we're doing? . . . A great honor, I swear . . . Just as I thought. His Lordship is joking.

DUKE. He is not joking.

MOYSHE. A move is a move. Checkmate, my lord!

DUKE. Damn! Wait, wait, try to make your next move. Ha ha ha, we're both mated, Moshek! Neither of us can move. It's a draw, Moshek!

MOYSHE. What are you saying, Your Excellency?

DUKE. A draw, a draw! Hey, Fool, a draw! (*Stands up.*)

MOYSHE. (*Kneeling.*) What does that mean, a draw? And what about my daughter, ha? Nobles, people! Is God in your hearts? Take a rifle and shoot me! Moshek wants a bullet in his heart. He fully deserves it

. . . Nobles, lords, gentle people! Here kneels before you a little Jew, some sort of Moshek, and begs for your mercy: shoot him! Because he hates himself, this Moshek! Do him a favor: trample him! Do you enjoy seeing a man, a creature made in God's image, curled up and writhing on the ground like a trampled worm? Moyshe staked his daughter, staked his own flesh and blood. Hey, nobles, fine people, do you think you've turned Moshek into a dog? He's turned himself into a dog, and now he can't stand his own smell. Help me, God— how much can one of your creations hate himself? My hatred is as strong as the strongest wine, as sharp as the sharpest sword. My lord, if you have a single spark of mercy for one of God's creatures, then make an end of me!

DUKE. Take this Jew away! Why is he crawling underfoot? Why are you wailing for the whole palace to hear? You're making me angry, my dear man. Foolish Jew! We fared equally: both lost . . .

BISHOP. (*Lifts Moyshe, leads him to the door.*) Come, Moshek, you'll calm down, have a drink of cold water. Come . . .

MOYSHE. (*Allows himself to be led.*) What can I do, holy Father, when I despise myself so much? It's like a heavy stone on my heart. *We have trespassed! We have betrayed! We have strayed!*[27] Hatred! Hatred! (*The Bishop leads him out.*)

DUKE. (*Watches them go. Turns right, to his son. Looks at him.*) Your friends . . . Shliama . . . (*Exits right. The Young Duke grabs the scimitar. With a muffled roar he takes a step toward his father, then holds back.*)

YOUNG DUKE. Be still, Esau, vanish, die in my heart. That's not the way, no . . . Lowly Moshek, a thousand Mosheks, a nation of Mosheks! And the sacred truth—the legacy of the great and the exalted—is plagued and debased along with them. Like you, Moshek, who has wagered your daughter, I am choking with shame. But I shall tear myself away. I'm still a goy. I may do what Moshek cannot! This sword is sharp enough, and my hand is bold enough, and my throat is bare, like Isaac's on the altar. For your debasement and insult. Moshek! Esau's way, the bloody way . . . and Moshek, the thousand-headed Moshek, will keep being driven across an alien world, will bet his daughter again and again, against nobleman after nobleman, will continue to drink deep of others' hatred—and his own self-loathing . . . (*In his excitement, he presses his hand against the sword and cuts open his finger. He quickly pulls his hand back and wipes the blood in the open book of Shlomo Molcho. Stares at the bloody book.*) Eureka! What a great idea! What a simple, brilliant way out! Shlomo Molcho! My

---

27. The language is taken from the *Vidui*, the confessional prayer recited on Yom Kippur as well as on other occasions.

brother across the generations! Are you speaking to me? Is that your voice? Surely that is the right path, surely I must raise the truth from dust and disgrace, raise it up over the hateful world like a sparkling diamond. Die? You are telling me not to die . . . . To live, like you lived, to do what you did, to walk in your footsteps . . . . I don't have your divine genius, but I am a knight. So am I any less bold? Is my arm any weaker? Will my heart tremble? Brother Shlomo! You speak to me through the veil of generations and I hear your voice. And I walk in your footsteps . . . . And you, father duke, can be satisfied. Your honor is washed clean. There will be blood between you and your son—your son's blood. That blood will carve out a deep abyss between us . . . . (*Exits left with the sword. Clown creeps out from stage right.*)

CLOWN. What will happen here, ha? Who will he slaughter? Himself? Moshek? Maybe even the holy Father? I'm shaking in every limb. Why am I shaking? From fear? From joy? Maybe it's started? Maybe this is the mighty vengeance for generations of pain and shame? For my deceased grandfather? My disgraced mother? For my own broken rib? Ay, Moshek is right: this place can make you hate yourself. Oy, it's hard to be a clown among clowns! A clown among clowns! A clown among clowns! (*Exits left.*)

Scene 6

(*The Duke enters from stage right leading in Nekhamele as if they were dancing a minuet. She is dressed in aristocratic clothing.*)

DUKE. Come, come, my queen! For the moment you are my queen. On this very spot, your father, Moshek, kissed my feet so that I would return you to him. Have I stolen you away? Now I want everyone to see you. Now I want you to tell the world that returning to your father's tavern is the last thing you want.

NEKHAMELE. I am ready, my beloved, I am ready, my most excellent duke! I have followed my desire—from the land of mourning to the land of abandon. I only thought to find refuge in your palace, but I've found a soul like glorious wine. Hold me tightly in your arms, Excellency—me, who your foolish son did not understand how to hold. Your son is old, Duke, and you are young! Young and handsome and radiant and joyful. And when you let me go, I'll fly away to the wide world, with smoke and wind and all of the dark angels; all the hidden springs of pleasure and abandon from my grandmother and great-grandmother are opening inside me. Everything that withered in their lifetimes and rotted in the earth has been revived in me. Dozens of lives cry out from my breast, dozens of women roar within

me! We were tormented, tormented, our lives unlived! Hold me
tight, glorious duke. Like champagne, I'll pour out of your arms.
Embrace me . . . or kill me . . .

DUKE. Me—kill you? I'm not so young, my queen, that I can spend my
treasures so freely. One hour of living is better than years of playing
games. Embracing a young woman—better than empty arms. Let's
laugh at the world, let's drink to abandon. Kiss me, kiss me, harder!
Bite! . . . Now . . . I will kiss you . . . (*He lifts her up in the air. The Clown
and Bishop run in.*)

Scene 7

CLOWN. A disaster, Excellency! The young duke . . .
DUKE. (*Puts Nekhamele down.*) What, what's happened?
CLOWN. A river of blood . . .
BISHOP. With his sword! With the Turkish scimitar!
DUKE. Has he killed himself?
BISHOP. Worse, Excellency! . . . He circumcised himself!
DUKE. Circumcised?
CLOWN. Circumcised . . .

Curtain.

Act III

*A deep wine cellar. A vaulted ceiling with supporting posts. Dark corners. From the
left, a wide passageway leads down into the cellar. Near it, a small door to a second
passageway. In the distant background, a rack with barrels of wine; to the right, a
door to another room. A couple of tables, barrels to sit on. From behind the righthand
door, the drunken singing of several male voices and a shrill female one.*

Shoshanes yankev tsahole ve'samekha—ha ha . . .
Biroysam yakhad tkheles mordkhe—he he . . .
Tshuasam hayiso, tshuasam hayiso le'netsakh,
Ve'tikvasam, ve'tikvasam b'khol dor va'dor.[28]

---

28. "Shoshanat yaakov," or "The Rose of Jacob," is a liturgical poem conventionally recited
by traditional Jews on the holiday of Purim after the reading of the book of Esther. The
first stanza cited here, referring to the exultation of the Jews of Shushan when they see
Mordechai riding triumphant through the city streets (cf. Esther: 6:11), can be translated:

The rose of Jacob thrilled with joy and exulted
When they beheld Mordechai robed in royal blue.
You have always been their salvation,
Their hope, their hope in every generation.

Scene 1

DVOYRE. (*Emerging, angry, from the righthand door.*) The girl has no shame! Go try to reason with that piece of filth . . .

WOMAN'S VOICE. (*Behind the door, right.*) Dvoyreshi! Dvoyretshke! Bring more ale, may you live and be well! My Litvaks are thirsty!

DVOYRE. Would it kill you to wait, my lady!? Oh, I'll serve her, alright! May my enemies be sick for as long as she'll be waiting . . . But on the other hand, what have the Litvaks done wrong? Came to the fair—wanted to have a little fun. And what's wrong with my doing an honest bit of business? (*She goes to the rack, taps a barrel, and fills a pitcher, which she passes through the righthand door.*) There's your ale, take it! Be a mentsh and keep a tab. Might the Litvaks want anything else? (*Shuts the door.*) Tfu!

Scene 2

(*Yoshke rushes in from the broad passageway at left and bars the door. Dvoyre is astonished.*)

DVOYRE. What's happening?

YOSHKE. (*Walking around in a rage.*) None of your business!

DVOYRE. Something's lit a fire under him . . .

YOSHKE. The whole town can go burn, and us along with it. Oy, God, why won't you send down a proper fire?

DVOYRE. He's gone completely mad.

YOSHKE. Of course, what did you expect? With you on one side and her (*Gesturing toward the door at right.*) on the other, do I even stand a chance of staying sane?

DVOYRE. You're comparing me to her? To the town's . . . girl? But my husband: if you're so willing to sacrifice yourself for her, why didn't you do it earlier? You're think you're so smart, but you're kidding yourself.

YOSHKE. Tfu! I'd certainly look great if I . . . and my enemies should end up the way I'd look to you. A laughingstock. Act like an important citizen, serve as a trustee, and behind my back every one of them gives me the finger.

DVOYRE. O wise one, how do you know what goes on behind your back?

YOSHKE. I can feel it, woman! The shame is eating me up. What do you think, I have no sense of honor?

DVOYRE. Just look at him, Yoshke with his honor, ha ha ha! If you had any sense of honor at all, you wouldn't have come to this. You wouldn't have let her come here, the town whore. Yoshke, prepare yourself for a bad end. Do you think the town's gonna keep quiet? They'll chew you up and spit you out. I'm so ashamed!

YOSHKE. So what do you want, woman? Should I drive her out? I just can't. Tear me to pieces, but I just can't do it! Women have already gone running to the rabbi, the whole town will be here soon, you fool!

DVOYRE. I'm cursed! That's why you barred the door? Where can we hide? Where can we run to? My God, you bastard, what do you want from poor little me?

YOSHKE. Maybe it wasn't worth it? Did you have a choice? (*A knock on the cellar door at left.*)

DVOYRE. Oy, they're here already, they're coming in through the cellar, through the back door. I'll die of shame . . . of shame . . . (*Runs out right.*)

YOSHKE. Who's knocking there? Who the hell is coming in through the cellar? You couldn't come in from the street?

Scene 3

(*The door opens. A nobleman slips in, his collar raised above his face. Yoshke backs away, frightened.*)

NOBLEMAN. No one's with you, Yoshke?

YOSHKE. What? Who should be here? A wine cellar . . . May I bring His Lordship a glass of ale?

NOBLEMAN. (*Folds down his coat collar.*) Don't you recognize me, Yoshke?

YOSHKE. (*Surprised.*) Oh my God! His Excellency! In my cellar! Here! I'll run and call my wife!

DUKE. Sh-sh! Stay, my dear man! No one need be here.

YOSHKE. But my God, Your Excellency!

DUKE. Why are staring like that, my dear man? I've come to repay my debt to you. Or have you already become wealthy? Do you still remember the debts that respectable people owe you?

YOSHKE. What sort of debts, Excellency?

DUKE. (*Throws him a purse full of money.*) Don't you remember the bear's trousers?

YOSHKE. But Excellency, that was just a joke. His Excellency was joking.

DUKE. You're not in on the joke, scoundrel! Take what's given to you! You're making me angry, my dear man! (*Yoshke picks up the purse.*) Now answer, Yoshke, and to the point: where is the young duke?

YOSHKE. Oh my God, what happened to the young duke?

DUKE. I'm asking you, my dear man. Where is he?

YOSHKE. (*Falls to his knees.*) My dear Lordship, how should a poor tailor know what to say? May I never be involved in such things. Perhaps— heh heh heh! Perhaps His Excellency is joking?

DUKE. I'm not joking. Answer me now: have you heard news of him? The duke can reward you richly, but woe to the man who makes him angry.

YOSHKE. Your Excellency, why should Yoshke take the fall for all the Jews? I haven't heard anything, haven't said anything—quiet as a mouse. The rabbi even forbade us to mention his name.

DUKE. What? Forbade you to say the duke's name?

YOSHKE. Excellency, I'm shaking like a leaf. I'll tell you everything I've heard the Jews saying. But . . . but it's just stuff that we Jews have made up, hee hee hee!

DUKE. Made up what?

YOSHKE. People are saying—please don't get angry—people are saying that the young duke was very ill, because . . . he converted, hee hee hee! That is, he became a Jew.

DUKE. Go on, my dear man, go on.

YOSHKE. His Excellency isn't angry? Nu, the rabbi forbade us to mention this; that way there wouldn't be any decrees against us, God forbid.

DUKE. And?

YOSHKE. What else? May I never hear such bad things. All we know is that the young duke got better and left the country.

DUKE. And you know nothing else, my dear man?

YOSHKE. What should I know? How should I know? (*The Duke pushes him away. Yoshke stays on the ground far from the Duke.*)

DUKE. Come here, Yoshke. Can you keep a secret?

YOSHKE. If His Excellency commands it!

DUKE. Listen carefully, my dear man, listen carefully. The young duke was ill when he left.

YOSHKE. He really *was* sick?

DUKE. Quiet, scoundrel! He went away because the air here was harmful to him.

YOSHKE. What do you mean?

DUKE. Quiet, my dear man! My son disappeared while abroad; I've learned that he returned home, but I don't know where he is. And the air here is harmful to him.

YOSHKE. The air is harmful . . .

DUKE. He must leave. He must leave here, my dear man.

YOSHKE. He must . . .

DUKE. So help me find him!

YOSHKE. Me?!

DUKE. You. Here's here . . . among you.

YOSHKE. Oy, my head!

DUKE. Shh!

YOSHKE. Excellency! How could you think that?

DUKE. Have you heard any news of him?

YOSHKE. Me? No, Excellency. But why doesn't His Excellency ask the innkeeper, Moshke? After all, he—His Excellency won't be angry?—he was a regular at Moshke's.

DUKE. I cannot ask Moshke.

YOSHKE. His Excellency can't? His Excellency can do anything.

DUKE. Not anything, my dear man, not anything. Moshke will ask me where his daughter is.

YOSHKE. And does His Excellency have to know?

DUKE. Apparently so.

YOSHKE. But, my God! That's easy to find out. I can find that out. (*A knock at the door.*)

DUKE. Yoskhe, none of your people can see me here.

YOSHKE. Fine, Excellency, fine. Oh my God . . . I understand everything . . .

DUKE. (*Gets ready to leave.*) But Yoshke!

YOSHKE. Fine, Excellency, fine. I'll find out. I'll take care of it.

DUKE. You scoundrel, my good man! (*Exits. Yoshke accompanies him out through the narrow cellar door. Dvoyre comes running in from the right.*)

Scene 4

DVOYRE. Where is Yoshke? Who's knocking there? I'm coming, I'm coming! (*Runs into Yoshke. He holds the purse up and shakes it. He looks very excited.*) Tfu! Tfu! Yoshke! Look at you, Yoshke! Have you killed someone? What's that money? Who was that nobleman?

YOSHKE. Money! Money! You have no idea! Quiet, woman! Earned it honestly, sweated for it. Maybe you think you've become so respectable—no, sister, this here is for the bear's trousers. A purse in the hand—a knife in the heart!

DVOYRE. *Vey iz mir!* The Jew is touched in the head. Yoshke, hide the money! Yoshke, someone's knocking!

YOSHKE. They can knock their heads against the wall! You think I'm afraid of them? I can buy and sell every one of them!

DVOYRE. What do we do, Yoshke? Should I open the door?

YOSHKE. Don't bother me, woman! For me, today's a holiday. Ha! Yoshke has a secret. Yoshke has the duke by the throat. Yoshke, be a man, Yoshke! Be a Jew, Yoshke! Be second to none! . . . Oy, Yoshke will run out into the marketplace, pick up a drum: People! Hear what can happen, people, ha ha ha! The air is harmful. Are you a Jew, Yoshke? You're despicable!

DVOYRE. *Vey iz mir,* what's going on here, people? (*From behind the righthand door, a song is suddenly heard.*)
Shoshanes yankev tsahole ve'samekha—ha ha . . .
Biroysam yakhad tkheles mordkhe—he he . . .

Scene 5

NEKHAMELE (*Dancing onstage with several drunken Litvaks.*) Take away the tables, clear away the benches! Here's a space to dance; I'll teach you how to dance right here! Just like the nobles, just like the goyim! Make a circle, good-for-nothings! Spin, spin, spin in a circle! The tailor and the barmaid, the warden and his wife! (*They dance in the circle, Yoshke and Dvoyre caught in the middle.*)
Shoshanes yankev tsahole ve'samekha—ha ha . . .

YOSHKE. Nekhamele, let me have a word with you, Nekhamele! It's important, very important!

NEKHAMELE. (*Dancing.*) Get away from me. Keep your tailor's paws off of me. I'm not here for your sake, but for these fine people. Look at how we dance, this is how we dance, this is how we kick up our feet! Like the goyim do, like princes do. Whoever looks down gets his eyes poked out. The first time, you go blind. The second time, you die.
Shoshanes yankev tsahole ve'samekha—ha ha . . .

DVOYRE. Let me out! No good can come of this! Let me out! I'll pour water all over you!

NEKHAMELE. You're a joke! No one listens to a word you say, newly-minted madame! *I'm* in charge here! Once you're in the circle, you'll never get out. Go wild, people! Into the circle! I'll bring everyone into the dance, the whole town, young and old! And all the big shots, and the rabbi and the bathhouse keeper! I've got a bone to pick with her: why do I have to wait 'til Sarah the warden's wife gets out of the bathhouse? She's just one person's wife; I belong to everyone! Ha ha ha!
Shoshanes yankev tsahole ve'samekha—ha ha . . .
And I swear to you, people—the holy oath of the town whore! I'll get the yeshiva itself! All the students will sin with me! Just you wait! Just let me get my hands on Avremele the Studious, the rabbi's treasure. He'll dance with me just like this, he'll hit the sky, he'll crash through the floor.
Shoshanes yankev tsahole ve'samekha—ha ha . . .

YOSHKE. Nekhamele, Nekhamele, just listen to me!

DVOYRE. Crazy, crazy, tfu! Worthless! (*The Litvaks and Nekhamele dance in a circle.*)

Tsahole ve'samekha, ha, ha, ha! . . . (*No one hears the knocking at the door. The door finally gives, bursts open.*)

Scene 6

(*Enter the Rabbi; two religious Jews, one a Hunchback, the other a Cripple; and following them, two Attendants from the Jewish court, one of them fat and the other one thin. All of them stand on the stairs, watching the drunken dance in a rage. Finally, the Rabbi makes a gesture and descends deeper into the cellar with the religious Jews. The Attendants stay by the door.*)

RABBI. So this is how the rabbi meets with the town's aristocrats? You bar the door to the public and commit adultery openly?

RELIGIOUS JEWS. Ach! Ach! . . .

NEKHAMELE. (*Continues leading the dance.*) Ignore him, people, ignore him! Spin, people! Spin in a circle, bring in the Rabbi and the community, everyone follow me, everyone follow me! *Shoshanes yankev tsahole ve'samekha—ha ha* . . . Ha ha ha! We've turned the rabbi into a rabbi-for-a-day! Turned the community into a Purim play![29] To hell with the community! To hell with the Jews—the pious, good Jews! We spin away from the Torah and into wantonness, into wantonness! It's about time, long overdue! (*The circle has by this point engulfed the Rabbi and the two religious Jews.*) See, people? What did I tell you, what did I say? Everyone will come, everyone will succumb to my power, to my spell. I'm a witch, a witch! Rabbi, Rabbi! A ransom, pay the woman her ransom! I want the most handsome student for my husband! I want the best scholar for my husband! Bring me Avremele the Studious! Bring Avremele the Studious down here! I want . . . I want the moon on a silver platter. If not, you'll stay and spin in the circle 'til the end of time, 'til the end of time! . . . *Shoshanes yankev tsahole ve'samekha—ha ha* . . .

RABBI. What! What! Wanton woman! Outcast! You vile piece of garbage! You dare mention the holy name of Avremele the Studious? (*To the Hunchback.*) Yerakhmiel, why don't you say something? Yerakhmiel, save me from this hell!

---

29. Literally, a "purim rabbi" and a "purim shpil." On the significance of these to the history of the Yiddish theatre, see the introduction.

HUNCHBACK. (*A booming voice.*) Quiet, drunkards, bastards, scoundrels! Respect for the town rabbi! (*The circle collapses as the drunken merchants leap into the corners.*)

MERCHANTS. (*Rubbing their eyes.*) The rabbi, it's the rabbi himself! Fantastic . . .

NEKHAMELE. The circle collapsed, ha ha ha! . . . Who will dance with me next? What are you afraid of? You're looking for somewhere to hide? Hide under my dress!

HUNCHBACK. (*To one of the Attendants.*) Go get the yeshiva students; we'll have a war on our hands with this bunch of drunks. (*The Assistant goes.*)

RABBI. (*To Yoshke.*) Nu, my treasure! Barred the door to the rabbi and the community, and thought he'd get away with it. The world's gone mad, no?

DVOYRE. *Oy, vey iz mir,* troubles are just raining down on us!

YOSHKE. Sha, woman! Rebbe, I'm . . . . I'm a truly sinful man . . . . Sit down, Rebbe . . . . Such guests . . . one could say . . . Such eminent guests . . . . Sit, Rebbe . . . . Why are you standing, Dvoyre? . . . What are you rolling your eyes for? . . . Bring something to sit on, my wife! . . . Something to nibble on . . . How are you, Rebbe? . . . Accept my best wishes! (*Left standing with his hand outstretched.*)

HUNCHBACK. You betrayer of Israel, you so-and-so! You crawl to the rabbi with "best wishes?"

CRIPPLE. Listen up, he really means it!

HUNCHBACK. The community leaders have come to you, do you understand, idiot? The leaders! A delegation of Jews has come to you, the town's leading lights, led by the rabbi, may he be well. For the time being, the merchants have stayed behind in the marketplace. There's some problem with tomorrow's fair. But just wait, they'll be coming.

CRIPPLE. Listen up, he really means it!

DVOYRE. Oh, I'm cursed!

HUNCHBACK. Not just cursed, woman, but cursed ten times over. When the town gets its hands on this dark lair of yours, it'll turn its guts inside out.

CRIPPLE. Listen up, he really means it!

YOSHKE. Rebbe, people, may God be with you! What do you want from me?

RABBI. Look at that impudent face of his. He has no idea what we want from him. Tell him, Yerakhmiel. Spell it out in black and white.

HUNCHBACK. You've turned this place into a whorehouse, you enemy of Israel! Men from their wives, fathers from children, young people from the Torah—all of them are torn away and dragged into the dark swamp.

NEKHAMELE. (*Pushes Yoshke away.*) Let me talk, Yoshke, let me speak! (*Stands with her hands on her hips.*) Just look at the destruction a town whore can cause—a laughingstock, I swear! Just tell me, Rebbe—you know how these things work: which counts more, the sin she brings into the town, or the sin for which she can . . .

RABBI. People, help, people . . . where have you brought me? Stop up her filthy mouth! . . .

HUNCHBACK. Quiet, tramp, quiet, Lilith! . . .

NEKHAMELE. I will not be quiet, that's what God gave me a mouth for . . . Jews want to sin, Jews have to sin, just like everyone else!

HUNCHBACK. Shut your mouth! (*Strikes her with his cane.*) You'll be tarred and feathered, and driven through the market to the sound of a drum . . .

NEKHAMELE. Aaah! . . . (*She runs into her room and shuts the door.*)

HUNCHBACK. You won't be able to hide from the town that way. People, attend to her. (*The Merchants emerge from the corners. The Attendant and the Cripple, led by the Hunchback, approach Nekhamele's door.*)

DVOYRE. Oy, this is a catastrophe . . . (*Retreats somewhere into the background.*)

CRIPPLE. Listen up, he really means it!

YOSHKE. (*Runs and blocks Nekhamele's door.*) People, Rabbi, don't disgrace me, don't bother the woman, don't lay a hand on her! I will . . . I'll pack her things myself, send her away—but quietly, without a scandal.

HUNCHBACK. Take him away, throw him out, twist his arms behind his back! What arrogance! Still getting in our way! (*Yoshke wrestles with the assailants. They drag him away from the door. The Cripple trips him with his big, thick cane. Yoshke falls.*)

CRIPPLE. Listen up, he really means it!

HUNCHBACK. (*Panting.*) As strong as five goyim. Bring your belts over here! Tie him to the post—to the post! (*They tie Yoshke's hands, stand him up, then bind him to the post.*)

RABBI. (*Sits turned away, covering his face with his hands.*) Oy, a shame, a disgrace! The things my eyes have seen!

HUNCHBACK. Now, people, we'll see to the other one! (*They push against the door. Nekhamele retreats. With each push and bang on the door, its hinges squeak. The rabbi looks at Yoshke, who is tied to the pillar.*)

RABBI. Nu, my treasure! You've done pretty well for yourself, eh? You won't get a pat on the head for this. You'll rot in prison like a dog, with a chain around your neck! "Whoever goes by, will spit in your eye."[30] What a scoundrel. Dying to be a big shot, ha? How do you like that, folks: Yoshke the big shot, eh?

---

30. This is rhymed in the original, giving the sense of a folk saying.

THE THREE ATTACKERS. Ha ha ha ha!

YOSHKE. (*Crying.*) Rabbi, I swear I'm not guilty—cross my heart, Rabbi. It's nothing, a hole in my heart. *Oy, vey iz mir!* Someone might think that . . . a man with two wives, *oy, vey iz mir!* Rabbi! I swear, I was a widower, and a widower I'll remain . . . (*In the meantime, the door has been torn off its hinges and Nekhamele has been dragged out and tied with belts to the other post.*)

HUNCHBACK. (*Panting.*) Well, you tramp? You want to scratch? We'll cut those nails down to size! . . .

NEKHAMELE. People, a terrible end awaits you—I'll rat you out to the duke.

ATTACKERS. Ha ha ha ha ha ha! . . .

YOSHKE. (*Shudders.*) Ha? . . . What? . . . To who? . . .

HUNCHBACK. As if he'll listen to you . . . The town, on the other hand . . . Throw out her filthy things, throw them out! Burn them in a pile in the middle of the marketplace! (*The Caretaker throws pillows, linens, various pieces of clothing out of the room. The Cripple bundles them up and hurls them out the door onto the staircase. Some of the things get scattered and trampled underfoot. Nekhamele bursts into tears. Yoshke tries to tear himself away from the pilllar.*)

YOSHKE. Rabbi, people, burn me, roast me alive! I can't stand this hell! As long as she doesn't cry! Just make her stop crying!

CRIPPLE. Listen up, he really means it! (*He tosses one of the bundles, which hits one of the town Merchants who enter at that very moment.*)

Scene 7

FIRST MERCHANT. (*Hit by the bundle.*) God damn it! What's going on here?

HUNCHBACK. We're driving out the whore.

CRIPPLE. (*Preparing to throw another bundle.*) Listen up . . .

FIRST MERCHANT. The things people have time for! We're in deep trouble, people—no fair tomorrow!

EVERYONE. What?

FIRST MERCHANT. The nobleman has issued a decree: the city gates are to be locked!

EVERYONE. A disaster!

FIRST MERCHANT. The city will collapse, we'll be left without a livelihood.

SECOND MERCHANT. Out-of-town merchants are scattering like mice.

THIRD MERCHANT. Craftsmen are howling like wolves.

RABBI. And why are you so quiet, ha? Why aren't you running straight to the duke? Why don't you beg for mercy? Jews are out of work, *vey iz mir!*

FIRST MERCHANT. What, you think he lets just anybody see him? No one can even find him. His coach is outside the town hall, all harnessed, ready to take off at any minute.

RABBI. So why so quiet, people? We're in great danger!

CRIPPLE. Listen up, he really means it!

FIRST MERCHANT. So what are you doing, genius, with women's clothes in your hands?

CRIPPLE. (*Throwing them aside.*) Tfu! . . . (*Everyone forgets about Yoshke and Nekhamele for a while. They look around, silently, perplexed, each hoping for an answer from the others.*)

YOSHKE. Ha ha ha! . . . What do you all think? That the nobleman won't let the fair go on? Untie my hands, I'll take care of it!

HUNCHBACK. You? You? What arrogance! Your elders have tried, better Jews than you.

RABBI. Sha, Yerachmiel, let him speak.

YOSHKE. I can, like I said, I probably can. You should know, the duke was here today!

HUNCHBACK. Liar! The duke was here in his cellar! Did you hear?

YOSHKE. You don't believe me? Then take a look at the purse he gave me—you'll see if it's his or not.

HUNCHBACK. (*Picks up the purse, which Yoshke had dropped during the scuffle. Examines the embroidered coat of arms. Astonished.*) The duke's coat of arms, as I live and breathe. Rabbi, look! (*The Rabbi and the others look at the purse, shaking their heads.*) A fortune!

YOSHKE. Nu, don't you think I can pull it off? If Yoshke says! . . .

FIRST MERCHANT. Untie his hands, untie him from the pillar!

RABBI. Wait, wait, it's a complicated matter.

FIRST MERCHANT. Rabbi, what else can we do? If you need a thief, you take him down from the gallows.[31]

YOSHKE. (*Annoyed.*) I'm no thief, people! Tell me what I've stolen, huh?

FIRST MERCHANT. (*Somewhat chastened.*) It's just an expression.

YOSHKE. Save your expressions for your friends!

HUNCHBACK. Some nerve!

YOSHKE. People, untie me! Why should I be stuck here, huh? If you don't, it'll be easier to see your own ears than tomorrow's fair.

HUNCHBACK. Well, rabbi? . . .

RABBI. (*Turns away. Makes a gesture with his hand.*) Let the people do as they wish.

CRIPPLE. Listen up, he really means it! (*He is the first to begin untying Yoshke. Others help him. Yoshke is freed.*)

---

31. This is in fact a Yiddish proverb: *Az men darf a ganef, nemt im arop fun der tlie.*

YOSHKE. (*Rubbing his wrists.*) Such cruelty! Those ropes cut my wrists.

RABBI. Well, my treasure, what do you say now?

YOSHKE. I say, Rabbi . . . I say to untie that woman. Without her there won't be any fair . . .

HUNCHBACK. Are you crazy, or feeble minded? People, he's mocking us.

YOSHKE. How is that mockery? I'm not mocking. You're making a mockery of yourselves. The coach is waiting, the duke can take off at any moment! Untie the woman, I tell you, let her go! You're taking the bread out of your own mouths.

HUNCHBACK. Nu, what do you say, Rabbi?

FIRST MERCHANT. I can't wait to see what will come of this.

RABBI. Tell me, Yoshke, what is this money for? It's a fortune!

YOSHKE. Kosher money, rabbi, not stolen goods. And I don't owe anyone an accounting. But if you really want to know, then I'll tell you: for this money I'm to prepare that woman for His Excellency.

NEKHAMELE. Who, me? . . . But I don't want to, no!

HUNCHBACK. Quiet, tramp, who's asking you?

RABBI. What does His Excellency have to do with this woman?

YOSHKE. That, Rabbi, is none of our business.

FIRST MERCHANT. But how do we get a fair out of this?

YOSHKE. All I'm hearing is a lot of chatter! If you set her free . . . if you beg her pardon—and ask her nicely—she is the only one who can prevail upon the duke.

HUNCHBACK. Tfu!

CRIPPLE. Listen up!

FIRST MERCHANT. Her, this one here, the people should beg *her* pardon?

RABBI. My children, the man is truly insane . . .

DVOYRE. (*Runs in, overjoyed.*) Ha, they let him go, they set him free? Well after all, he's innocent as a lamb, he's . . .

NEKHAMELE. (*Cutting her off.*) But who said I would go to the duke? Who said I would plead for your fair? Go ahead: strip me naked, tar and feather me, drive me through the marketplace to the beat of a drum. I want nothing to do with your fairs, I won't plead to the duke for you!

DVOYRE. What? You're making her our envoy?

FIRST MERCHANT. (*To Nekhamele.*) Listen, what's this all about? It's beneath you all of a sudden?

NEKHAMELE. (*Shouting, tearfully.*) I don't want to go, people, I can't go, I can't go to the duke.

DVOYRE. Damn! You mean we *are* sending her to the duke? And begging her, to boot?

HUNCHBACK. No one's begging yet.

FIRST MERCHANT. No? Why not? If she can really do something . . . What do I care who the help comes from?

YOSHKE. Bring her things back in.

HUNCHBACK. People, throw her things back here.

CRIPPLE. Listen up . . . (*She is untied. Scattered bundles and things are tossed back into the cellar.*)

FIRST MERCHANT. (*To the Rabbi.*) Well, what does the Rabbi have to say?

RABBI. What should I say, my dear people? . . . When it comes to business, I'm sure the people will listen to me like—well, like a rabbi . . . but I must tell you the truth: I'm hardly pleased with the messenger. . . . Through *her* the city must be saved?

NEKHAMELE. Oy, Rabbi, you're right, it's the absolute truth. The town won't be saved through me. I won't go to the duke, even if I knew . . .

FIRST MERCHANT. What do you mean, you won't go? What is this about not going? What if we ask you nicely? Sort out her things there, don't leave them lying around! (*No one does it.*)

DVOYRE. (*Calming down somewhat.*) What's with you, Nekhamele? If the people ask you nicely, you shouldn't be a pig about it.

HUNCHBACK. And no one's forcing you. What do you think, Rabbi? If she behaves herself, she won't embarrass anyone, will she? Nonsense, nonsense. If you don't want something, it doesn't tempt you.

CRIPPLE. Listen up, he really means it!

Scene 8

(*The Warden's Wife and other women enter, singing a melody from a women's prayer book.*)

WARDEN'S WIFE. Oy, what can we do? We're cursed! People, people, what are you doing here? . . . Children are crying in their cradles! A catastrophe has descended upon us! Children will die, poor things, for lack of a drop of milk! And there won't be any flour, or cornmeal either. Nothing but crumbs.

HUNCHBACK. Sha, what's happened?

WARDEN'S WIFE. (*Bluntly.*) What do you mean, what's happened? The city has lost its livelihood! The duke is leaving, and the fair's called off! You think the women will keep quiet? We'll tear your beards out, stupid men! How did you let this happen? How could you let this happen?

FIRST MERCHANT. Nu, Rabbi?

RABBI. I beg of you, people, don't ask for my advice. Do as you see fit. I'm an old man, a shell. Why have you latched onto me? Can I squeeze blood from a stone? Can I guarantee the town a livelihood? You heard—this is no laughing matter!

CRIPPLE. Listen up, he really means it!

FIRST MERCHANT. (*To Nekhamele.*) That means you'll go to the duke, woman. Right, Rabbi?

NEKHAMELE. But people, tear me to shreds, I can't go to the duke, I can't ask him!

FIRST MERCHANT. What do you mean, you can't? Aren't you a Jewish girl, God forbid? Don't you feel anything when a town loses its livelihood? You don't mind if little children are snuffed out like candles? If the town has to go begging from fellow Jews from town to town? Don't you have a Jewish heart?

NEKHAMELE. I don't know what sort of heart I have. I must have some sort of heart, because I can't go to the Duke.

FIRST MERCHANT. What, have you robbed him, God forbid?

NEKHAMELE. Maybe I've robbed him, maybe even assaulted him . . .

FIRST MERCHANT. Ha ha! Assaulted him? Well, he's alive and well—all Jews should be so lucky. He was just here at Yoshke's today.

NEKHAMELE. (*Crying.*) If you don't understand, people, what can I do? You just don't understand.

FIRST MERCHANT. Okay, we're simple people, maybe we don't understand. But the Rabbi, may he be well, he probably does. What do you say, Rabbi?

NEKHAMELE. (*Laughing through her tears.*) Who, the Rabbi?

RABBI. Yes, woman, don't be so surprised. I think I have some idea. I suspect you broke the duke's heart. You have a Jewish heart, so it's hard for you to face him?

NEKHAMELE. Rabbi, Rabbi! God bless you, that's it!

FIRST MERCHANT. But the town is asking you—the whole town is begging you—to be our emissary, and may God be with you. Isn't that right, people?

EVERYONE. Of course, of course!

CRIPPLE. (*Separately.*) Listen up . . .

HUNCHBACK. It wouldn't be the first time that a woman saved the Jews from an evil decree.[32]

FIRST MERCHANT. Go, the whole town is begging you, go . . .

WARDEN'S WIFE. My child . . . I can see that you can save the town. Do you want us to cry at your feet? Do you want us to bring you our little infants in our arms? Fine, that's what we'll do! I'm telling you, people, may my entire life be as beautiful as she is. She is a queen, a real queen! No more . . . (*She blows her nose and goes silent.*)

---

32. The reference—given the situation of a Jewish woman going to attend to a non-Jewish ruler—is almost certainly to Esther's unwillingness, then decision, to go to Ahasuerus. See Esther 4:8-17.

DVOYRE. Beautiful? She should only act as beautiful as she looks.

HUNCHBACK. Sha, woman . . .

CRIPPLE. Listen up . . .

RABBI. Nu, my child, you see, it's turned out for the best. The people must turn to you for help. Doesn't that mean something to you? Doesn't it make you feel powerful?

NEKHAMELE. No, Rabbi, I don't have any power at all.

RABBI. It will all work out.

YOSHKE. Enough, enough, the duke won't wait! Won't you get going already?

NEKHAMELE. Hmm . . . You see how it's turned out? I'm actually the messenger. Should I really go? It's so hard for a person like me to rise to the occasion. I'll try, I'll go. I'll appeal to the duke. But I'm afraid no good will come of it, people.

ALL. Why not?

NEKHAMELE. I don't know. I'll go. Jews need to make a living.

WARDEN'S WIFE. Wait, my child. That's how you're going to His Excellency the duke? That's how you'll appear before his royal presence—tattered and torn? Wait, let me fix you up a little. Women, what are you waiting for? Let's fix her up like a lady. (*The women, led by the Warden's Wife and Dvoyre, gather around her in a circle and arrange her clothes. One of them picks up a piece of cloth from the floor, dusts it off, and fastens it on her. Another throws a shawl around her shoulders. Dvoyre begins to take off her own rings and the Warden's Wife takes off her own earrings to put them on Nekhamele.*) Just wait, my child. You'll shine like the sun, you really will! Well, people? Take a look, is there anything to be ashamed of, ha?

NEKHAMELE. I don't need any jewelry, I don't need it. (*With the dark shawl covering her head and shoulders, she has come to look modest. Her expression is solemn and sad. She walks slowly to the staircase, turns back to the crowd, and looks down. Everyone looks at her silently. Yoshke jumps into her path. He stands by the open door.*)

YOSHKE. Enough, enough. The duke won't wait!

NEKHAMELE. People, maybe there's another emissary? A better one than me? I'm afraid that . . .

VOICES. No, no! You have nothing to be afraid of, we don't need anyone better. The town asks, the town sends you.

Scene 9

(*At that very moment the Attendant and Yeshiva Students come in, led by Avremele the Studious.*)

RABBI. (*Leaps to his feet. To Avremele.*) You? Avrom? What do I see? *Vey iz mir*, what are you doing here—in this swamp? This hell? Go back to the house of study, that's an order! (*Looks around.*) Who sent for these boys?

HUNCHBACK. I did, Rabbi. I thought we'd have a war on our hands.

AVREMELE. (*Descending the stairs.*) Why do you hide me from the world like this, Rabbi? Why do you think I mustn't set foot in this swamp, Rabbi? Why must I avoid this place, where Jews must do battle? Is that why I came to you—so you could treat me like a precious object, so you could admire me in private? I'm cut off from the Jewish community, even more than I was before. I want to suffer along with everyone else, share in the sufferings of all Israel. And that was all I wanted, after all. Rest and comfort, wealth and honor— I had all of that at home. I spat on all of that, turned my back on it. And although I'm a convert, I'm still among my own people, among Jews!

ALL. (*Quietly astonished.*) A convert? A convert? (*Some back away, some move closer to him.*)

AVREMELE. A convert, Avrom ben Avrom[33]—let the world know, people! The Rabbi has known for a long time, but kept it a secret. And I don't need secrets any longer. I don't want to live in hiding any more, for I am among Jews here, among brothers! . . .

RABBI. Avrom! God be with you! Quiet, people! Ask no more questions! Something terrible could happen, God forbid. Ever since this man came to me with a letter from distant rabbis, I haven't asked him a single question more than necessary. Sha, quiet! Have mercy! Settle down! I sincerely confess to you, God in Heaven, that I am a weak person, an old man. What sort of leader can I be if I'm afraid of my own shadow? Avrom! Avrom! Do me a favor, my friend! I beg of you, go away from here, keep all this quiet.

AVREMELE. No, Rabbi, you can't defeat evil by being quiet and fearful— all the evil around us, Rabbi! I wanted to be the quietest among you, I wanted to lock my young heart away within the four walls of the study house, I wanted to immerse myself, body and soul, in the sea of the holy books. But I'm not—people, I'm not the prodigy who uncovers the Torah's secrets, and who finds them his only solace. And I'm not—people, I'm not the saint, the recluse, who has the remedy for the broken world in the quiet depths of his heart. I can no longer live the quiet life; my forefathers were knights. And I want to live among you like a Jew, a man of valor. I want to wage war on the evil that faces us, and on the evil among us. We Jews have many prodigies and geniuses, but I cannot see the man who will raise a

---

33. The traditional Hebrew name given to a convert; "Abraham son of Abraham," after the figure considered to be the first Jew.

steady voice and a strong fist against the enemy without and the evil growing within.

RABBI. (*Trembling.*) Avrom, what do you want to do, Avrom? We are Jews, Avrom!

AVREMELE. I want . . . First of all I want to root out the evil among us. I've descended into this dark cave, this den of iniquity, not with a blessing on my lips, but with a fiery curse. All the evil growing within Israel must be stamped out! I want—first of all I want the Jews to be a chosen people. I want the people who carry the Torah inside them—God's word in the world—I want them to be pure as a newborn, as an angel; may we be a people of angels! May we be pure and holy! Torah and whoring, Torah and wine cellars, Torah and selling dusty old things in the marketplace—how can that be? The Torah is holy and holy are its bearers—the people Israel. And if the people become sullied, they must be sanctified once more—with strong words, with a strong fist and with a strong curse! What are Jews doing in this dark netherworld? Our fine leaders have come here—to make what sort of deal with whores? Cursed be the Jewish hands who have done their filthy business in this cellar. May their children's heads be stopped up so that none of them become scholars! May they be ripped away from the Jewish people!

YOSKHE. (*On the stairs.*) Ah ah ah! Children! . . . (*Disappears. His distant cries can still be heard. Avremele the Studious takes a cat-o'nine-tails out of his shirt, unfurls it, and begins flailing left and right—at the women, at the Litvaks, at the remaining Merchants.*)

AVREMELE. Get out of the cellar, you sinful Jews who aren't worthy to bear that name. Out of the dark cellar, out of the ugly swamp, into the brilliant world, toward the brilliant sunshine! There we'll see which of you are black and which are white. (*He aims a blow at Nekhamele. She covers her face with her hands and bursts out laughing. Her laughter startles the entire group of Jews out of their paralysis.*)

NEKHAMELE. Ha ha! Me too? Oy, my dear people, the way things turn out! I've been standing here in shock. I couldn't speak, I was so astonished. So this is Avremele the Studious? This is who I've had sinful dreams about? He's the one I was dying to lead astray from the righteous path? This goy? But then I recognized his voice!

RABBI. (*Shouts with a voice that isn't his.*) Keep back, whore, don't go near him!

NEKHAMELE. Keep back? But we're old friends. How is His Excellency the young duke? Does the duke still remember the fiery kiss with which he honored a young Jewish girl, and ignited a great, sinful flame in her? Come, scholar. Not even a real scholar. Come dance with your old friend. With the town whore. I have the town's approval; you'll make them tremble. Come, Duke, dance with me. (*All the Jews remain as if frozen in place. The Rabbi approaches Nekhamele with his cane in the air.*)

RABBI. Get away, you and your crazy talk! What do you talking about, a duke? People, tear her away from him, she will defile him!

AVREMELE. Don't touch her, people, don't touch her—it's *my* sin! What she says is true. A goy once held her close, and that goy was the young duke. And the young duke—that was me. (*The crowd is frozen with fear.*)

NEKHAMELE. Ha ha ha! You won't let them? Well, if not, then not. I hate him, because he ruined me while he himself has been purified! Nothing will appease my hatred. Unless (*Cries.*) you give me the Scholar, the true Scholar, and let me lead him astray. (*She dances around Avremele, claps her hands and breaks into hysterical sobbing.*)

A VOICE FROM THE CORNER. (*Grating.*) And what about tomorrow's fair?

AVREMELE. (*Covering his face the whole time. Cries out.*) Oy, Jews!

Scene 10

(*A commotion by the doorway. All the Jews turn to the door, then back away in fear into the depths of the cellar. Only Avremele, Nekhamele, and the Rabbi remain in the middle. Two Christian Hermits dressed in black appear in the doorway, with black hoods pulled low over their eyes.*)

FIRST HERMIT. (*Raises an arm.*) There is an unbeliever here. In the name of the Church . . . we have come to demand . . .

AVREMELE. (*Shudders. Looks around. Turns.*) They've come for me. It's about time. Go, I'll follow you! (*Exits following the Hermits. A death-like silence falls over the crowd. Finally we hear men and women sobbing quietly as well as Nekhamele's scattered laughter.*)

RABBI. (*With a lost voice.*) Who . . . who informed?

HUNCHBACK. Yoshke's work!

CRIPPLE. Listen up . . .

Curtain.

Act 4

Scene 1

(*Distant church bells. An organ. Women's voices singing in unison. A bridge.*)

HERALD (*Goes up onto the bridge. Fanfare right, left. Calls out.*) A man will soon be burned according to the holy law of the Church. His body will return to dust and ashes, for from dust and ashes was he created; and his soul will return to God, for in God is its eternal rest. Had this man recognized His ways and not strayed neither to the right or to the left—all would have gone well for him in the bosom of the holy faith. For, approaching the end of his days, this man would have rejoiced at his deeds. And God the Almighty would have sent His angel and messenger to separate body from soul at the appointed time.

But this person did not recognize God's ways; he turned away from the true faith and cleaved to a false one. And the holy tribunal realized that this vessel of God's presence had been shattered. That a godly soul was imperiled in such a sinful body. And in its justice and mercy, the holy tribunal decided thus: to halt the blind gallop toward the gates of eternal suffering; to separate the divine soul from the sinful body before its appointed time; to return the body to dust and ashes, so the soul may return purified to its Creator.

A man will soon be burned according to the holy law of the Church. For the eternal praise of almighty God. For the comfort and joy of all believers. For the fear and trembling of all secret enemies, of all hidden enemies, of all open and concealed unbelievers. Amen!

Scene 2

WOODCUTTER (*Entering from stage right with a load of wood.*) Amen! I'm not too late, am I, gracious lord?

HERALD. No, not too late.

WOODCUTTER. Praise the Eternal One! All my life I'm dying to do a good deed, but someone quicker than me always grabs it right from under my nose. I try and I try, and what will I have to show for it in the next world? Nothin'. And you gotta prepare. I'm an old man, waited my whole life to do a good deed, heh heh heh! And not for nothing either. This here load of wood, for lighting the holy flame, to roast that sinful creature. Fine wood, dry wood, wood like almonds, wood like sweet ale, gathered branch by branch, white, brown. I'm a wood-cutter. With my sweat I've carved out a good deed. Heh heh heh! Thanks to God in Heaven. Here on Earth—may he be praised, eternally praised. I'm a woodcutter . . .

HERALD. Go with God, O diligent one, go with God! And may all God-fearing servants take example from your humble sincerity. (*Both exit left.*)

Scene 3

(*Two Noblemen enter stage right.*)

FIRST NOBLEMAN. We'll wait for the judges right here.

SECOND. And if we have to, we'll kneel to them.

FIRST. And if we must, we'll unsheathe our swords.

SECOND. It goes without saying that the punishment is too harsh—how can they let a nobleman be burned?

FIRST. Even if he is an unbeliever.

SECOND. Even the Holy Father would have mercy on him.

FIRST. But God is great. And Rome is far away. Until the old duke returns with the pardon, they'll have to delay the sentence.

SECOND. The messengers from Rome have already arrived, and the judges feign ignorance. They are hasty in their zeal.

Scene 4

(From stage right enter two Judges, one with the verdict on an unfurled scroll.)

FIRST NOBLEMAN. Halt, holy judges.

SECOND. In the name of all nobles, we beg for clemency for the accused.

FIRST JUDGE. Can earthly clemency be greater than Heaven's? For Heaven's mercy will be done.

FIRST NOBLEMAN. But the punishment is too harsh and the sinner is too young—and the time he has been given to repent is too short.

FIRST JUDGE. We would rather be accused of being too diligent, than of being too lenient. We have done what we could; we have spoken to the lost soul as to our own son. And with tears in our eyes, we have begged him to reconsider, to openly confess his error. But he proudly turned away from us. We shall see how proudly he turns his gaze to the fire of justice.

SECOND NOBLEMAN. But we ourselves should be his judges.

FIRST JUDGE. You are right, my lords, to wish to judge one of your own noble line. But when is this done? When, though shaming his line, the accused does not entirely uproot himself from it. This sinner, however, smashed his golden coat of arms just as he had stained the golden garb of the true faith. This sinner is a stranger to you, gentlemen. And only Almighty God in His eternal compassion remains the suffering Father of this lost soul.

Gentlemen, time is short. God's flock grows impatient, and we are standing here debating in the middle of the bridge. Let us leave this bridge, gentlemen. Thousands of impatient eyes are waiting to witness the fire of justice. And how fine that is! And how noble that is! Let us leave this bridge, gentlemen.

FIRST NOBLEMAN. We will not let you pass.

SECOND. If justice wavers, we will rely on the sword!

FIRST JUDGE. And how regrettable that would be! Do you wish to show, gentlemen, that the sword can subdue God himself? Noblemen! Do you wish to weaken the branch on which you sit, ignorant of how unsound and unsure it is? Noblemen! Don't you know that the fear of God—is the fear of you? That without fear there is no justice? No followers and no leaders? No slaves? No nobles? . . . (*The Noblemen are astonished. They let the judges pass.*)

Scene 5

SECOND NOBLEMAN. Is all lost?

FIRST. They're bringing the condemned this way. Let's speak to him ourselves. Stay, unhappy man, stay! (*The Young Duke, in a white robe and chains, enters from the right.*)

SECOND. And this was the pride of our line!

FIRST. Young nobleman! Drag your feet. Say nothing, do nothing. Stay here. Maybe a thought of repentance will blossom in the rocky soil of your heart. After all, you're too young to die—the time isn't ripe yet.

YOUNG DUKE. Who are you and what do you want, noble sirs? Why are you torturing a poor Jew on the last steps of his life's journey? Everything that could possibly be said to me has been said. Every argument that could be made, has been made. With threats and promises. All the gates of Heaven and Hell have been opened for me, and they have breathed on my stony heart with their flames and their ointments, with the fragrance of perfumes and the stench of sulfur. It seems that my heart is made of sterner stuff; it didn't give in, neither through fear nor through sweetness. But I am still a human being. I must submit to the rule of law. Is this your idea of nobility, my lords, to increase the pain of a condemned man beyond that? Do not impede my final, difficult journey, gentlemen.

FIRST NOBLEMAN. Young Duke! We are noblemen. We wish to help you, not torture you. Nobility is precious to us, and you still are one of us. We wish to save your life. Your father the duke has sped to Rome to plead for mercy. He will surely win you a pardon. But we must gain time, a bit of time. We must outwit your judges. Tell them your heart shuddered! Tell them you need to consider, that you still need to think things over. Your judges will be happy to hear it, and will order the crowd to disperse.

YOUNG DUKE. I thank the gentleman for his good intentions. But I have nothing to consider. See how large the mob has grown, gentlemen? Today my judges offer up a fiery sacrifice, but I offer one of my own, and the day I set foot on the pyre will burn in people's hearts for generations to come.

SECOND NOBLEMAN. Young Duke! You are more learned than we in the holy books of both faiths. But it is not your soul we wish to save, but your body. And if a fiery sacrifice is as important for you as for your judges—then just say the word, young Duke, and someone else will be burned in your place, under your name—someone who's broken man's laws, if not God's. The prisons are full of murderers and criminals.

YOUNG DUKE. (*Astonished.*) Gentlemen! Whose words are these? Whose messengers are you? Molcho! Holy brother in pain! You have granted me the beginning of your journey—give me its fiery end. Make me avoid the shadow of the middle of your journey. I cannot follow in your footsteps, I lack your strength. And I do not believe—no, I do not believe, that you could have known that in your place, oh Molcho, someone else was thrown into the fire. Though perhaps you needed to. Perhaps you had to. You had to live. Your life was necessary. But I . . . it is not my life, but my death, that is necessary, for myself and for my Jewish faith. Listen, gentlemen, I want to die. I want to die now, for my whole life's work lies in these last few steps to the pyre. Listen, gentlemen, you have not come here as my enemies, and so I make my final confession to you. My brothers cannot hear me, and they may not understand me. Though I have immersed my soul in the waters of Judaism, my back has not borne the Jewish yoke, and my aristocratic spine remains unbent. I carry the old, proud Judaism myself on behalf of a host of bowed Jewish backs. I am strong and noble enough to give up my soul in the fire. Before all the world, in the name of God almighty. I am strong enough to die as a Jew, but too weak to live as one. To live, dying limb by limb, in dust and in yearning, in all the marketplaces of the world, under horses' hooves; to gasp under the boots of the mighty; to utter the holy Name with bloody lips as one expires; all this heroism of the holy stones that pave the world. I was not made for that. Generations of hammer blows have not bent my back. And God knows my strengths and my weaknesses. I want to go to my death like a knight, to die like a Jewish knight, to die, to die before the world, for Jewish honor, for the greatness of God, who sanctifies His name in the crowd, blesses them—O God, who sanctifies Your name in the crowd! (*Exits left.*)

Scene 6

FIRST NOBLEMAN. All is lost!

SECOND. There was witchcraft in the judge's words. Even more witchcraft in his. Ach, if only a miracle would happen; if only night would suddenly fall!

FIRST. Or a flood would come and engulf the world.

SECOND. It will come, but when? . . . I hear wheels whirring.

FIRST. Me too. Could that be the duke? I can't believe it. (*From the right a whirring like thunder or music. The Noblemen strain to see. The Clown dances onto the stage with a drum.*)

CLOWN.   Tram tam tam, tram tam tam!
               For my grandpa, for my mother,
               And a family full of slaves!
               Oh, I will not tarry, brother!
               Tram tam tam, tram tam tam!
               When they burn him, when they roast him,
               I will run to see them toast him,
               Just to see that sight.
               Just to see it with my own eyes,
               How that proud one will be chastised,
               When he gets what he once gave.
               Oh, the vengeance of a slave!
               Many slaves!
               Oh, I'll take it to my grave!
               Tram tam tam!
               I will dance and I will skip,
               With my dislocated ribs,
               Always clapping as I go.
               You—enjoy your fancy things,
               Of your wife and child go sing—I
               Get to burn my foe!
               Who needs pity? What good's mercy?
               My long fast has made me thirsty,
               It's my holiday today.
               Devour, my eyes, the orange flame!
               Burn, branch of a noble name!
               Tram tam tam, tram tam tam!

(*The Noblemen let him pass, looking on in amazement. The Clown with his drum disappears stage left; meanwhile, we hear a violin from the right. The tune: "Shmaye mitn fidele" [Shmaye with His Violin].[34] Reb Zadok enters in tattered clothes and his Sabbath fur hat.*)

---

34. Musicologist Chana Mlotek notes that this is a variant of the refrain of the folksong, "Tsen brider" (Ten Brothers), in which the number of brothers is reduced, one per verse, until no one is left. Ginsburg and Marek's authoritative collection of Yiddish folksongs renders the chorus as "Shmerl mit dem fidl, / Yankl mit dem bas, / Shpilt mir oyf a lidl / Oyfn mitn gas!" (Shmerl with his violin, Yankl with his bass, play me a song in the middle of the street.) Y. L. Cahan's folksong collection changes the names to "Yokl with his violin, Berl with his bass." And Mlotek's own collection has Shmerl on violin, Tevye on bass. See S. M. Ginsburg and P. S. Marek, *Evreiskiya narodniya piesni v rossii* (St. Petersburg, Voskhod', 1901), 102–103; Y. L. Cahan, *Yidishe folkslider mit melodyes* (1912; repr. New York: YIVO, 1957), 340; and Eleanor and Joseph Mlotek, *Pearls of Yiddish Song: Favorite Folk, Art and Theatre Songs* (New York: Education Department of the Workmen's Circle, 1988), 121–123.

Scene 7

REB ZADOK. Once upon a time I had two faithful grandchildren.

A boy and a girl—both, you see.

Now their granddad's leading them to the wedding canopy . . .

Where are you running to with your drum, jester? I can't keep up with you. The whole orchestra is disappearing . . .

I married off two loyal children.

Now I'm alone, I'm left all alone.

What will become of my old bones?

Jester, jester! Where did you and your drum run off to? Ran away and left me here alone—all alone. At sea. (*Exits.*)

FIRST NOBLEMAN. Let's get out of here. We'll run wherever our legs take us.

SECOND. Stay, stay,—the whole world has gone mad. There's nowhere to run.

Scene 8

(*From the right an Old Woman in white enters with a little pot of water and a cane. Crosses herself.*)

OLD WOMAN. Still not too late, children? God preserve us, God preserve us! You think I'm walking? I'm running, I'm flying. 'Cause these old feet don't work. Go ahead, laugh at me, children, with my little pot of water. What's the water for, children? Heh heh heh! Once upon a time I had children of my own, grandchildren too. Dead. All dead. Some by plague, some slaughtered in wars. And I'm still alive—all alone—and carrying a whole cemetery in my heart. And he once had a mother too—that sinner, I mean. I know what it means to be a mother. I'm standing up to God. So I'll go against God. I'll go there with my pot of water. This water is holy. They'll light the fire under him and I'll drip a drop of water on it—and it'll go out. They'll light it again—and I'll drip another drop of water, making sure nobody sees. And that's how I'm going to stand up to God and put out the terrible fire. And if I'm called to God and He asks me why I'm doing this, I'll tell Him: never You mind, I was also a mother. A mother . . . (*The Noblemen cover their faces. The Old Lady moves on. Voices from left.*)

VOICES. Fire! Fire! Fire!

FIRST NOBLEMAN. (*Terrified.*) Fire?

SECOND. Fire?

Scene 9

(*From the right enters Nekhamele, disheveled, almost naked, with a candle in her hand.*)

NEKHAMELE. Who wanted fire? Here's your fire, take it! Let's burn the newest growth on the old cancer. Who thought up the Jews, anyway? I could have been a goy like any goy, could have been your goyish wife, and ridden around with you to lots of fancy places in a coach with a big cross on it.

And now? Like a white fish out from the dark sea, I leaped up to meet the sun and was left hanging in the air. Now I no longer know where the sun is and where the abyss, whether I'm your wife or the guide leading you to the fiery wedding canopy. I ran away from home to the goyish world, to the wanton world. Judaism made its way into foreign temples, Judaism turned inside out. So if I ran away from there, then why am I running after you? What do I want from you? I know—because I'm losing someone to hate. We're a match made in hatred, and I can't part from you. Take your fire, set it ablaze! Light the red wedding canopy! Let it make the whole world brighter and brighter.

Scene 10

OLD DUKE'S VOICE. (*From offstage right.*) Nobles! Nobles!

FIRST NOBLEMAN. (*Coming to.*) Here he comes! It's a miracle.

SECOND. There had to be a miracle. Run faster, Duke, time is running out. (*Old Duke enters from right, running, holding a signed document.*)

FIRST NOBLEMAN. Pardoned?

SECOND. His Holiness himself?

DUKE. Pardoned. He's still alive, my dear sirs?

FIRST NOBLEMAN. Just in time, Duke. Run! And may God's angel light your way.

DUKE. Where should I run to, nobles? What should I run for? I really must ask you a couple of questions . . .

FIRST NOBLEMAN. What are you waiting for, duke? Save your son!

DUKE. Have you seen him?

BOTH NOBLEMEN. We have.

DUKE. Spoken to him?

BOTH. Yes.

DUKE. What did he say?

FIRST. Now is no time to talk. Save your son!

DUKE. Later will be too late.

SECOND. You're stubborn, Excellency!

DUKE. Stubborn, my dear sir, stubborn.

FIRST. You're a father, for God's sake.

DUKE. There are higher duties. Hurry, my dear sir, don't keep me in suspense. What did he say?

FIRST. He said he had no regrets.

DUKE. That I know. What else?

SECOND. He said he will remain a Jew.

DUKE. I understand that. Go on, go on . . .

FIRST. He can't live in chains, he said. He'd prefer a brilliant death to a dismal life.

DUKE. That's what he said?

FIRST. But why do you listen to him, Duke?!

DUKE. Who should I listen to? You? The court? The mob? I listen to my son. Alone in that dark room, in Rome, without witnesses, I fell to one knee, bent my gray head, kissed the holy slipper and begged for mercy for my son. A father may do that. But he, before the judges, before the mob, should he back off, retreat, go against his own will, his own beliefs? Were my son to run from the battlefield, what would I say? Were he to be shot in the back, what would I say? And if others were to see it, how could I bear it? A father—yes. But the honor of my son, the honor of the young duke! Nobles! That's what he said? To die a brilliant death? Nobles! Help me tear this father's heart out of my chest! I want to understand him, I need to understand him, to be close to him at this decisive moment! His honor is preferable to me than his life. Because . . . he wants it this way. Nobles! See how a duke behaves; if death is dearer to him . . . then let it take him. (*He tears up the pardon. The Noblemen make a move to stop him, then stop, amazed. Distant church bells. Singing in unison. The roar of the crowd grows louder.*)

Scene 11[35]

(*First Nobleman bares his head. Crosses himself in the red glow of the pyre. Second Nobleman picks up the torn pardon, and mechanically tries to put it back together. The Duke, hunched over, slowly exits left. The Noblemen follow. The*

---

35. Because the production was running too long, the following two scenes were cut from the original production of *The Duke*. We have chosen to restore Kacyzne's original ending.

roar of the crowd. Yoshke stumbles in from the right, having just been beaten by the crowd. Stones are thrown at him. He falls to the middle of the bridge, gets up, sees the flames, cries out, and covers his face. Slowly gets up once more.)

YOSHKE. What did I do to deserve this? What did I want, after all? A little corner. A little tiny corner of this big world. To live an honest living. To be a Jewish tailor. But they won't even let me do that, won't let me make an honest living. (*Pounds his chest. Looks at the flames.*) Go ahead, burn! Burn my eyes out! Stones! Poke them out! A dog—yes, yes, even a dog also wants better scraps. Oo hoo hoo! (*Howls.*)

Scene 12

(*Nekhamele runs on from left. What's left of her clothing is burned. Her body bears the black marks of the bonfire's coals. Stones are hurled at her. Voices.*)

VOICES. A witch! A witch! Stone her!

VOICES. A saint! A saint, was in the fire!

NEKHAMELE. (*Retreating backward. Looks at the stones.*) I owed you one—now a weight's taken off my shoulders. Paid off my debt, gave you back your flaming kiss. Crept into the fire and gave it back to you! That's what drove me back to you, that's what bound me to you. The flaming kiss with which you burned up a Jewish daughter! I don't owe you any more. Gave it back! I would have paid interest, but those bastards dragged me away from the fire by my feet! I'm no longer in your debt! And they bur-r-r! (*Freezes, her fist raised in a curse.*)

YOSHKE. (*Crawls to her on all fours.*) You—you—you! You, my one and only! You won't push me away, I crawled into hell for you. You won't curse me. You're silent? You're mute? Made of stone? (*He looks at her, amazed. Tableau.*)

Curtain.

Made in the USA
Middletown, DE
28 December 2019